GOD OF WAR

CONTENTS

THE TALE SO FAR

Kratos returns to the field of battle! You've been waiting for this for some time, but need wait no longer. The war against the Olympians rages and you'll be at the forefront, helping Kratos change the entire course of history once more. With the aid of the Titans, he hopes to unseat the rulers of Olympus, but is this a path to glory or a fool's errand? Only time will tell.

God of War III promises to be the biggest yet in this epic franchise, and you won't want to miss a thing. Our guide contains maps of all the areas, the locations of each and every chest, and the top tricks for overcoming your enemies in battle. We'll show you the easiest - and some of the hardest - routes through the story. Whether you like gaining experience and purchasing upgrades, collecting all the items, or earning all the trophies, this guide has the information.

Series History

TITLE	RELEASE DATE	PLATFORM
God of War I	3/22/05	Playstation 2
God of War II	3/13/07	Playstation 2
God of War: Betrayal	6/20/07	Mobile Phones
God of War: Chains of Olympus	3/04/08	PSP
God of War Collection	11/17/09	Playstation 3

As you can see, *God of War III* is actually the fifth entry in the storyline of the series. Obviously, *God of War I* was the incredible unveiling of what would turn out to be one of the most recognizable icons in gaming. The second release of the game further entrenched Kratos as a force to be reckoned with. The Mobile and PSP versions of the series provide insight into more of Kratos' backstory that helped define him as the Ghost of Sparta. The *God of War Collection* was a re-release of the first two console titles remastered for the PS3.

CHRONOLOGICAL HISTORY OF THE GOD OF WAR

The *God of War* series has stretched over five years of real time, and it covers several periods from the life of Kratos.

The epic story of Kratos begins during his service to the gods as a Spartan warrior willing to do their bidding. Through the game, he is often challenged by mortals and immortals alike, eventually falling prey to their machinations due to his driving desire to be cleansed of his nightmares and reunited with his dead family.

Persephone, Queen of the Underworld, is revealed to be behind the scheming and in collaboration with the Titan Atlas to get revenge against the Olympians for her yearly incarceration in Hades. She planned to kill everyone, including herself, in an attempt at revenge and to finally be free of the Underworld. Kratos rises to challenge her at the cost of his own chance at redemption and future with his daughter, Calliope, in the fields of Elysium. Persephone falls to Kratos, a brutal foretelling of things to come, and Atlas himself foresees a reunion with Kratos at a later date.

Victory achieved, Kratos returns Helios' Chariot to the heavens and, drained from his many battles, falls from the skies only to be stopped at the last instant above the ground. Helios and Athena strip the Spartan of his weapons and adornments and leave him atop a cliff overlooking the Aegean Sea.

Our Byronic hero begins *God of War I* cursed by the Gods of Olympus, for reasons that unfold during his unexplained quest for vengeance. His duty is to stop a rebellious war between Ares and the people of Athens. Ares, the God of War, was jealous of Athena's favored city and the good will shown to it by Zeus. Kratos eventually succeeded in gaining enough power to eventually face and kill the Olympian, Ares, and assume his mantle as the new God of War. This did not sit well with the remaining Olympians. After all, a mere mortal should not sit beside them as an equal. One could surmise that the Olympians find his presence nearly as frightening as it is galling. After all, one of their number fell by his hand.

The story continued in *God of War: Betrayal* through a story where Kratos must prove his innocence from the crime of killing Hera's pet, Argos. The Ghost of Sparta finds that he was framed by an unknown assassin whom is tasked with defacing Kratos in the eyes of the Olympian Gods. Through this part of his tale, concern is shown by Zeus regarding the wake of absolute destruction left by Kratos during his attempt to establish his innocence. The God of War refuses to be chained and continues on a path not within the plans and without the approval of the other gods of Olympus.

So, in *God of War II*, a trap was set for Kratos, which resulted in the Olympians recapturing the Ghost of Sparta's godly powers. Left to die, our anti-hero should have fallen victim to the passage of time and disappeared into history. He did not...

Kratos was told of the Fates and their ability to change the path that each person takes. A Titan named Gaia, an old enemy of Zeus, explained to Kratos how he might find the Fates and alter his past, avoiding death at the hands of Zeus. So, Kratos bared his teeth and sought the Fates. Finding them, he avoided his death and forced Zeus to flee back to Olympus.

That wasn't enough for the fallen God of War. He used the Fates' loom to gather all the Titans from the past to relaunch their battle against the Olympians. His hope is to bring down the very halls of Olympus, ending the reign of Zeus. It's entirely possible that he'll succeed, but there are many gods waiting to stop him.

CONTROLLING YOUR FATE

You won't get awfully far in *God of War III* without knowing how to move around and keep Kratos in fighting shape. This chapter explains the basic controls of the game. Not much has changed from the earlier iterations of the series, though experienced players should still glance over this section to re-familiarize themselves with everything.

UNDERSTANDING THE INTERFACE

INTERFACE LEGEND

NUMBER	LABEL
I	Current Weapon Equipped
II	Health Bar
III	Magic Bar
IV	Item Bar
V	Red Orbs (Experience)
VI	Rage of Sparta

God of War games only have a few areas taken up by aspects of the interface. Most of these are in the upper left side of the screen. The circle in that area indicates which weapon Kratos has equipped. Three colored bars are right next to that symbol. The top bar (green) shows Kratos' health, both the health maximum and his current status. The bar diminishes as Kratos takes damage, and if it reaches the far left, you lose your life and must restart from the last checkpoint.

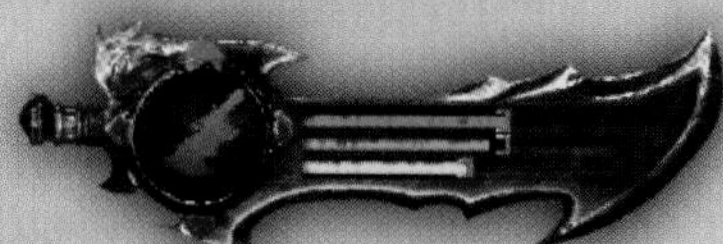

The yellow bar, third, reflects Kratos' energy levels. Unlike magic or health, this bar restores itself quickly over time. Items consume the yellow bar, but the benefit is that they can be used incessantly due to the automatic replenishment of the bar. The Bow of Apollo is a great example. Firing a barrage of arrows to drop an enemy is a great tactic. Follow this up with some evasive rolls or even melee combat and before you know it, the bar is filled and Kratos is ready to unleash the bow's awesome abilities once more.

Kratos will eventually learn to use the Rage of Sparta. Once this becomes available, a special icon appears in the bottom right of the screen. The icon fills as Kratos fights, kills, and incurs damage. Pressing both of the analog sticks activates this power. While using Rage of Sparta, Kratos inflicts far more damage, moves more quickly, and is much harder to kill. Save this for extremely challenging fights to give yourself an edge. Mixed Orb Chests also provide an opportunity to fill the gauge with a specific Orb. Lastly, know that you can deactivate the Rage of Sparta in the same way you activated it: **L3** + **R3**.

The second bar, middle, is blue and shows Kratos' magic pool and maximum magic storage. Using spells and attacks reduces Kratos' magic pool, but these are replenished by opening Blue Orb chests or killing certain creatures, such as Gorgons and Gorgon Serpents.

THE CONTROLLER LAYOUT

Look at this picture of the PS3 SIXAXIS Controller to learn the immediate controls in *God of War III*. The controls should be familiar to returning players. Newcomers to the series don't need to memorize this system; the game walks you through many of the standard features during the first hour of play, so it's quite user-friendly.

MOVEMENT

Kratos is not a static warrior. He'll be challenged with difficult battles, tests of agility, and endless exploration. As such, the very basic concept is movement. The following entries explain how the Ghost of Sparta can run, dodge, jump, fight, swing around, and even fly to achieve his goals, dark though they may be.

RUNNING

Use the left analog stick to control Kratos' movement. Press left to have him run left, pull back to have him head toward the camera, and so forth. This is a obvious and intuitive, and it only gets tricky if you're trying to move while the camera is altering its angle. When that happens, try to slow down for a second and get your bearings. Otherwise Kratos may end up shifting to the left when the ledge is straight ahead. There are plenty of obstacles to be conquered by the fallen God of War.

Later on, after defeating a certain enemy, Kratos gets a special set of footwear that allow him to run up walls or dash even while he's airborne. That's when things get really interesting...

Running can be more than just explorative, it can be defensive. Kratos has considerable range with his blades, and even gains even more when you grab the Bow of Apollo. Because most enemies rely on melee attacks for the bulk of their damage, Kratos has an edge if he stays away from his targets. Attack enemies from your maximum range and stop your combos to run away from enemies if they start crowding Kratos en masse. This prolongs encounters, but it provides Kratos with more a higher survivability.

EVASIVE ROLLS

For even more defensive options, use the right analog stick to have Kratos perform a defensive roll. Mastering this is invaluable for people who play on higher difficulty levels. Kratos can block certain attacks and avoid damage in that manner, but some enemy abilities can break through this defense and slam Kratos whether he's attacking, standing still, or blocking. When these attacks are too quick to avoid by simply running away or in another direction, you must roll aside. Wait until the attack is about to land and then tap the right analog stick in the direction you want to roll. This is an absolutely critical tactic to master!

JUMPS AND THE ICARUS LIFT (DOUBLE-JUMPS)

The ⊗ button commands Kratos to jump. He's an amazing athlete and even his normal jump is high enough to clear a small pit or leap over an enemy. But that's not all Kratos can do. While airborne, tap ⊗ again - ideally at the apex of the initial leap - to jump even higher. This double-jump, or Icarus Lift, has no cost, no downside, and can be done at almost any time during a normal jump. Icarus Lifts are useful for avoiding ground-based attacks, especially if they affect an entire area. This maneuver is also essential for clearing larger pits, obstacles, and troublesome targets.

Kratos has the ability to fight quite viciously while jumping. Knock enemies into the air with various attacks, then follow them up to savage them before they land and recover. This is one technique for isolating enemies from their allies.

THE WINGS OF ICARUS AND THE ICARUS GLIDE

Sometimes you must leap between areas that aren't within range of a normal jump or even an Icarus Lift. That's where the Wings of Icarus come into play. Kratos "acquired" these from Icarus in *God of War II* and he still has them strapped to his back at the beginning of *God of War III*.

To unfurl the Wings of Icarus, perform an Icarus Lift but hold down ⊗ the second time you press it instead of tapping. Kratos deploys the Wings of Icarus and glides toward his target. Technically, this is called the Icarus Glide. You can control the direction Kratos is heading, making it possible to swerve around obstacles. However, this is not true flight. You usually can't rise or sustain your glide indefinitely. Make haste and get to your goal before Kratos potentially plummets to his death!

In some locations there are air vents that throw Kratos high into the air while he's using his Wings of Icarus. Look for these spouts; they're easy to see because of the turbulence around them. Burning pots of oil or brambles serve this function several times in *God of War III*. Jump over them with your Wings unfurled to reach secret areas and even solve puzzles.

AERIAL ASSAULTS

Kratos can launch enemies into the air with a variety of moves. One of the strongest is accomplished by holding down △. Though this takes time and exposes Kratos to enemy attacks, it's a superb way to control and eventually decimate small groups with larger targets (Gorgon Serpents and Minotaurs are wonderful targets).

Once airborne, Kratos has the ability to slam his enemies without much fear of reprisal. Few targets have aerial attacks of their own, and enemies on the ground are too far away to aid their comrades.

Against large enemies, such as Cyclopes, Kratos can attack from the air and still strike his targets. When Cyclopes sweep the ground, have Kratos jump and attack. Attacking leaves Kratos airborne for much longer, aiding in his defense. In addition, he'll cut through his victims while they flail uselessly at the dirt.

GRAPPLE POINTS

Kratos has always known how to latch onto objects with his blades. This makes it easy to swing between certain points at high speed. Grapple Points are easily spotted; they shine with a white glow to indicate appropriate targets for a chain grapple. When Kratos is near enough to one of these points, an **R1** indicator appears on the top of the screen. Press **R1** to grapple onto the target and hold **R1** to have Kratos swing back and forth. When you're ready to let go, use ⊗ to jump. It is possible to double-jump and deploy your Wings of Icarus during the dismount.

Kratos can chain these together to leap to another Grapple Point and so on. It's fun to grapple across several targets in tandem, losing as little time as possible between each. If you're comfortable with the controls, don't let Kratos swing backward at all. Grapple, wait until you get to the other side of your first swing, release, and grapple again.

The trickiest grappling points are located on vertical objects. Instead of swinging back and forth, Kratos uses centrifugal force to rotate around the grapple point. It's harder to tell exactly where to release when you're on one of these. Usually, it's better to release early rather than late with such grapple points because momentum helps you reach your target. If you wait too long, Kratos' momentum carries him away from the target and this often can't be corrected in time.

CLIMBING

No mountain is too high for Kratos. Since the God of War is planning another trip to Mount Olympus, you can bet that climbing will be rather important to his progress. When it's time to climb, look for vines or other surfaces that stand out. These places are often quite visible; you might even see the camera pan over your intended path when Kratos enters an area—common in trickier sections.

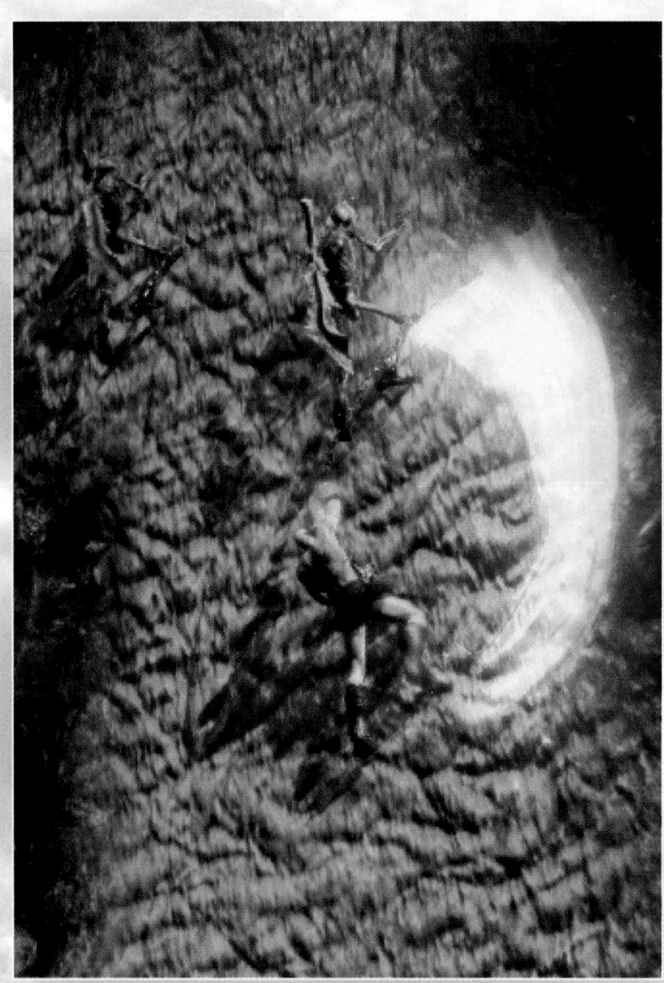

To climb, leap over the intended surface. Kratos latches on with astounding strength, and he won't fall until you tell him to let go. Press **R1** to release or jump off the surface with ⊗. If you're on a vertical surface, hold **R1** to initiate a controlled slide down the surface rapidly.

Now that you're climbing, use the left analog stick to climb up, down, left, or right. It's much like normal movement. The key differences are they you're much slower and that Kratos can't evade while climbing. It's much harder to defend yourself from enemies in this state. Press up on the left analog stick and tap ⊗ to jump up quickly. This is the fastest way to get around when you're climbing.

Enemies sometimes follow Kratos onto the cliffs. Your weapon attacks knock targets around well enough, but an even more enjoyable way to kill people is to grab them (◎) and throw them to their doom. This is a wonderful method when enemies are spread out and you can afford the extra time it takes. When enemies clump together, use heavy attacks (△) to fight several at once.

Kratos can even move along certain ceilings. If a section of vines or other climbable material extends onto a ceiling, Kratos can stab his way across. The controls are exactly the same as with normal climbing except for one difference; you can't use **R1** to descend quickly. Pressing this releases Kratos' grip on the ceiling and he drops off the ceiling instantly. That might be a bad thing, depending on what's beneath the white warrior.

SHUFFLING ALONG LEDGES

Narrow ledges might frighten lesser heroes, but Kratos isn't daunted. Walk up to a cliff that has tiny footholds and watch Kratos change his stance. He'll automatically shuffle onto the ledge and carefully make his way across. Press left or right on the left analog stick to send Kratos in either direction. If you're blocked and need to ascend, jump up a tier with ⊗. If instead you must descend a level and continue, use **R1**.

Kratos uses this to shuffle on ledges or to go hand over hand when necessary. The controls function similarly in either case. The same is true when you're crossing suspended rope lines.

MOVABLE OBJECTS

Many of the puzzles in *God of War* involve moving objects into various positions and figuring out what needs to go where. That hasn't changed in *God of War III*, but there are a few new tricks that are quite convenient. One major difference is that many objects that Kratos can grab and drag can now be rotated. While holding onto the object, press the right analog stick in either direction to rotate your target clockwise or counterclockwise.

As in previous games in the series, you know which items to grab by looking for a white glow on the handle. Kratos can grab and drag oil pots, blocks of stone, and similar objects.

OPENING DOORS AND REMOVING OBSTACLES

The Ghost of Sparta can force open most doors without needing to look for keys and such. By the same token, Kratos won't have to call for help just because a tree falls across his path. Approach these obstacles and watch the top of the screen to see if a button indicator pops up. This lets you know that a Context-Sensitive Action can be made there. Use the on-screen directions to move the obstacle, open the gate, or whatever else needs to be done. This is usually an easy process. However, there are times when Kratos is surrounded by enemies and can't complete the action unless he's either quick or massacres everything nearby ahead of time. Thus, engaging in wholesale slaughter has an additional benefit—you won't be interrupted in the middle of your attempt to open something.

SWIMMING

Quite some time ago, Kratos found Poseidon's Trident. This artifact allowed Kratos to dive underwater and swim indefinitely. Without worrying about air, Kratos could explore any aquatic passage.

This doesn't work in *God of War III* until you've defeated a boss in the Underworld and taken his soul. In areas with deep water, press ⊡ to dive beneath the surface and swim around. You can't evade while submerged, but there isn't any fighting to worry about either. Use △ when you're ready to breach the surface.

COMBAT

There are many times when brutality is necessary to get things done in the world of *God of War*. Kratos is a master of combat, and the following techniques are often all he needs to survive encounters against mortals and gods alike.

BASIC ATTACKS

The most basic attacks in the game are light attacks (used by pressing □) and heavy attacks (△). Light attacks are extremely quick, don't disrupt enemies much, and inflict modest damage. They're good for defensive fighting or for killing softer, quicker, more agile targets. Heavy attacks have a much longer windup, meaning that you have to start your attack sooner and know where your enemy is going to be ahead of time. To compensate, heavy attacks hit harder and are involved in combos that are better for knocking enemies around and stunning them.

It's fine if you only use a single light or heavy attack at a time, but that isn't how Kratos normally joins a battle. Instead, he's driven to launch combinations of attacks. Not only do these combos do more damage over time, but they can also be strung into special moves that have a variety of effects.

Your current weapon and the level of that weapon determine which special moves are available to Kratos. Each weapon he acquires starts at level 1 and can be improved by spending Red Orbs in the menu. The Blades of Exile are the first choice for upgrades, and they're one of the most versatile and reliable weapon options in the game.

LIGHT COMBOS

Light combos are the series of attacks that focus primarily on faster hits. These combos have almost no startup time and can often be cancelled midstream by pressing any direction on the right analog stick. You can usually get Kratos to block quickly as well, even when he's in the middle of a light combo. That is why these are fantastic for defensive fighting. Kratos is better at retaining maneuverability and avoiding damage while engaged in these.

The most simple and basic light combo is to tap ◻ again and again as you push Kratos toward his enemies. Even new players to the series are likely to use this combo because it couldn't be more intuitive; it's button mashing at its finest. This is still a relatively powerful and effective method of killing enemies that don't have terribly high health.

Light combos are used heavily against bosses as well. Boss fights are usually quite dangerous; the enemies have high damage output, and you can't afford to let Kratos eat too many attacks. Heavy combos have the disadvantage of leaving Kratos exposed some of the time. Though boss fights are long, it's better to focus on evasion and general defense. Get in a few light attacks, roll away, and watch for openings. That's a proper approach when facing a new enemy and you aren't exactly sure what to do against them.

As a weapon's level rises, Kratos learns new moves and does more damage with his other attacks. Look in the menu if you want to know which attacks you've learned and how to initiate them.

HEAVY COMBOS

Obviously there are major advantages to using light attack combos. Since they're good for weak enemies and bosses, you might wonder if heavy combos are useful. The answer is that they have a major place in Kratos' arsenal. Tougher monsters and mini-bosses sometimes pose as much of a threat as their leaders. There are many fights that involve multiple weaker enemies and several nastier beasts. Heavy combos are wonderful against these monsters for several reasons.

The best thing about them is their ability to toss your targets around. Light combos typically leave enemies free to attack or counterattack. That's bad with tough enemies because they won't fall quickly and their damage output is high enough that they shouldn't be ignored. You must use moves with stopping power! Heavy combos have that in spades. These maneuvers end with blows that stun, disrupt, throw targets in the air, and otherwise give you the opportunity to press the attack or retreat.

Try a basic heavy combo. Use the following sequence: △, △, △. Watch specifically for the long startup time of the combo, but see how far the enemies are thrown when you finish. Combine the high damage and the splatter effect of this move and you can understand why it's a winner. Heavier enemies are pinned down with a heavy combo. While the big guys are disrupted, kill a few of their lesser troops and get ready to repeat the process.

GRABBING ENEMIES

Kratos does most of his best work while he's up close and personal. Use ○ to grab enemies and have your way with them. Lighter targets can be grabbed even when they haven't been damaged. For example, Kratos can grab some creatures right off the bat and kill them instantly. However, stronger enemies must be weakened before Kratos has enough of an advantage in strength to grab and hold them. In these cases, Kratos must wait until a spinning circle appears over the creature's head. That's your indication that the beast is dazed and weak enough to be thrown around.

Most targets are slain when Kratos grapples with them. There may be a mini-game to finish them off, but once you learn how to execute each mini-game it becomes relatively easy to dispatch any target. Some bosses and tougher enemies require you to grapple with them several times, perhaps using different button combinations each time you grapple. As always, follow the onscreen directions to know what to do.

POSSIBLE BUTTON COMMANDS DURING GRAPPLING MINI-GAMES

ACTION	INDICATOR
Press ◻	A ◻ appears on the left side of the screen
Press △	A △ appears on the top side of the screen
Press ○	A ○ appears on the right side of the screen
Press ✕	An ✕ appears on the bottom of the screen
Tap Circle Repeatedly	○ appears again and again in the lower right
Give the Left Analog Stick a Half Rotation	An arrow appears in the bottom center showing the direction of your 180-degree circle
Rotate the Left Analog Stick	The left analog stick appears in the lower left
Tap **L1** and **R1** Quickly	**L1** and **R1** appear in the top corners of the screen
Hold **L2** and **R2**	**L2** and **R2** appear in the top corners of the screen
Press Down on both analog sticks	**L3** and **R3** appears on the screen

With weaker enemies you have a choice in your grappling attacks. Some enemies can be dispatched at leisure, but you also have the option to use their bodies as living shields. This new attack, called the Battering Ram, is initiated by grabbing the target and pressing ◻ immediately afterward. Kratos runs around the screen smashing through everything in his way.

Another interesting grab attack is the Combat Grapple. Hold down **L1** and press ○ to use this move. Kratos disables his targets temporarily, leaving them exposed. Siren Seductresses are easy to silence and kill in this fashion.

BLOCKING AND COUNTERATTACKS

When standing still, Kratos blocks as long as you hold down **R1**. This negates the damage from the majority of fast attacks that enemies make. Certain types of special attacks or heavy blows can break through your block and damage Kratos regardless of what he's doing defensively. Use the right analog stick to roll out of the way.

Blocking is most effective when there are only a few enemies nearby. Because you can't move while blocking, it's risky to block while facing larger groups. The enemies get time to circle around, flank Kratos, and launch additional attacks. At that point you're forced to continue blocking and it's hard to get away or launch a counteroffensive without incurring substantial damage.

If there's an onslaught of attacks, or if your reflexes are especially good, counterattack. The Golden Fleece allows Kratos to instantly counter if he blocks a fraction of a second before the strike lands. Wait until the enemies are done with their wind up and block as the attack launches. This inflicts damage to all nearby enemies and throws them back, giving Kratos room to recover and get to a better position.

MENUS, OPTIONS, AND MISCELLANY

In case you're wondering about anything else, we've answered a number of miscellaneous questions here. Many more issues about gameplay, tactics, and more involved system mechanics are dealt with in the next chapter!

THE OPTIONS MENU

Before starting your first game, look at the Options Menu. If you prefer inverted controls for flight or special camera activities, this is the place to set those. You can also take a peek at the controller display here. The Gameplay Options in this menu allow you to toggle the tips seen in the early game. Players that have gone through the game already may prefer to turn off Hints and Tutorial Messages. Subtitles are also toggled in this part of the menu.

In addition, you can set the various volume controls and speaker output. There is also a graphical option if you have a specific setup and need to fine tune the visual output on your television or monitor. This menu is also available in game. Press **SELECT** to access these options. While in game, you can also "Restart from the Last Checkpoint" or "Quit" to exit the game.

THE PAUSE MENU

God of War III keeps track of quite a few things for you. Press **START** when playing to open the Pause Menu. Several pages of information provide data on your progress.

Power Up

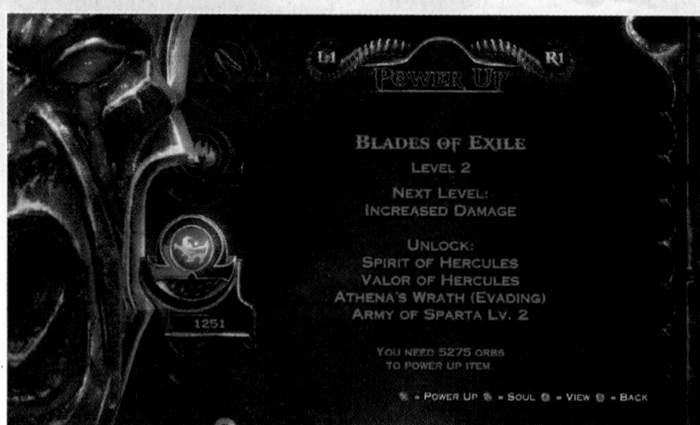

The initial page shows how many Red Orbs you've collected. After the first area is complete, Kratos is allowed to start spending Red Orbs to upgrade his magic and weapons. Cycle up and down through the items you've collected to find out how many Red Orbs you need for any upgrades as well as to see the current status of your abilities.

Items

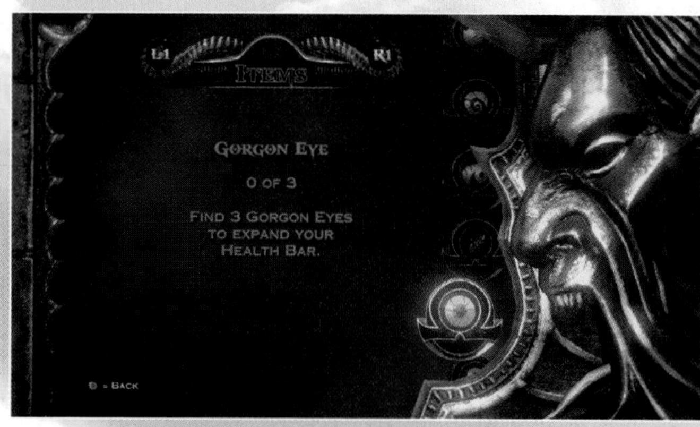

Press **R1** to cycle the pages to the right. This opens the Items Screen. Here you find out how many collectible objects Kratos has recovered. Some items permanently upgrade Kratos; these are especially nice to collect. Others affect post-game play or add different abilities as part of the story. You can't alter anything in this screen.

Status

The third screen is a record of several pertinent stats. None of these are important for upgrading Kratos or beating the game. Instead, they serve as a tally to let you know how well you're progressing.

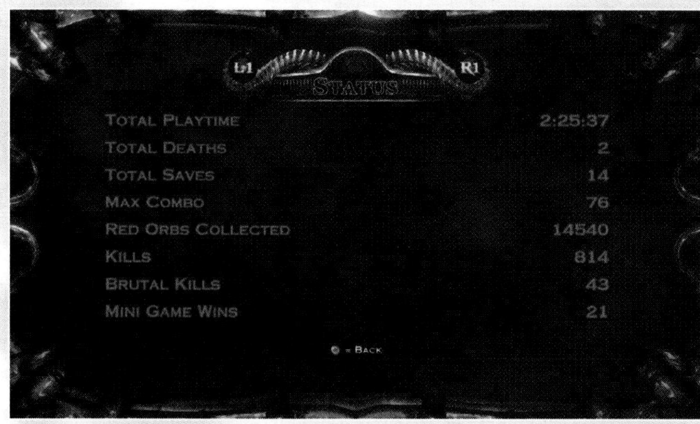

STATUS SCREEN INFORMATION

Total Playtime	Red Orbs Collected
Total Deaths	Kills
Total Saves	Brutal Kills
Max Combo	Mini-Game Wins

Moves

The final screen lists all of the weapons and items you have at your disposal. Move up or down to view each, and press ⊗ to find out what attacks or abilities you gain from these tools.

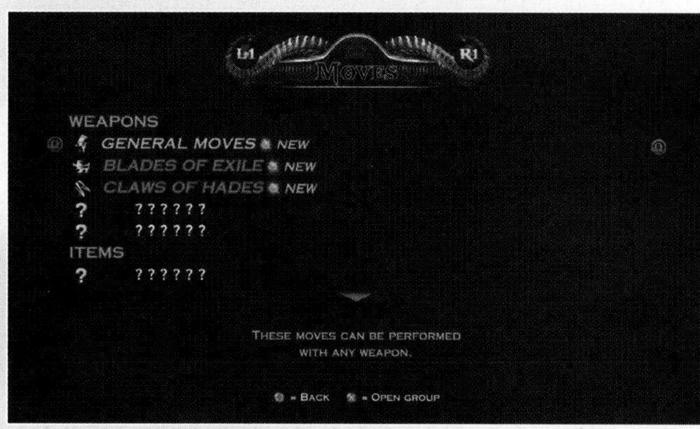

SAVING YOUR GAME

God of War III has two options for saving your game. First, the game saves automatically at every checkpoint to the Autosave Slot. You can't manually save to this spot and it's overwritten at every checkpoint. Secondly, there are glowing yellow Save Altars throughout the world. Stop at one to access the save system.

A SPARTAN'S TACTICS

It's important to understand the controls for the game, but it's even more essential to see the tactics behind various moves and attacks in *God of War III*. This chapter delves deeper in the weapons, magic, and specific moves that Kratos learns throughout his quest for vengeance.

A NOTE ON DIFFICULTY

The difficulty you select when starting a game makes a dramatic difference on several fronts. Kratos incurs more damage and has a much more difficult time damaging enemies on higher levels. In addition to that, Kratos will receive fewer resources as he progresses through a higher level game as well. If you take on more than you can handle (and die repeatedly) the game offers you an opportunity to lower the difficulty.

This is good, but note that you can't crank the difficulty back up later on. Find the best setting for your current play level. Use the table below to find out much more about these options. None of this data is available in-game, so it's quite useful for understanding what attempting the game on higher difficulties entails.

LEVEL	KRATOS DAMAGE OUTPUT	ENEMY DAMAGE OUTPUT	HEALTH ORB WORTH	MAGIC ORB WORTH	TITAN ORB WORTH	RED ORB WORTH	ENEMY AGGRESSION	ENEMY RECOVERY RATE
Spartan (Easy)*	200%	50%	150%	150%	150%	150%	Normal	200%
God (Normal)	100%	100%	100%	100%	100%	100%	Normal	100%
Titan (Hard)	100%	250%	75%	75%	75%	100%	Doubled	50%
Chaos (Very Hard)	75%	500%	25%	25%	25%	75%	Merciless	Immediate

*** MAGIC COST IS 25% CHEAPER AND THE RAGE OF SPARTA METER DRAIN IS 25% SLOWER ON SPARTAN (EASY) ONLY.**

THE FINEST WEAPONS

GENERAL MOVES

ACTION	COMMAND	EFFECT
Orion's Snare	○	Press ○ to grab a nearby enemy
Orion's Snare (Air)	○	While airborne, Press ○ to grab a nearby airborne enemy
Orion's Harpoon (Enemy Airborne)	○	Press ○ while an enemy is airborne to slam them back to the ground
Rapid Switch	L1 + □	Quickly switch to your next weapon and attack
Rapid Switch (Air)	L1 + □	While airborne, quickly switch to your next weapon and attack

These moves can be performed with any weapon. Kratos starts with all these actions and can use them at almost any point in the game.

ORION'S SNARE

Orion's Snare is often referred to as "grabbing an enemy." These actions cause Kratos to grapple with his targets, often killing the foes in the process. Weak foes can be attacked with Orion's Snare at any time. Many others, however, most be weakened before they can be attacked in this manner.

Dazed enemies can be grabbed at any time. You know that a target is dazed because a large, rotating circle appears above their heads. This happens with bosses, extremely powerful enemies, and a number of heavier troops.

Doing this while airborne allows Kratos to throw his target to the ground, inflicting damage and causing the victim to bounce for moment. Use this as a finisher after you've already beaten a target for several attacks while they're in the air.

ORION'S HARPOON

The attack isn't as essential as it was in *God of War I*. Still, it's a fantastic move that lets you slam enemies after launching them into the air. Lighter enemies can be repeatedly juggled while Kratos remains on the ground. Heavier targets don't bounce quite high enough for repeated uses of this ability without making additional launch attacks.

BLADES OF ATHENA

Athena gifted Kratos with magical blades to replace his previous weapons, the blades that Ares made for him a long time ago. Kratos starts *God of War III* wielding the golden Blades of Athena. These aren't always available to Kratos; in fact, they're only used in the early part of the game. However, obtaining a certain Godly Possession from a lovely goddess allows Kratos to use these later in the game as well.

As with the Blades of Exile, these chained blades are extremely fast and give Kratos the ability to attack enemies from moderate range, even though they are melee weapons. Hit fast, stay mobile, and remember that you are, and always will be, the God of War.

Many of the moves used with the Blades of Athena are exactly the same as those used with the Blades of Exile. Read both sections thoroughly to get an idea what Kratos is capable of unleashing. The moves listed here are the unique powers provided by the Blades of Athena.

RAMPAGE OF THE FURIES

- **Command:** **L1** + ◎
- **Summary:** Focus your rage on one enemy with this multiple hit attack.

This is primarily used against powerful single targets. The damage output from the attack is quite high, but Kratos can't cancel the combo and switch into block or evade. Thus, you shouldn't try this when there are multiple enemies surrounding Kratos. Instead, try this as a finishing attack after you've cleared the lighter troops from a battle.

RAMPAGE OF THE FURIES (AIR)

- **Command:** **L1** + ◎
- **Summary:** Quickly swing your blades in this multiple hit aerial attack.

The airborne version of this attack is quite different from the land-based variety. Kratos is able to avoid attacks to some extent because he stays above the enemies and rains attacks vertically down into them. Avoid using the attack if there are Archers around or other troops that are good at countering aerial attacks—like Satyrs.

HYPERION CHARGE (RUN)

- **Command:** Hold ◻
- **Summary:** Hold ◻ to slash your blades in an arc, continue to hold ◻ to initiate a running charge.

This "attack" doesn't do anything by itself. Instead, it sets Kratos in motion and prepares for a secondary command. Chain this into Hyperion Rush or Hyperion Rise.

HYPERION RUSH (RUNNING)

- **Command:** ◻
- **Summary:** During a Hyperion Charge press ◻ to slam your shoulder into an enemy.

Kratos knocks enemies around with Hyperion Rush, doing modest damage and giving himself a slight edge in the fight. This isn't a necessary opener for many enemies, but it's a good and flashy way to close the distance with targets that aren't especially threatening. Don't try this against enemies that are hard to disrupt; they recover too slowly and have a chance to pound Kratos before you lead into your next set of attacks.

HYPERION RISE (RUNNING)

- **Command:** △
- **Summary:** During a Hyperion Charge press △ to deliver an uppercut to launch enemies.

Hyperion Rise is an even more effective finisher to Hyperion Charge. You throw the target into the air, getting a chance to jump after them and juggle the victim while his buddies stay below, helplessly watching their friend get ripped to shreds.

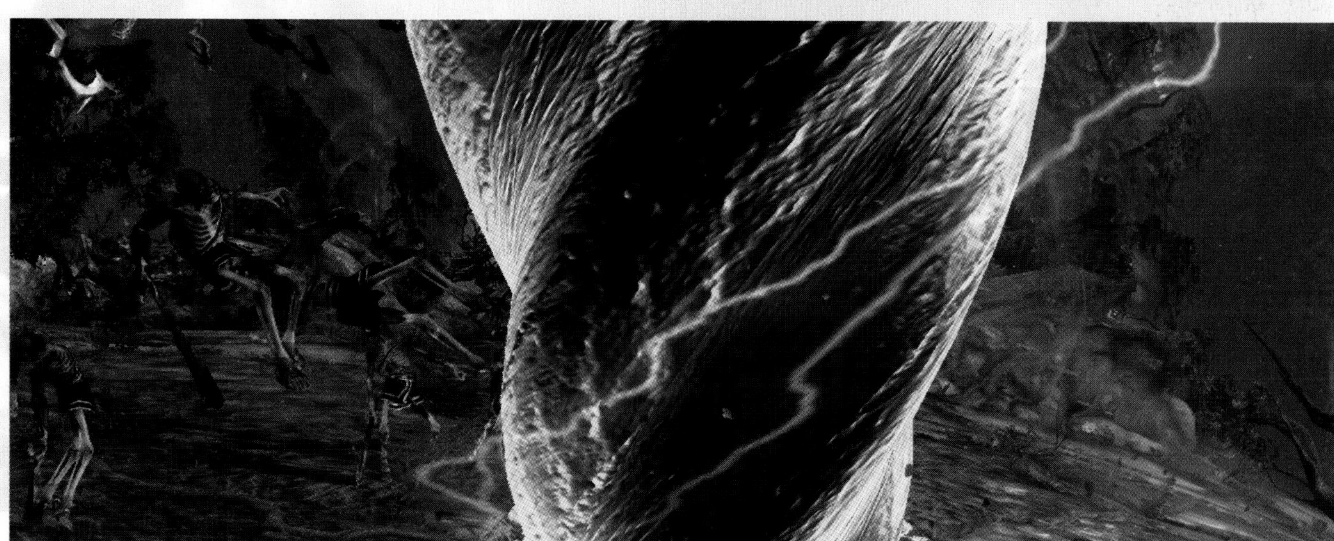

DIVINE RECKONING (GROUND OR AIR)

- **Command: R2**
- **Summary:** Drive the Blade of Olympus into the ground and launch enemies into the air with a powerful vortex.

Kratos drives the legendary Blade of Olympus into the ground creating a deadly swirling vortex. All surrounding enemies take damage and are launched into the air. The extremely large area of effect, combined with Kratos' completely powered up Magic bar at the beginning of the game creates a brutally devastating attack.

THE BLADES OF EXILE

These blades are tremendous assets against the Gods of Olympus. The Blades of Exile act like previous versions of Kratos' chained blades. They offer surprising range and still allow Kratos to block, counter, evade, and use Orion's Snare.

If you don't know exactly what's in an upcoming encounter, leave these weapons out. They don't have any weaknesses! Also, their magic attack (Army of Sparta) is reliable under almost all conditions.

UPGRADE LEVEL	RED ORB COST	POWER MULTIPLIER	BASE/MASH DAMAGE	MAGIC COST	NEW MOVES
1	N/A	100%	25	30	Plume of Prometheus, Olympic Fury, Olympic Ascension, Hyperion Ram, Hyperion Ram (Air), Army of Sparta
2	4,000	150%	25	30	Increased Damage, Cyclone of Chaos, Argo's Ram
3	7,000	200%	35-40	35	Increased Damage, Valor of Hercules, Hyperion Fury, Athena's Wrath, Army of Sparta Lv. 2
4	8,000	250%	35-40	35	Increased Damage, Cyclone of Chaos Lv. 2, Tartarus Rage, Argo's Rise
5	10,000	300%	50-70	40	Increased Damage, Tartarus Rage Lv. 2, Army of Sparta Lv. 3

CUMULATIVE ORBS REQUIRED TO MAX OUT 29,000

PLUME OF PROMETHEUS

- **Command:** □, □, △
- **Summary:** A quick and powerful combo ending in a fiery finish.

This move is great at taking out groups of mixed troops. The combo starts quickly and keeps enemies from interrupting you. The final strike inflicts a fair amount of damage over a wide area. It also knocks some enemies off their feet.

OLYMPIC FURY

- **Command:** □, □, □, □, □
- **Summary:** A quick combo that strikes all surrounding enemies.

The light attacks stagger weaker enemies and Kratos is exposed for quite some time if he lets heavier enemies get close, or if there are targets on his flanks. Use this to finish off lighter groups or to hit enemies on the periphery of a larger group.

OLYMPIC ASCENSION

- **Command:** Hold △
- **Summary:** Hold △ to launch enemies and jump into the air after them.

This move singles out an enemy and removes them from their group. While mutually airborne, Kratos can slaughter his victim without worrying about counterattacks from his side or back.

HYPERION RAM

- **Command: L1** + ○
- **Summary:** Pull yourself toward an enemy, ramming them, and launching them backward.

This attack is also known as combat grappling. It's a useful technique for controlling enemy positioning. Use Hyperion Ram against faster enemies (like Siren Seductresses) to stop their momentum and inflict a few free strikes against them. Another perk of Hyperion Ram is that you draw Kratos and the target toward each other. It drags burrowing targets out of the ground, or is used with the aerial version to ground those annoying Harpies.

HYPERION RAM (AIR)

- **Command: L1** + ○
- **Summary:** While airborne, pull yourself toward an enemy, ramming them.

This combat grapple can target aerial or grounded enemies. It's extremely effective against Harpies.

CYCLONE OF CHAOS

- **Command: L1** + □
- **Summary:** Rapidly swing your blades, striking all surrounding enemies multiple times.

This attack flays everything around Kratos. The range is superb and the blows stagger weaker targets. At higher levels, you can continue tapping □ to sustain the assault. Don't use this often against heavier enemies, as they tend to wade through the damage.

CYCLONE OF CHAOS (AIR)

- **Command: L1** + □
- **Summary:** While airborne, rapidly swing your blades, hitting all surrounding enemies multiple times.

This attack functions much like the grounded counterpart, but it has added utility. In some fights, Kratos is safer in the air. This attack can be spammed to keep Kratos aloft longer while inflicting damage to both aerial targets and taller enemies (like Cyclopes).

SPIRIT OF HERCULES

- **Command:** △, △, △
- **Summary:** A powerful, albeit slow, combo with an explosive finish that launches enemies into the air.

This combo provides an immense amount of damage per hit. That makes Spirit of Hercules effective against grouped enemies or heavier targets. The final slam covers a fair amount of territory, so that's also an incredible benefit.

The only problem with Spirit of Hercules is the windup time for the combo. The first hit is especially slow, and the remainder of the combo isn't fast either. Start Spirit of Hercules from maximum range, or even while standing out of range, to give Kratos the time he needs to pull it off.

VALOR OF HERCULES

- **Command:** △, △, □
- **Summary:** A powerful, slow combo that sends enemies flying back.

Valor of Hercules has many of the same functions as Spirit of Hercules. Instead of slamming the ground at the end of the series, this move throws Kratos into targets with his Blades of Exile. This is better when you want to push targets around. For example, it's amazing when you want to throw them off ledges or keep them away from something.

HYPERION FURY

- **Command:** Hold □
- **Summary:** Slam into an enemy and deliver a devastating combo.

Kratos charges a single target and brutalizes them with light attacks. The move has a lot of flash, but it's risky if you have multiple enemies attempting to engage Kratos, as is often the case.

ATHENA'S WRATH (USED WHILE EVADING)

- **Command:** Evade + △
- **Summary:** While evading, press △ to create an explosive wave along the ground, launching those enemies in front of you into the air.

This attack targets the closest enemy to Kratos as he regains his footing after an evasive roll. Use the attack to damage enemies that are a major threat to Kratos. He can roll between two targets, damaging both of them while staying so mobile that neither can retaliate effectively. You won't throw enemies around substantially, but you're essentially causing damage without risking reprisal.

TARTARUS RAGE

- **Command:** L1 + △
- **Summary:** Rip your blades down onto multiple enemies, launching them into the air.

This attack strikes all enemies within weapon range. Everything incurs damage and suffers a modest launch. At higher levels you can charge this attack by holding △. Once that becomes available, ignore Olympic Ascension in favor of launching entire groups into the air, reducing their effectiveness. This raises your damage output and makes it easier to maintain long combos while juggling your targets.

TARTARUS RAGE (AIR)

- **Command:** L1 + △
- **Summary:** While airborne, rain down multiple attacks and land with an explosive finish, launching enemies into the air.

Combine this with the grounded version of the attack for an enjoyable one-two punch. Launch surrounding foes, leap after them, and then finish with another Tartarus Rage to decimate your adversaries. Holding △ allows you to charge the attack at higher levels.

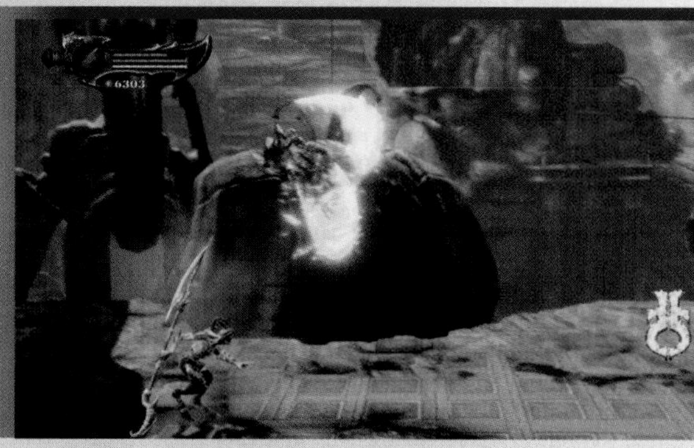

ARMY OF SPARTA (GROUND AND AIR)

- **Command:** R2
- **Summary:** Summon a protective phalanx of shields, spears, and arrows to drive back your enemies.

Summons Spartan Warriors to surround Kratos with shields and spears. This renders Kratos immune to damage for the duration of the casting; the spell also damages all nearby foes. At higher levels, tapping ○ summons a flight of arrows to rain down upon all targets within range as well.

Though the damage from Army of Sparta isn't high enough to make it a great boss killer, this spell has such a perfect blend of offense and defense that it never wears itself out. If you think you're going to get splattered by an unblockable attack, hit Army of Sparta and prepare for a retaliatory attack of your own!

CLAWS OF HADES

Ripped from Lord Hades, these cruel hooks grant you power over souls. The Claws are both similar and different compared with the Blades of Exile. The similarity is actually one of their weaknesses. Kratos doesn't gain many vastly different powers by using the Claws of Hades, so they don't have a uniquely specific use.

Their greatest strength is for people who are trying to upgrade as many items and weapons as possible. To do that, players need to accumulate Red Orbs. A mix of high combos, the bonus from the Claws of Hades, and cautious searching (for Red Orb Chests) is the best way to go about it. For those players, it's worth investing in this weapon early, to maintain their benefit for the longest period.

UPGRADE LEVEL	ORB COST	POWER MULTIPLIER	BASE/MASH DAMAGE	MAGIC COST	NEW MOVES
1	N/A	100%	Special	Special	Hades Agony, Hades Curse, Hades Ascension, Soul Rip, Soul Rip (Air), Soul Summon
2	3,000	135%	Special	Special	Increased Damage, Tormenting Lash
3	5,000	160%	Special	Special	Increased Damage, Hades Bane, Soul Summon Lv. 2, Souls Unlocked: Chimera, Gorgon Serpent, and Olympus Fiend
4	6,000	190%	Special	Special	Increased Damage, Unending Sorrow
5	9,000	225%	Special	Special	Increased Damage, Soul Summon Lv. 3, Souls Unlocked: Cyclops Berserker, Siren Seductress and Centaur General

CUMULATIVE ORBS REQUIRED TO MAX OUT: 23,000

SOUL SUMMONED	LEVEL REQUIRED	ATTACK TYPE	DAMAGE	CASTING COST
Cerberus Mongrel	1	Melee	15–25	15
Olympus Sentry	1	Melee	5-7 per hit	15
Olympus Archer	1	Projectile	2-3 per hit	10
Gorgon Serpent	3	Stone Enemies	Special: Beam	70
Olympus Fiend	3	Explosive	15-25	15
Chimera	3	Explosive	10-15 per hit	30
Cyclops Berserker	5	Melee	45-55	30
Centaur General	5	Melee	30	20
Siren Seductress	5	Explosive	25	20

***LOWER LEVEL SOULS RECEIVE DAMAGE BONUSES WHEN THE CLAWS OF HADES REACH LEVELS 3 AND 5.**

HADES AGONY

Command: ◻, ◻, ◻, ◻, ◻

Summary: A quick combo that hits all surrounding enemies.

This attack is useful when Kratos is surrounded. Though the damage is light, it's easy to lash out at multiple targets. Slash through groups of weaker enemies, but avoid using this against Minotaurs, Gorgons, and other targets with high health or a strong defense.

HADES CURSE

- **Command:** △, △, △
- **Summary:** A powerful and slow combo with an explosive finish that launches the enemies into the air.

Hades Curse is a heavy attack for juggling enemies. Kratos pops them into the air and can repeatedly use the same attack to juggle the enemies, preventing them from getting back to the ground.

HADES ASCENSION

- **Command:** Hold △
- **Summary:** Hold △ to launch enemies and jump into the air after them.

This is the Claws of Hades version of Olympic Ascension. The Claws aren't quite as good at bringing direct damage or aerial combos to the mix, but that isn't a horrible hindrance against most enemies. This attack still slaughters light or medium troops without a hassle.

SOUL RIP

- **Command:** L1 + ○
- **Summary:** Rips a demonic soul from your enemy that will viciously attack those nearby.

The souls brought forth by Soul Rip don't inflict much damage, but they're good for increasing your Hit Counter. Use this to buy yourself time while setting up bigger combos.

SOUL RIP (AIR)

- **Command:** L1 + ○
- **Summary:** Rips a demonic soul from your enemy that will viciously attack those nearby.

This aerial version of Soul Rip has no major advantages over its normal variant. The attack won't keep Kratos aloft (an unfortunate weakness) and there are more effective ways to deal damage against launched enemies.

TORMENTING LASH

- **Command:** L1 + □
- **Summary:** Whirls the Claws of Hades at surrounding enemies multiple times.

This routine is very effective against large groups of enemies. Lighter targets are hit over a wide area and are often knocked down. Using this in the air hits enemies in all directions, including above and below Kratos.

TORMENTING LASH (AIR)

- **Command:** L1 + □
- **Summary:** While airborne, whirls in a deadly frenzy, hitting surrounding enemies multiple times.

Compare this attack with Cyclone of Chaos, as both have a similar function. Tormenting Lash won't keep Kratos in the air as long. It also has somewhat shorter range. However, the ability to hit enemies both above and below Kratos is quite enjoyable; not many attacks strike enemies from this many angles.

MOURNER'S LAMENT

- **Command:** Hold □
- **Summary:** Begins a vicious attack that slams an enemy to the ground.

After several light, sweeping attacks Kratos picks up a single target and then slams it to the ground. The first few attacks are too light to daze anything, so Kratos is often interrupted before he gets to the ground slam. Do not try this against heavier opponents or large groups. This is a better attack to save for a flashy finish.

HADES BANE (EVADING)

- **Command:** Evade + △
- **Summary:** While evading, press △ to attack with a powerful overhead slam.

Hades Bane is slow, so you won't use it against maneuverable enemies. Instead, try it while rolling to the flank of a heavier opponent, such as a Talos or Cyclops.

UNENDING SORROW

- **Command:** L1 + △
- **Summary:** Summons your Claws and launches enemies into the air.

Use Unending Sorrow to repeatedly launch light or medium foes. The initial attack throws the target up, but Kratos recovers before they land. Thus, it's possible to repeat the attack and keep the enemy bouncing until they die. This is an ideal attack for finishing off resilient enemies that aren't too heavy to launch in the first place.

UNENDING SORROW (AIR)

- **Command:** L1 + △
- **Summary:** While airborne, slams your Claws into the ground, launching enemies into the air.

This is just as effective as the ground version. Avoid an enemy attack by double-jumping over the target. Launch the victim with Unending Sorrow before you land, and then chain into the ground version to continue the attack until your target falls.

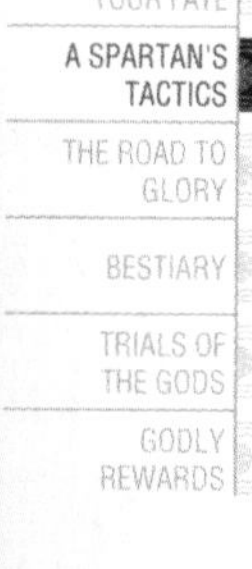

SOUL SUMMON

- **Command: R2**
- **Summary:** Summons the spirit of a monster to attack your enemies.

Press **START** and look in the Power Up menu before you play with this spell. There are a number of spirits you can summon, and this option expands as you level the Claws of Hades.

Kratos doesn't become immune to damage while Soul Summon is active. That makes this one of the least defensive uses of your magic. The spell is much more situational than Army of Sparta, Nemean Roar, and other magic. Summoning the right soul at the perfect time could change the course of a battle.

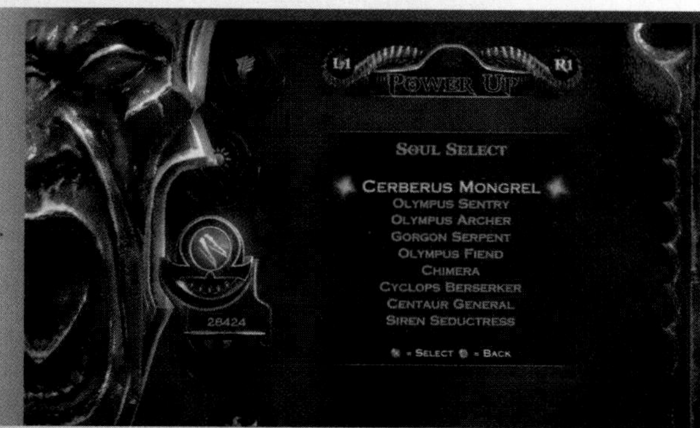

Cerberus Mongrel

Unleashes a Cerberus Mongrel that charges your enemies and makes a sweeping claw strike. The attack inflicts moderate damage and can stagger even heavier enemies.

Olympus Sentry

Summons several Olympus Sentries to attack nearby foes. These attacks deal moderate damage and knock enemies off their feet.

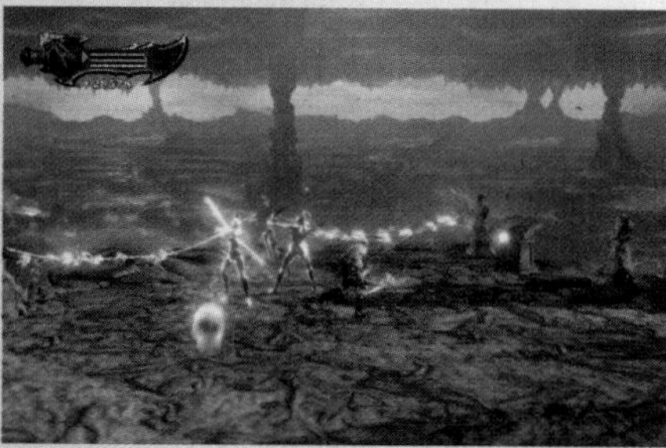

Olympus Archer

Summons an Olympus Archer to provide covering fire. The Archer shoots several times and knocks down the targeted enemy and anything nearby.

Gorgon Serpent

Commands a Gorgon Serpent to attack enemies near Kratos. The Gorgon Serpent partially petrifies enemies in a small radius, and for a short duration. The enemies aren't fully turned to stone, so they'll break free before Kratos has a chance to finish them off.

Olympus Fiend

Sacrifices an Olympus Fiend to knock a couple enemies into the air. This is a close-range attack that only affects targets in melee with the Ghost of Sparta.

Chimera

Summons a Chimera to hit nearby foes and breathe fire at others. This is quite useful against groups of weaker opponents as it knocks the enemies down while dishing out the damage.

Cyclops Berserker

Calls a monstrous Cyclops Berserker to kick the first enemy in front of Kratos and then to smash its club into the ground. The ground slam knocks down everything in a fairly large area-of-effect.

Centaur General

Orders a Centaur General to charge your enemies. This mows down all targets in straight line, knocking them prone in the process.

Siren Seductress

Brings forth a Siren Seductress to blast your enemies. After a moment, the Siren unleashes her attack, striking everything and blasting them away from Kratos. This is even effective against heavy enemies, but the amount of time it takes is troublesome. Kratos is left out in the open while the Seductress prepares her attack. Never use this when enemies are already mauling Kratos.

NEMEAN CESTUS

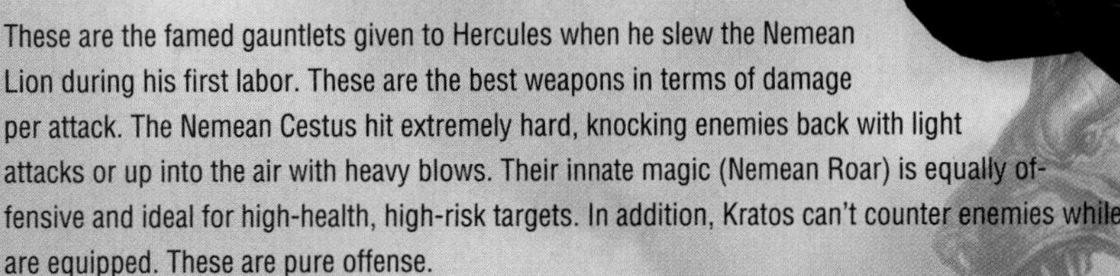

These are the famed gauntlets given to Hercules when he slew the Nemean Lion during his first labor. These are the best weapons in terms of damage per attack. The Nemean Cestus hit extremely hard, knocking enemies back with light attacks or up into the air with heavy blows. Their innate magic (Nemean Roar) is equally offensive and ideal for high-health, high-risk targets. In addition, Kratos can't counter enemies while they are equipped. These are pure offense.

The Nemean Cestus have almost no range, and they're limited in their ability to destroy groups of light enemies that can surround Kratos. A proper mix of a faster weapon and the Cestus combine to make Kratos almost unconquerable.

UPGRADE LEVEL	ORB COST	POWER MULTIPLIER	BASE/MASH DAMAGE	MAGIC COST	NEW MOVES
1	N/A	100%	25	33	Triumphant Labor, Erymanthion Rage, Augean Stampede, Augean Stampede (Air), Brutal Ascension, Ferocious Bite, Ferocious Bite (Air), Nemean Roar
2	3,000	110%	25	33	Increased Damage, Vicious Maul
3	5,000	120%	40	33	Increased Damage, Savage Charge, Nemean Roar Lv. 2
4	5,000	130%	40	33	Increased Damage, Crushing Strike
5	8,000	140%	65	33	Increased Damage, Nemean Roar Lv. 3

CUMULATIVE ORBS REQUIRED TO MAX OUT: 21,000

TRIUMPHANT LABOR

- **Command:** □, □, □
- **Summary:** A quick combo of punches ending in a powerful dash.

Kratos moves forward with each attack during this combo driving his opponent back. This combo compensates for some of the limited range with the Nemean Cestus. It's also fast enough to keep enemies on their toes. Don't mistake it for being too light; nothing with the Cestus is light on damage or pushing power.

ERYMANTHION RAGE

- **Command:** △, △
- **Summary:** A powerful, slow multiple hit combo with an explosive finish that launches enemies into the air.

Kratos takes a step forward and slams one hand into the ground for the first attack, inflicting damage to everything nearby. He then takes a second step and slams his other hand into the ground. This attack destroys weaker troops, bosses, and just about anything in between. It's repeatable, deadly, and easy to use.

AUGEAN STAMPEDE

- **Command:** Hold □
- **Summary:** Hold □ to rush forward; continue holding □ to viciously pummel an enemy.

Augean Stampede ends up being overkill for weaker enemies. The buildup is wasted on them because they're too easily thrown around or slaughtered. Save this for enemies that blocked often or have higher health—like Minotaurs.

AUGEAN STAMPEDE (AIR)

- **Command:** Hold □
- **Summary:** Hold □ to viciously pummel an enemy.

The enemy must already be in the air for this attack to work. It's a beautiful way to break apart enemies that you've already launched.

BRUTAL ASCENSION

- **Command:** Hold △
- **Summary:** Hold △ to launch enemies and jump into the air.

This launches nearby enemies into the air and Kratos springs up to join them. Follow up with Augean Stampede and decimate Kratos' forsaken victims.

FEROCIOUS BITE

- **Command:** L1 + ○
- **Summary:** Pull an enemy toward you and then send them flying back with a powerful blow.

This won't work against enemies that are too heavy, but it's not made for them. Use Ferocious Bite as a repeatable attack against light or medium targets.

FEROCIOUS BITE (AIR)

- **Command:** L1 + ○
- **Summary:** While airborne, pull an enemy toward you and send them flying back with a devastating punch.

Though similar in function, it's good to know that this version of the attack can hit aerial or grounded targets.

VICIOUS MAUL

- **Command:** L1 + □
- **Summary:** Rapidly swings your Cestus, hitting all surrounding enemies multiple times.

Though slow to initiate, this attack is similar to Cyclone of Chaos. Kratos strikes many enemies and builds his Hit Counter rapidly. Clear groups of foes by rolling into their midst and initiating this attack before they're even ready to launch their own attack.

VICIOUS MAUL (AIR)

- **Command:** L1 + □
- **Summary:** While airborne, rapidly swings your Cestus, hitting all surrounding enemies multiple times.

This has a similar attack pattern to Cyclone of Chaos, but be aware that it can't be used it keep Kratos airborne for more than one combo. If you're trying to attack and keep the Spartan above his enemies, switch to your Blades of Exile instead.

SAVAGE CHARGE (EVADING)

- **Command:** Evade + △
- **Summary:** While evading, press △ to launch the Cestus forward, striking all in your path.

Most evasive attacks inflict modest damage and don't wade through multiple foes. This is different. Kratos comes up and charges into his targets, hitting several of them with fair damage if they're grouped together.

CRUSHING STRIKE

- **Command:** L1 + △
- **Summary:** Slams your Cestus together, crushing all in their path.

Kratos tosses his Cestus out to the sides, hitting any enemies in the way. He then whips them together in a sweeping attack. Use this while enemies are charging Kratos. It takes too long to engage if enemies are already attacking, but the move is perfect for slapping down massive groups before they organize.

CRUSHING STRIKE (AIR)

- **Command:** L1 + △
- **Summary:** While airborne, Crushing Strike slams the Cestus into the ground with an explosive finish, launching enemies into the air.

This attack allows Kratos to land with a bang! This clears the landing area beneath Kratos with this attack; it has enough impact to get rid of any enemies that would otherwise counterattack Kratos during his recovery from the maneuver.

NEMEAN ROAR (GROUND OR AIR)

- **Command:** R2
- **Summary:** Slams your Cestus on the ground multiple times to create explosive waves.

The Nemean Cestus are not subtle weapons. Kratos deals direct damage to enemies in a relatively tight area. This isn't as good for clearing groups as Army of Sparta, nor does it last as long or protect Kratos as well.

However, the damage to individual targets is higher with Nemean Roar. That makes this a better boss-killer than Army of Sparta. You also have more throwing power. That gives Kratos more room to maneuver as he finishes the attack.

NEMESIS WHIP

The Nemesis Whip was crafted from the Omphalos Stone by Hephaestus himself. It offers high-speed damage and the ability to shred soft targets regardless of their numbers. Kratos must position himself well with the Whip, because its damage focuses on a tighter area than the Blades of Exile. However, the results are worthwhile for clearing swarms.

As the Nemesis Whip levels up, its ability to maintain combos increases. Eventually, you can leave the Whip at full length for several seconds in a row, inflicting damage on anything and everything that approaches from that direction. It's also fantastic for pulling enemies around corners to lure them into danger!

UPGRADE LEVEL	ORB COST	POWER MULTIPLIER	BASE/MASH DAMAGE	MAGIC COST	NEW MOVES
1	N/A	100%	18	20	Righteous Tirade, Righteous Ascension, Furious Contempt, Harsh Penance, Surging Lash, Surging Lash (Air), Nemesis Rage
2	3,000	110%	18	20	Increased Damage, Severe Judgment, Increased Righteous Tirade/Ascension Duration
3	5,000	120%	30	20	Increased Damage, Avenging Strike, Nemesis Rage Lv. 2, Increased Righteous Tirade/ Ascension Duration
4	5,000	130%	30	20	Increased Damage, Deadly Reprisal, Increased Righteous Tirade/Ascension Duration
5	8,000	140%	48	20	Increased Damage, Nemesis Rage Lv. 3, Increased Righteous Tirade/Ascension Duration

CUMULATIVE ORBS REQUIRED TO MAX OUT: 21,000

*** THE NEMESIS WHIP GIVES KRATOS A LOW CHANCE OF OBTAINING GOD AND MAGIC ORBS DURING RIGHTEOUS TIRADE AND ASCENSION**

FURIOUS CONTEMPT

- **Command:** □, □, □, □, □
- **Summary:** A quick combo that hits all surrounding enemies.

Kratos walks forward unleashing the Whip in front of himself and driving opponents back with a storm of blades. It's wonderful against mobs of weaker enemies although the Whip won't strike enemies behind Kratos. Roll away from groups to herd them all onto one of Kratos' flanks before initiating your attack.

HARSH PENANCE

- **Command:** △, △
- **Summary:** A multiple-hit combo that launches enemies and Kratos into the air.

This attack is effective against small clusters, but it leaves Kratos vulnerable during his landing. Use with caution.

RIGHTEOUS TIRADE

- **Command:** Hold □
- **Summary:** Continue to hold □ at the end of a combo, to keep the Whip's blades.

Kratos throws the Nemesis Whip to full range and the blades spin around in a blender-style attack. This is marvelous against enemies without ranged attacks; they simply walk into the shredder and soak up the damage. Be warned that the hits are light, so heavier enemies walk through the storm of blades without trouble.

RIGHTEOUS ASCENSION

- **Command:** Hold △
- **Summary:** Continue to hold △ at the end of a combo to launch an enemy into the air and continue spinning the blades of the Whip.

Launches weaker opponents into the air and uses a blender attack against them while they're suspended. Don't use this when additional enemies can strike at Kratos. Instead, use it to flay individual enemies without giving them a chance to respond.

SURGING LASH

- **Command:** L1 + ○
- **Summary:** Whips an enemy, delivering a deadly shock.

This strikes an enemy with a light attack and pulls Kratos to the target. When he gets there, Kratos hits all nearby enemies for moderate damage. Surging Lash has a much different feel from the Blades of Exile's combat grapple. Though offering less utility, the overall damage output is much higher, because it hits multiple targets.

SURGING LASH (AIR)

- **Command:** L1 + ○
- **Summary:** While airborne, this whips an enemy, delivering a deadly shock.

This is the same as the grounded version of the attack with all the same strengths and weaknesses.

SEVERE JUDGMENT

- **Command:** L1 + □
- **Summary:** Lashes the Whip into enemies and launches them into the air.

Use this to launch individual enemies into the air. Afterward, hit them with Severe Judgment in the air a few more times before they land.

SEVERE JUDGMENT (AIR)

- **Command:** L1 + ◻
- **Summary:** While airborne, lashes an enemy multiple times.

You won't stay airborne for too long, but Kratos has enough time to shred his enemies on the way down. Use this attack for extra damage against enemies that you just launched. It's nice because you can leave your finger on **L1** and press ◻ repeatedly to maintain the entire combo.

AVENGING STRIKE (EVADING)

- **Command:** Evade + △
- **Summary:** While evading, press △ to deliver a powerful rising attack.

After evading, Kratos spins the Whip around himself, damaging nearby foes. This attack has minimal range, and is mostly dwarfed by the evasion moves of other weapons, especially the Nemean Cestus.

DEADLY REPRISAL

- **Command:** L1 + △
- **Summary:** Kratos leaps forward, hitting all enemies in his path.

Use Deadly Reprisal as a powerful opener. Kratos staggers most targets when they're hit, providing plenty of time to follow up with group attacks or launches.

DEADLY REPRISAL (AIR)

- **Command:** L1 + △
- **Summary:** While airborne, Kratos rapidly swings his Whip, damaging nearby enemies.

Kratos focuses on a nearby target. He'll descend toward the victim and land on top of them, initiating a Deadly Reprisal against all nearby foes.

NEMESIS RAGE (GROUND AND AIR)

- **Command:** R2
- **Summary:** Shocks all surrounding enemies with a blast of energy.

Kratos eats through magic quickly with this fast-casting attack. However, he can decimate entire swaths of foes and knock them prone in just moments. If you're trying to massacre enemies quickly, this is a good way to do it.

ITEMS

Kratos can use a number of items in *God of War III*. Unlike earlier titles in the series, Kratos has an Item Gauge that allows you use his equipment without losing magic. The Item Gauge refills quickly, so all items are available whenever you need them.

HEAD OF HELIOS

This is simply the God of the Sun's head, ripped screaming from his body. This item serves as both a tool and a weapon. The Head of Helios lights dark areas, reveals hidden items, and can stun/push away enemies when its powers are charged and released.

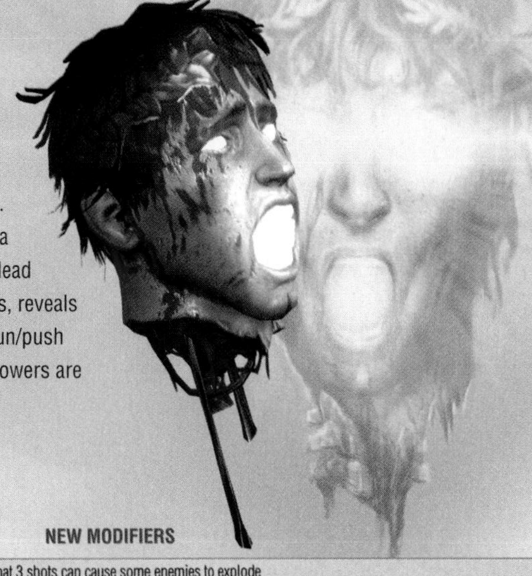

UPGRADE LEVEL	ORB COST	POWER MULTIPLIER	SHOT/FLASH DAMAGE	NEW MODIFIERS
1	N/A	100%	25 shot / 50 flash	Note that 3 shots can cause some enemies to explode
2	2,500	300%	25 shot / 50 flash	Increased Damage, Reduced Charge Time, More Helios energy (causes enemies to explode after taking fewer shots from the Head)

CUMULATIVE ORBS REQUIRED TO MAX OUT: 2,500

SOLAR BEAM

- **Command: L2**
- **Summary:** When the Head is equipped, press **L2** to shine a beam of light that reveals hidden secrets.

Aim the beam with your right analog stick. Light shines from the eyes and mouth of Helios and can light your way in dark areas. The gods have hidden plenty of items away. Keep the Head out as you walk around to look for hidden chests or to see through unlit caverns.

If you see gold dust shimmering in the air, shine the light toward it. This is often the sign that a hidden object is close by. To uncover concealed doors, shine the light on them and use the right analog stick to expose the entire surface of the door.

SOLAR FLASH

- **Command: L2** + ◬
- **Summary:** Releases a burst of blinding light that briefly stuns enemies and illuminate your surroundings.

This attack gives Kratos a moment to recover when there are too many enemies closing in. Another use is to pull Siren Seductresses out of the shadows, revealing them and making them vulnerable to damage again.

SOLAR FLARE

- **Command: L2** + Hold ◬
- **Summary:** Hold and release ◬ to charge a burst of blinding light that will stun enemies and illuminate your surroundings.

The charged version of this attack pushes enemies back, even throwing them off edges in a few areas. The stun duration is also more noticeable, giving Kratos a chance to initiate additional attacks before his enemies recover.

BOW OF APOLLO

This is a fiery bow that once belonged to Apollo. Though this weapon only delivers modest damage, it's often safe to use and offers damaging opportunities from range when your enemies may not be able to counter the attack right away. Kratos can fire the bow while moving; this is even true of the bow's charged attack, which deals increased damage.

A targeting column appears when Kratos holds down **L2** with the bow equipped. Look for this column of light. It automatically seeks the nearest, powerful enemy. Flick the right analog to either side to change Kratos' target.

UPGRADE LEVEL	ORB COST	POWER MULTIPLIER	MAGIC COST	NEW MODIFIERS
1	N/A	100%	10 per shot, 45 when charged	Bow Attacks
2	2,500	200%	10 per shot, 30 when charged	Increased Damage, Reduced Cost for Charged Attacks

CUMULATIVE ORBS REQUIRED TO MAX OUT: 2,500

FLAME BURST

- **Command:** L2 + ◎
- **Summary:** Fire a flaming arrow.

The Bow of Apollo inflicts trivial damage if you don't charge your attacks, but its firing rate is godly. Tap ◎ quickly to fire again and again. Use this to burn through Olympus Archers at an impressive clip.

FLAME BURST (AIR)

- **Command:** L2 + ◎
- **Summary:** While airborne, fire a flaming arrow.

These attacks are exactly the same as the normal attacks with the bow. The only difference is that Kratos can fire while he's airborne, potentially avoiding enemy attacks on the ground as he attacks.

FIERY INFERNO

- **Command:** L2 + Hold ◎
- **Summary:** Hold and release ◎ to launch an arrow that engulfs enemies in flames.

This attack has two major uses. It removes weaker enemies from the fight for a brief time. They'll struggle to put out the flames before re-engaging. The attack also is useful for clearing brambles, an obstacle that is primarily found in Hades.

BOOTS OF HERMES

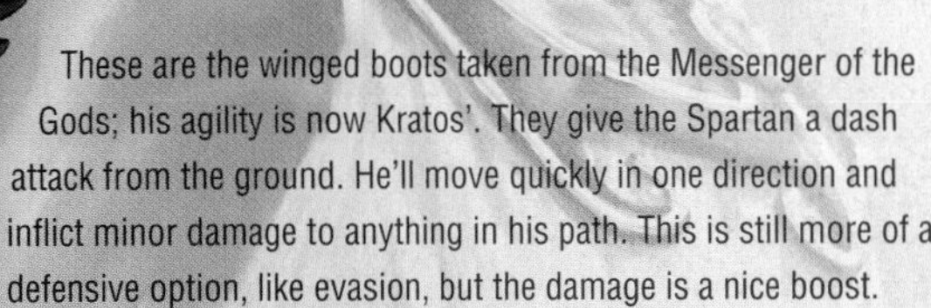

These are the winged boots taken from the Messenger of the Gods; his agility is now Kratos'. They give the Spartan a dash attack from the ground. He'll move quickly in one direction and inflict minor damage to anything in his path. This is still more of a defensive option, like evasion, but the damage is a nice boost.

The Boots of Hermes also allow for an aerial evade. That is an extremely effective option, and it's one that you can't mimic with other abilities in the game. The speed and defensive potential of this maneuver are truly a blessing. Use aerial attacks to slam enemies safely, and then dodge aside before landing to avoid reprisal.

Finally, the boots allow Kratos to run along walls and dash up certain surfaces. These locations are always marked with the Hermes Brand Symbol (sets of foot-prints that glow as you approach).

UPGRADE LEVEL	ORB COST	POWER MULTIPLIER	MAGIC COST	NEW MOVES
1	N/A	100%	50	Hermes Dash, Hermes Rush
2	2,500	100% + Explosions	50 Dash / 65 Charge	Hermes Jest

CUMULATIVE ORBS REQUIRED TO MAX OUT: 2,500

HERMES DASH (AIR)

- **Command:** Use the right analog stick while dodging
- **Summary:** While airborne, evade your enemies.

Using Hermes Dash from the air is probably the best combative function of the Boots of Hermes'. Kratos becomes almost as agile in the air as he is on the ground. Most enemies already have trouble hitting Kratos when he's springing around, and this compounds that advantage.

HERMES RUSH

- **Command: L2** + ◎
- **Summary:** Rush forward, slamming into an enemy.

You won't inflict much damage, but this is a good way to close the gap against enemies that are out of range. Players who enjoy the Nemean Cestus can use Hermes Rush to engage enemies quickly.

HERMES JEST

- **Command: L2** + Hold ◎
- **Summary:** Rush forward and slam into multiple enemies, launching them into the air.

Hermes Jest is a major improvement over Hermes Rush. Though you need more time to set up the attack, it proves to be a non-issue. You don't need to use this during a fight. Instead, charge the attack while you're running toward a fresh group of foes. Kratos gets to start off with a solid attack, throw his enemies around, and pay no real price.

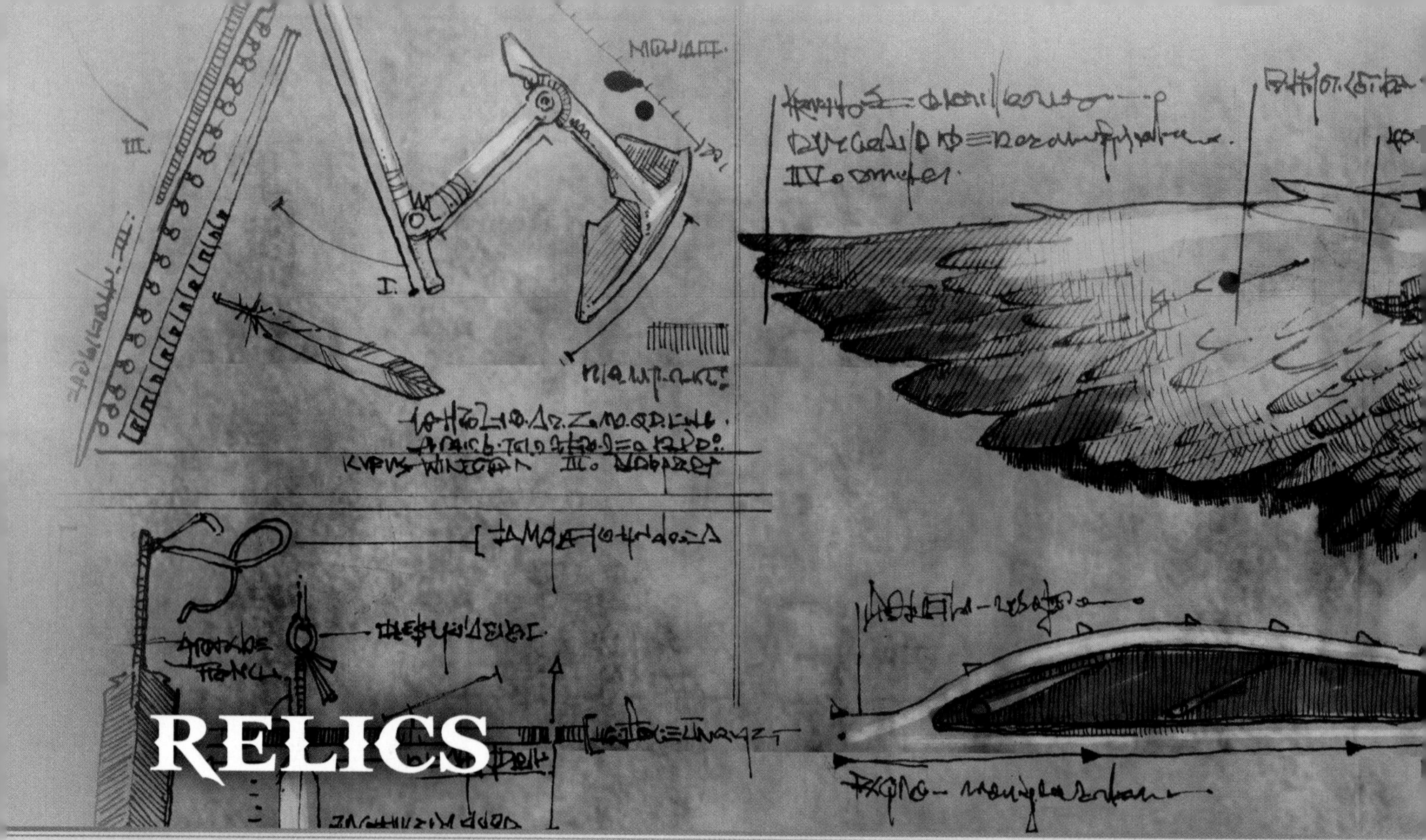

RELICS

POSEIDON'S TRIDENT

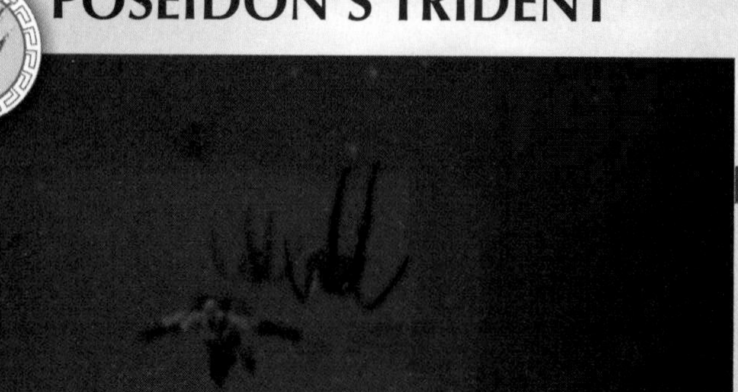

This symbol of Poseidon's power allows you to breathe underwater. However, you won't be able to use that power until you've collected the soul of a major god...

SWIMMING CONTROLS

COMMAND	CONTROL
Swim	Press the left analog stick in the direction you would like to swim
Swim Up	Press △ or ⊗
Swim Down	Press □
Swim Dash	Hold R1 and then release it to dash forward underwater and destroy objects blocking your path

THE WINGS OF ICARUS

These are the wings torn from Icarus in *God of War II*; they grant you brief flight. Kratos can double-jump with the wings, leaping twice into the air with equal strength. Afterward, hold ⊗ to deploy the wings and glide to safety.

GLIDING CONTROLS

COMMAND	CONTROL
Icarus Lift	While airborne, press ⊗ to jump even higher
Icarus Glide	While completing Icarus Lift, hold ⊗ to glide

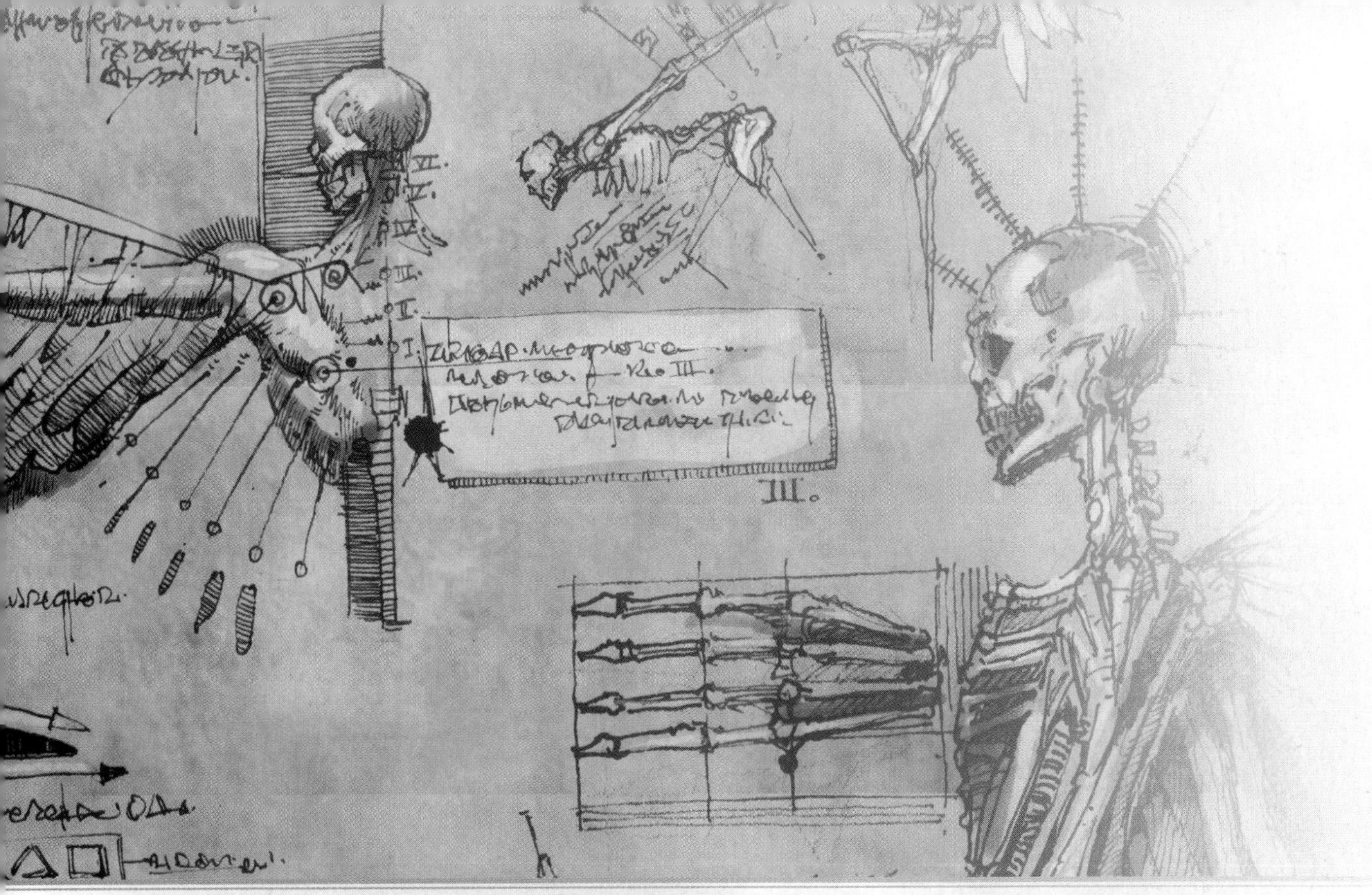

THE BLADE OF OLYMPUS

Let your foes feel the wrath of the blade that ended The Great War. You won't be able to wield this weapon normally. Instead, it's tied to the Rage of Sparta, a power that builds while Kratos fights and defeats his enemies. Save this for boss fights and other serious encounters. Kratos massacres enemies with brutal efficiency when he's wielding the Blade of Olympus.

CONTROLS FOR THE RAGE OF SPARTA

COMMAND	CONTROL
Rage of Sparta	Press L3 and R3 simultaneously to call forth the Rage of Sparta
Spartan Fury	Tap □ and use the Blade of Olympus to decimate your enemies
Spartan Spirit	Tap △ and use the Blade of Olympus to launch your enemies
Spartan Glory	Press ⊗ to create an explosive wave that launches enemies into the air

GOLDEN FLEECE

This legendary armor allows you to reflect enemies' attacks, projectiles, and beams, but requires careful timing. Wait to block enemy attacks until the last moment. Then, hit **L1** to activate the Golden Fleece. The action slows briefly when you succeed. During this time, press □ to perform Argo's Ram. Once you learn Argo's Rise (at higher levels of the Blades of Exile) use △ for an even better counter.

The Golden Fleece demands careful attention to enemy attacks and positioning. Some players love it and its utility is never in question. Try these blocks and counters in large battles and watch how easy it is to punish many enemies at once.

CONTROLS FOR BLOCKING AND COUNTERING

COMMAND	CONTROL
Argo's Return	Press L1 just before being hit to reflect an attack, projectile, or beam
Argo's Ram	After a successful parry, press □ to ram into nearby enemies and send them flying backward
Argo's Rise	After a successful parry, press △ to do a powerful counterattack, launching nearby enemies into the air

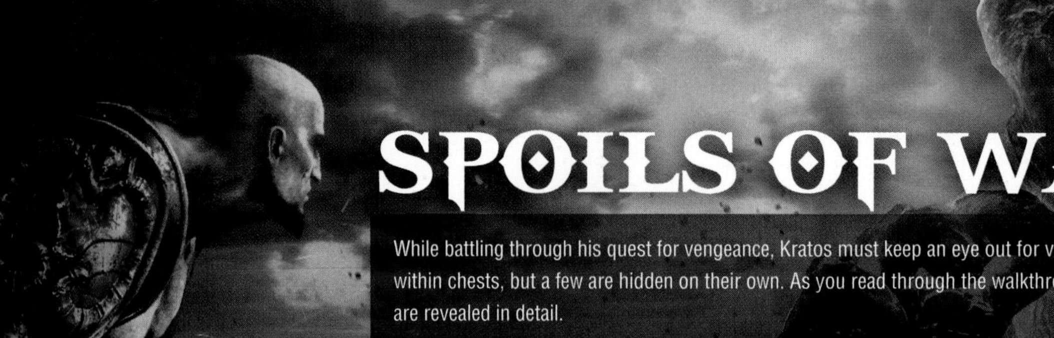

SPOILS OF WAR

While battling through his quest for vengeance, Kratos must keep an eye out for various treasures. Most are kept within chests, but a few are hidden on their own. As you read through the walkthrough, the locations of all these items are revealed in detail.

RED ORB CHESTS

Red Orb chests boost your experience after they're opened. Kratos uses Red Orbs to upgrade his weapons and items. Early on, these chests provide relatively few Red Orbs. Later in the game, some chests release hundreds of Red Orbs, making it much easier to purchase upgrades.

GAINING EXPERIENCE

Kratos gains Red Orbs from fighting as well as from finding chests. All enemies grant some Red Orbs when they're slain, but the amount you get in each level may differ. Kratos gets bonus Red Orbs for Brutal Kills, kills made by grabbing enemies. He also gets bonus Red Orbs by reaching high combos on the Hit Counter.

Maintaining a high-hit combo is all about staying in motion, acting quickly without pulling away from enemies. The counter disappears if you stop attacking for more than a moment or two. Evading doesn't count against this timer, so you don't have to risk Kratos' life at every turn.

Magic that hits groups or attacks that affect a wide area are amazing for building your hit combo. Army of Sparta, Cyclone of Chaos, and even general hits from the Nemesis Whip are all examples of attacks that rack up the hits quickly.

Watch the right side of the screen when you're in a combo. The Hit Counter is there, but the rewards for your combos are also displayed in that location. Watch for a positive number to appear briefly next to a Red Orb icon. That's your bonus!

People who want to upgrade weapons early and hit the eventual upgrading cap need to kill every enemy possible and maintain consistent combos while doing it!

HEALTH CHESTS

Health Chests have an omega symbol (Ω) that radiates with a green light; they release Green Orbs when opened. If Kratos is wounded, these Orbs restore his lost health. Don't open a health chest if Kratos is already at full health because that wastes the Green Orbs that could come in useful later...

MAGIC CHESTS

Magic Chests glow with a blue light from the omega symbol (Ω). The Blue Orbs they contain restore Kratos' magic. Magic is lost when Kratos casts spells and uses attacks with his weapons. It's hard to restore magic without these chests because there are only a few enemies in the game that provide Blue Orbs on their own.

ALTERNATING CHESTS

Alternating chests switch between green and blue light and offer the respective Orb, depending on when you loot them. Wait for either green to glow if Kratos is low on health, or blue for magic. Simply open the chest when it's glowing with the color the Spartan needs.

MIXED CHESTS

Mixed chests have a white appearance. They have a spread of Orb types that are instantly acquired when you open them. These usually restore Kratos in several ways and raise his Rage of Sparta gauge.

ITEM CHESTS

Items chests quite vary greatly, differing in appearance from the other chest types. You won't know what is inside an item chest until you open it. There aren't any reasons for leaving one of these unsearched; always open them as soon as you find them. These chests contain either Gorgon Eyes, Phoenix Feathers, or Minotaur Horns—all items that should be gathered when found.

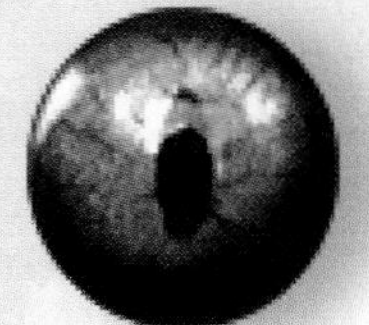

GORGON EYES

Gorgon Eyes eventually improve Kratos' maximum health. Every three Gorgon Eyes give you a permanent boost.

PHOENIX FEATHERS

Phoenix Feathers are similar to Gorgon Eyes in how they work, but they increase Kratos' maximum magic instead. Again, three Phoenix Feathers can make a world of difference.

MINOTAUR HORNS

Minotaur Horns are both useful and coveted, but don't increase Kratos' two main stats. These upgrade his item gauge, allowing him to fire more arrows and use other items without needing frequent recharge time.

TREASURES OF THE GODS

The rarest items in the game are the Treasures of the Gods. Almost all are found after you've defeated one of the Olympians or their greatest heroes, though sometimes the items are just lying around. Search the area every time you see a mysterious sparkle and hope that you find something marvelous.

These items can be turned on and off after you've completed the game. Note that it's impossible to get Trophies/Achievements after using one of these treasures in your current game. Many of the items have a dramatic (and usually positive) effect on gameplay.

APHRODITE'S GARTER
Lets Kratos continue to use Athena's Blades

DAEDALUS' SCHEMATICS
Grants infinite Item use

HADES' HELM
Maxes Health, Magic, and Item Meters

HELIOS' SHIELD
Triples the number on your Hits Counter

HEPHAESTUS' RING
Kratos automatically wins all Context Sensitive Attacks

HERA'S CHALICE
Causes your Health Meter to slowly drain over time, never completely emptying it

HERCULES' SHOULDER GUARD
Decreases damage taken by one-third

HERMES' COIN
Kratos collects ten times the amount of Red Orbs

POSEIDON'S CONCH SHELL
Grants infinite Magic

ZEUS' EAGLE
Grants infinite Rage of Sparta

THE ROAD TO GLORY

ACT I

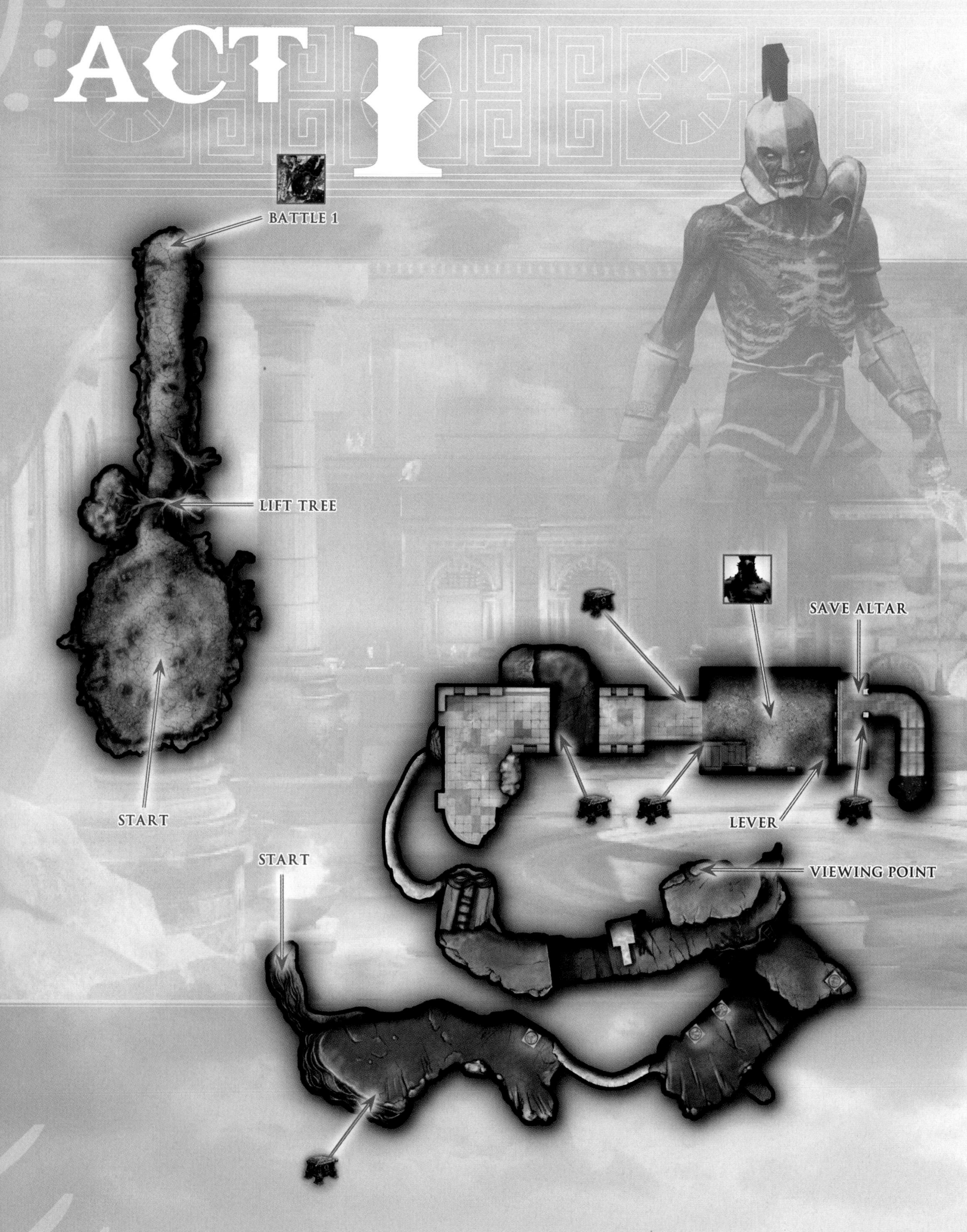

BATTLE 1
LIFT TREE
START
SAVE ALTAR
LEVER
START
VIEWING POINT

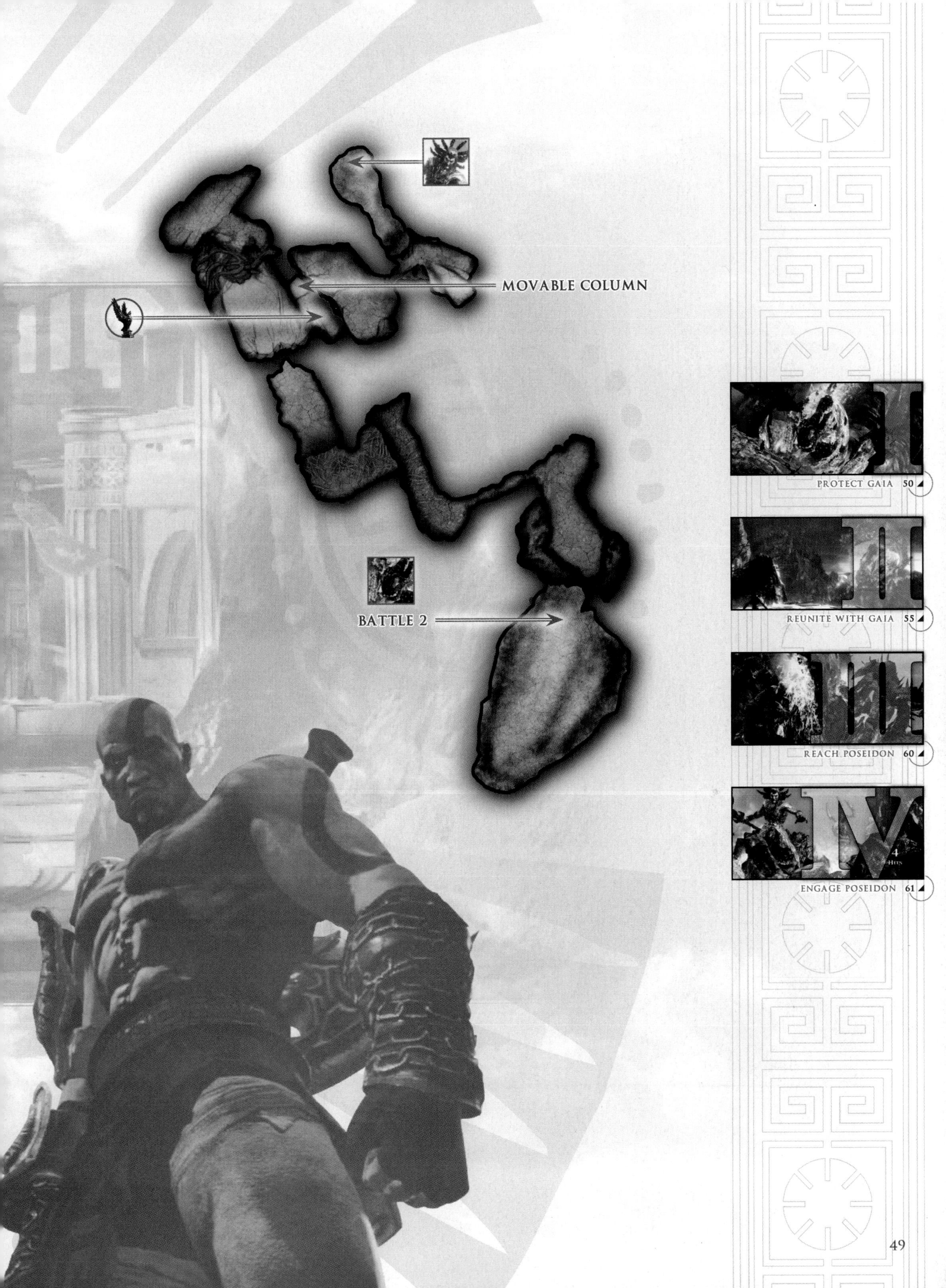

MOVABLE COLUMN
BATTLE 2
PROTECT GAIA 50
REUNITE WITH GAIA 55
REACH POSEIDON 60
ENGAGE POSEIDON 61

MOUNT OLYMPUS

Kratos begins his assault on Olympus just moments after the events ending *God of War II*. Gaia is climbing the cliffs of Mount Olympus with Kratos riding on her shoulder, helping to lead the charge. Though the Gods above may feel the earliest tinge of nervous energy, they are far from defeated. Zeus stands defiantly at the summit and the other Olympians are beside him, ready to defend their home.

Kratos has a nigh unquenchable thirst for blood that will drown them all in a sea of hate.

THE PRODIGAL SON RETURNS

PROTECT GAIA

First Assault

Just as one of the Titans is thrown off the cliff in a sudden counterassault, Gaia holds firm and continues her advance. Kratos must help her when the need arises; just wait for the chance! There isn't a long delay before the action begins. A mob of Olympus Sentries lands on Gaia's arm and swarms over Kratos. These enemies are weak and provide you the perfect opportunity to experiment with Kratos' extraordinary combat abilities. Eliminate all the Olympus Sentries using a mix of light attacks (■), combos, and a few throws for good measure.

THE NEW ART OF WAR

Kratos has new and powerful moves to inflict on those barring his path. After grabbing an opponent, Kratos can use the poor soul as a **Battering Ram** by pressing ■ and running toward his new target(s). Kratos can also use his **Icarus Wings** in a deadly area attack. Hold **L1** and press ✖ to launch enemies into the air with a deadly wind attack.

THE NEW ART OF RETALIATION

All enemies, from the smallest grunt to the Gods of Olympus, have gained new attacks and tactics for the battlefield. Kratos may notice that the Olympus Sentries can now pile on top of him, crushing him under their sheer weight and then stabbing him while he is down. To break free of the pile, quickly move the left analog stick back and forth until Kratos is able to break free.

OLYMPUS SENTRY 228

After you slice through the legion of Olympus Sentries, it becomes clear that the riffraff won't be enough to slow Kratos. Acting on Zeus' orders, Poseidon dives into the Aegean Sea to join the battle. He rises with a herd of monstrous Leviathan Tentacles. Before long, one of Poseidon's Tentacles latches onto Gaia. Kratos must find a way to save Gaia or risk losing his chance to kill Zeus. It's time to advance.

Clearing the Brush

After the wave of Olympus Sentries is decimated, Gaia blows out the flames on her shoulder providing Kratos with a path onward. Advance down the length of her right arm, crushing any new Olympus Sentries that arrive on the scene and testing out Kratos' magic. Use **R2** to damage any enemies unfortunate enough to be near Kratos. Afterward, approach the fallen tree nearby and move it out of the way before you continue.

KRATOS IN ACTION

Kratos' brute strength is useful for more than separating limbs and torsos. There are many obstacles scattered throughout the world that allow Kratos to interact with the environment in unique ways. To find these, look for white glowing beacons on objects and press **R1** to latch onto them. Kratos can perform various actions depending on the object with which he is interacting.

In this case, press ◎ repeatedly to lift the tangled trees into the air and clear the path along Gaia's arm.

Gaia

Gaia was seen by the Greeks as a personification of creation and the spirit of Mother Earth. She came before the Titans, when there was only Chaos, and she bore many children that eventually settled the land and the skies.

The Greeks worshipped forces that were meant to be understandable. Wisdom (Athena), justice and rule (Zeus), culture (Apollo) and so on. Gaia was not heavily worshipped because she was seen more as a force than a being. Her power was too great and too terrible to truly comprehend.

Ancient Greeks believed that the universe was becoming more organized and more civilized as time went on. The earliest creatures were little more than manifestations of nature, while their children were more like people. This process was meant to continue, and was an intuitive evolution of the cosmos.

Gaia mothered the skies (Uranus) and the oceans (Pontus) by herself. She soon became Uranus' lover, and with him conceived the Titans as well as the line that sired the Olympians.

In time, Gaia tired of the Titans and of Uranus. She crafted a stone sickle and showed it to some of her children. She asked if one would hide and then castrate Uranus the next time he approached her for lovemaking. Only Cronos had the courage to accept the task.

He did this and threw the resulting waste into the sea. Uranus was ripped apart, and his lost pieces and blood were forged (by Gaia) into new children.

Poseidon and the Hippocampi

Poseidon was the brother of Hades and Zeus, a child of the Titans Cronos and Rhea. When Zeus overthrew Cronos, Poseidon battled alongside his brothers against the Titans. In return, he was given a share of the spoils. He drew lots with Zeus and Hades for a domain: Zeus won the Heavens, Hades was given the Underworld, and Poseidon claimed the Seas.

Poseidon was known for his unstable, mercurial temper. He could be completely affable one moment, enraged and aggressive the next. Sometimes he was extremely considerate and welcoming, only to suddenly become vindictive. In short, he was not someone that could be trusted to be reasonable.

Poseidon's nature was mirrored by his domain, and he was prayed to by sailors and fishermen. He was sought for both his blessing and as a precaution, for it was easy to anger Poseidon. There were many dangers in the water, and the God could be merciless.

Still, Poseidon didn't usually care much about mortals. He was more than willing to leave them to their own devices. There was one exception, though: Poseidon was taken with the ladies. He was as much a philanderer as his brother Zeus; he had countless affairs with just about anything that he liked.

Fortunately for Poseidon, however, his wife Amphitrite was much more forgiving than Hera, and she didn't cause any problems for Poseidon. With his wife, Poseidon had two noteworthy children, a girl (Rhode) and a boy (Triton), as well as countless others, the Water Nymphs. Most of them stayed beneath the waves, in Poseidon's undersea palace.

He also had a number of children with human women and most of them became heroes. Of them, Theseus is the most well-known, and Poseidon took an active interest in protecting him. For instance, he ensured that the boy received proper weapons and armor and made certain he received warrior training. When Theseus was in trouble on the ocean, he prayed to Poseidon, who calmed the waves and tamed the winds for his son.

Some of Poseidon's children were monsters. He once decided that he'd try his luck with the Goddess Demeter. Demeter, being his sister, and knowing Poseidon's nature all too well, wasn't interested at all. But he wouldn't be dissuaded. Finally, she turned herself into a mare and hid in a herd of horses. Poseidon, though, was not one to be denied easily. He saw through her disguise and turned himself into a stallion. Their child was horse, Arion, that had human reasoning and speech.

Poseidon was always fascinated with horses, and they were his special animal. In many poems, the white-capped waves going into shore have been compared with white-maned horses. His chariot was pulled by hippocampus: creatures with the bodies of a horse and the tail of a fish. Poseidon would give special horses to those that pleased him, and it was considered a great honor to receive such a prestigious gift.

Once the path has been cleared, hurry along Gaia's arm. Along the way, Kratos is ambushed by a few more Olympus Sentries. Dispatch them with any attacks that suit your style. This fight isn't especially dangerous and is still a chance to experiment, getting used to Kratos' fighting techniques. The foes ahead are much stronger.

This is also a good time to start practicing evasive maneuvers. Olympus Sentries aren't tough by themselves, but there are many enemies in the game that require finesse. Use the right analog stick to roll around and get a feel for Kratos' dexterously defensive options. You'll be glad you did!

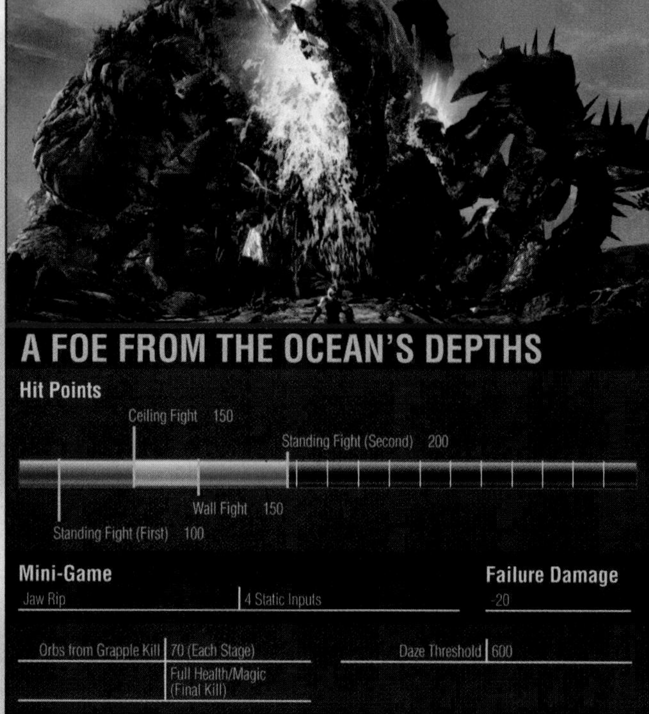

A FOE FROM THE OCEAN'S DEPTHS

Hit Points

Stage	Hit Points
Standing Fight (First)	100
Ceiling Fight	150
Wall Fight	150
Standing Fight (Second)	200

Mini-Game		Failure Damage
Jaw Rip	4 Static Inputs	-20

Orbs from Grapple Kill	70 (Each Stage)
	Full Health/Magic (Final Kill)
Daze Threshold	600

Kratos reaches the end of the path and gets an up close and personal look at one of Poseidon's pets. This aquatic monster bears deadly claws and unleashes water-based attacks that can rip Kratos to shreds in mere seconds. Rush the monstrous Leviathan Tentacle and attack it with a series of quick combos. Soon after Kratos initiates an attack against the beast, the steed prepares a counterattack.

Watch the Tentacle's head and prepare to dodge when it rears back. Its brutal water attack is imminent. You can't block these attacks; it's not worth even trying. Instead, roll out of the way and scramble back into attack range as soon as possible. The water pushes Kratos back, even if you avoid damage, but this is only a temporary setback.

To wound the beast, slash at its stony chest. Once Kratos has injured the monstrous foe it will pull away, writhing in agony. This motion causes Gaia to lose her grip on Mount Olympus, nearly sending Kratos and the Tentacle back into the ocean far below.

Kratos is flipped upside down and must hang from Gaia while he attempts to finish off the Tentacle. Move to the edge of Gaia's arm, closest to the steed, and continue attacking. The monstrosity can't use its watery breath from this angle, so watch the creature's crab-like claws instead.

While upside down, Kratos cannot roll, but retains his ability to dodge incoming attacks. Press ⊗ while moving in a direction to quickly dash away from the beast's claws.

Give yourself a bit of extra time to dodge; Kratos can't move quickly while hanging, and it takes a couple seconds to evade the oncoming attack. Be conservative with your attacks! Usually, three or four light attacks make a good combo. Stop after these, speed out of the way, and then continue the attack.

Keep attacking until Gaia regains her grasp on Mount Olympus. Though Gaia's arm is back in place, Kratos is still holding on for his life—but at least now he isn't upside down. Pinned by Gaia's arm, the Tentacle returns to its water attacks, though it also has a new claw attack. Crawl to the top of Gaia's arm and resume your light attacks. When you see the steed's head arch or its claw rise, quickly pull to the side and use ⊗ to get out of the way.

Gaia is eventually able to completely regain her grasp and Kratos gets back to even ground. The same patterns of attacks and evasion you've been using remain viable here. Stick to them, but add one or two blasts of magic for extra damage. The Tentacle finally succumbs to Kratos' onslaught and he is able to perform a devastating finishing move. Initiate the Context-Sensitive Action (◎) and silence the beast once and for all. The onscreen commands let you know what to do.

CONTEXT-SENSITIVE ACTIONS

Context-Sensitive Actions normally occur when giant enemies have been weakened to a state of submission. Once this happens, press ◎ to initiate the attack. Press the corresponding buttons or perform the appropriate analog stick movements that follow to successfully complete the motions of the devastating attack.

A major change from the earlier *God of War* games is that these commands appear in different parts of the screen that correspond to the locations of the face buttons on the PS3 Sixaxis™ controller. This is intended to help you know what to do without taking your eyes off the action. For example, ◎ commands appear on the right side of the screen and on the controller.

Keep your eyes centered use your peripheral vision to watch for input commands. For some monsters, these button combinations are random. For this Tentacle, however, the button sequence is □, □, □, □.

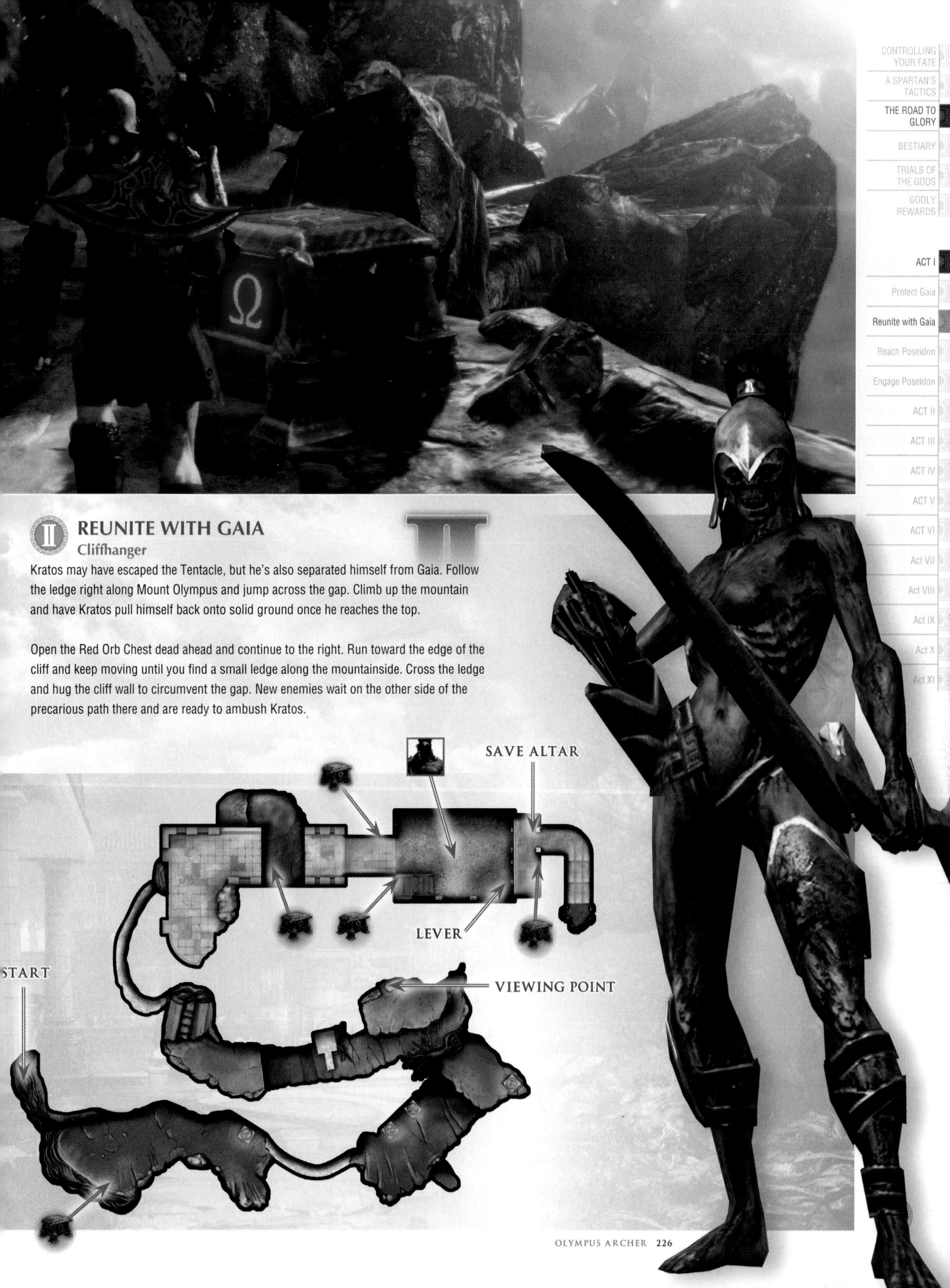

II REUNITE WITH GAIA

Cliffhanger

Kratos may have escaped the Tentacle, but he's also separated himself from Gaia. Follow the ledge right along Mount Olympus and jump across the gap. Climb up the mountain and have Kratos pull himself back onto solid ground once he reaches the top.

Open the Red Orb Chest dead ahead and continue to the right. Run toward the edge of the cliff and keep moving until you find a small ledge along the mountainside. Cross the ledge and hug the cliff wall to circumvent the gap. New enemies wait on the other side of the precarious path there and are ready to ambush Kratos.

GIFT OF THE GODS

Kratos can use magic to create a widespread attack that obliterates lesser enemies. Use Divine Reckoning by pressing **R2**.

An old trick from earlier games is to use magic attacks defensively. Kratos is immune to damage while he's unleashing this spell. Thus, you can avoid unblockable attacks *and* inflict damage to nastier enemies by unleashing Divine Reckoning just before the moment of impact.

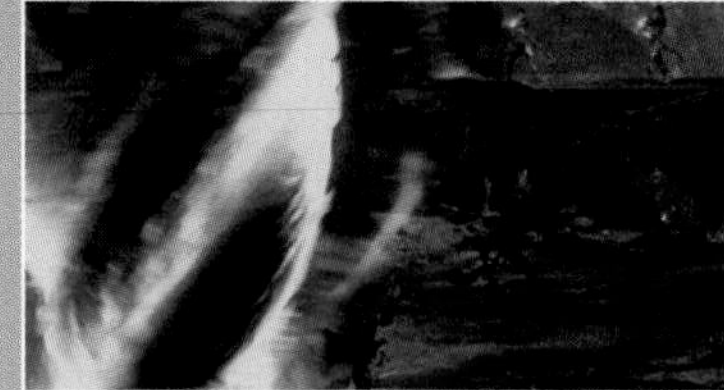

There is a small group of Olympus Sentries ahead of Kratos, and two Olympus Archers stand on the higher area behind them. The Olympus Sentries are closest, but the Archers should be Kratos' primary targets. Archers are a cowardly breed, and Kratos has little respect for them. They disrupt combos and make it harder for Kratos to stay at full health even when fighting defensively. Bring the fight to them!

Run toward the Olympus Sentries and use a quick combo, such as **Tartarus Rage** (**L1** + ◎), to scatter the foes. Alternatively, perform two evasive rolls to dodge past the troops. After creating a temporary clearing, jump onto the ledge and attack the Olympus Archers at close range. Kratos can easily grab the Archers and tear them in half to rid himself of their annoying presence. After killing the Archers, jump back to the lower level and eliminate the remaining enemies at your leisure.

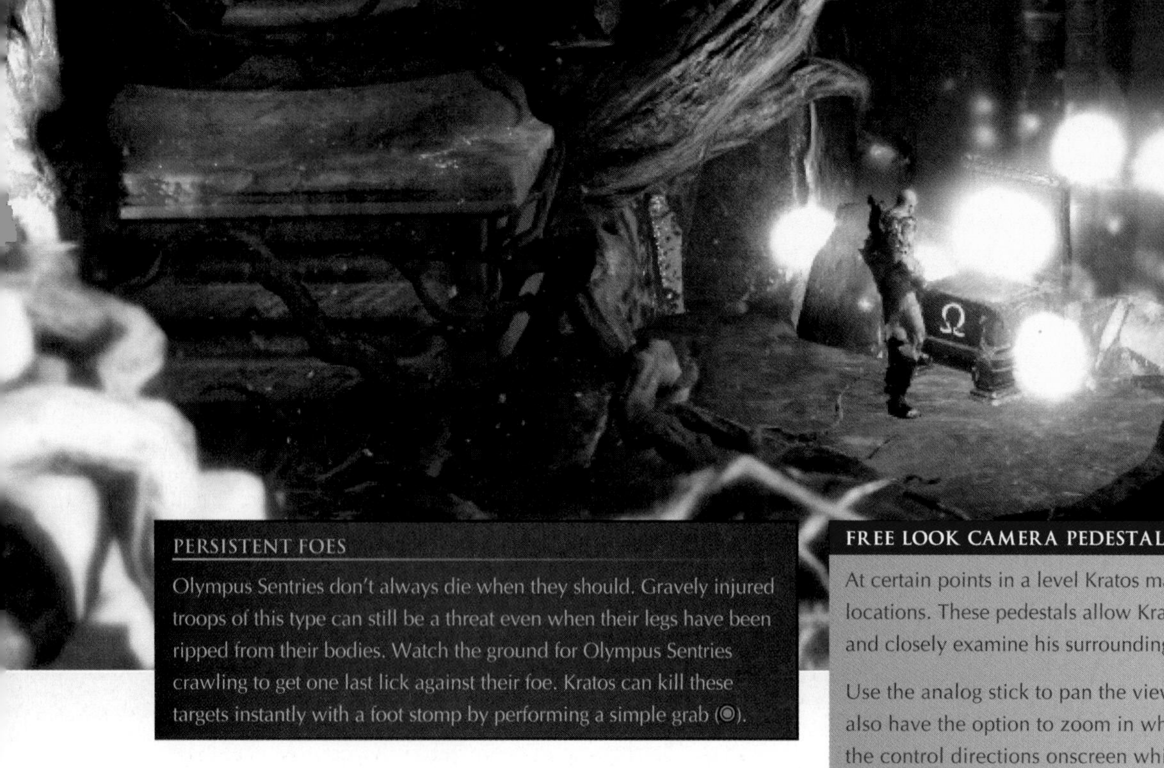

PERSISTENT FOES

Olympus Sentries don't always die when they should. Gravely injured troops of this type can still be a threat even when their legs have been ripped from their bodies. Watch the ground for Olympus Sentries crawling to get one last lick against their foe. Kratos can kill these targets instantly with a foot stomp by performing a simple grab (◎).

After clearing the area, climb up the ladder on the Olympus Archers' ledge and continue up the vines. Kratos encounters more Olympus Sentries at the top. Quickly dispatch these troops and take a moment to explore the area. Grab the Green Orbs from the chest on the lower level and jump up to the higher platform on the right side. Once on the platform, access your first Pedestal to get a glimpse of the Chain of Balance.

After using the Pedestal, run to the western edge of the platform and double-jump toward the broken stone arch. Grapple onto the stone arch (**R1**) and then double jump to the other side. This process can be completed without jumping toward the grapple point, if you prefer to start from the edge of the ledge.

FREE LOOK CAMERA PEDESTALS

At certain points in a level Kratos may locate Free Look Camera locations. These pedestals allow Kratos to take control of the camera and closely examine his surroundings.

Use the analog stick to pan the view in any direction you like. You also have the option to zoom in when you press forward. Look at the control directions onscreen while getting acquainted with this first pedestal.

GRAPPLING

Kratos uses his blades to grapple onto glowing Grapple Points. These glowing objects provide Kratos a way to swing across large chasms. Look for the bright targets and jump toward them. When Kratos is near the Grapple Point, press **R1** to latch on. Hold **R1** to continue swinging and press ⊗ to jump out of the grapple. A double-jump will provide extra height during the leap.

This can be chained between multiple Grapple Points. For instance, a jump across an extremely dangerous gap might require Kratos to jump, grapple, jump, and immediately grapple a new target. It's not as hard as it sounds once you're used to the controls.

There are three types of grapple points. We've just described the regular version, but the other two varieties are trickier. One spins Kratos in a 360 degree circle. Watch these carefully to ensure that Kratos dismounts as he's coming around to the desired side of the circle. The final type is a launch point. These won't let Kratos hold on; they pull him up and throw him out toward other targets.

Two Olympus Archers and a gang of Olympus Sentries spawn from the ground as soon as Kratos' feet touch ground. To eliminate the enemies, grab onto one of the Sentries and use him as a Battering Ram to knock down the Archers and any other enemies who happen to get in the way. After Kratos violently rids himself of the makeshift ram, use **Cyclone of Chaos** (**L1** + ◎) and other attacks to decimate the remaining troops. Once Kratos is alone, climb the ladder and continue on the vines to the right.

Get onto the ledge at the end of the vines and carefully proceed to the left. Jump across the gap in the path and watch as Kratos automatically nails the landing on the other side. Any time there is a gap jump you won't have to worry about controlling Kratos' direction in the air; he'll automatically leap the far side without trying to dive away from the cliff face.

As Kratos reaches the end of the ledge, jump up to the vines directly above. Keep climbing until you reach the top. In the distance, Kratos can see that Gaia is in dire need of his help. Run toward the bridge ahead, but be wary. The way across might have problems.

After an event takes place, a hole opens in front of Kratos. Before jumping across the newly created chasm, drop down to the new pit and open the chest in the southern corner. Climb out of the pit by jumping on the steps behind Kratos and then double-jump and release the Icarus Wings to cross the pit to the other side. Collect the Blue and Green Orbs from the two chests ahead if you need them.

WASTE NOT, WANT NOT

It's not always wise to open Health or Magic Chests if you're full on either. Kratos can often return to areas that he's recently passed. If he isn't badly hurt or hasn't used much magic, leave unneeded chests closed. That way you can return and loot the chests later if you fight a sudden battle that leaves you weakened.

On the flipside, it's never good to leave Red Orb Chests behind. Experience is *never* a bad thing to have in abundance. You get to upgrade both weapons and items with Red Orbs, so they're vital to Kratos' progress.

Proceed into the interior of Mount Olympus. When Kratos reaches the doorway, grab the bottom of the door and wrench it open. The screen directs you to tap ◎ repeatedly until the door is fully opened. Do this quickly or Kratos won't have the strength to proceed (and you have to repeat the mini game).

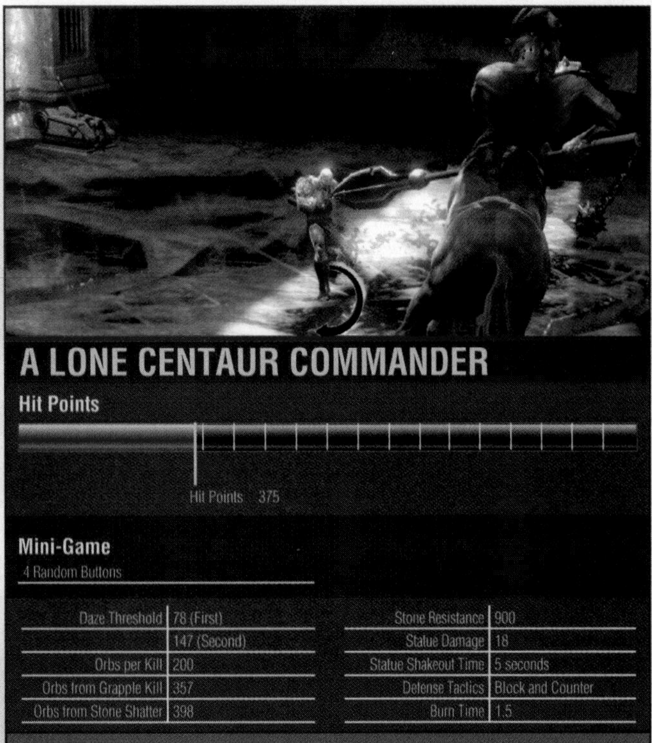

A LONE CENTAUR COMMANDER

Hit Points

Hit Points 375

Mini-Game

4 Random Buttons

Daze Threshold	78 (First)	Stone Resistance	900
	147 (Second)	Statue Damage	18
Orbs per Kill	200	Statue Shakeout Time	5 seconds
Orbs from Grapple Kill	357	Defense Tactics	Block and Counter
Orbs from Stone Shatter	398	Burn Time	1.5

Kratos finds himself inside Ares' tomb, but he's not the only one there. A Centaur Commander stalks in behind Kratos. Before he can react, the monster charges and catches him on the end of his spear. Quickly rotate the left analog stick, as displayed onscreen (clockwise from 12 o'clock to 6 o'clock) to counter the beast and get the fight started.

The Centaur Commander soon summons a group of Olympus Sentries to his side. Kratos can easily take care of this fodder, but having the Centaur in the room makes executing long combos more difficult. The Commander can order Sentries to pile onto Kratos, wearing him down with their numbers. If this starts to happen, dodge aside to avoid the pile (and use magic if possible to clear the enemies). When Kratos gets tackled, shift the left analog stick back and forth rapidly to escape the attack.

Use quick air combos and the Battering Ram technique to quickly eliminate the lesser Sentries. If you're lucky, the Centaur's brutish attacks will even damage his allies.

WARE THE KICK

Kratos isn't terribly safe when circling the Centaur Commander. Centaurs can unleash a brutal rear kick. Distance and speed are better defensively than outflanking these horsemen.

The Centaur Commander may also attempt to impale Kratos again, which can be a blessing in disguise. If the Centaur catches Kratos with his spear, quickly rotate the left analog stick to counter the attack and throw the Centaur off balance. The Centaur doesn't stay down for long, so take full advantage of the opportunity and unleash a barrage of attacks.

Practice blocking and parrying with the Golden Fleece during this fight. Kratos can block normal attacks when you hold down **L1**, but the Golden Fleece lets you avoid heavier blows and launch counterattacks! To do this, wait until an attack is about to hit Kratos. Don't press **L1** until the last second, and watch as the action slows down briefly. This lets you know that the Golden Fleece activated successfully. Later, Kratos learns how to respond with incredibly powerful counterattacks after he's uses the Fleece.

Golden Fleece upgrades are purchased when you improve the Blades of Exile. You should find these soon enough. The Centaur falls over in agony once Kratos inflicts enough damage. Close for the kill and use a Context-Sensitive Action to finish him off.

DOMINANT VICTORY

If you want to give yourself a challenge, try beating the Centaur Commander before taking on any of the Olympus Sentries. It's entirely possible, especially on earlier difficulty levels. Trying to do it this way on Chaos difficulty is a real treat.

A Quick Getaway

Take a moment to use the Pedestal on the northern wall once all the enemies are dead. Using this, Kratos can see Ares' corpse resting beneath the ice. After looking at Ares, study the layout of the tomb. There's a ladder leading up a wooden platform in the northeastern corner. There's also a lever against the western wall.

Pull the lever and quickly scale the eastern ladder to the platform above. A hanging scaffold is temporarily there and will provide transport for Kratos. Quickly jump onto the scaffold. Within seconds, it carries Kratos to the far side of the tomb. If Kratos doesn't make it in time to catch the ride, hop down and pull the lever again to call it back.

Once the scaffold stops, jump onto the upper level of the tomb and collect the Red Orbs from the nearby chest and use the Save Altar. Once Kratos is ready, run down the hall and throw open the gate to be reunited with Gaia.

SAVE ALTARS

These glowing pillars record your progress throughout the game, and there aren't any penalties for using them. Unlike survival horror and other similar games, you're free to save repeatedly without harming your score or your chance to get rewards. Thus, it's always good to take full advantage of these points when you reach them. In fact, it's even worth backtracking to save in a few rare cases.

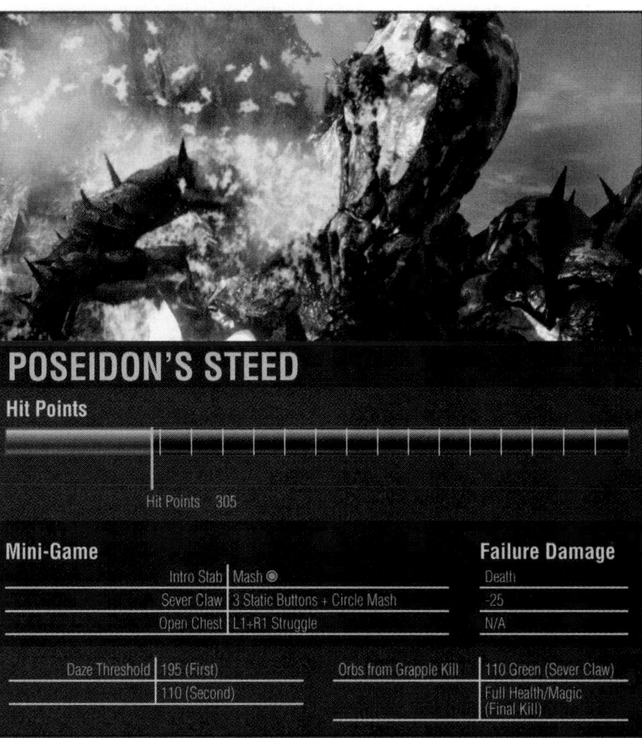

POSEIDON'S STEED

Hit Points

Hit Points 305

Mini-Game		Failure Damage
Intro Stab	Mash ◉	Death
Sever Claw	3 Static Buttons + Circle Mash	-25
Open Chest	L1+R1 Struggle	N/A

Daze Threshold	195 (First)	Orbs from Grapple Kill	110 Green (Sever Claw)
	110 (Second)		Full Health/Magic (Final Kill)

Kratos rides one of Poseidon's watery beasts back onto Gaia's chest. This battle is similar to the fight against Poseidon's previous Tentacle, but this one has the freedom to perform some new attacks. The Tentacle may charge toward one side or the other. Stay roughly in the middle of the screen and avoid each swing while inflicting as much damage as possible. The Tentacle will force Kratos back several steps and then try to breathe water over him. Attack quickly and attempt to break the Tentacle's routine. If that fails, use a magical attack at the last moment to avoid damage.

Between the Tentacle's normal attacks, counter with combos and heavy attacks. Eventually the beast weakens and Kratos can initiate a Context-Sensitive Action.

Follow the onscreen commands to sever one of the beast's claws from its torso. Take notice of the claw and that it falls on the "ground" behind Kratos.

Now that the beast is severely injured, it begins using fast, frantic attacks as well as the water attacks you've seen before. Quickly dodge the water attacks and block any claw attacks. When there is an opening, move in and unleash the full fury of an enraged Spartan. After a series of blows, the Tentacle is stunned once again.

With the enemy reeling, perform a Context-Sensitive Action to rip open its rib cage and expose its beating heart. Quickly run back to the severed claw and grab it to have Kratos throw the claw straight into the steed's heart. This automatically delivers the final blow, ridding Gaia of another nuisance.

Centaur

Centaurs were half-man, half-horse, and they were reputed for having bad reputations. Often viewed as brutal, savage creatures, most people stayed well away from them. There were few people capable of defending themselves from a rampaging Centaur.

The Centaurs were indirectly created by Zeus. There was a mortal king who fell in love with Hera, the Queen of the Gods and Zeus' wife. He resolved that he would have her, no matter the cost. He invited Zeus and Hera to a dinner, with the plan of stealing her away from her husband. Zeus, however, was not fooled. Instead of taking Hera, he created a woman made of clouds, one that looked exactly like his wife, and took her with him. The king was completely fooled, and his attempts to lure away the false Hera were completely successful. The two were married, and in due course, they had children. Zeus, though, arranged to receive a bit of revenge: the children were born as half-horse monsters.

Centaurs had a fondness for good, strong wine, and they got drunk quickly and became violent. On one occasion, a village decided to throw a huge wedding banquet for a newly married couple. Out of courtesy, they invited the local centaurs who drank their fill at the feast and started to cause trouble. They instigated fights, turned over tables, and were generally loud and obnoxious. That's when things got really ugly; they decided to carry away the bride and all the other nearby women.

Fortunately, one of the wedding guests was none other than Hercules. He took offense at the Centaurs' attitude, and he wasn't about to let them have their way. He fought off the entire Centaur band that quickly fled from the village. The centaurs in that area were never a problem again.

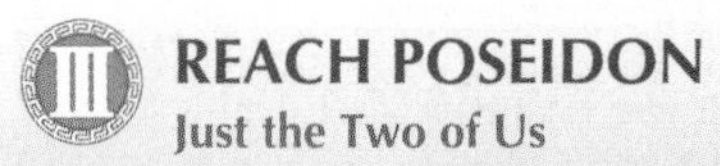

REACH POSEIDON

Just the Two of Us

After defeating the Tentacle, climb up Gaia's chest and drop into the wound caused by the monster's attack. Kratos finds himself within the Titan's body. Proceed through a dark cavern and squeeze through the tiny opening in the wall. Climb up the vines ahead of Kratos and continue along the ceiling. Slide down the far wall and then drop back onto ground level.

Kratos ends up inside Gaia's chest, near her heart. Head toward the eastern wall and climb the vines onto an elevated platform. On the platform is an Ancient Mural. Beneath it is **Zeus' Eagle**, a special treasure.

GODLY POSSESSIONS

The Gods have a number of special items that Kratos should collect while fighting his way through their ranks. They're all detailed in the walkthrough, so you won't miss a single one.

After viewing Zeus' drawing, drop back to the lower level. Grab onto the stone column inside the eastern wall and drag it to the center of the room. Rotate the column 180 degrees and place it within the indentation on the western wall.

ROTATING OBJECTS

Kratos can rotate objects that he can drag. Hold onto the object and push left or right on the right analog stick to change the object's orientation. It's fast and convenient. Turn the block 180 degrees, so that Kratos is pushing it instead of pulling. This makes for a faster trip to the other side of the room.

Climb up the western wall and continue along the vines toward the right. Kratos quickly reaches a gap in the wall; use the Grapple Point to swing across. Keep climbing until you find a new, elevated path.

Move down the path and keep your guard up. Olympus Sentries spawn from the ground and initiate a new assault. Grab the first Sentry that reaches Kratos and use it as a Battering Ram to topple the rest of the squad. Once Kratos discards his unwilling partner, eliminate any remaining Sentries with fast combos. Kill everyone in the way, walk to the end of the corridor, and climb onto the vine path.

Scale the vines on the wall and jump the gap to reach a new platform. A glowing Grapple Point is above Kratos. Jump up and grapple to reach a higher tier. Kratos finds some company on the vines in the form of more Olympus Sentries.

It's easy to avoid the Olympus Sentries. Fast jumps take you past them without any fighting. Alternatively, you can attack the group by grabbing them or using regular weapon attacks and combos.

If any Sentries are straggling behind, take them out with quick, sweeping attacks (◎). Use the Grapple Point at the top of the vines to exit Gaia and land on the outside of her head.

ENGAGE POSEIDON

Save a Titan

IV

As you reach the top of Gaia's head, she intercepts another of Poseidon's minions. However, the true threat reveals itself as Poseidon rises into view in all his glory and questions the act of challenging a true God of Olympus. It's time to battle a god!

DEFEAT THE GOD OF THE SEAS

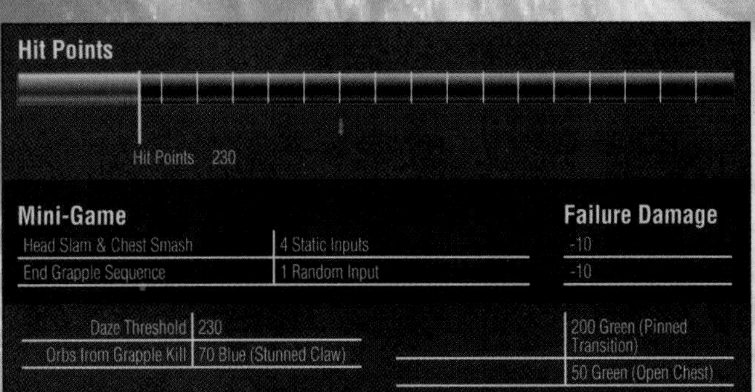

Hit Points

Hit Points 230

Mini-Game		Failure Damage
Head Slam & Chest Smash	4 Static Inputs	-10
End Grapple Sequence	1 Random Input	-10

Daze Threshold	230
Orbs from Grapple Kill	70 Blue (Stunned Claw)
	200 Green (Pinned Transition)
	50 Green (Open Chest)

Poseidon is done hiding, and it's time for Kratos to put an end to his tyranny. Unfortunately, Poseidon has dug his crustacean-like claws into Gaia's head, keeping Kratos at bay for the moment. Start attacking the claws on both sides to release Gaia from Poseidon's grasp.

The Olympian won't let Kratos unleash his full fury unchallenged, however. Poseidon has two attacks to defy the Spartan: one is a lightning attack with his trident and the other is a stab with his claws. Roll out of the way if the ground radiates with blue sparks. This lets you avoid Poseidon's electrical attack. Watch carefully to see where to dodge. The lightning covers a fair amount of territory, so you have to react very quickly. If the sparks are close to Poseidon, roll away. If they're to your side, roll to the other.

If Gaia's head lolls to the side, be ready for an incoming claw attack from either the right or left; roll to the opposite side to avoid a crushing blow.

Continue attacking the claws between evasive maneuvers. Eventually Gaia will turn the tables on Poseidon and Kratos lends his considerable assistance.

Freed of the claws, Gaia grabs Poseidon. Follow her orders and grapple onto her hand (**R1**). Kratos swings onto Gaia's fist while she pins Poseidon against Mount Olympus. It's a telling blow, but this isn't enough to end the fight.

Poseidon is trapped and doesn't have much maneuvering room. Poseidon chooses to either punch quickly, stab multiple times with his trident, or thrust his weapon into the "ground" and dig around to punish Gaia.

The nastiest attack is the trident's triple stab. Poseidon adjusts his aim from left to right as the combo progresses, so evade to the left when you can. Or, use magic to avoid the damage and open Poseidon to counterattacks.

When Poseidon finishes each swing, rush in toward his body and lay into him with your blades. Remember that Poseidon won't wait long before attacking once more; stay on the lookout for the indication that he's about to do so. It's smart to play the long game and rely on a few hits here and there. Continue attacking until Poseidon is dazed.

With the Olympian winded, climb up Gaia's finger and initiate a Context-Sensitive Action. Kratos inflicts massive damage on Poseidon. Nearly crippled and in desperation, the God of the Sea orders his minions to renew their attack on Gaia once more.

HESITATION KILLS

Poseidon recovers if Kratos takes too long to climb Gaia's finger and initiate the next attack. This provides a minor breather for the God and heals him a bit. Poseidon also takes advantage of the delay to snatch Kratos off Gaia's fingers and toss him around. Avoid this by leaping up Gaia's finger instead of climbing cautiously and diving into the Context-Sensitive Action.

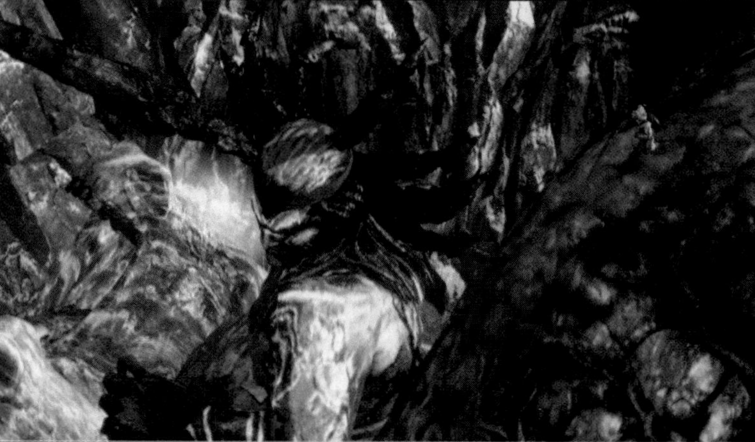

Kratos returns to Gaia's scalp and tries to free her from the claws once again. Poseidon's attacks have grown more powerful and frenetic, but they're quite similar to his original attack types during the first stage of the fight. The lightning blast is now a combo move that sweeps across the ground.

If the sparks appear on the left, dodge to the right and then roll left after the first blast hits. The lightning covers the whole screen, but there is enough of a delay to avoid both blasts.

When the lightning appears in front, get to the back of the screen and wait for the lightning to come toward you. It covers the front third, then the middle, and finally the rear portion of the screen. Roll to the top after either stage to avoid being trapped and struck down.

Use Divine Reckoning and quick combos to eliminate the claws while dodging and avoiding Poseidon's attacks. As the claws retreat again, Gaia winds up to slam Poseidon; she's stopped once more by the tentacles, but Kratos has the opening he needs.

Approach the grapple point that is sparkling to your side. Press **R1** to start a chain of grappling events. There are several of these in a row, and be prepared to press **R1** to access each as quick time events. Immediately after Kratos leaves the third tentacle, perform a Context-Sensitive Action to cut Gaia loose. With Gaia's help, Kratos delivers the coup de grace to the mighty Poseidon.

Kratos and Poseidon end up alone on Mount Olympus. The Sea God's powers are depleted, and he's left at the Spartan's mercy. Another Context-Sensitive Action reveals the end to the skirmish.

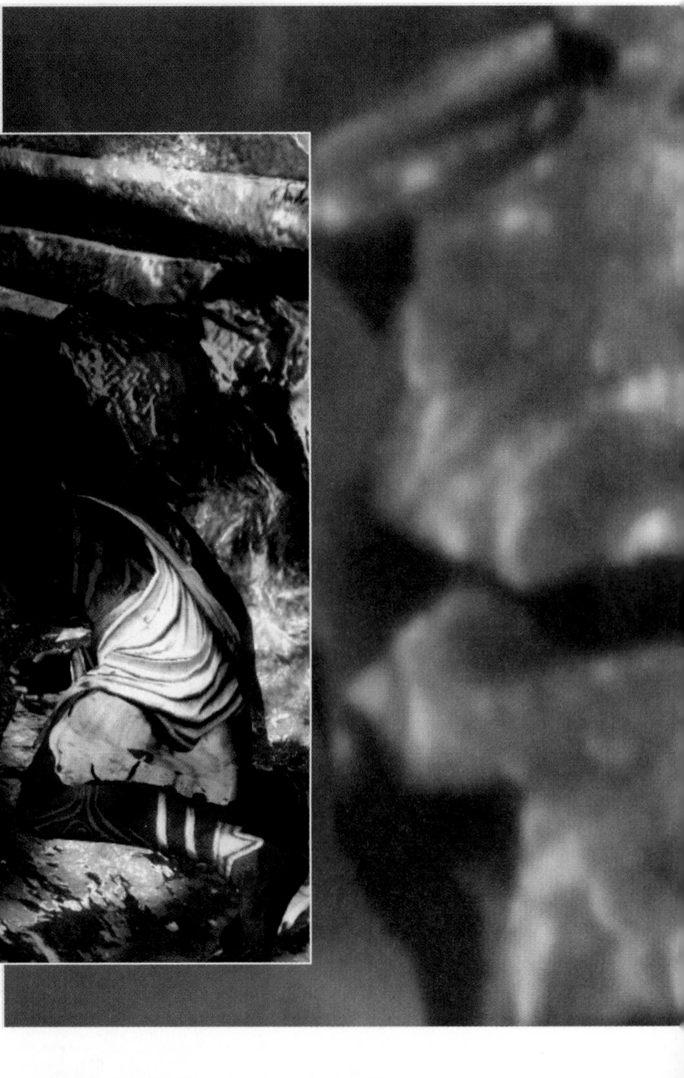

Vengeance Denied

Once the story sequence ends, look around for a Save Altar. Avail yourself of the Altar before leaping onto Gaia's hand. She carries Kratos to the top of Mount Olympus, where Kratos has an important confrontation. But within moments, Kratos is forced to leave Mount Olympus and descend into the depths of the Underworld once more.

ACT II

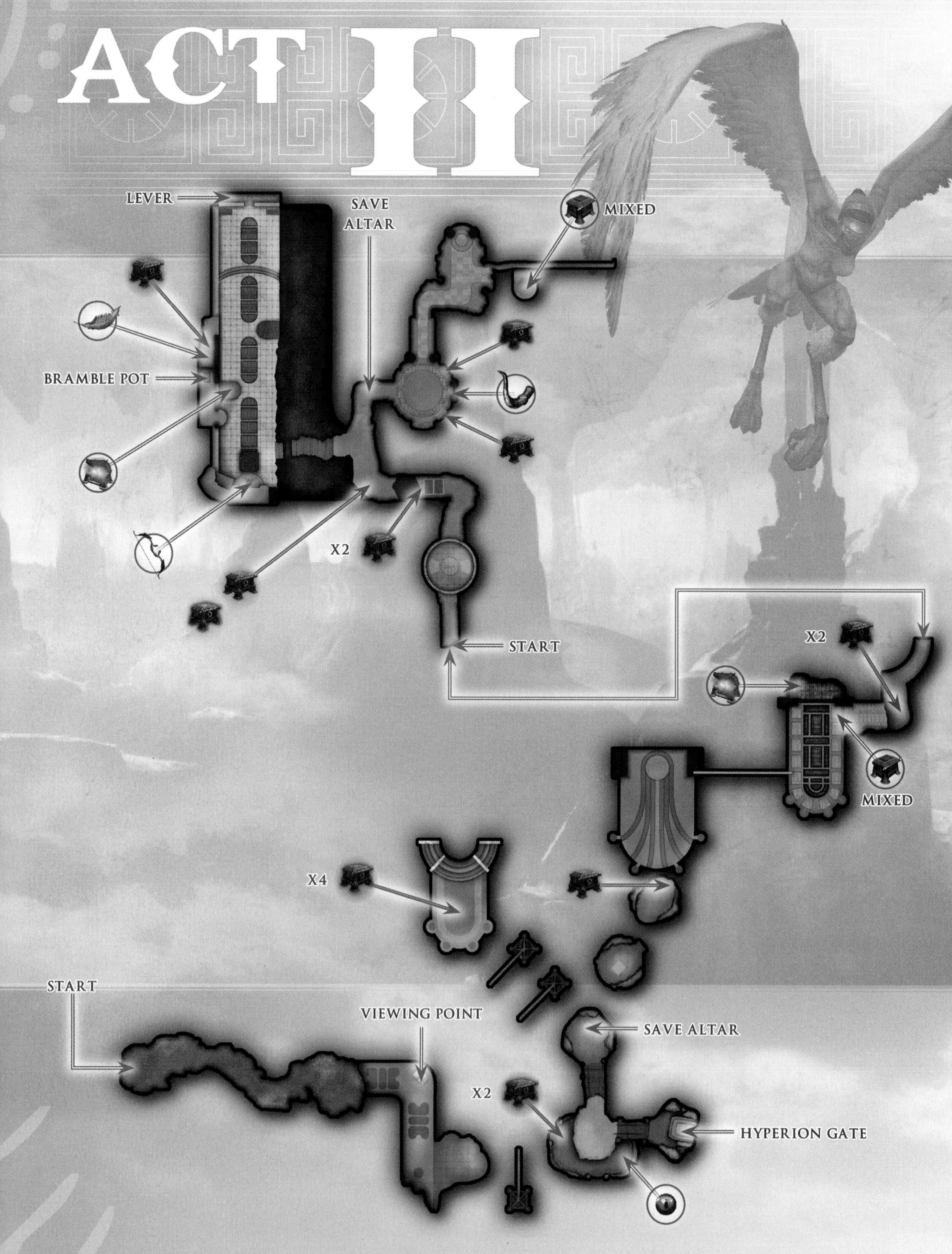

LEVER
SAVE ALTAR
MIXED
BRAMBLE POT
X2
START
X2
MIXED
X4
START
VIEWING POINT
SAVE ALTAR
X2
HYPERION GATE

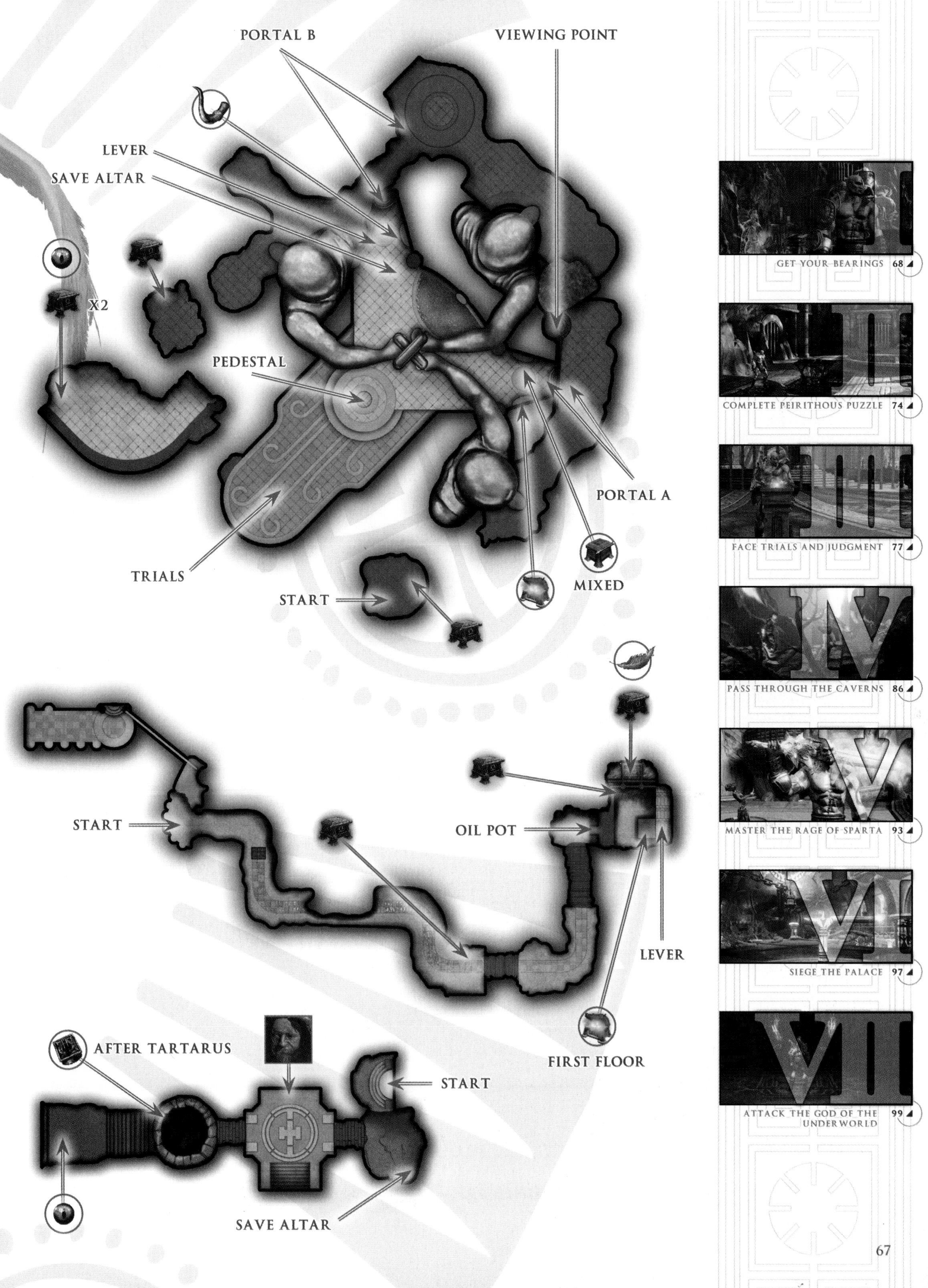
PORTAL B
VIEWING POINT
LEVER
SAVE ALTAR
X2
PEDESTAL
PORTAL A
TRIALS
MIXED
START
START
OIL POT
LEVER
FIRST FLOOR
AFTER TARTARUS
START
SAVE ALTAR

HADES

THE ROAD OUT OF HADES

GET YOUR BEARINGS

Cursed River

Swim down the River Styx without fear of attack. The Lost Souls in the water are victims of fate. Though they can't kill Kratos, they desire something of him. They greedily strip away his health, magic, and experience. This is unavoidable. Use the left analog stick to swim to the nearby embankment and climb out to reach the entrance of Hades' domain.

LOST SOULS

These souls, damned to Hades, roam the landscape. They cause little harm and usually avoid attacking unless provoked. Almost any damage Kratos inflicts kills them. Grab Lost Souls to crush them and restore some of Kratos' health if he is injured.

Stagger to the right and give Kratos a moment to regain his composure. As he slowly walks forward, a spirit from his past arrives and greets him. After an important conversation, the spirit alters Kratos' blades and dubs them the Blades of Exile. Though Kratos is weakened, he must continue his quest.

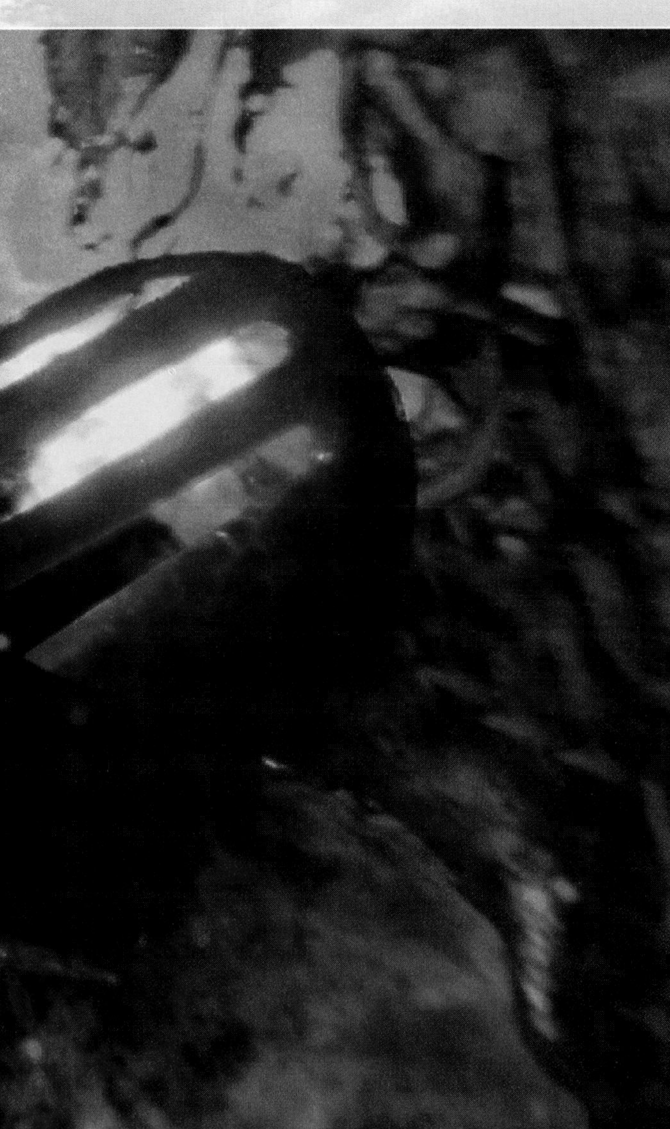

Welcome to Hades

Use the pedestal on the left to look at the Gates of Hades and the surrounding Underworld. Continue along the main path until the walkway comes to a sudden halt. Fortunately, there's a Grapple Point hanging over the cavern ahead. Use Kratos' new blades to latch onto the extended beam and swing to the next ledge.

Fall short of the upper ledge after releasing from the Grapple Point. Kratos lands on lower ground near two Red Orb Chests and a lone Item Chest. Open them and revel in their offerings. You've found a **Gorgon Eye**.

GORGON EYE

The chest on the right side of this hidden spot contains a Gorgon Eye. These rare items provide Kratos with exceptional health. If he gathers three of them he'll receive a permanent boost to his maximum health!

The River Styx

Styx is probably the best known of the great rivers of the Underworld. The ancient river's water has various magical properties. Foremost, it would normally slay any being that drank from it. However, Kratos is hardly a normal being, and his thirst for vengeance drives him on!

Above, the path leads off in several directions. To the right is the Hyperion Gate. Kratos can't use this yet, but must return here later. Take the left path instead. Continue looking left and leap toward a series of Grapple Points. Swing across these to reach a treasure area with a few Lost Souls. Open the four Red Orb Chests for a modest reward. Afterward, return via the Grapple Points and head to the right. This leads deeper into the Underworld.

As you proceed, Kratos remembers how to use a move known as combat grappling. This is an form of attack that works well against enemies that can't be grabbed automatically. Instead of pressing ◎ by itself, hold down **L1** and then press ◎ to snag enemies and disrupt their attack routines. This technique is extremely useful against faster enemies!

Hades

Hades is one of the three Olympians who divided all creation between themselves. His brothers are Zeus and Poseidon. It is said that Cronos once flung Hades into the depths of Tartarus, and so that was fated to be his kingdom when the three divine brothers drew lots to see where each would rule.

As the ruler of the Underworld, Hades became the God that presided over the afterlife. Using Hades' name directly was thought to be bad luck. It was thought that doing so called the god's attention, and let him learn of the affairs of the living world. Instead he was called "the wealthy one" or "receiver of many guests."

Hades left his kingdom so rarely and became so identified with his kingship that, in time, even the Underworld itself was simply called Hades. Referred to as the "Zeus of the Underworld," Hades' power within his realm was absolute. The other Olympians rarely dared go there, save for Hermes, who was allowed to escort the souls of the departed as part of his role as the Psychopompos.

Geographically, the great river Styx served to mark the boundary between the mortal world and the Underworld. The river flowed directly from Pontus, the Ocean himself. Styx's waters were so potent that the Gods swore oaths upon them, and suffered a host of torments if they dared to break their word.

A host of rivers that sprang from the Styx ran through the Underworld: the Phlegethon, a river of burning fire, Acheron, the river of woe, Lethe, the river of forgetfulness, and Cocytus, the river of lament.

To enter Hades, souls of the dead had to be ferried across the Styx by the ferryman, Charon. However, he charged to take passengers across. That is why Greeks buried their dead with a coin beneath their tongue (to pay the ferryman). Anyone who wasn't attended in this way was left on the riverbank to wait for all eternity.

Hades was the kingdom of the dead. Virtuous dead went on the Elysian Fields (a very different realm that was not under Hades' control). Those who found themselves in the Underworld were lost, wicked, or insufficiently virtuous.

Souls were judged by the shades of the three great kings: Minos, Radamanthus, and Aegeus. These are the spirits that would decide where each spirit would go. Once a person's soul entered Hades, it could never escape save by special dispensation from Hades himself. Those who attempted to leave were menaced by Cerberus.

Failing to reach the Elysian Fields was not the end of a person's judgment. These remaining souls were divided into two groups. Those who weren't wicked were allowed to roam freely in the Asphodel Fields, a stand of black poplars and sterile willows. This area was sacred to Persephone, and it stood on the edge of the kingdom.

There, the shades of the dead gathered in great throngs. These spirits could no longer do harm (or good). They only found pleasure in drinking the blood of black rams and bulls sacrificed to Hades.

The result was much worse for the truly wicked. Their time in Hades became an eternity of tortures designed to prevent them from ever forgetting their crimes. Perhaps the most famous example was Tantalos, who had greedily stolen nectar and ambrosia from the Gods. In his afterlife he was tortured by hunger and thirst that could never be quenched. Water flowed up to his lips only to ebb away if he tried to drink, and fruits that grew on the trees above his head would lift away as he tried to reach them.

Kratos soon reaches an open area with a statue of mighty Hades seated above him. The voice of Hades calls out to Kratos as he presses ahead, but no god appears. Instead, he sends many of his warriors to stop you. These Olympus Sentries are spoiling for a fight, but Kratos suddenly learns the **Army of Sparta** maneuver. This spell is cast by pressing **R2** while the Blades of Exile are readied. It inflicts damage in a circle around Kratos; it's perfect for killing light, swarming enemies like this.

You effectively have an infinite supply of magic during this encounter, so test the new spell to your heart's content. Use it repeatedly to decimate the Olympus Sentries.

The magic boost ends when the last of the Olympus Sentries dies. Locate the suspended chain on the right side of the platform. That's your path forward. Jump and grab the chain and use ⊗ to move quickly right. Don't stop to think about the Olympus Sentries that are approaching behind you. There are more of them ahead, and those are the foes to beat. Stop briefly to knock the Sentries ahead of you to their deaths; it's easy to use weapon attacks to drop two at a time.

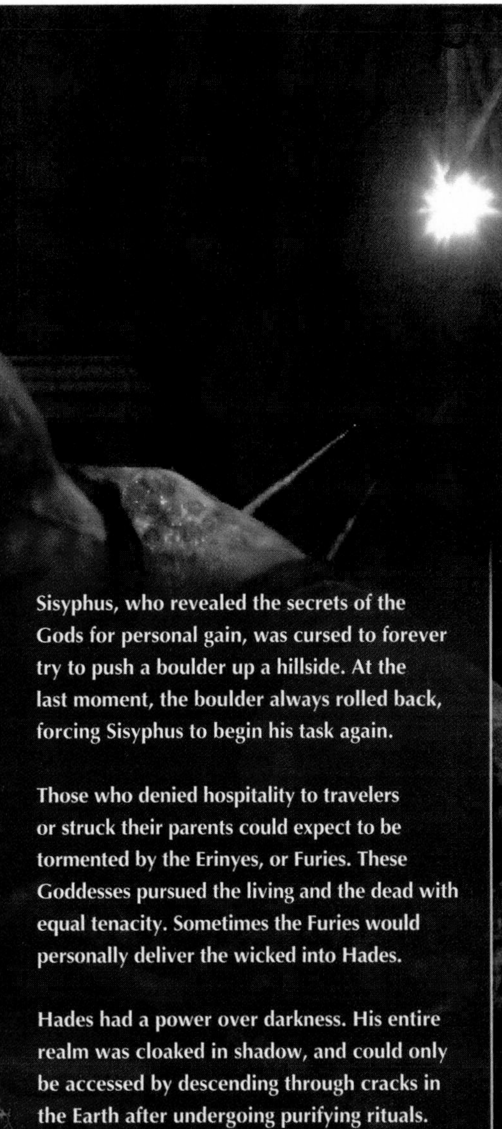

Sisyphus, who revealed the secrets of the Gods for personal gain, was cursed to forever try to push a boulder up a hillside. At the last moment, the boulder always rolled back, forcing Sisyphus to begin his task again.

Those who denied hospitality to travelers or struck their parents could expect to be tormented by the Erinyes, or Furies. These Goddesses pursued the living and the dead with equal tenacity. Sometimes the Furies would personally deliver the wicked into Hades.

Hades had a power over darkness. His entire realm was cloaked in shadow, and could only be accessed by descending through cracks in the Earth after undergoing purifying rituals. Hades himself wore an enchanted helmet that let him cloak himself from all eyes, mortal and immortal. Hades used this during battle to great effect. The only opponent known to ever wound him is Hercules who was such a good archer that he could hit even Hades.

A RACE FOR SURVIVAL

If you hurry, you can beat both impeding, attacking squads and drop off the chain before the pursuing troops catch you. It's much easier to fight the remaining warriors on the ground after they catch up!

Climb across the chain, killing the Olympus Sentries that dangle there. Weapon attacks are good for doing this at range safely, but at higher difficulty levels it's harder to kill enemies before they get close to you. Remember that Kratos can grapple with the Sentries and throw them off!

ROPE/CHAIN NAVIGATION

The left stick moves Kratos along the rope or chain and ⊗ allows him to move more quickly. Press ▢ for a quick kick, press △ for a long swipe, and press ◯ to grab an enemy. If an enemy latches on to Kratos, wiggle the left analog stick to escape. Press **R1** to let go.

Jump off the chain at the far end to land on the next platform. Open the Alternating Chest and Mixed Orb Chest. The path continues on a lower plane to the right.

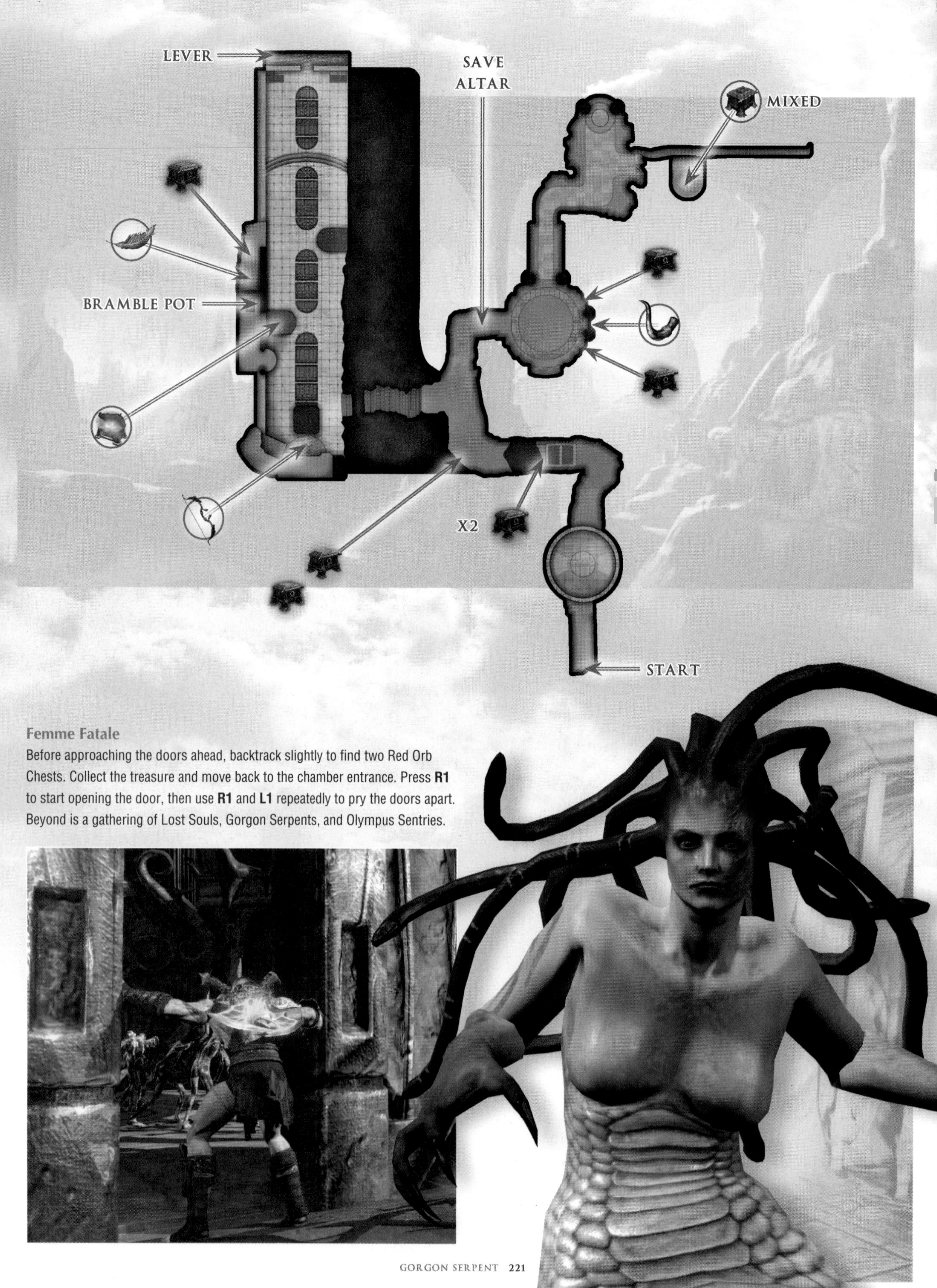

Femme Fatale

Before approaching the doors ahead, backtrack slightly to find two Red Orb Chests. Collect the treasure and move back to the chamber entrance. Press **R1** to start opening the door, then use **R1** and **L1** repeatedly to pry the doors apart. Beyond is a gathering of Lost Souls, Gorgon Serpents, and Olympus Sentries.

GORGON SERPENT 221

GORGON SERPENT

These half-woman, half-serpent creatures are famous for their stony gaze. When Gorgon Serpents concentrate, the beams from their eyes become more intense and turn most living things into stone.

When you see the creature's eyes begin to glow, roll away from these beams using the right analog stick, but don't give up hope if the serpentine witch turns Kratos to stone. Move the left analog stick back and forth very quickly. Kratos can break out of his stone prison and prevent the Gorgons from killing him in a single hit!

After wearing Gorgon Serpents down, Kratos can grapple with them to rip their heads off. This temporarily petrifies any surrounding foes. In addition, you receive a number of Blue Orbs for this, restoring some of Kratos' magic. The downside of this is that your experience for the fight is slightly reduced.

The first Gorgon Serpent turns the room's inhabitants to stone as she enters. The creature then proceeds to rush Kratos; answer this insult with a barrage of light attacks and start pummeling her. She may periodically ensnare Kratos with her serpent tail; rip away from her grasp by using **R1** and **L1**. Escaping in this manner inflicts damage on the monster instead of Kratos, so it's not particularly bad to be ensnared. As an added bonus, he can't be struck by other creatures while in her grasp.

Olympus Sentries and Shades enter the chamber during your fight. Focus on the Gorgon Serpent and let the others fall in the crossfire. Soon Kratos can perform a Context-Sensitive Action to rip off the creature's head and use it to petrify the crowding attackers.

Here's an advanced technique for those who favor the counterattack. Prepare for the Gorgon Serpent to use her petrifying beam attack. When she does, press **L1** when the beam hits Kratos and a random button prompt will appear on the screen. Press the button to reflect the beam and petrify all those around you.

Another Gorgon Serpent makes an appearance after the first falls. Destroy the new foe just as Kratos did with the other sister and clear the room of all enemies. Victory opens the path on the left side. Force open the next set of doors to continue.

PUZZLE OF PEIRITHOUS

Thorns and Fire

The path veers left and leads into a cave. There is a pit just inside the entrance, but don't leap over and ignore it. It's safe to fall into the pit and look around. There are two Red Orb Chests in the lower part of the pit. Loot the chests and climb back to the top. Look deeper into the cave to find a Health Chest as well.

Pressing forward, you should notice that the main path is blocked by thorn-ridden brambles. There is no way to get past these for now. Turn down the left walkway instead. This path leads back into an open area.

Soon, Kratos encounters Peirithous strapped to a stone chair. The two of them talk, and a deal is reached. He must set Peirithous free; in return he'll give Kratos the Bow of Apollo. That sounds quite useful, especially here, where so many of Kratos' powers were stolen.

Gorgons

Medusa is the most well-known of the Gorgons, but the term actually refers to group of creatures. Athena turned Medusa into a Gorgon because of a slight inferred by the mortal. Medusa was once a beautiful woman with gorgeous, auburn hair. Unfortunately, she had a romantic tryst with Poseidon in one of Athena's temples, earning the goddess' everlasting wrath.

The Gorgons were Medusa's sisters. Some stories said there were three Gorgons in all, counting Medusa herself; some described the Gorgons as an entire tribe of creatures. At the very least, Medusa's two sisters were named Stheno and Euryale. They were part of a group of lesser divinities called the Phorcides, or "Grey Goddesses." All of them were monstrous in appearance.

Gorgons were hideous to look upon. They all had scales covering their bodies which made them resemble serpents or dragons. Instead of hair, these women had writhing snakes on their heads. Gorgons were said to have tusks like a boar, hands made of sharpened brass, and either one or two pairs of sharpened, golden wings. Anyone who looked directly at the Gorgons would be so overwhelmed that they would be instantly turned to stone.

Perseus, a Greek hero, slew Medusa using considerable guile. The hero took a shield and polished it until the shield reflected whatever image shone upon it. He waited until the Gorgons slept, and then approached while looking only at the image in his shield. When he saw the reflection of Medusa, he cut off her head.

Afterward, the Gorgons wailed from both their human-like mouths and each of their serpent heads. The high-pitched keening noise inspired Athena to create the pan flute, to mock the Gorgons' suffering.

The inspiration for the Gorgons probably came from ritual masks worn by ancient priestesses who worshiped mysterious Goddesses rather than Zeus. The masks warned people away from trying to examine anything they guarded. Ancient Greek bakers, for instance, painted Gorgon faces on their ovens to warn curious passers-by from opening them.

WOULD YOU LIKE TO SOLVE THE PUZZLES ON YOUR OWN?

Some people prefer to finish puzzles without our help, while others want to crash through and get things done as quickly as possible. We've provided options for everyone. Below are a series of hints. The first gives a mild suggestion for what to do. The following hint offers more substantial information. And if that's not what you want, we finish with a complete step-by-step guide for what to do. It's up to you if you want to use any (or all) of them.

SMALL HINT

The Cerberus Mongrel is known to have some nasty breath.

BIG HINT

The bramble pot, the hanging lamp, and the Cerberus are all Kratos needs to make Peirithous feel the heat.

1. *Climb up the two shallow ledges above Peirithous and jump onto the kindling lamp.*
2. *Kratos' weight causes the lamp to slowly drop from the ceiling. Before it can drop too far, leap to the small balcony on the left.*
3. *Climb up the ledge and slip inside. Follow the corridor until you find a pot containing highly flammable brambles. Grab the pot with **R1** and move it into the gap in the railing.*

4. *Kick the pot over the edge by holding onto it with R1 and pressing ⊗. Hold down ⊗ for several seconds to charge a more powerful kick before releasing the button.*
5. *Drop to the lower level.*
6. *Grab the pot and drag it to the far end of the area (to the right), where a Cerberus Mongrel is caged. The creature unleashes a blast of fire when he sees Kratos approaching.*
7. *The pot ignites and creates a geyser of hot air. Place the pot to the left, beneath the lever above.*
8. *Leave the geyser for now and return to the hanging lamp at the other end of the area.*
9. *Stand on the lamp until the gate on the upper section of the far wall is completely open. Leap off the lamp and race to the hot air geyser.*
10. *Leap into the rising column of hot air and deploy the Wings of Icarus. Kratos flies high enough to reach the ledge above. Dash through the open gate before it closes.*
11. *Pull the lever there by pressing **R1**. This completely opens the upper level gate as well as the gate restraining the Cerberus Mongrel.*
12. *Drop down to the creature and begin beating the beast into submission.*
13. *When the beast is stunned, bring the canine around with a Context-Sensitive Action. Hop onto the Cerberus Mongrel and rein it in.*

CONTROLLING CERBERUS

Move Cerberus with the left analog stick. Press □ to launch its fireball attack or press △ to use its fire breath.

14. *Move back toward Peirithous, obliterating the Olympus Sentries and Olympus Archers along the way. Attack aggressively to eliminate your targets without allowing your mount to incur much damage.*
15. *Once you've returned to Peirithous' prison, use one of the Cerberus Mongrel's attacks to set the trapped man's cage ablaze. The flames remove the brambles—and anything else.*
16. *Retrieve the Bow of Apollo as a reward.*

The Story of Peirithous

Peirithous was the type of guy who had more guts than brains in Greek mythology. This fellow decided that he wanted to have Persephone as a bride. The only problem with this longing was that Hades had already taken her for his own. What's more is that Hades had already gone through quite a bit of negotiation just to keep Persephone in Hades, so he wasn't likely to give her up.

Peirithous convinced Theseus to come into the Underworld with him. Surprisingly (to the two of them), Hades greeted them and was quite friendly. But it was all a trick. Both men sat down in front of a fine banquet but were frozen to their seats by magic. Heracles eventually freed Theseus, who hadn't really done anything wrong (at least, not yet). But Peirithous was sentenced to live a life of endless suffering.

In *God of War III*, Peirithous is in endless fear of flames, as the embers of a fire continually fall around him, threatening to set his bramble cage on fire.

IF YOUR MOUNT FALLS IN BATTLE

The Cerberus Mongrel that Kratos rides is not immune to damage just because it's part of a puzzle. It can indeed fall beneath its rider. If it's attacked for too long, the creature can shake Kratos off. If this happens, Kratos has no choice but to kill the disobedient dog. Another Cerberus Mongrel will spawn in its place, but Kratos must begin his taming anew.

Now that you have a bow, it's best to try it out. Fire it into the nearby Olympus Sentries and Olympus Archers. The bow has an auto-aim feature that allows Kratos to locate the target at which he's aiming. Targets are highlighted by a beam of light. Switch between highlighted targets by pressing left or right on the right analog stick. Use this function if the auto-target grabs an enemy that you don't want to shoot.

Move the hot air geyser as close as possible to the newly opened balcony. Jump over the geyser and deploy the Wings of Icarus once again. Wait until you are as high as possible and glide toward the upper balcony. A Red Orb Chest and an Item Chest with a **Phoenix Feather** are inside the alcove. Take these and drop to the ground floor.

PHOENIX FEATHER

The Item Chest beyond the opened balcony contains a Phoenix Feather.

CERBERUS MONGREL 216

THE BOW OF APOLLO

Press and hold **L2** to arm the bow and press □ to fire. If Kratos knocks an arrow and holds the draw, the attack charges and becomes more powerful on release; charged arrows set your targets on fire, confusing them while they try to put themselves out. Charged arrows also destroy flammable obstacles.

The bow's arrows are not exactly unlimited, but they do replenish over time. The yellow bar that appears below Kratos' magic gauge indicates the number of arrows in his quiver (the yellow strip is called your Item Gauge). The gauge depletes as Kratos fires each arrow, but soon after he stops it starts to refill.

In terms of damage, the Bow of Apollo isn't exceptional, but it's not meant for mowing down swaths of bad guys. Rather, it's a way to provide supplemental damage when your enemies are at range. Pick off targets when it's convenient and switch to your blades when the foes close for the kill.

Now would be a good time to open the Health Chest along the ground floor. Kratos could probably use a dose of Green Orbs after his endeavor with the Cerberus Mongrel.

FACE TRIALS AND JUDGMENT

From on High

Backtrack to the cave and locate the path that is blocked by brambles. Use the Bow of Apollo to clear the vines and open the walkway. Beyond the corridor is a small, open area with a few Shades, a Magic Chest, and a Health Chest. Destroy the Shades and open the two chests before turning to the small cluster of brambles against the north wall. Take aim with the Bow of Apollo and clear the vines. An Item Chest is revealed. This time you get a **Minotaur Horn**! There is also a Save Altar in this area. Stop there before moving forward; the fights ahead get much tougher.

MINOTAUR HORN

The Item Chest behind the bramble contains a Minotaur Horn. These items improve Kratos' Item Gauge when enough are collected.

Take the west exit and follow the corridor to another stopping point. Harpies and Shades stand in Kratos' way— a foolish move. The Harpies take to the air, and they're fairly hard to hit from the ground. It's easier to leap into the air and slash the fell beasts. In either case, don't leave the Harpies to their own devices. They will dive at Kratos and can deal a surprising amount of damage, especially on higher difficulty levels.

Use Army of Sparta to eliminate the ground enemies. You can also launch the magic attack and take to the air or pull out the bow to slay the Harpies. Another trick is to automatically kill Harpies after they dive. Harpies are vulnerable while grounded. Grapple with them for a free kill.

You must defeat several waves of Harpies to finish the battle.

Scaling the Underworld

Once the area is clear, take the opportunity to look around at the nearby scenery before continuing to the end of the path. A small platform containing a Mixed Orb Chest is across the vast opening. Climb along the wall to the right and leap over the narrow waterfall before dropping onto the crumbled molding. Continue to the right over the next two gaps. Scale up the stone facade and climb along the left handholds. Soon, the left path ends and Kratos has nowhere to go but up.

KNOW WHEN TO LEAP AND WHEN TO LOOK

It's not always clear where Kratos can jump when he's clinging to the side of a cliff. One wrong move could kill you, but there are ways to know if a jump is safe before you leap. If Kratos arrives at the end of a ledge and reaches out toward a far point, that's a safe jump. If he doesn't lean out, don't jump!

Pull onto the overhead ledge and leap to the next strip of decorative molding. Follow the handholds to the left and pull Kratos up when the molding runs out. After attaining the shallow stone ledge, continue left. A small alcove containing an Item Chest is at the end of the path, across two gaps. It contains a **Gorgon Eye**.

GORGON EYE

The Item Chest in the small alcove contains a Gorgon Eye.

HARPY QUEEN 223

Return to the place where you pulled yourself up and follow the shallow outcropping to the right. Jump across another narrow waterfall onto the far stone facade and ascend to the platform above.

Harpies

The Harpies are a group of sisters who prey upon those unfortunate enough to incur Zeus' wrath. Their name means "snatcher" and they were believed to have hands twisted into grasping claws. Harpies prefer to live in dark caves. Many are thought to be in underground caves beneath Crete. Because of their speed and power, Harpies were thought to be personifications of storm winds. Early stories described them as being fair, but the majority of tails describe them as foul creatures.

Harpies are like many servants of the Gods; they are distantly related to the Furies that serve Hades, and the beautiful Nereids that serve Poseidon. The Harpies have a beautiful winged sister, Iris (the rainbow goddess). She acts as one of the Gods' lesser messengers. Both the Furies and Iris figure prominently in the Harpy myths.

The most famous myth about the Harpies is part of a much longer story about the Greek heroes called the Argonauts. The Argonauts wished to consult the famous seer Phineas. Unfortunately, Phineas had become such a skilled diviner that he thought he knew the mind of Zeus. That's a dangerous thing for any mortal. In punishment, Zeus blinded Phineas. Zeus couldn't take away the seer's gift (because it came from Apollo), but he could torment the man on a whim.

Zeus sent Harpies to harass Phineas at the temple on the outskirts of Bithynia. Whenever Phineas tried to eat food of any sort, the Harpies would fly down from the sky and snatch it from his hands. What little remained, the Harpies would soil with a hideous liquid that streamed from their eyes. The food smelled and tasted so horrible that no person could stand to come near until it had either been consumed or rotted away.

Phineas agreed to tell the Argonauts their futures if they could end his troubles with the Harpies. The Argonauts prepared an enormous meal and waited for the Harpies to descend.

As the Harpies went for the food, the Argonauts rattled their spears against their shields and shouted. The noise frightened the cowardly Harpies and sent them retreating into the sky.

Two of the Argonauts present were Zetes and Kalais, twin sons of Boreas, the North Wind. These winged demigods flew into the air to pursue the harassing Harpies. Iris intervened to protect her sisters. She called them the "hounds of Zeus" and said that to kill them would be unlawful. Instead, she swore that the Harpies would harass Phineas no more if Zetes and Kalais would swear to spare their lives. The two heroes agreed, and the oath was sealed with water from the river Styx.

When people disappeared, it was often believed that Harpies had snatched them away. Some writers claimed the Harpies and Furies were so similar that they could be mistaken for each other, and that the Harpies frequently brought people they seized to the Furies to receive horrible punishments.

The two Harpies who harassed Phineas were called Aello and Okypete. Another, called Podarge, gave birth to a pair of legendary horses called Xanthos and Balios. Some legends mention another Harpy named Kelaino.

Jump to the root-covered ceiling and scale its path using the Blades of Exile. Don't drop down until there is a small platform beneath Kratos. Next, move across to the pillar wrapped in roots. Climb to the top of it and get a look at the area around Kratos.

Trials and Tribulations

Two chains are to the left of Kratos. Use these Grapple Points to swing to the platform below. Step on the plate at the center of the area. The Three Judges of the Underworld are here, but they won't offer wisdom or judgment until you've completed their trials.

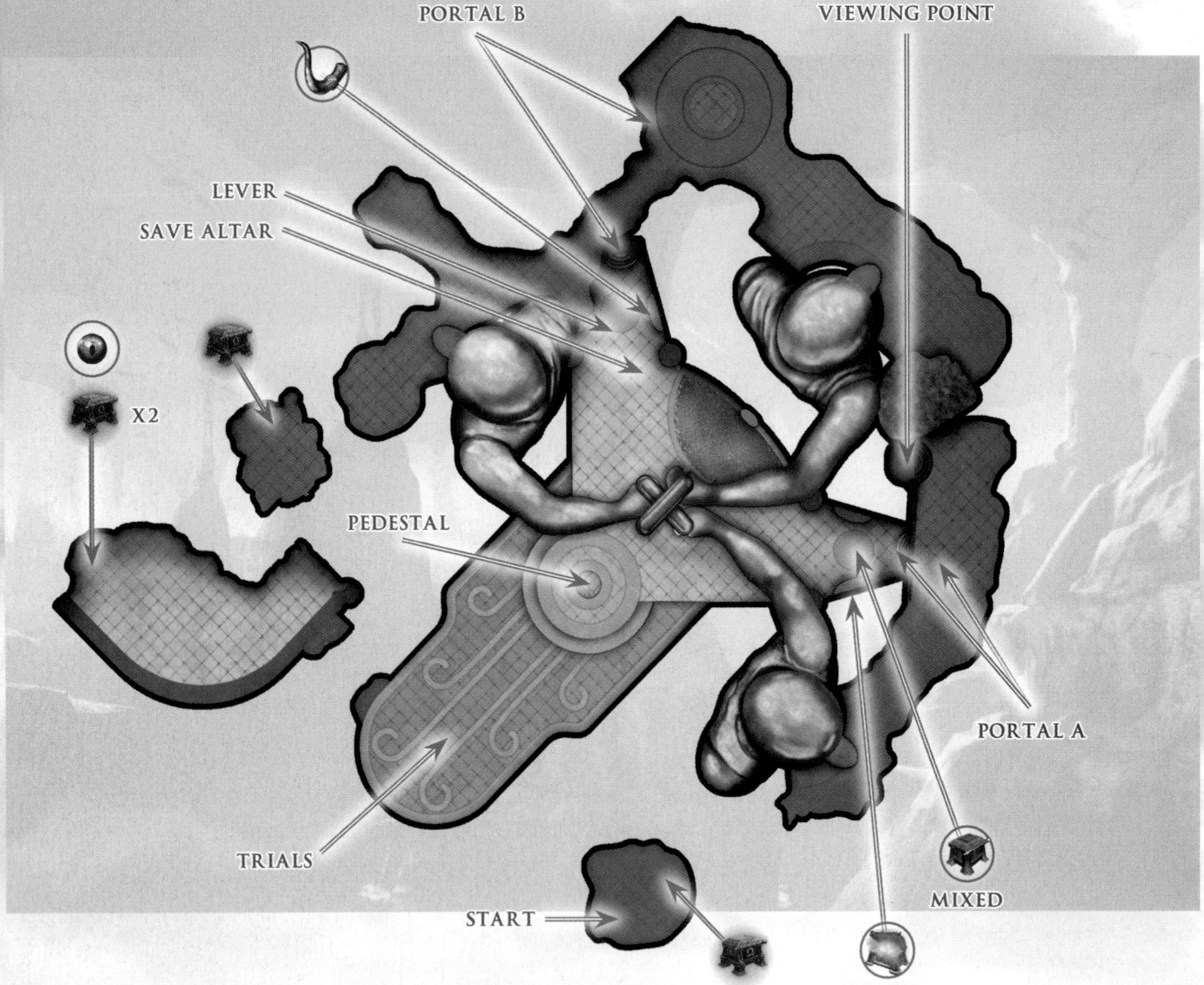

PORTAL B
VIEWING POINT
LEVER
SAVE ALTAR
X2
PEDESTAL
PORTAL A
TRIALS
MIXED
START

Swim across the pool to the north and admire the beautiful statue there. Head to the left when you get out and use the Save Altar before starting the trials. When you're ready, run south and read the book on the pedestal that initiates the first challenge.

A series of confused souls drops into the enclosed area, along with a group of Hades Arms. This warm-up trial is completed once all the Hades Arms are destroyed. Focus on them with the Blades of Exile and lay waste. The confused citizens are transformed into Shades if touched by the hands, but do little harm thereafter. Once all the enemies are eliminated, return to the book for the next trial.

Shades appear along the edge of the enclosed area. They lurch slowly toward the blue wall of flame. If they reach the wall, they transform into either a Minotaur Brute or a Olympus Sentry. A lone Minotaur Brute is already standing at the blue wall of flame. To complete this trial as quickly as possible, avoid the charging creature and eliminate all the Shades using the Plume of Prometheus or other area-of-effect attacks. Save magic if you can, because the next trial is even more troublesome.

Once all the Shades are dust, destroy the Minotaur and return to the book one last time. This isn't necessarily easy. Minotaur Brutes are faster than many of the Minotaurs in earlier *God of War* titles. They can charge Kratos at high speed, and even after missing they have a chance to redirect their charge and press the attack. Roll out of their way and stay in the open when possible. Being close to a wall makes it more likely that the Minotaur Brute will correct its off-target trajectory and hit you afterward!

LOST SOUL 218

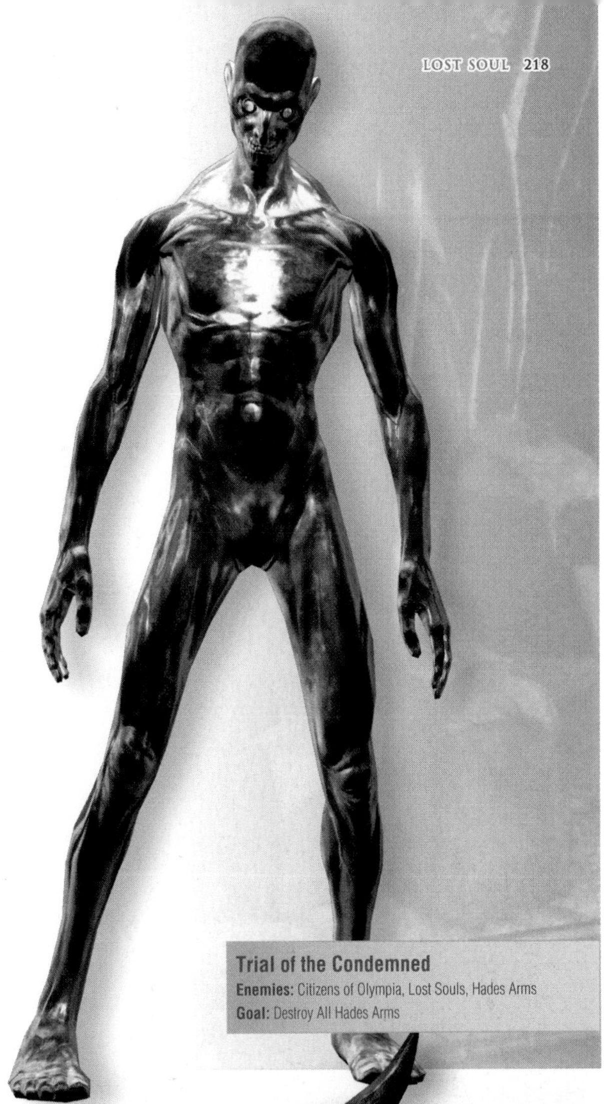

Trial of the Condemned

Enemies: Citizens of Olympia, Lost Souls, Hades Arms

Goal: Destroy All Hades Arms

MINOTAUR BRUTE 224

Trial of the Lost

Enemies: Lost Souls, Olympus Sentries, Minotaur Brutes

Goal: Destroy the Lost Souls and Kill the Original Minotaur Brute

The fight starts with just four Harpies and the Gorgon Serpent. Things seem easy initially, but don't underestimate your foes. Ignore the Gorgon Serpent (offensively) and focus on the Harpies. Kill them when they're grounded and dash evasively when you aren't pulling one apart. Watch the Gorgon Serpent's head for signs that she's about to glare at everything. Roll aside and see if any Harpies get stoned. Take advantage of this opportunity to obliterate petrified Harpies.

Trial of the Chosen
Enemies: Harpies, Minotaur Brutes, and a Gorgon Serpent
Goal: Kill All Your Enemies

KRATOS IS FRAGILE

Shake your analog stick as quickly as possible if the Gorgon Serpent manages to petrify Kratos. There are many enemies and it's easy to get killed if you're encased in stone.

In addition, be wary of jumping when the gaze might affect Kratos. If you're turned to stone while airborne it's likely that Kratos will shatter when his statue hits the ground.

Be wary of the Gorgon Serpent's tail swipe. Veteran players are likely to underestimate the reach of this attack because it's so much longer in *God of War III* than in previous adventures. Block this attack if you see it coming.

The first Minotaur Brute appears after the Harpies die. Slay him with normal attacks and leave the creature between yourself and the Gorgon Serpent. This gives the beast a chance to get petrified by the witch's attack. If this occurs, shatter the Minotaur with heavy attacks.

A second Minotaur Brute and more Harpies appear when the first falls. Continue using the Gorgon Serpent to your advantage. Let her petrify your enemies, but start whittling her health down now. If she incurs enough damage and becomes dazed, go for the kill. Her final burst of energy petrifies most targets anyway, offering you a simple chance to cleanup afterward.

DEATH FROM ABOVE

Gorgon Serpents and Minotaur Brutes are susceptible to Olympic Ascension (hold down ▲ for your launch). Watch Kratos rise with his victim for an aerial dance of destruction. You're relatively safe while hovering over the battlefield and this is a great way to execute tougher enemies without getting stabbed in the back.

When the bloodbath is over you're free to collect your rewards. To the west is a small ledge. Leap to a platform that is barely out of your sight and walk back to a set of chests. Two contain Red Orbs and the third has a powerful item: a **Gorgon Eye**. Collect everything before leaving the area.

GORGON EYE

 The middle chest in this trio contains a Gorgon Eye.

Use the Save Altar again after the trials have been completed. After saving, step on the dais between the Three Judges to face your final judgment. King Minos holds the final decision, and he deems that Kratos is not yet ready for the realm of the afterlife. Minos opens the gate to the right of the well, allowing Kratos to advance. Before passing through the portal beyond the gate, pick up Orbs from the mixed and Alternating Chests nearby. Walk through the portal to be teleported above the Judges.

The Three Judges

The Three Judges of the Underworld were once mortal kings, three brothers: King Radamanthus, King Aeacus, and King Minos. They were sons of Zeus and a mortal woman named Europa. Zeus had spied the girl walking on the shoreline and was immediately smitten with her. He transformed into a beautiful white bull, and she was impressed with its gentleness. When she climbed upon the bull, Zeus seized his chance and carried her off into the waves. He eventually carried her to Crete, where she was treated with great reverence. The boys were born soon afterward.

Each of the brothers ruled Crete, and they all gained a reputation for great intelligence coupled with inflexibility. The codes of laws they set in place were firm, fair, and held little compassion.

At some point, Minos seized power from his brothers and exiled them. Little is known of Rhadamanythys and Aeacus after their exile. Minos, however, features prominently as a villain in a number of stories. This was the King that ordered Daedalus to construct the Labyrinth to hide the Minotaur and sacrificed countless numbers of people. He continued to terrorize Crete and the surrounding countries until he was eventually killed.

Still, Hades decided that the souls of the men had some use. After their deaths, the God of the Underworld had them set aside as Judges. The souls of the dead had to come before them and plead their cases. Each had to explain their life and whether they had lived up to their ideals and the Gods' morality. It was up to the Judges, then, to decide if they had lived acceptably. If the person had been true, they were sent to the Elysian Fields, to live in contentment. If the person had been evil in life, though, they were sent to Tartarus, where they would suffer without purpose.

A Higher Plane

After exiting the portal, run to the right and enter a small alcove beside Kratos. Use a Free Look Camera to see the Judges. Leave the room and continue down the path to the right. Double-jump over a gap in the road and land ready to face two Minotaur Brutes. Quickly take on the Minotaur Brutes one at a time and slay them both. Be cognizant of the oil pots in this area. These are useful during the fight with the Brutes because they do considerable damage when detonated. Charge arrows from the Bow of Apollo when the Brutes are near an oil pots. Shoot the pots to scorch the foul Minotaurs!

Continue down the path until Kratos passes through a tunnel. Two Shades are there; kill them if you wish, and turn around to discover a portal hidden inside the wall. Walk through the portal to steal chests with all manner of Orbs. In addition, there is a **Minotaur Horn**! Ignore the Shades in the room unless they get in your way or annoy you, then pull the lever inside the room which releases a gate. Take the portal back when you're done.

MINOTAUR HORN

The portal room has many chests, including one with a Minotaur Horn.

Jump to the platform ahead and open a Red Orb Chest. Double-jump to the northern platform and continue until a familiar voice calls out to Kratos.

After listening to the conversation, jump up to the chain above Kratos and climb to the other side of the chamber. Use the vines on the rock face and slide all the way down the edge. Follow the path to the right to enter the caverns outside Hades' Palace.

CAVERNS OF HADES

VENGEANCE NEARS

PASS THROUGH THE CAVERNS

The Elite of the Underworld

IV

OLYMPUS FIEND 226

Squeezing through the gap between the rocks, Kratos emerges inside the caverns near Hades' Palace. Some familiar enemies stand between Kratos and your goal, but there are new threats as well. Be prepared!

Continue down the path after beating the Hades Arms and look for a bridge ahead. Ignore the Shades and get ready to face the true threat. Olympus Fiends are a bit farther down and they're dying to introduce themselves to Kratos. They charge your position; hold back instead of rushing to meet them.

Pull out the Bow of Apollo and shoot the oil pots as enemies run past them. Once the Olympus Fiends are too close for missile attacks, retreat and use charged arrows to further thin their ranks. This demolishes the Olympus Fiends and keeps you out of harm's way.

OIL POTS

Oil pots appear throughout the world. Kratos can drag them into different locations while on level ground. When enemies are close to the pots, use the Bow of Apollo to destroy the pot and light the oil.

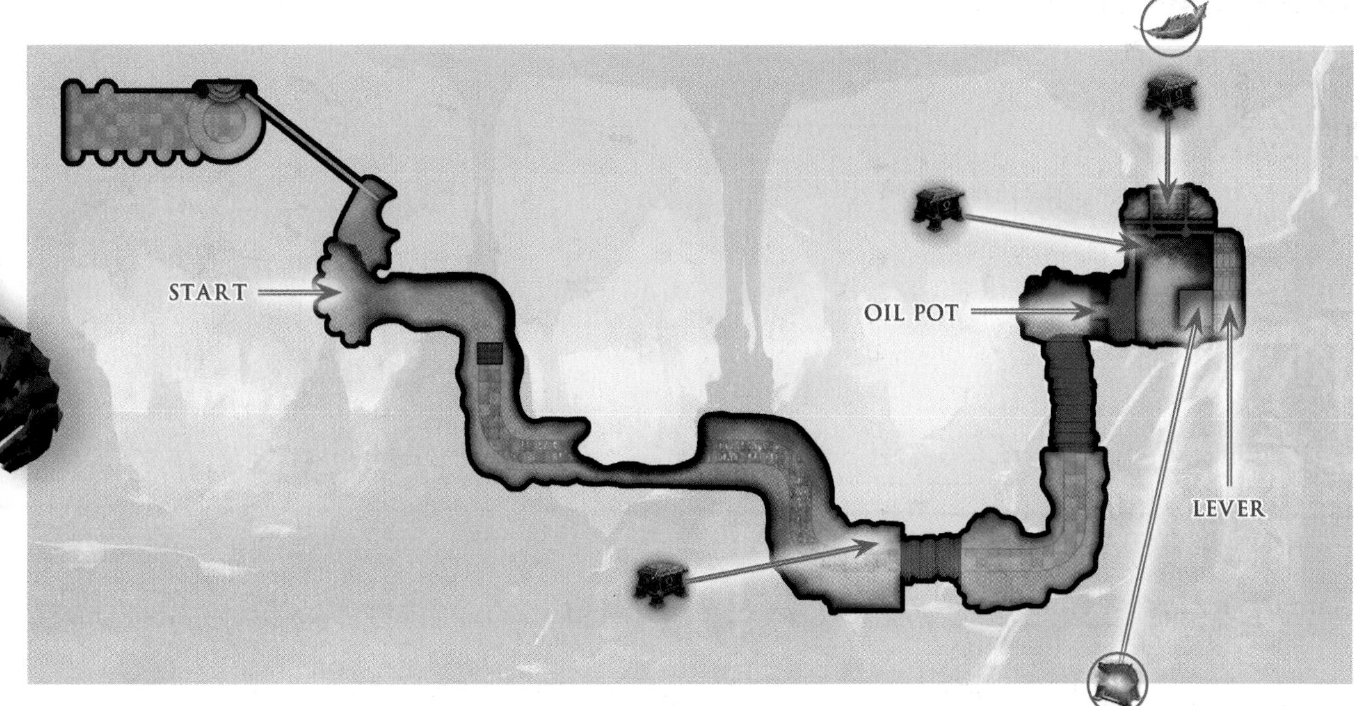

OLYMPUS FIENDS

These warriors are much more deadly than Olympus Sentries. Not only are they armed with better weapons, including grenades, but they're also well-trained and won't stop trying to kill the Ghost of Sparta until they're entirely destroyed. Don't underestimate them.

At close range, Olympus Fiends use sword combos to deal out their damage. You're forced to block or use evasion to keep Kratos from being overwhelmed.

At range, the Soldiers lob grenades that explode in a modest area-of-effect. Leap over the blasts to avoid damage and the knockback effect of the explosions.

Grab Olympus Fiends to get an advantage over them. If you switch the targets quickly between grappling attacks, it's easy to avoid the Olympus Fiends' counterstrikes.

Heavier combos are also effective, though you must launch these attacks sooner. A nice trick is to roll away from Olympus Fiends and start the initial hits of a heavy combo. The enemies won't even be in range for that first strike, but by the time they close in, they'll be jumping right into the teeth of the chain's damage.

Watch carefully when Olympus Fiends fall; they aren't always out of the fight. Glowing Olympus Fiends can explode, inflicting a fair amount of damage if you stick around. Pull enemies away from their downed comrades to continue the fight without having to walk on eggshells.

Temperature Rising

Once the Olympus Fiends have been slain, open the Red Orb Chest to the left and head across the bridge. Some Olympus Sentries appear farther down the path, but they don't pose much of a threat. Decimate them and continue on until Kratos reaches a metal grate with brambles beneath it.

BRING THE HEAT

Without a change in the wind, Kratos remains grounded.

FUEL THE FIRE

There must be a way for Kratos to heat up the flight pad. Maybe a bit more fuel for the fire...

1. *Charge the Bow of Apollo and fire a flaming arrow into the heart of the kindling. This ignites the wood and creates a hot air geyser.*
2. *Leap into the geyser and use the Wings of Icarus to fly to the upper platform to the right.*
3. *Kill the two Olympus Fiends that spawn behind Kratos and then pull the lever opposite the elevator.*
4. *Quickly jump onto the elevator and ride it to the third tier of the room.*
5. *Grab the oil pot across from the elevator and pull it onto the platform.*

6. *Leave the oil pot and kill the three Olympus Fiends that spawn by the far wall.*

ACCIDENTS HAPPEN

You won't fail the puzzle if the oil pot gets destroyed. However, you must then get the replacement that appears.

Use this to your advantage. Push the oil pot toward the Olympus Fiends as they spawn and back off. Let the fools grenade the oil pot and kill themselves in the process.

7. *The elevator has probably returned to the second level, but Kratos can prepare for the next step. Drag/push the oil pot to the edge of the platform where the elevator used to be.*
8. *Drop to the second level, pull the lever, and ride the elevator back up to the oil pot.*
9. *Pull the oil pot onto the elevator and ride down to the second level.*
10. *Leave the oil pot on the elevator and eliminate the two Olympus Fiends that spawn to the north. Keep the fight away from the oil pot, or else you'll need to retrieve another.*

11. *Drag the oil pot to the north wall and push it off the unguarded ledge into the hot air geyser.*

This stokes the fire even further allowing Kratos to fly higher than ever on the augmented thermal. Use the Wings of Icarus to reach the metal grating above. Kratos grabs on and the addition of his weight causes the metal box to plummet, but its chains stop it from crushing the Spartan. Climb to the top of the metal box and lift the ominous metal door that is now accessible.

Two chests are ahead of Kratos. One contains a **Phoenix Feather** and the other is a Red Orb Chest. You must clear a path to reach them. Hades Arms spawn below, beside, and above Kratos. Use sweeping attacks to quickly eliminate these pests and reap the rewards of their demise. After clearing the path, open the chests in the back and return to the metal box.

PHOENIX FEATHER

The eastern route from the gazebo has a Phoenix Feather.

HADES ARMS

Upon entering the caverns, Kratos encounters Hades Arms. These immobile appendages lash out at Kratos but do little damage. It's a simple matter to run right past them.

That said, it's easy to destroy them in droves, and they provide a small amount of Red Orbs. If you're interested in getting as much experience as possible, stop to destroy them all.

Start from the metal box and jump as high as you can. Fly through the hole in the ceiling and then float to the new path. Continue down the winding hallway until Kratos reaches the first set of stairs. There are two more chests here: a Health Chest and a Magic Chest. Loot what you need and move up the stairs to reach the outer atrium of Hades' Palace. Turn right at the intersection and collect the Red Orbs from another chest.

The Talos

Move along the outer path of the Atrium and pass the first statue to reach a viewing point. Use the pedestal to catch a glimpse of the charred landscape. Move farther down the path, but beware! The statues aren't what they seem. These are Talos. Though slow and ungainly, these powerful creatures are tough to kill and can splatter most things that get in their way.

STONE TALOS

These stone giants have been brought to life by the Gods. Their single-minded purpose is to smash and destroy intruders. If Kratos finds himself on the wrong end of their mallets, he may bid goodbye to his chance at vengeance. Talos attacks, while powerful, are slow and easy to dodge. Use evasive rolls and jumps to move around the Stone Talos and attack them with combos before they turn around. Keep an eye on the Talos' movements to predict their next move and plant Kratos behind them before attacking.

STONE TALOS 230

GORGON EYE

The path to the left has an Item Chest containing a Gorgon Eye.

Circle around the Stone Talos and unleash your fiercest combos. Position Kratos so that all the Talos stand to one side of him. This makes it much easier to damage them simultaneously. It also lets you know where to dodge before any of the Talos make their attacks.

A third Talos animates after the first two have been destroyed. Three Olympus Sentries arrive with this final enemy, and it's best to kill the weaker soldiers first. This leaves you free to kill the nastiest target without additional concerns.

Once all the Stone Talos have been reduced to rubble, continue down the hallway and use the Wings of Icarus to glide to the cave below. If Kratos needs a little pick-me-up and hasn't already accessed the Health and Magic Chests at the bottom of the stairs, return to the previous hallway and get what you need.

OPTIONS

Kratos has Gods to kill. Stone Talos take quite a beating before they go down, and maybe you aren't in the mood to deal with them. As an alternative, run past these constructs to reach the next area. Use this option if you're in a hurry.

Shaped by the Flames

After landing, pick up the Green Orbs from the Health Chest to the left and continue down the path. At its end, jump down to Hephaestus' workshop. Things are quiet for the moment, but you won't be able to count on that for long. Walk up the pathway and Hephaestus soon recognizes Kratos' presence. The God gives Kratos some clues about the Flame of Olympus. From the circular dais in front of Hephaestus, turn right and walk across to a rock ledge on the eastern side. Use the Save Altar and then pull a lever to open the way forward.

Look down the path on the left before leaving. This quickly leads to an Item Chest with a **Gorgon Eye**. The doors there can't be opened right now. Return to the previous room and run down the eastern stairs.

Run through the underground hallways until Kratos arrives at a stone gazebo. The doorway that Kratos used to enter the gazebo is the only exit available, so Kratos must use the winch in the center of the room to open the way. The winch rotates to determine which direction the opening faces.

Turn to the east path first. Follow this to its end and eliminate the Hounds that challenge Kratos. Absorb the orbs from the Red Orb Chest and return to the gazebo. Rotate the opening until it faces north; this exposes flammable brambles. Use the Bow of Apollo to light the brambles on fire and pass through this pathway.

Hephaestus

Hephaestus was the God of the Forge. He was the patron of smiths and craftsmen, and his work was beyond compare. His forge was said to reside in an immense volcano, which would spew out molten lava as he worked. As such, he was the God of Fire as well as technology.

He was the son of Zeus and Hera, but it took a while before they accepted him. Hephaestus was born with a lame foot, and his parents were ashamed of his deformity—and their son. He was also an amazingly ugly baby. To keep anyone from realizing his birth, the infant was disposed of, dropped from Mount Olympus. He fell for nine days and landed in the ocean where he was cared for by two ocean nymphs: Thetis (the future mother of Achilles) and Eurynome. He grew up under their tutelage and quickly demonstrated his prowess in metalworking and smithcraft.

Once the Olympian Gods realized what Hephaestus was capable of, they welcomed him back and asserted his divine status. He was treated with great respect and Zeus gave him a magnificent forge. In return, Hephaestus forged thrones for all the Gods, and each was a marvel in and of itself. In fact, Hephaestus' status was such that he was even given the most beautiful of Goddesses as a bride: Aphrodite, Goddess of Love. Although he was more than satisfied by this union, she was not. It was something that was a source of unhappiness to Hephaestus, but he dealt with it by putting much of his emotion into his craft.

Most of the famous weapons and armor used by Gods and heroes were once created by Hephaestus. Zeus' Thunderbolts, Hermes' Winged Boots, and Helios' Chariot are all said to be his work. In addition, Hephaestus also created arms and armor for Achilles, Perseus, and Theseus, to name a few heroes.

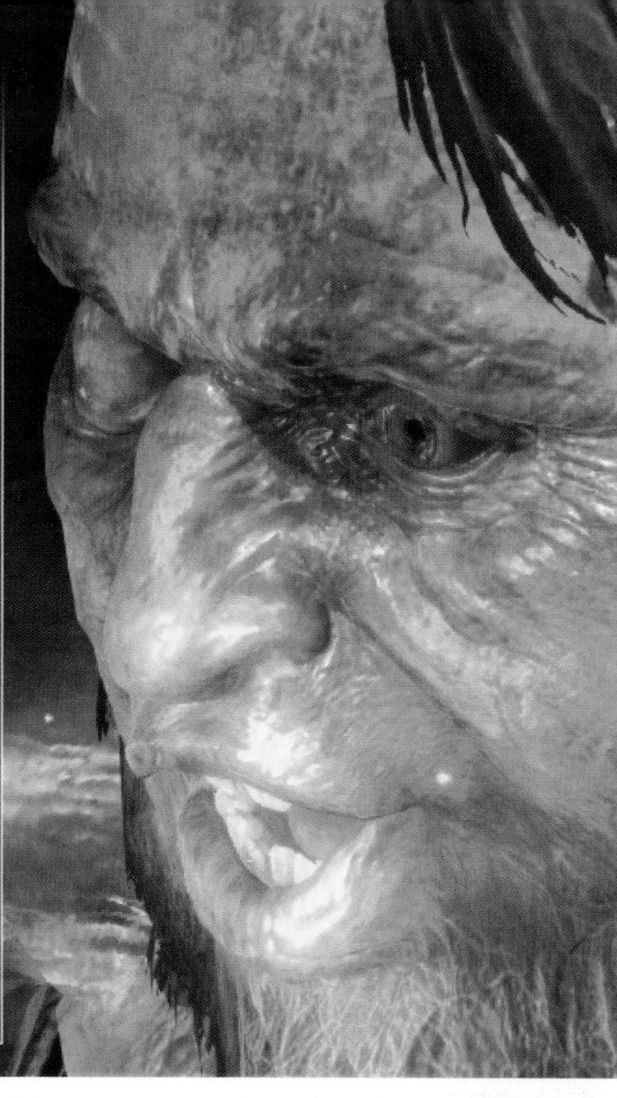

MASTER THE RAGE OF SPARTA

Reunion

There is a Health Chest here. Pilfer what's inside as needed and prepare for a serious confrontation. Move past several Shades and continue down the passageway until Kratos reaches a statue. There is a familiar item imprisoned within it. Kratos converses with a spirit. Afterward, collect the **Blade of Olympus** once more. A small army of Olympus Sentries attacks, but that's no punishment. It's practically a reward!

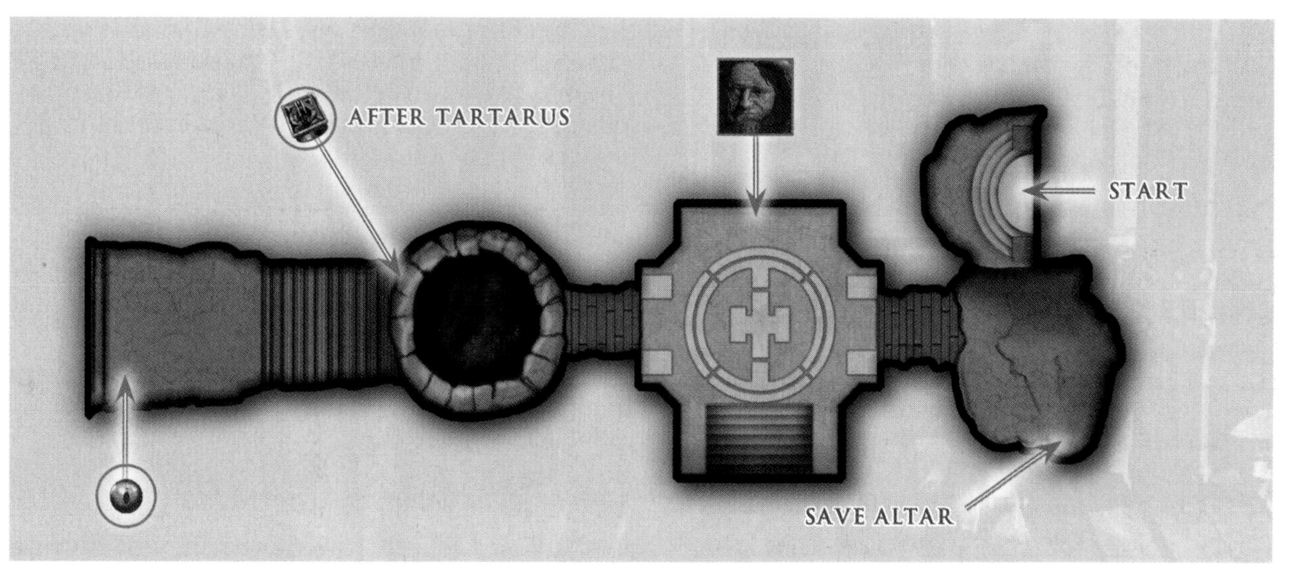

THE RAGE OF SPARTA

Now that Kratos has the Blade of Olympus, he can unleash the Rage of Sparta upon his enemies, by simultaneously clicking **L3** and **R3**. While empowered by the Rage of Sparta, Kratos' devastating attacks become absolutely godly; not many enemies can stand more than a few attacks before falling to his sword.

Also, Kratos takes less damage when he's filled with the Rage of Sparta. Being able to survive heavy hits while dishing out immense damage is essential in large battles and boss encounters. Save your strength for these "make-or-break" moments.

The Rage of Sparta is only temporary. When the meter in the bottom right of the screen is depleted, Kratos regains his normal fighting abilities. Refill the Rage of Sparta by collecting Gold Orbs.

If you really want to try out this new power, initiate the Rage of Sparta and massacre the Olympus Sentries. Kratos should be able to eviscerate all his enemies in mere moments.

THE BLADE OF OLYMPUS

The Blade of Olympus is not a weapon from Greek mythology. This sword was introduced in the *God of War* series and was said to embody the power of the Olympians. Zeus, from this mythos, used the weapon to end the Great War with the Titans. He turned the blade's powers against Kratos and tried to kill him with it. This failed because Kratos returned from death; he used the power of the Fates to rewrite history and save himself from Zeus' treachery.

Traditionally, swords are often associated with power, authority, justice, and brutality. While magic swords rarely appear in the ancient Greek myths, swords do appear frequently as symbols of incredible power and inevitable death.

An example of a symbolic blade would be the Sword of Damocles: a blade that was said to hang over a ruler's head and could fall at any time. The symbolism reflects the weight of leadership and the possibility for sudden and catastrophic change that comes with it,

When Aphrodite appears as the Goddess of Victory, she bears the sword, helmet, and shield of Ares. Ares was worshipped by the Scythians in the form of a divine sword. Nemesis, the grim goddess of vengeance, bears a wheel in one hand and a sword in the other.

Among the mortals there are fewer examples of this power. Heracles was given a divine sword as a reward for defeating Erginus. The hero Peleus carried a divine sword forged by Hephaestus. Theseus used a divine sword hidden for years in a shrine to Zeus to prove he was the true son and rightful heir of Aegeus, King of Athens.

After the area is clear, move past the statue and jump off the ledge. You wind up back near the beginning of the region, where you first fell into the Underworld. Use the two Grapple Points to the northeast to swing back toward the main path. After Kratos has landed, draw the Bow of Apollo and shoot the Olympus Archers in the distance.

Walk along the path and open the next Health Chest. Return to the platform where Kratos learned the Army of Sparta special attack. Hades is taking you much more seriously this time, and he dispatches two of his mighty Hades Cerberus Breeders to stop Kratos.

CERBERUS

Cerberus, the three-headed Hound of Hades, is one of the most famous Greek monsters. This beast was born of the union between Typhon and Echidna, and was among many such monsters to be raised by Echidna.

Cerberus became known as the Watchdog of Hades. He is sometimes described as having a horde of serpents instead of a tail, more serpents for his mane, and fierce claws like a lion's. As Hades' watchdog, Cerberus' duty was both to prevent the living from entering Hades and the dead from leaving. Both living and dead feared him equally. He was said to be so fierce that the dead would have to bribe him with a honey-cake in order to pass by.

Because Cerberus had three heads he could stay awake at all times. Only a few heroes were able to slip past the hound without drawing its aggression. Orpheus managed this using a lullaby to put the fierce creature to sleep. Other legends mention heroes finding ways of drugging or stupefying the beast.

Cerberus is the focus of the Twelfth Labor of Heracles. King Eurystheus ordered Heracles to descend into Hades and return with Cerberus as his captive. Instead of doing this violently, Heracles was cautious in his approach. He completed rituals to descend into the Underworld as a living being. Once there, he visited Hades and Persephone as a proper guest. He asked Hades if he could borrow Cerberus. Hades agreed, on the condition that Heracles not harm the great hound.

So, using only his bare hands, Heracles wrestled with Cerberus and dragged the creature into the upper world. Cerberus was accustomed to the darkness of Hades, and he panicked furiously once in the upper world. Heracles succeeded in his task, but was immediately ordered by the King to take the hound back in the Underworld.

Greek legends say that Cerberus' saliva dripped on the ground as he was dragged above ground. A deadly plant grew from this tainted area; it was named Aconite, also known as Wolfsbane.

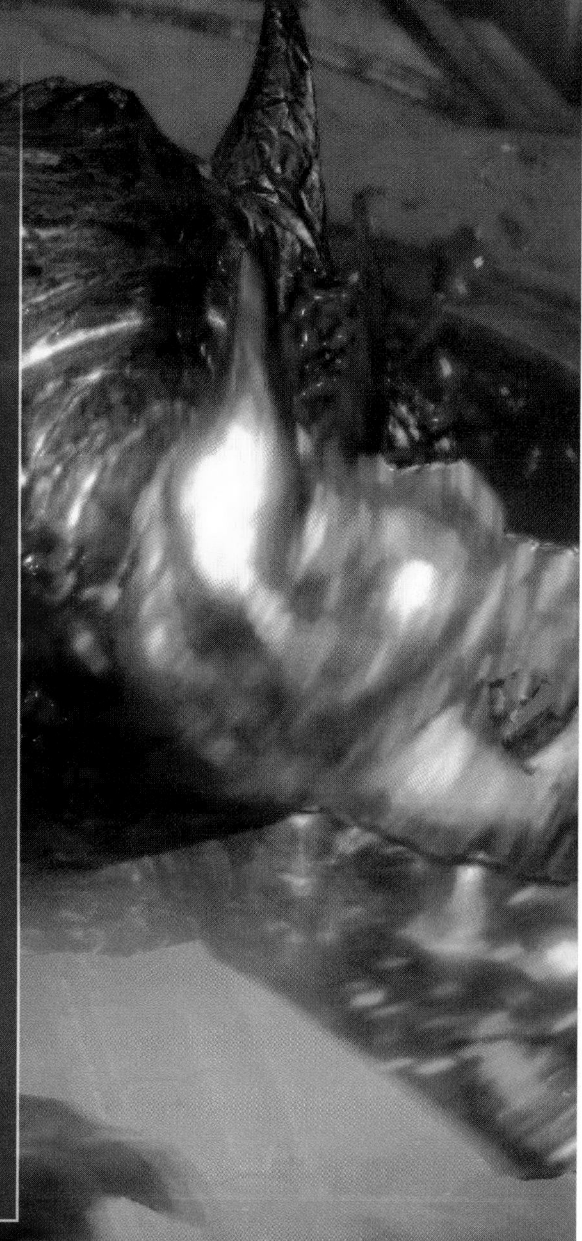

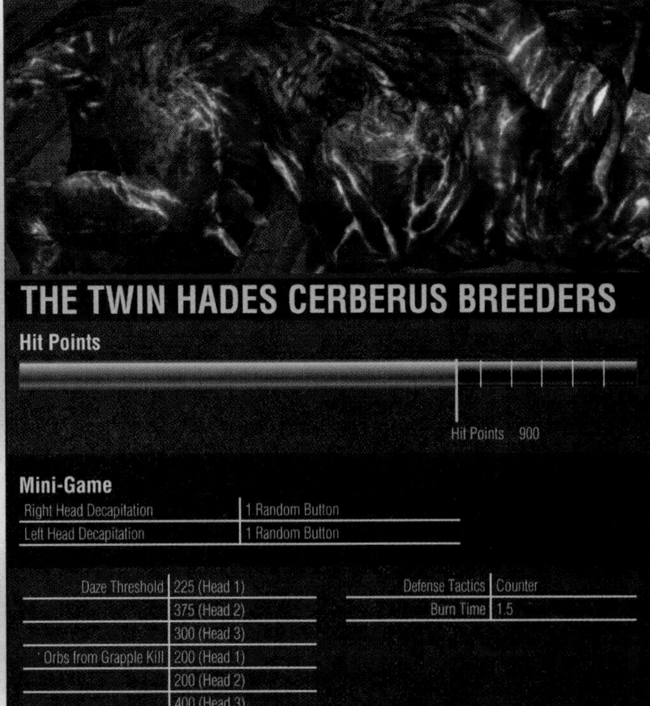

THE TWIN HADES CERBERUS BREEDERS

Hit Points

Hit Points 900

Mini-Game

Right Head Decapitation	1 Random Button
Left Head Decapitation	1 Random Button

Daze Threshold	225 (Head 1)
	375 (Head 2)
	300 (Head 3)
' Orbs from Grapple Kill	200 (Head 1)
	200 (Head 2)
	400 (Head 3)

Defense Tactics	Counter
Burn Time	1.5

Both creatures are at full strength, so neither is a better target than the other. Despite this, you must pick one and attack that monster as aggressively as possible. This provides the best chance for survival because you get to eliminate half of the incoming damage much earlier in the battle. Splitting up your damage between the two simply prolongs the toughest portion of the battle.

Keep one of the Hades Cerberus Breeders between Kratos and the other as often as possible. This forces the dogs to shoot their partners in the back, stunning the victim briefly and inflicting some damage. This also protects Kratos from some attacks.

CHALLENGE BOTH

Don't be gentle on either Hades Cerberus Breeder. Instead of playing it safe, go after both simultaneously. Rip the head off one and then hit the other next. This makes the fight more dangerous because you face both until the very end. Test your positioning skills to the limit in preparation for challenges to come.

The Cerberus Breeders have claw swipes, a melee charge, and fireball attacks. Evasion works wonders against them all. Provided you don't get greedy with combos it's possible to evade everything that these monsters throw at you. Their fireballs can be spotted a mile away. They'll throw their remaining heads in the air while charging, and all you have to do is move to either side.

Remember to use the Golden Fleece if you have a good sense of timing. Cerberus' fireballs can be reflected back at their senders, burning the massive beasts and making your battle shorter—and easier.

For the other attacks, roll away from the dogs as they approach and use light attacks at long range to punish the creatures. This is a slower method, but it's reliable at all difficulty levels.

If Kratos is hit with a charge, he'll have to wiggle free while the Cerberus Breeder on top of him attacks repeatedly. Push left and right quickly on the left analog stick to escape. Even skilled players are going to take damage from this if they are struck in the initial charge, so be conservative with your dodging.

Each Hades Cerberus Breeder has to be grappled three times to destroy all their heads. These are short sequences; don't let your guard down. The first two heads require a single button command each, and the third is automatically torn off when you engage in the final grapple.

Once the first flaming creature falls, the fight drastically becomes easier. Dodge, attack with double light blows, or a single heavy blow, and repeat the process. Use the Bow of Apollo for damage at range until the monster falls at your feet.

Now that you're in the clear, the Spartan must put his back into the door to open it completely.

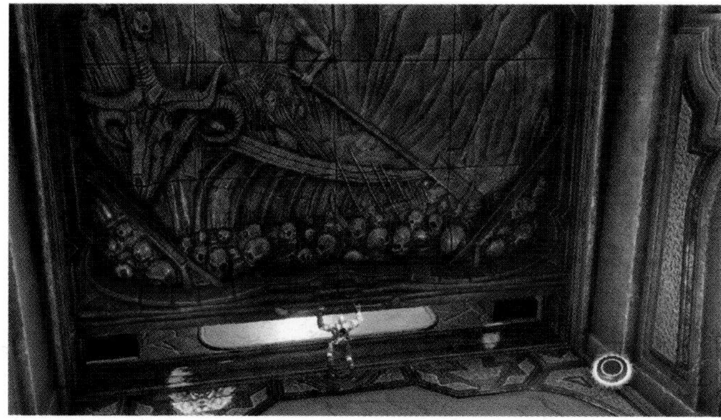

Hades' Door

Head toward the back of the next room. Olympus Sentries and Cerberus Mongrels spawn from the floor as you advance. Use the Olympus Sentries as Battering Rams while trying to kill the Cerberus Mongrels. Quickly finish the Olympus Sentries and tear down the canines afterward. The only thing to fear from the mongrels is their dog pile. The entire group jumps onto Kratos and pins him down. If this happens, wiggle the left analog stick to free the Spartan. When you're done, open the Alternating Chest in the room before leaving. Hades' Palace is ahead.

SIEGE THE PALACE

For Whom the Bell Tolls

After entering the palace, Hades' spectral voice greets Kratos. Look around and get a feel for the place. There is a Save Altar to the left to record your progress. Once you've taken in the surroundings, there is a puzzle to solve.

FAMILY BONDS

Persephone and Hades were together in life. Perhaps they can be together in death as well.

REUNION

If you plan on re-shackling Hades, the stacked stone brace is going to need to pull double duty. Only then can husband and wife be reunited.

1. *Dash to the small alcove in the northeast. If Kratos' health is low, open the Health Chest in the room.*
2. *Grab the stacked stone brace in the center of the room and pull it to the northwestern corner of the main chamber.*

3. *Harpies launch an attack when Kratos gets the brace into position. Use grapple attacks from the ground or reliable air attacks, such as Cyclone of Chaos (a level 2 Blades of Exile maneuver) to kill the Harpies.*
4. *Turn the wheel in the northwest and push the brace into position to block the wheel from resetting. Before moving on, open the Red Orb Chest next to the locked gate.*
5. *Climb the tree to the mezzanine.*
6. *Open the two Mixed Orb Chests to your right before heading into the gated room. As you enter, two Minotaur Brutes and two Cerberus Mongrels appear. Use heavier combos to kill the mongrels while damaging the Minotaur Brutes. If the canines grab you, throw them off and hope that the Minotaurs are close enough to incur damage as well.*

7. *Open the Magic Chest near the entrance to the southern hallway and proceed to the second level.*

8. *Use the winch at the entrance to the second level to draw back the corpse of Persephone. This winch also opens the manacles that bind Hades' arms. As soon as the corpse is lifted, the statue's arms move down to cover its chest.*

9. *Move toward the suspended casket of Persephone. Use R1 to swing the coffin at the statue of Hades. The resulting crash knocks two ladders free in the small alcoves to either side.*

DON'T SLIP

It's possible to fall off the ledge here as there is no railing. Your fall will leave you in the room below. Simply climb the tree and run up the ramp to return. Three Olympus Sentries and two Harpies attack during your return.

10. *Before using either ladder, move to the end of the northeast hallway and open both the Mixed Orb and Red Orb Chests there.*

11. *Walk down the northwest hallway and climb the ladder. Open the chests housed in this small observation room. There are two Red Orb Chests here. More importantly, you find a Phoenix Feather as well.*

PHOENIX FEATHER

The supply room in the northwest has a Phoenix Feather.

12. *Climb the ladder in the western alcove.*

13. *Use the lever on the left to activate an elevator; ride this down to the ground floor.*

14. *You arrive in the room beside the initial chamber. Open the gate to get back into the main room. Retrieve the stone brace, but release it to fight off the wave of Harpies that appears. Open the Health Chest next to the elevator if you incur too much damage.*

15. *Retrieve the stone brace and take it up the elevator with you. Place it next to the cracked wheel and move back down to the second floor.*
16. *Return to the winch at the entrance of the second floor and use it to open the arm braces.*
17. *Climb back up the western ladder and use the crank wheel to drag Hades' arm into the manacle before it resets.*
18. *Move the stone brace to hold the arm in place and head back down to reopen the manacles.*

19. *Finally, move up the eastern ladder and use the winch there to bind Hades' other arm. Before returning to the second floor, open the Magic Chest at the back of the room.*
20. *You are now free to use Persephone's casket to topple this wicked statue and move on.*

ATTACK THE GOD OF THE UNDERWORLD

Use the Save Altar at the beginning of the puzzle before entering the statue. When you head inside, Hades has a frank conversation with Kratos. Afterward, he'll try to rip the soul out of Kratos' body. Alternately press **L1** and **R1** quickly to save yourself. The battle now begins in earnest.

CONQUERING THE UNDERWORLD

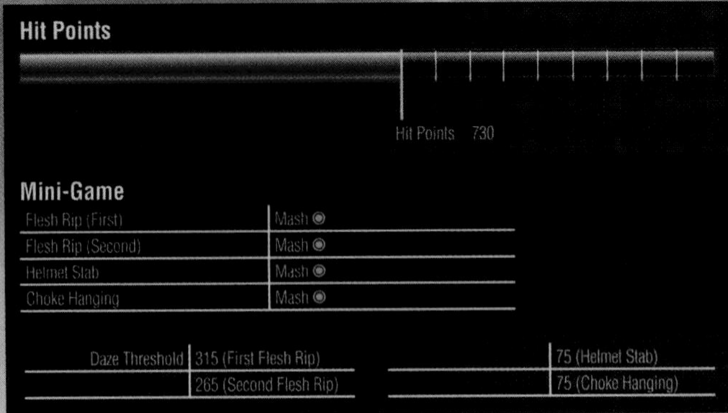

Hit Points

Hit Points 730

Mini-Game

Flesh Rip (First)	Mash ◉
Flesh Rip (Second)	Mash ◉
Helmet Stab	Mash ◉
Choke Hanging	Mash ◉

Daze Threshold	315 (First Flesh Rip)		75 (Helmet Stab)
	265 (Second Flesh Rip)		75 (Choke Hanging)

The First Phase

Activate the Rage of Sparta and tear into Hades. The Olympian uses his blades to grapple to the back of the room and then lashes out with a number of long-range, fast attacks. Avoid these by rolling to either side. After several attacks, Hades reveals a new tactic. He'll sweep his blade along the floor, covering a huge area. Double-jump to get over his weapon and stay in the air as long as possible by continuing your own attack. If you have mastered the Cyclone of Chaos, use its airborne variant to inflict considerable damage.

These tactics soon daze Hades. Land and grapple with the god to begin the next stage of the fight. Kratos rips off some of Hades' flesh. To restore some health, destroy this fleshy bit as it attempts to reunite with Hades. Avoid the Hades Arms throughout this challenge.

After this, Hades gathers his chains. The ground starts to darken in most of the room and you must wait and see where a clear spot beckons. At the last moment before the assault, a circle opens in either the left, right, or central portion of the room. Get over there as soon as possible. This avoids Hades' mighty strike.

Jumps and Stomps

Hades pulls himself to the ceiling after his attacks fail. He'll drop down to the floor in another part of the room; this releases a shockwave. Avoid it by leaping over the danger.

Hades also stomps during this part of the fight. He'll gather himself for a couple of seconds to prepare and then smashes his foot into the floor. Back off to avoid both the damage and the stunning effect of the blast.

Punish Hades between these sets of attacks and wait for him to show weakness. Once he's dazed, grapple with him again and tear out another piece of Hades' body. Destroy this while avoiding the Hades Arms.

Hades unleashes another super chain attack. Stay in the center of the room to ensure that you're fairly close to whatever safe point appears. There won't be much time to dodge.

Beware the Chain

Now Hades uses his chains in a burrowing attack. He'll send the chain into the floor and have it shoot up at random targets. A purple circle appears just before the chain breaks the surface; ensure that Kratos gets away before the chain comes up.

It's hard to counterattack during this phase because Kratos has to stay on the move most of the time. To compensate, use charged shots from the Bow of Apollo to hit Hades on the move.

After enough hits, Hades summons two spectral Cerberus Breeders. These canines charge at Kratos and attack before disappearing. Dodge them and return to the fight.

Eventually Hades shrugs off your attentions and carves a chasm in the ground. Kratos and Hades get their chained blades tangled, and they wrestle in a lethal tug-of-war. Evade while tossing attacks at the God of the Underworld. Don't worry if you fall in; a simple tap of ◎ lets you climb back up.

Evade and attack repeatedly until you get a chance to grapple Hades again. Kratos tears Hades' Claws off as the god falls into the chasm.

Premature Victory

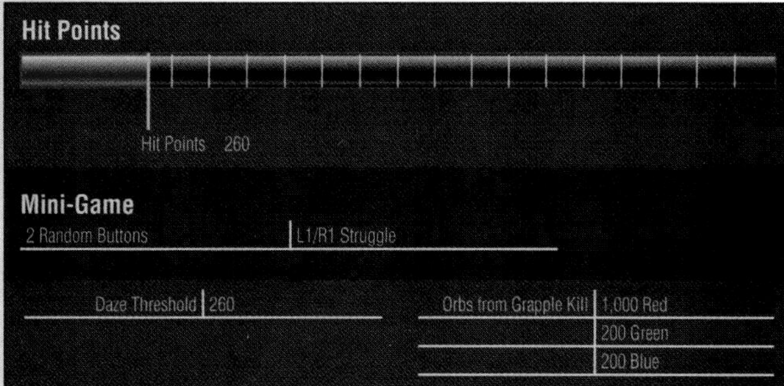

Hit Points

Hit Points 260

Mini-Game

2 Random Buttons	L1/R1 Struggle

Daze Threshold	260	Orbs from Grapple Kill	1,000 Red
			200 Green
			200 Blue

Olympus Sentries appear to avenge the Lord of Hades. Use the Claws to kill these newcomers while Hades climbs back out of the pit. The Olympian is torn up rather badly, and he's lost his weapons. Still, gods never die easily.

Hades unveils a squashing tactic and a new breath attack. Run to the sides of the ledge and watch for Grapple Points to appear. Grapple across when they do, and then land behind Hades. Tear into the god until he turns around.

Hades can shift into a number of attacks at this time. The trickiest to avoid is a two-arm smash that covers the entire platform. If that happens, jump and deploy the Wings of Icarus to float above the attack. You must dodge for a while before the Grapple Points appear again. When they do, repeat the entire process to score more strikes against Hades. Beyond this, the left/right palm smashes are your only concern. Avoid these and cut into the god again and again. He has almost nothing left!

After several rounds of these tactics, Hades loses the will to fight. A circle appears over his head and Kratos is ready for the kill. Finish the battle.

You've stolen Hades' Soul. This allows Kratos to swim safely in the River Styx. Also, the death of Hades has released a number of spirits previously imprisoned. That's not really your concern, so cross the river and use the Save Altar on the other side.

Dive into the River Styx and search the bottom for **Hades' Helm**. Follow the shades downstream and through the corpse of Hades; swim through the hole in his chest. Rise into a small room with a grate in the center and another pool of water on the other side.

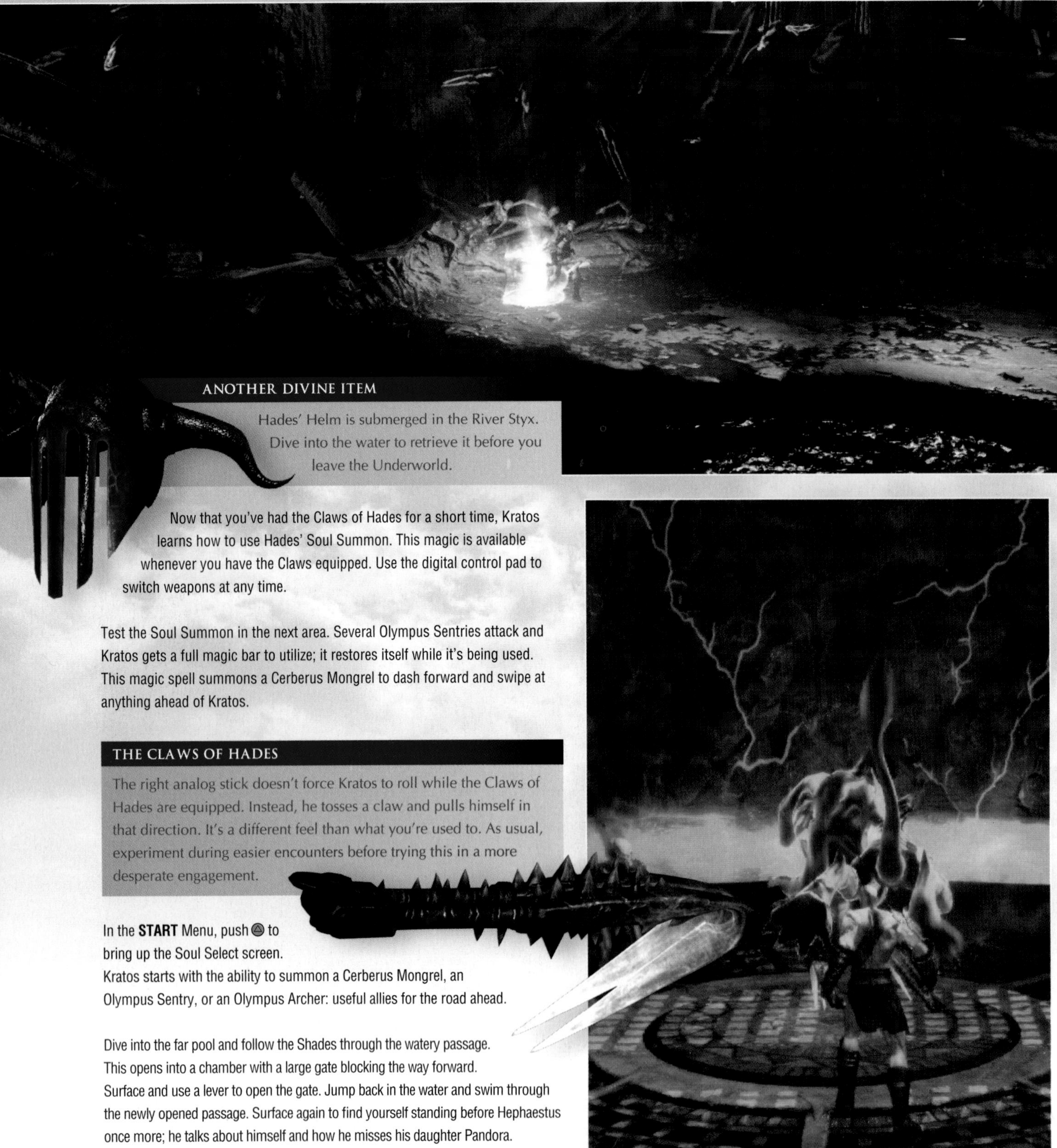

ANOTHER DIVINE ITEM

Hades' Helm is submerged in the River Styx. Dive into the water to retrieve it before you leave the Underworld.

Now that you've had the Claws of Hades for a short time, Kratos learns how to use Hades' Soul Summon. This magic is available whenever you have the Claws equipped. Use the digital control pad to switch weapons at any time.

Test the Soul Summon in the next area. Several Olympus Sentries attack and Kratos gets a full magic bar to utilize; it restores itself while it's being used. This magic spell summons a Cerberus Mongrel to dash forward and swipe at anything ahead of Kratos.

THE CLAWS OF HADES

The right analog stick doesn't force Kratos to roll while the Claws of Hades are equipped. Instead, he tosses a claw and pulls himself in that direction. It's a different feel than what you're used to. As usual, experiment during easier encounters before trying this in a more desperate engagement.

In the **START** Menu, push ⊚ to bring up the Soul Select screen. Kratos starts with the ability to summon a Cerberus Mongrel, an Olympus Sentry, or an Olympus Archer: useful allies for the road ahead.

Dive into the far pool and follow the Shades through the watery passage. This opens into a chamber with a large gate blocking the way forward. Surface and use a lever to open the gate. Jump back in the water and swim through the newly opened passage. Surface again to find yourself standing before Hephaestus once more; he talks about himself and how he misses his daughter Pandora.

Dash down the steps to exit the Forge. Kratos is back at the gazebo. Two Stone Talos spawn when you grab the crank. Use hit-and-run tactics to demolish these brutes. Five Cerberus Mongrels and another Talos appear when the first Talos falls. Use the Blades of Exile in this fight, as Army of Sparta is much better for clearing out the Mongrels. It's pretty easy to kill the Talos once the four-legged creatures are dead.

Afterward, turn the crank until the opening faces north. Exit the chamber and follow the path until the Hyperion Gate comes into view. Kratos can use the gate now that he has the soul of Hades. Jump down to the lower tier. Two Grapple Points bring you to a Save Altar. A pair of Olympus Archers stands beside it, and there are two more across a bridge. Dispatch the nearby archers and then shoot their companions before stopping to save your game.

You're done with the Underworld now. Approach the Hyperion Gate and listen to some advice before leaving this realm.

ACT III

DOOR TO OLYMPIA

START

SAVE ALTAR

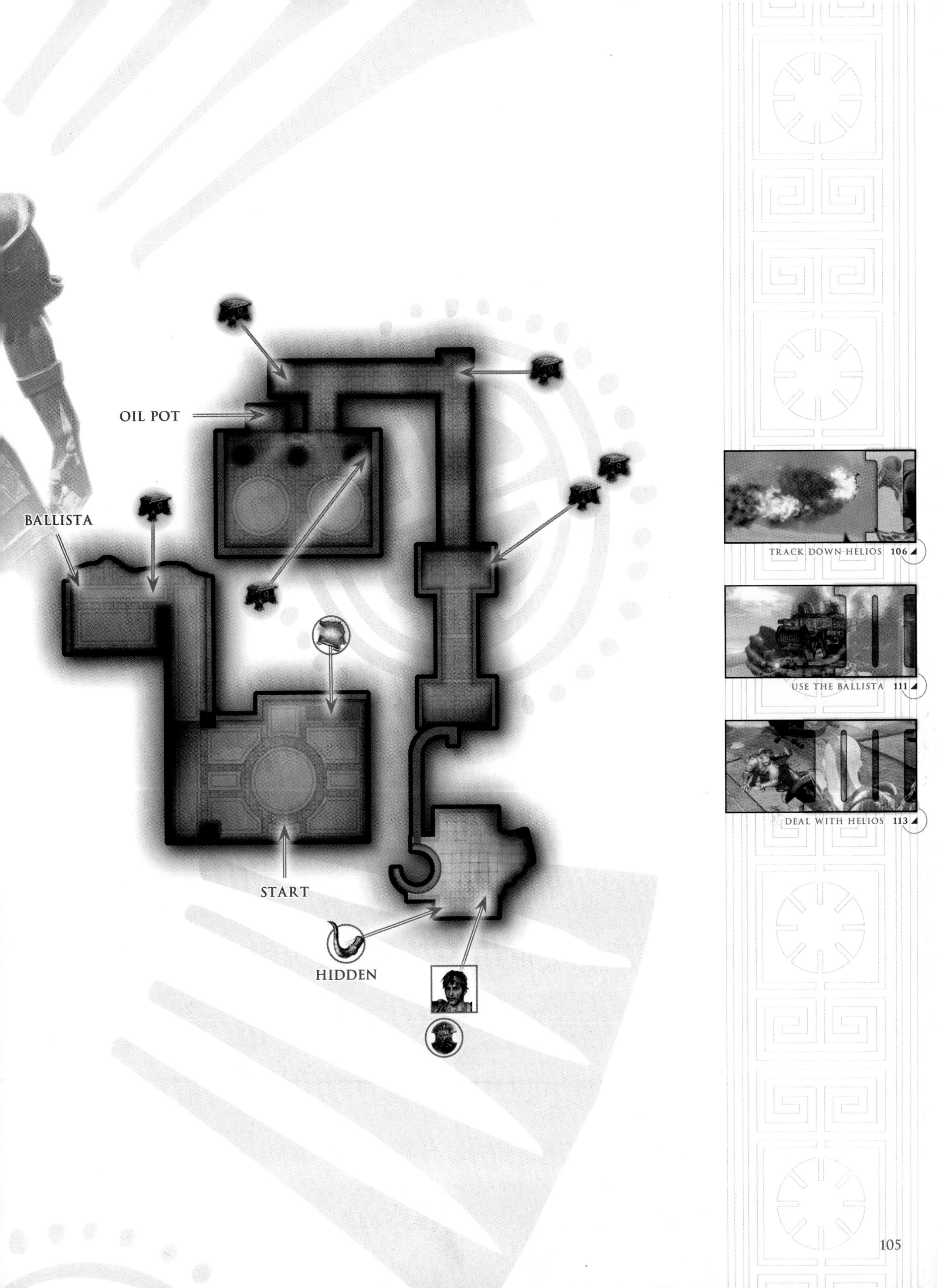

TRACK DOWN HELIOS 106
USE THE BALLISTA 111
DEAL WITH HELIOS 113

CITY OF OLYMPIA

OLYMPIA IN RUINS

I TRACK DOWN HELIOS

An Old Ally

Kratos exits the Hyperion Gate and finds himself on the path toward Olympia, a city of mortals that rests beneath the glory of Mount Olympus. Continue down the path until Kratos meets with an old "friend." This powerful being is broken and battered, begging for help, but Kratos rarely offers mercy. Cut through the traitor's wrist and perform the Context-Sensitive Action to dig deep into the tendons. Grab onto the thumb and push the hand over the edge. With that done, continue on the path and examine the door to Olympia.

Olympus Legionnaires climb up and over the cliff to challenge the God of War. Equip the Claws of Hades and start attacking. Stay in motion and keep all the Spartan soldiers in front of Kratos instead of planting Kratos in the center of them. Use the Claws' strong attacks to throw the soldiers off balance. If Kratos becomes overwhelmed, use magic to repel the enemies and regain the upper hand. Feral Hounds are thrown into the mix, but Kratos' attacks on the Spartans should take care of them as well.

Be wary of the Olympus Legionnaires' attacks. These troops are better trained and have axes that cut deep. Their charged swings have a slight area-of-effect, so Kratos is forced to evade even if he isn't in melee range. If you've invested points heavily in one weapon over another, switch to the more advanced weapon as the fight progresses. Circle the groups of enemies if they begin spreading out; this clumps the enemies together again and makes your heavy combos more effective.

Fight until the area clears. With everyone else dead, the statues around the door are deactivated. The door to Olympia is now unlocked. Open the Health Chest to the right of the statues and then open the door to Olympia. Cross the threshold when you're ready.

OLYMPUS LEGIONNAIRE 228

The Caves of Olympia

Kratos enters a dark cave where there are only a few enemies. You aren't supposed to kill the Harpy Queens in here at first. There's a trick if you want to get to the other side of the cave.

HOW TO HITCH A RIDE

Use the Bow of Apollo to upset the Harpy Queens inside the cave. They'll fly to Kratos after he's gotten their attention. Instead of killing them, leap into the air and latch onto them with a combat grapple (**L1** + ◎). This gives Kratos a free ride.

Guide your Harpy Queen with the left analog stick; once they've reached the end of their flight, press ⊗ to jump off. If the Harpy Queen becomes unruly, use quick attacks to force it back in line. Be careful though. Too many attacks can kill the Harpy Queen, leaving you hanging.

Cross the first gap using your captured Harpy Queen. Stop at the next gap and look down. Instead of immediately grabbing onto a new mount, drop to the lower level and turn around. There is a Red Orb Chest for you to loot. Look beneath the wooden scaffold and return to the upper level where the Harpy Queen waits. Grab onto the winged monstrosity and ride it toward the second. Jump from the first to the second to complete your trip across.

After dismounting – dismembering - the second Harpy Queen, walk around the corner and return to find a replacement. Shoot the new bird with your bow and draw it toward the cliffside behind Kratos. Grab onto the Harpy Queen and ride it into the air to access a hidden alcove containing two chests: one has a **Minotaur Horn** and the other a **Gorgon Eye**. There is also a Red Orb Chest!

DOUBLE THE LOOT

Ride the second Harpy Queen from the second gap. Take this one to the hidden niche described here to find both a Minotaur Horn and a Gorgon Eye.

Walk along the main path until you locate a Save Altar. Search here for a Health Chest and a Magic Chest before continuing. Afterward, the path leads into the city proper.

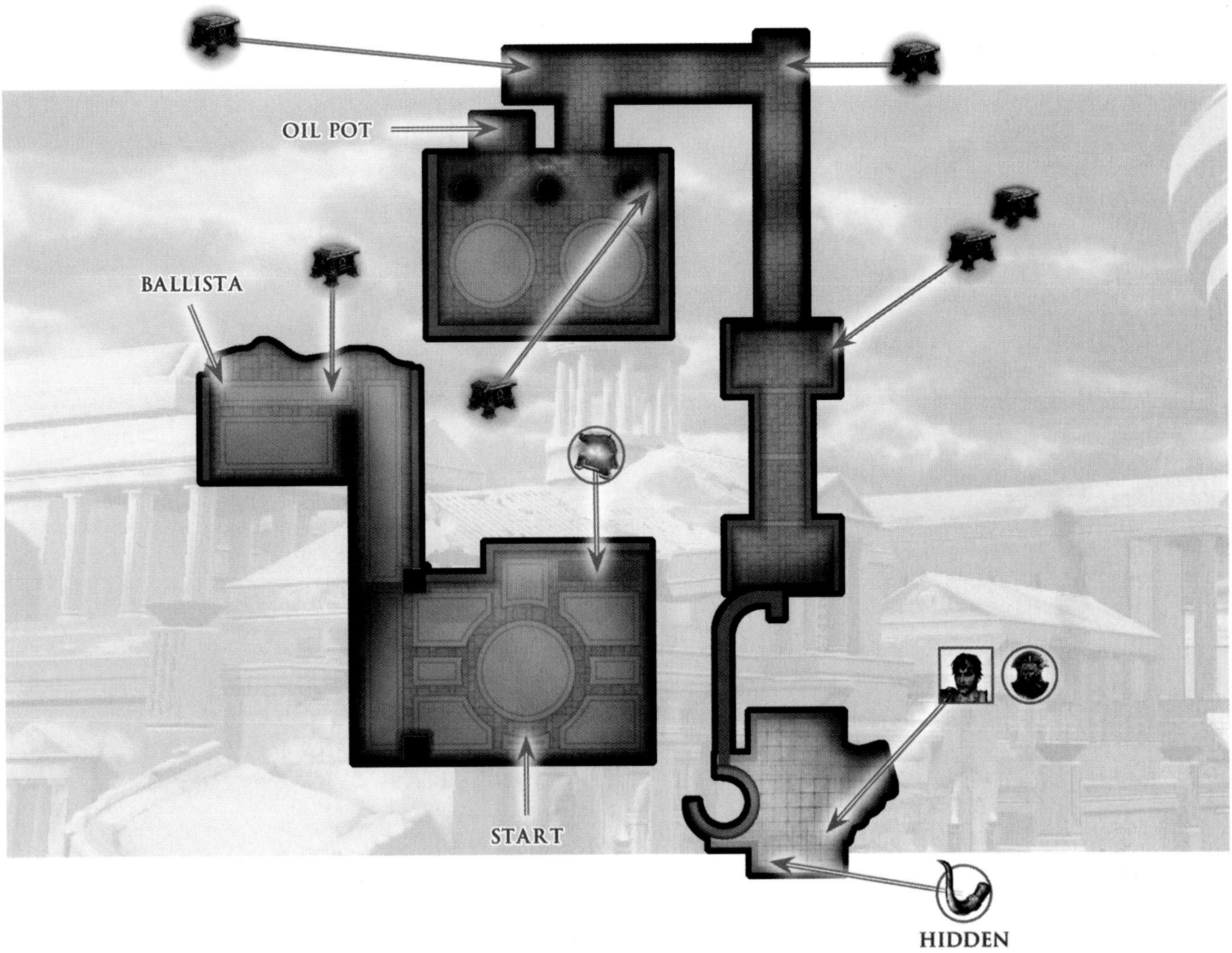

OIL POT

BALLISTA

START

HIDDEN

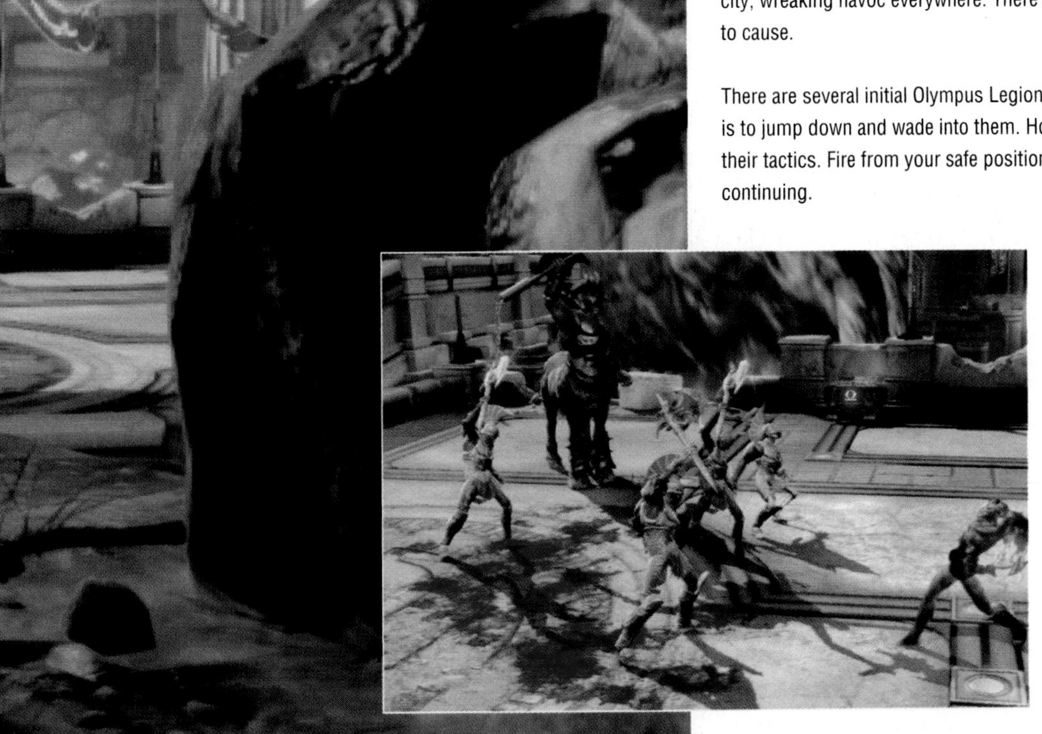

The Last to Arrive

Kratos arrives to witness Olympia in ruins. Helios and a Titan battle over the city, wreaking havoc everywhere. There's still plenty of destruction for Kratos to cause.

There are several initial Olympus Legionnaires waiting to greet you. One option is to jump down and wade into them. However, a cautious player should exploit their tactics. Fire from your safe position and decimate their ranks before continuing.

After ripping through the Olympus Legionnaires, another wave begins. This time you must jump down to initiate the battle; you can't get back up once you're down there.

Centaur General arrives with more Olympus Legionnaires at his side. This Centaur fights just like the one on Mount Olympus, but his armor much more resilient and harder to kill. Ignore the Centaur General at first and focus on his troops. Use the Blades of Exile during this fight, as they are faster than the Claws of Hades.

SEVER THE HEAD AND THE BODY WILL FOLLOW

Kill this Centaur General before taking out a single Olympus Legionnaire. Sounds too much like your last Centaur fight? Fair enough. Try doing it without magic or the Rage of Sparta.

There is an Alternating Chest on the upper right side of this area. Because of this, you're free to use Army of Sparta heavily throughout the fight. This slaughters the Olympus Legionnaires, leaving you alone with the Centaur and any stragglers. Finish the wounded Olympus Legionnaires and then attack the Centaur General with all your might.

Remember that Kratos can block the faster attacks from the Centaur. Only its slower, charged attacks should be dodged. Soon enough the Centaur General's health bottoms out, and you can use a Context-Sensitive Action to eviscerate the beast.

Now is a good time to loot the Alternating Chest nearby if you haven't opened it already. Consider taking magic from it, because there is a Health Chest not far ahead. Climb the stairs on the left side and continue until Kratos spots a ballista. There are a few civilians fleeing the battle. Kratos passes them on the way up the stairs. Although you get nothing from killing them normally, Kratos receives a slight health boost if he grabs and slaughters these civilians.

A Surprise Guest

Open the Health Chest at the top of the ramp if necessary, and then grab the ballista to take down Helios. While winding up, Kratos' progress is cut short by an approaching Chimera. That's fine; this won't take long.

CHIMERA

Chimera were monsters born from the mating of Typhoon, the great serpent, and Echidne. A Chimera is made of three different animals, combined with monstrous results. It has the head and body of a lion, a goat's head along the top of its torso, and the tail of a snake. It can also breathe fire and spit poison.

The most famous Chimera was known for terrorizing the country of Lycia. It ate most of the livestock and set fire to the region. Most people fled. It was clear that a hero was needed to slay the beast.

King Iobates of Lycia sent out a call for help. It was answered by Bellerophon. With aid from Athena, he received a magical golden bridle. This he used to tame a flying horse, the great Pegasus. Now that he could control the air, the Chimera was little threat to Bellerophon. He flew above the monster, and it couldn't reach him with either its poison spit or flames. Bellerophon then took a long spear and skewered the creature, quickly becoming the savior of the Lycian people.

Unfortunately, Bellerophon wasn't satisfied with that. He decided, against Athena's pleas, that he wanted to be god. He took Pegasus and began to fly higher, up to Mount Olympus. Zeus wasn't about to let that happen; it was all well and good for a mortal to be a hero, but Bellerophon was being far too uppity. He waited until the warrior was high above the world, and then he sent out a lowly gadfly. The gadfly stung Pegasus on the rear; the flying horse bucked. It was with such force that Bellerophon was flung off, and he fell to his death.

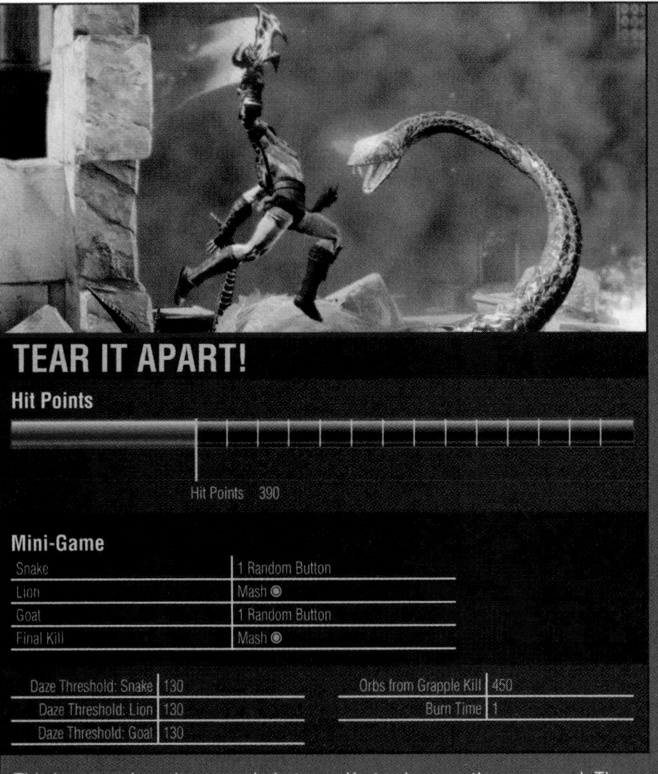

TEAR IT APART!

Hit Points

Hit Points 390

Mini-Game

Snake	1 Random Button
Lion	Mash ◉
Goat	1 Random Button
Final Kill	Mash ◉

Daze Threshold: Snake	130
Daze Threshold: Lion	130
Daze Threshold: Goat	130

Orbs from Grapple Kill	450
Burn Time	1

This beast packs quite a punch, but now Kratos is more than prepared. The Chimera rushes in with a series of quick attacks. Meanwhile, Helios throws fireballs from the sky. Both of these attacks are easily dodged. Avoid the Chimera's attacks and counter them until the beast is stunned. Once dazed, initiate a Context-Sensitive Action and rip the creature's tail off.

DEATH FROM ABOVE

Helios can't help but stick his nose where it doesn't belong. It's wise to avoid Helios' fireballs; stay clear of the glowing circles on the ground, and Kratos should escape unscathed.

Wounded and in great pain, the Chimera throws itself back into the fight. The beast rears up and begins launching fire attacks. Kratos could counter these short-range fireballs, but it's easier to dodge them unless your sense of timing is especially keen.

Dodge and counter for the easiest kill, and then destroy the lion's portion of the body as soon as you can.

Back on four legs, the Chimera is looking for vengeance. Its fire attack has more range now, and it's gained a slower, charge attack. Always dodge left to right, and get in quick combos after the Chimera attacks. Don't let your combos last too long. End the combos early and wait for the ideal time to dodge. This increases your chance of survival. It won't seem important during lower-difficulty playthroughs, but this fight is quite taxing on the highest difficulty.

Now is a good time to use magic or the Rage of Sparta. Burst damage like this brings the Chimera down quickly, avoiding its most dangerous form. Once the Chimera is dazed, initiate a final Context-Sensitive Action to destroy the abomination.

USE THE BALLISTA

Fire in the Sky

After defeating the Chimera, grab the ballista again and wait for Helios to fly directly in front of it. When the moment is right, release the ballista to damage Helios' Chariot. With Helios off balance, the nearby Titan is able to seize the opportunity and cripple the Sun God.

ZEROING IN ON YOUR TARGET

If you're having trouble hitting Helios with the ballista, keep your finger pointed at a spot on the screen where Helios passes. Fire as soon as Helios reaches your chosen point. If that fails, move your finger slightly to adjust your timing. It's not an automatic shot, but you're likely to score a hit after a couple tries.

To the Rescue

Helios is down but not out. Kratos must find this god before he escapes. Return to the platform where Kratos fought the Centaur General and look to the north. A flock of Harpies is over the large gap. Use the Bow of Apollo to lure a Harpy Queen over to Kratos and hop onto it. Fly north and jump onto another Harpy Queen, then another after that. It takes a few flights to make it all the way across, but you should be fine as long as you stay calm and look ahead to know where to fly. Always aim for the next Harpy Queen in the chain to ensure that you have a path and something to grab.

After dismounting, Kratos lands on the other side of the city and is greeted by three Olympus Legionnaires. Kill one at a time and these foes should pose no threat. More Olympus Legionnaires rise to take their place, totaling six enemies. The good news is that there is a Health Chest to the right. After looting it, open the gate nearby.

WATCH WHERE YOU'RE GOING!

An oil pot it behind the gate on the left. Pull it into the next hallway and use it as a ram all the way to the ladder at the end of the path.

Run through the gate on the right and turn left at the first junction. Open the Red Orb Chest and then turn around. Continue down the corridor until the fighting starts; Olympus Sentries and Olympus Legionnaires spawn in front of Kratos. In these tight quarters, either use magic or grab one of the Sentries to use as a Battering Ram. Fight your way to the end of the path and take another left to find a Red Orb Chest.

Turn around and walk down the hallway onto the outer pathway. Continue until Kratos hits a dead end; there is a Health Chest and a Magic Chest to the left of Kratos if needed. After using those, climb the nearby ladder.

Move along the outer edge of the building and stop before you reach the flaming windows. An unfortunate Olympian is in Kratos' way ahead. Climb next to the Olympian and initiate a Context-Sensitive Action to remove him from the situation.

The fire in front of Kratos prevents him from continuing on the same level. Use **R1** to drop down and then shimmy past the fire. Climb back up and gap jump off the building and into a column on the other side. Continue along the wall until Kratos reaches another dead end. When Kratos can't move to the side anymore, start climbing. Jump or climb to the top to reach Helios' broken chariot.

DEAL WITH HELIOS

Destroying the Phalanx

Before Kratos can reach Helios, a small army of Olympus Guardians form a phalanx around the wounded god. Don't even try attacking because there is no way that Kratos is going to break their line. Dash left to see if there's anything over there that might help. There is! It's a Cyclops Berserker.

OLYMPUS GUARDIAN

CYCLOPS BERSERKER

Cyclopes are all brawn and no brains. Their lumbering attacks are easily dodged, but any successful hits wound heavily. Run circles around the Cyclops and use heavy combos when you're in the clear. Once a Cyclops turns, it's time to run again.

If Kratos has any magic or the Rage of Sparta, use it on the Cyclops Berserker to end the battle quickly. Once the Cyclops is crippled, perform a Context-Sensitive Action to ride the beast. Move the Cyclops towards the phalanx and ignore the new Olympus Legionnaires that appear. Launch strong attacks to break the Olympus Guardians' defenses and keep attacking whoever is closest to the Cyclops Berserker. Eventually, the Cyclops succumbs to the blows and Kratos has to dismount. Once Kratos is back on the ground, defeat any remaining troops. Grab the Health Chest on the left side of the ledge when the fighting ends.

Cyclops

The earliest Cyclopes were children of Uranus. These mighty beings were strong, but they were also quite skilled at smithing—and war. The most famous of these ancient Cyclopes were Brontes (thunder), Steropes (lightning), and Arges (flash).

The Cyclopes grew to be so powerful that they rebelled against Uranus and tried to take over the heavens. Uranus defeated them and cast the group into Tartarus. They were freed when Cronus overthrew Uranus, but it wasn't long before these fellows got into trouble again. Cronus ended up exiling them back Tartarus.

During the war between the Olympians and the Titans, Zeus freed the Cyclopes from Tartarus and begged them to forge weapons mighty enough to defeat the Titans. These Cyclopes crafted a thunderbolt for Zeus; it was a weapon that he'd use throughout the war and after. The original legends of Cyclopes were probably inspired by ancient blacksmiths, who frequently wore a patch over one eye as they worked to protect it from flames. Cyclops also means "ring-eyed." Most Cyclopes had a great single eye in their forehead. Similarly, ancient blacksmiths sometimes had tattoos shaped like a series of concentric rings. Rings were the emblem of ancient blacksmiths because the shapes were necessary in forging round objects like bowls and dishes.

The most famous Cyclops of Greek mythology was Polyphemus, the giant one-eyed monster whom Odysseus encountered on the way back from the Trojan War. Polyphemus was a herdsman. He lived in a cave that Odysseus and 12 members of his crew investigated. When Polyphemus came upon them in his cave, he responded to Odysseus' request for hospitality by seizing two sailors, dashing their brains out against the cave's stone floor, and then eating them whole.

Odysseus got his revenge by giving Polyphemus some strong wine he had brought with him from his ship. Polyphemus had never had alcohol before, and was drunk senseless after only a few cups. Odysseus then got together with his men, sharpened a stake, and then hardened the tip in a fire. While Polyphemus slept, they got together to heft the stake and ram it, full-bore, into Polyphemus' eye. Blinded, Polyphemus was unable to find Odysseus and his men despite his murderous fury. Odysseus had given his name to Polyphemus as Oudeis—"Nobody"—so when Polyphemus' neighbors heard his screams for help, it sounded to them like "Nobody is hurting me!" Thus, they ignored him.

Polyphemus ordinarily sealed the door into his cave with an enormous stone, and doing so had trapped Odysseus and his men inside. Odysseus had refrained from killing Polyphemus outright, because only the Cyclops could open the door to release them. Polyphemus eventually had to open the door to let his flock out to graze. Odysseus and his men cleverly snuck out by sliding beneath the giant animals and clinging to their stomachs. Polyphemus patted each creature that left the cave, but he found nothing except sheep's wool beneath his hands.

When Polyphemus trudged back into his cave, Odysseus and his men stole Polyphemus' flock by herding them onto their ship. They sailed away for a distance, and then Odysseus foolishly shouted back to Polyphemus, announcing his true name and mocking the monster. Polyphemus hurled huge rocks after their ship. The boulders raised enormous waves that nearly smashed the ship against a cliff. The ship survived. Polyphemus could only pray to his father Poseidon to curse Odysseus' journey. Poseidon hated Odysseus anyway, and this only increased that god's rage. The journey home would be long indeed for Odysseus.

Helios

In the first days of the universe, there was no light. No one could see anything, and the crops couldn't grow, and most living things were completely miserable. Then the gods created the Sun and the Moon, and things significantly improved. However, they needed someone to watch over the celestial bodies, and they assigned Helios and his sister Selene to guide them. Helios pulled the Sun behind him across the sky on a chariot, and Selene did the same with the Moon.

There came a point when Helios fell in love with a beautiful mortal woman. But he couldn't stay with her, and he left before she could tell him that she was pregnant. She gave birth to a son, who she named Phaeton.

When Phaeton grew into a boy, he began pestering his mother. Who was his father? Why wasn't he here? What happened to him? Finally, his mother gave in. She pointed to the sky and replied that Phaeton's father was Helios, God of the Sun. At this, Phaeton was amazed. He had to visit his father.

When Phaeton arrived at Helios' palace, he was welcomed and Helios was thrilled. He offered the boy all sorts of wonderful things and entertained him. Phaeton was given the run of the castle, with the exception that he not bother Helios' chariot and horses. But Phaeton wasn't content. There was nothing that would satisfy him but to be just like his father. When Helios wasn't around, he snuck into the stables, harnessed the horses, and began to drive the chariot.

Phaeton wasn't prepared for how difficult it was. The horses were wild and nearly uncontrollable, and he couldn't handle the chariot. The Sun began to meander across the sky, burning everything. In desperation, Zeus called a thunderbolt and smashed Phaeton out of the sky. The boy fell to earth, dead.

In grief, Helios blamed Zeus for his son's death. He refused to leave the palace or drive the Sun's chariot, and the world was plunged into darkness. Finally, however, the other gods were able to convince Helios to resume his duties by showing that all would remember the boy's sacrifice. Those that mourned him were turned into trees, and their tears became amber.

Helios isn't about to let Kratos get close to him. When you try to approach he unleashes a blinding beam of light. Use the right analog stick to orient Kratos' hand in front of the beam and slowly continue toward Helios. Once Kratos is close enough to strike, perform a Context-Sensitive Action to receive a special gift. The **Head of Helios** is a useful tool that will come up many times in the areas ahead.

THE HEAD OF HELIOS

Kratos is quite resourceful with the Head of Helios and can use it for many things. By holding **L2** and tapping ⊚, Kratos can use the head as a torch to illuminate his path. If you hold down ⊚ while using the Head of Helios, Kratos can create a Solar Flash that stuns weaker enemies and damages all nearby foes.

Beyond that, there are hidden treasures and areas on the path ahead. Shine the light from the Head of Helios on sparkling areas to reveal their secrets.

Search the area to your right to find the **Shield of Helios**. Next, look along the railing to the right. A dusty gold image shimmers in the air. Shine the light from your head onto the spot to reveal an Item Chest with a **Minotaur Horn**.

MINOTAUR HORN

Uncover a hidden Item Chest with the Head of Helios; it's on the right side of the railing where you killed the God of the Sun. This gets you a Minotaur Horn.

Use the Head of Helios to unveil a hidden doorway to the left. Open the door by shining Helios' light all over the doorway until it becomes substantial; the right analog stick controls where you shine the beam. Go inside, into a dark mountain pass. This is an ideal place to test out the powers of the Head of Helios. Walk forward with the Head raised so that Kratos can see where he's going. Then, try out the Head's Solar Flash on two Olympus Sentries you meet in the narrow passage. Now that you've seen what the Head can do, continue down the corridor until you reach the Path of Eos.

ACT IV

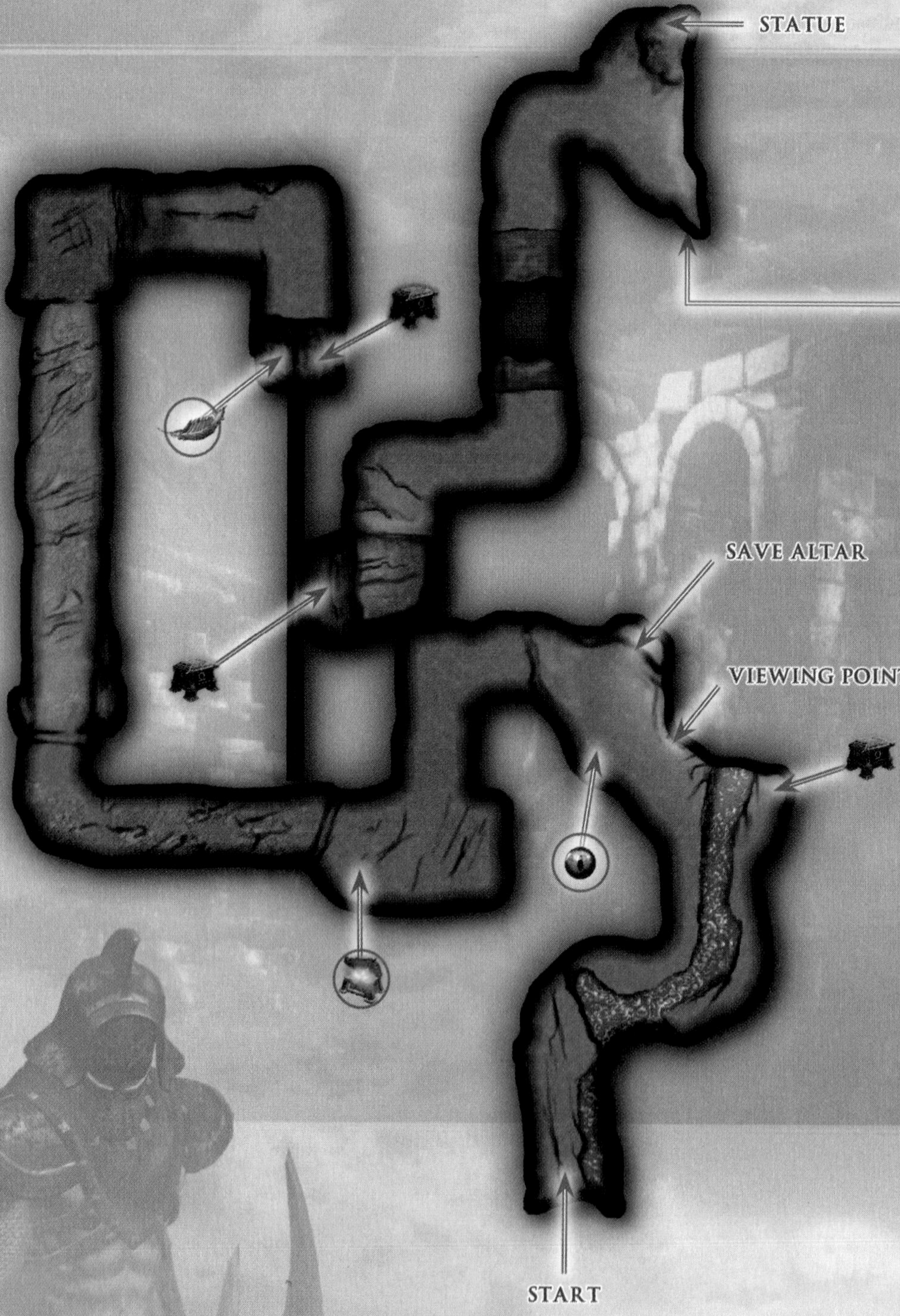

STATUE

SAVE ALTAR

VIEWING POINT

START

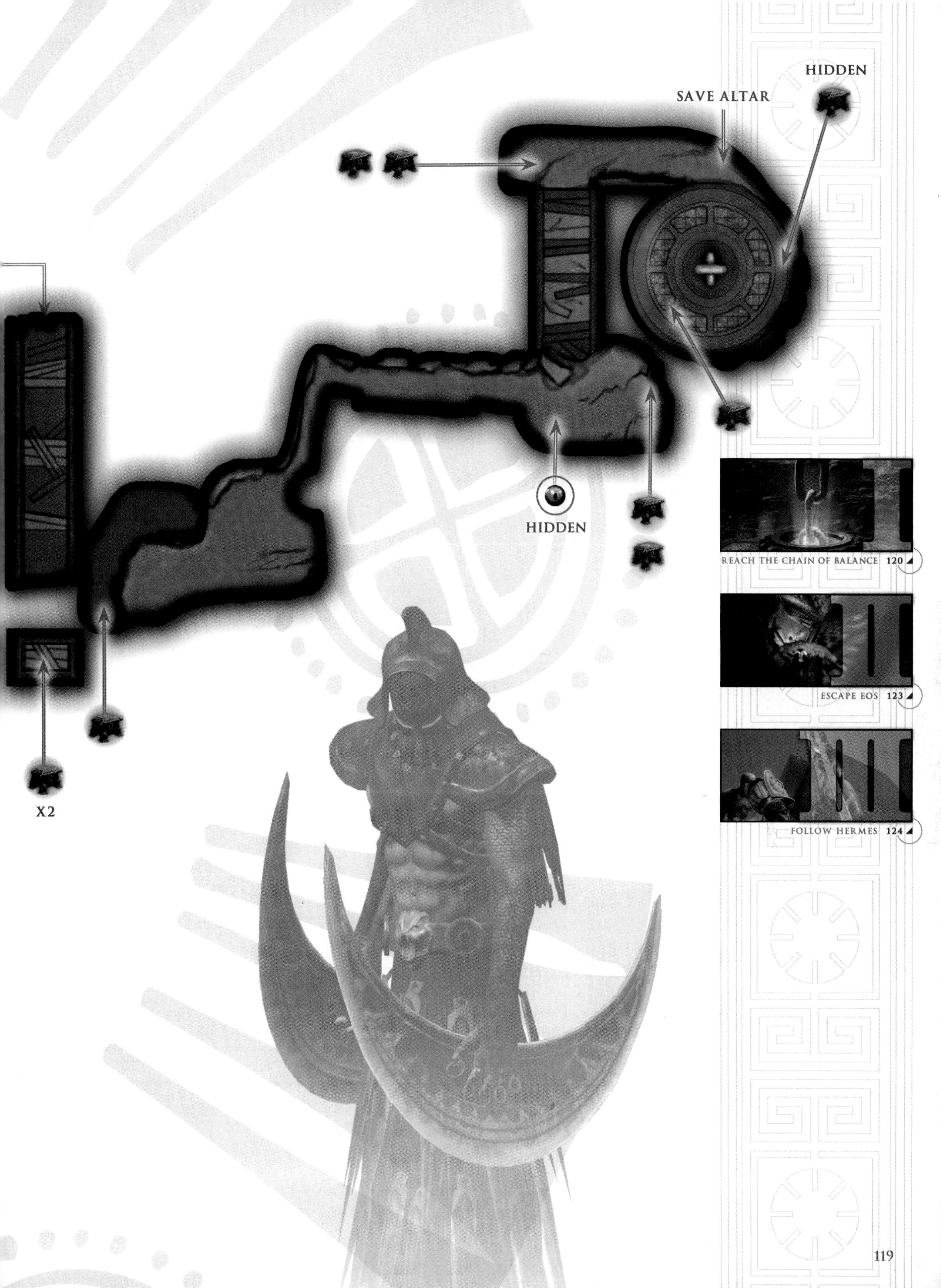
HIDDEN
SAVE ALTAR
HIDDEN
X2
REACH THE CHAIN OF BALANCE 120
ESCAPE EOS 123
FOLLOW HERMES 124

THE PATH OF EOS

A HIDDEN PASSAGE

REACH THE CHAIN OF BALANCE

The Mountain Pass

A Health Chest is ahead of Kratos, on the right. Look around for the viewing point and a Save Altar. Search the alcove to your left before heading out. The camera hides this area well, so look carefully to find it. Inside the small area is an item chest with a **Gorgon Eye**. Take the path on the left when you're ready.

Keep using the Head of Helios to light the way. Move into a small room with an Alternating Chest. Open it if needed and continue along the path. More Olympus Sentries appear, but they're as lambs to the slaughter. Treat them as an appetizer to appease Kratos' craving for vengeance and move on.

Kratos soon reaches a catwalk where he's ambushed by a flock of Harpies. Either draw the Bow of Apollo or use the Head of Helios' Solar Flare to blind the Harpies. Strafe along the catwalk and press the attack. If you can manage to retain your location and orientation in your head without the presence of light, leap into the air and fight blind with the Blades of Exile—it's surprisingly effective.

Once the Harpies are dealt with, use the Head of Helios to reveal a path to the left. Follow this path and slaughter every Olympus Sentry in the way. This leads to a ledge. Climb down to locate two chests. One has Red Orbs and the other contains a **Phoenix Feather**.

PHOENIX FEATHER

Don't miss the area beneath the ledge. There is a Phoenix Feather down there.

Jump to the rope at the end of the path; it's over Kratos' head. Climb to the other side of the gap and massacre the Olympus Sentries along the way. Once you're clear, drop onto the ground at the far end. Climb the rock platforms and keep your eyes peeled for a Health Chest.

A lone Olympus Sentry is at the top of the set of platforms. Kill this foe and continue forward. Pull out the Head of Helios again and use that to light the way. Kratos eventually reaches a gaping hole in the floor. There's nothing but death in that void, so don't leap in looking for treasure. Instead, use the Wings of Icarus to safely glide to the other side. Continue sprinting forward until Kratos begins to hear a familiar song.

Eos' End

A friend is here and Kratos takes a moment to speak with her. Afterward, use the Bow of Apollo to lure over a Harpy Queen. When she gets close, grab onto it and use the Harpy Queen to reach the stone path in the center of the cave. Jump out, to the right, to find a small area with two Red Orb chests. Then, run across the path and jump back onto the cave's cliff side. Two Wraiths of Olympus arrive as Kratos lands.

Before you worry about those guys, drop over the left edge of the cliff. While approaching this area you might have noticed the climbable spot that you're standing over. It's not visible from where you are now, but trust that it IS there.

Climb down this hidden spot. Look around the corner for a Red Orb Chest and then climb back to the top.

WRAITH OF OLYMPUS 231

WRAITHS OF OLYMPUS

They may look fierce, but they are quite easy to kill once you learn their rhythm. All of their attacks are light, which means that Kratos can block anything they throw at him. You won't need to stay mobile (a rarity for most encounters).

The Wraiths of Olympus' strength comes from their speed, but this can be countered with a combat grapple. Grab the Wraiths with (L1 + ◎) to push them away and expose them to a few free strikes. This even works when the enemies are burrowing underground.

Start blocking and wait for the Wraiths of Olympus to attack. After their swipes fail, counter by combat grappling a Wraith to knock him away. Then, go to town with your Blades of Exile. Alternatively, launch the Wraith into the air and flay him until you both land. It's possible to juggle them for quite some time, making it difficult for the Wraiths to get any attacks in edgewise. Another combo is block, combat grapple, Cyclone of Chaos, and back to block.

Once the Wraiths of Olympus are dead, head up the path and refresh Kratos with a Health Chest and a Magic Chest. Look behind the wooden scaffolding in this area. There is a secret wall that should be illuminated with the Head of Helios. A chest containing a **Gorgon Eye** is inside the secret opening.

GORGON EYE

Use the Head of Helios to find a secret wall behind some scaffolding. Take the Gorgon Eye from within.

A bridge is farther down the road. Two more Wraiths of Olympus attack Kratos as he's crossing the span and several Olympus Archers attack from long range. Upon stepping on the bridge, draw and charge your bow and target the oil pot ahead. This way you can shift to the Olympus Archers as soon as they spawn with just a tap of the right analog stick. Hit them as soon as possible to simplify the encounter. Aim for the oil pots next to them and take out two birds with one detonation.

Once at least half the Olympus Archers are killed, start on the Wraiths of Olympus. The bridge doesn't offer the same area in which to maneuver as the last area, but this won't be a problem if you juggle the Wraiths effectively.

Once everything in the vicinity lies dead at Kratos' feet, cross the remainder of the bridge. Open the Health and Magic Chests on the other side before moving on. Continue walking forward until you discover a Save Altar. Record your progress and look around.

Search the area before leaving. Behind the Chain of Balance is another wall hiding a chest. Use the Head of Helios to reveal your latest treasure trove of Red Orbs. Another chest is to the right of the Chain of Balance.

An Icarus Vent is next to Kratos and it can transport him out of the caves; prepare for a bumpy ride. The way up is fraught with danger, and you must react quickly to escape without taking major damage.

ESCAPE EOS

A Turbulent Take-Off

The ascending aerial journey seems straightforward at first, but this flight takes tremendous concentration, foresight, and reactions to survive. A number of players are likely to die their first time, but the recent checkpoint ensures that you won't lose much time to an accident or two.

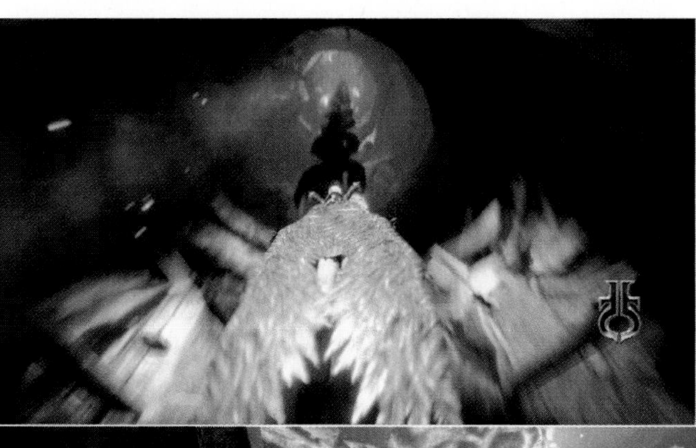

THE PERFECT FLIGHT

Can you make it up the passage ahead without a single bump? Practice for a few runs and use the "Restart from Previous Checkpoint" option if you slam Kratos into any obstacles. For a better challenge, repeat this when you try the second flying section!

Use the left analog stick to control Kratos' flight. In the first phase, your goal is to dodge the wooden planks. Look as far ahead as possible to predict where Kratos needs to be. You can't move Kratos quickly. Start moving as soon as the path is divined to stay ahead of the game.

Keep your maneuvers smooth. Kratos may hit the walls and take more damage with jerky movements. During the journey, there are two falling boulders that rush toward Kratos, but for the most part Kratos' obstacles are stationary. At the end of this section, Kratos passes a Titan and lands on the scaffolding surrounding a large column.

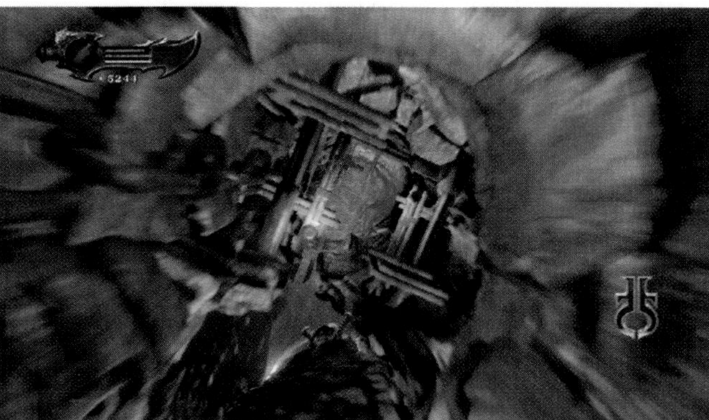

Proceed along the wooden planks on the side of the column. Next, climb up the netting along the cliff. Boulders start falling from above and they're heading straight for Kratos. Quickly jump from side to side to avoid the boulders and continue the ascent until Kratos is standing on wooden platforms higher up.

Pick up the pace. Sprint and jump along the platforms that line the walls. Boulders continue falling and some are going to hit the wooden platforms. Hurry or risk watching the way forward destroyed in the blink of an eye. If you stand for too long in one place, the planks break and doom Kratos.

When Kratos reaches a Grapple Point, use it to cross to the opposite wall and then resume climbing. As with the planks, you must move quickly here. The Grapple Points collapse if you hang on them for more than a few moments.

DON'T BE FOOLED

There are rocks jutting out of the wall as you climb. These look like they provide cover, but don't trust them. You can still take damage from boulders even if you're tucked under these overhanging rocks.

Continue climbing until Kratos regains his footing on the platforms. Stop for a moment. Do you see a faint light here? You're not imagining things. Shine the Head of Helios around to uncover another Item Chest. This one has a **Phoenix Feather**. Next, follow the platforms and use the Grapple Points ahead until you're able to take flight again.

This second flight makes the last one appear silly by comparison. The openings are now smaller, boulders are constantly falling toward you, and the route ahead is not clear. Have Kratos duck and weave between the wooden planks. Sometimes it looks like there is a dead end ahead. Stay calm. Falling debris breaks through the wooden platforms with just enough time for you to avoid the falling material *and* still reach the new hole.

Quickly orient Kratos into a position that allows him to fly through unscathed. It's fun, but challenging. There are four sections like this. The openings that you reach are in the following order: center, left, bottom, center.

PHOENIX FEATHER

This tricky item is found when you hit the second series of platforms during Kratos' ascent.

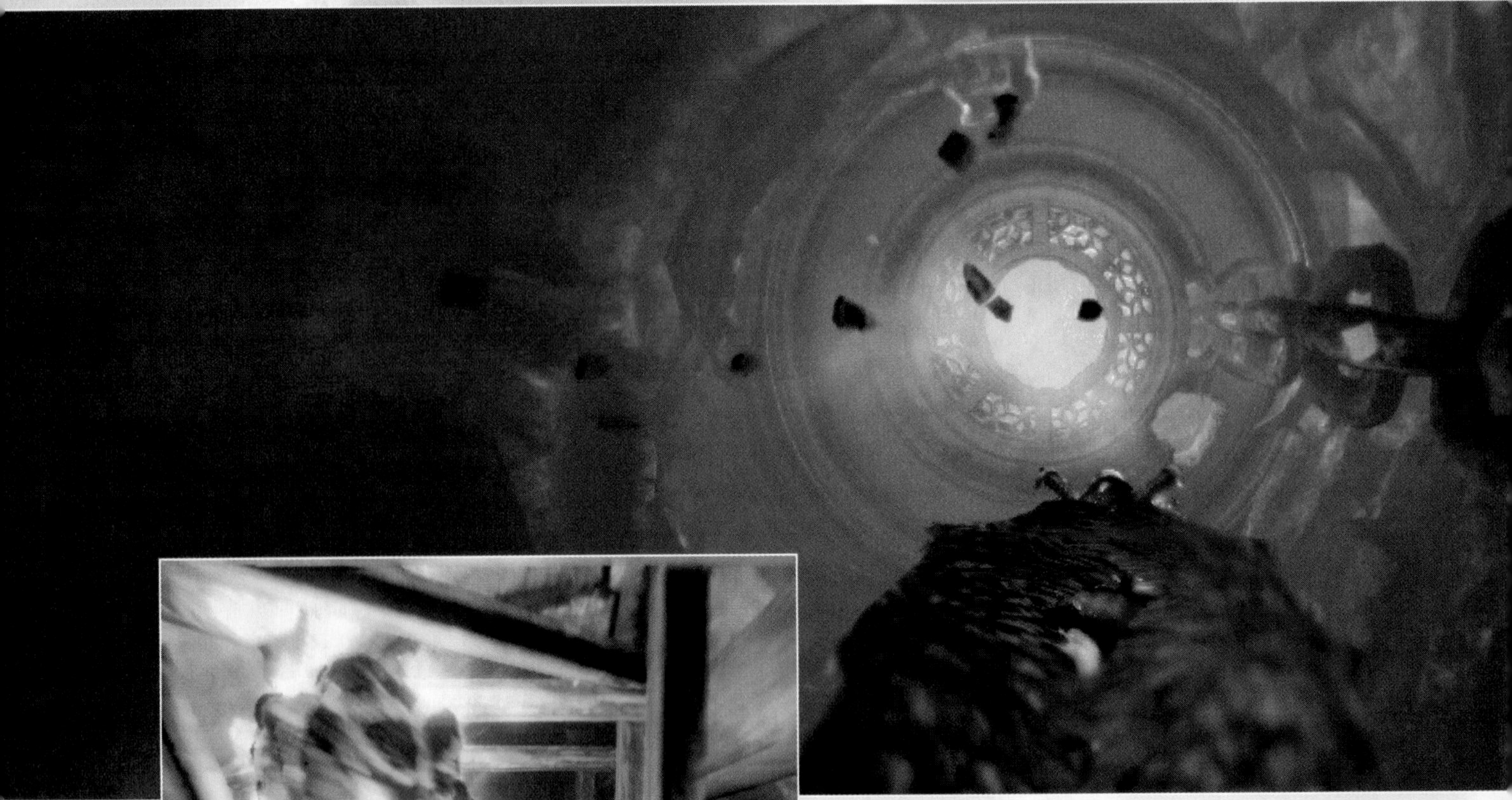

Kratos soon flies through a square column of falling boulders. It looks like death is imminent, but there is always an open quadrant for Kratos to squeeze through. Keep moving and stay one step ahead of the falling debris. Eventually there is light at the end of the tunnel, and Kratos is able to escape.

III FOLLOW HERMES

The Gauntlet

Dust yourself off. Look to the right and shine the Head of Helios over there to reveal an Item Chest containing a **Minotaur Horn**.

MINOTAUR HORN

The Head of Helios reveals an Item Chest with a Minotaur Horn just after you land.

Shoot a flaming arrow into the brambles ahead. A large platform is released when the debris burns away. Mount the container and ride it until it stops. Use a nearby Grapple Point to swing to a ledge. Afterward, swing to two more Grapple Points and leap to safety. The last Grapple Point has Kratos spinning in circles, so time your jump carefully. Aim for the last platform and use the Bow of Apollo again. Burn through the brambles to free another container.

While the crate is in motion, take a moment to stretch and center yourself. The following three fights are quite difficult, especially when you're first getting used to them. Olympus Sentries begin climbing over the edge of the platform. Eliminate some of these peons, but leave about half of the group alive for a short time. Evade them until their larger buddies arrive! Two Minotaur Elites show up and start hacking at the chain in the center of the platform.

CUT LOOSE

That chain is the only thing supporting the ride beneath Kratos' feet. If the Minotaur Elites sever it, everything on top of the platform goes for a long drop. It seems that these minotaurs are willing to die for their masters. That's fine. Help them die sooner than expected.

THINK OUTSIDE THE BOX

Killing the Minotaur Elites not only takes a lot of time but it's also hazardous to Kratos' health. There's a better way to get things done.

Use the Olympus Sentries as Battering Rams. Try to lure the Minotaurs toward the edge of the container by hitting them and backing away. Then, ram the Minotaurs off the sides for instant kills!

The technique takes practice, but this strategy is literally a lifesaver and can be applied to all battles taking place on the cart.

Immediately shift focus to the Minotaur Elites and start attacking them. Kratos' highest priority is keeping the Minotaurs away from the chain. It may be tempting, but do not use magic or the Rage of Sparta unless you're hard-pressed. The next stage of the fight is much nastier.

If you can't throw the Minotaurs off the platform, try to counter their quick attacks and return with strong hits of your own when they're blocking. Position Kratos at medium range in regard to the Minotaurs. Press and hold down △ to launch the Minotaur Elites and then pummel them in the air. Concentrate on one Minotaur at a time and beat it into submission. Perform a Context-Sensitive Action to finish off the Minotaur and then start working on its partner. Kratos gets health back if he kills Minotaurs by grabbing them, and every Green Orb counts in this fight.

Round Two

The platform continues moving once the Minotaur Elites are sent to the Underworld. Rush to the northern side of the container and charge the Bow of Apollo. Olympus Archers quickly appear on a distant crate. Kill them as soon as possible to decrease the challenge for this skirmish. Olympus Sentries appear as well—Minotaur Elites aren't far behind.

Again, use the Olympus Sentries as Battering Rams to damage, or kill, the Minotaur Elites. Once the Olympus Sentries are eliminated, begin attacking the Minotaurs head on. Unleash Kratos' magic this time, or even some of your Rage. The third fight is bigger, but there are ways to defeat it quickly and - somewhat - safely.

The Breaking Point

The cart jerks into motion once again, but this time a Cerberus Mongrel bursts into life. Fight this enemy quickly as Olympus Sentries rise. One quick Battering Ram is often enough to daze the beast. Mount the creature and use it to burn the Sentries and Minotaur Elites before they have a chance. This makes the final stage much easier.

If you're dismounted, use all Kratos' remaining magic first and then turn to the Rage of Sparta if that wasn't enough. The end is near, so any resources you have can be used without fear.

Hermes

The Messenger of the Gods, Hermes was also called "fleet footed" or "quick as thought." He owed this to his magical shoes made for him by Hephaestus; these winged boots allowed him to fly through the air and move faster than anyone else. He was the patron of travelers and wanderers, and he protected those far from home. As such, he served as a guide to the dead, watching over souls and taking them to Hades.

Hermes was also a trickster. He had a clever mind, a quick tongue, and a great deal of wit. In fact, it was the earliest sign of his divine nature. Hermes was the son of Zeus and a Nymph named Maia. Maia didn't want anyone to know about little Hermes, and she kept him safe in a cave far away from Mount Olympus. However, baby Hermes was precocious, and he wasn't content with staying in a cold, boring cave. He crept out one evening while his mother was sleeping.

Hermes then set out to see the surrounding region. Soon enough, he found a beautiful pasture, with a number of marvelous cows grazing upon it. He was impressed with them and decided to take them home. It occurred to him that someone might follow the cattle tracks and find them. Hermes thought about it and tied rushes to the cows' hooves, hiding their tracks.

As he was taking the cattle home, Hermes found a tortoise shell. This was also pretty interesting to him, and he began playing with it. He found that when he put a few strings on the shell and stroked them, a beautiful melody emerged. He called this new instrument a lyre.

Soon after Hermes left, the god Apollo (another son of Zeus) noticed that his beautiful cattle were missing. He looked around for some time but could find no sight of them. It was only after a while of searching that he discovered them outside a cave, in the care of a toddler. Amazed, he could only think that the child was responsible. Hermes' mother Maia told Apollo that it couldn't have been her baby; he was with her all night, and, besides, he was far too young. Then Hermes spoke up and said that, yes, he stole them. Apollo was amazed and fascinated with the whole event.

As he was speaking, Hermes was quietly playing his lyre. Apollo, the God of Music, had never heard anything like it, and he was quite intrigued by the song. Soon Hermes and Apollo reached an agreeable compromise: Hermes would keep the cattle and Apollo would be given the lyre.

After that, Apollo couldn't help but show off the new instrument, and soon all of Olympus had heard about the gifted child. There was no real point in trying to keep him secret, and Hermes was readily welcomed.

Stop whatever you are doing immediately if any Minotaur Elites get to the chain and start hacking at it. It only takes a single blow from Kratos to distract the Minotaurs—don't hesitate! Strike them or shoot them, then back off to avoid their counterattack.

Tortoise Meets the Hare

Once the battle is over, ride the platform to the top of the cavern and jump to an adjacent platform. Sprint to the center of the crate to meet Kratos' latest tormenter. It's Hermes. After insulting Kratos, Hermes flees the scene at an astounding clip.

Before giving chase, open the Health Chest to the right. Use the Grapple Point in the center of the crate to reach the Chain of Balance. Climb up the chain and enter the Chamber of the Flame.

ACT V

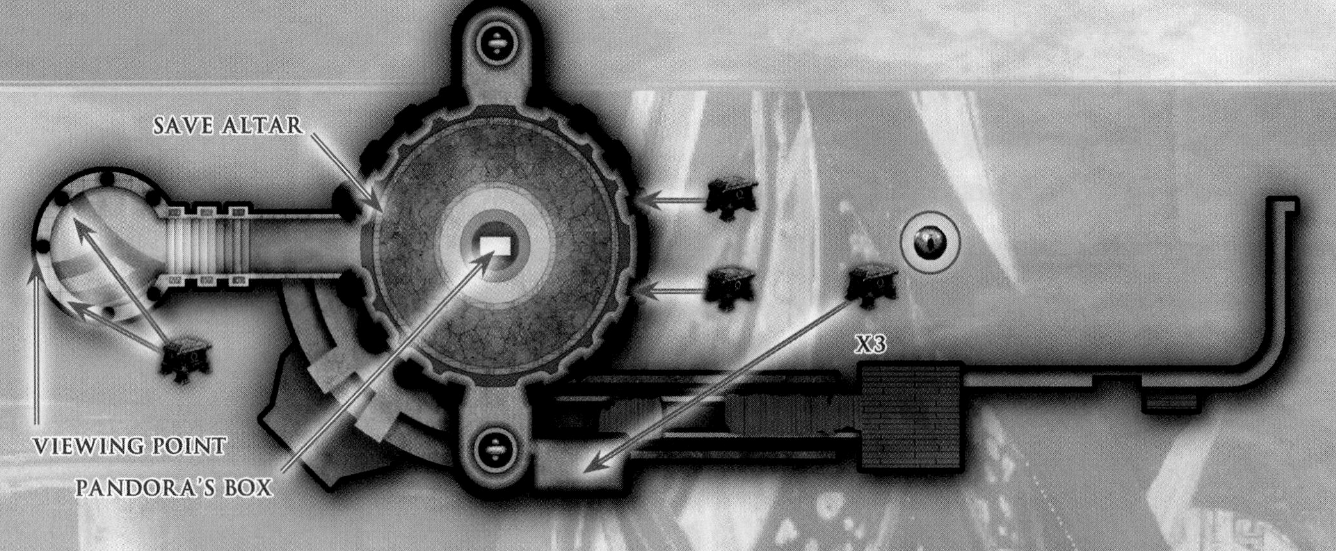

SAVE ALTAR
X3
VIEWING POINT
PANDORA'S BOX

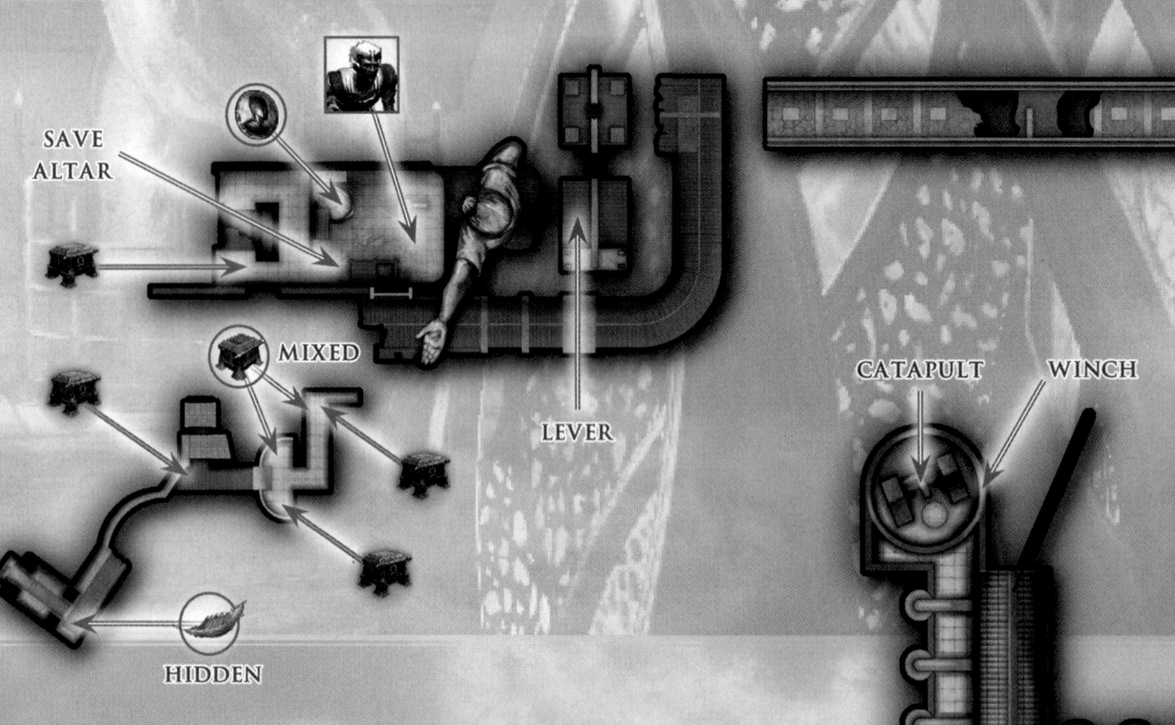

SAVE
ALTAR
START
MIXED
LEVER
CATAPULT
WINCH
HIDDEN
START

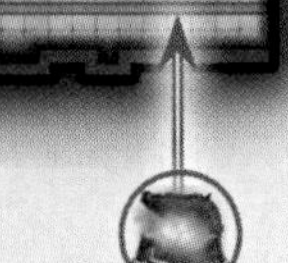

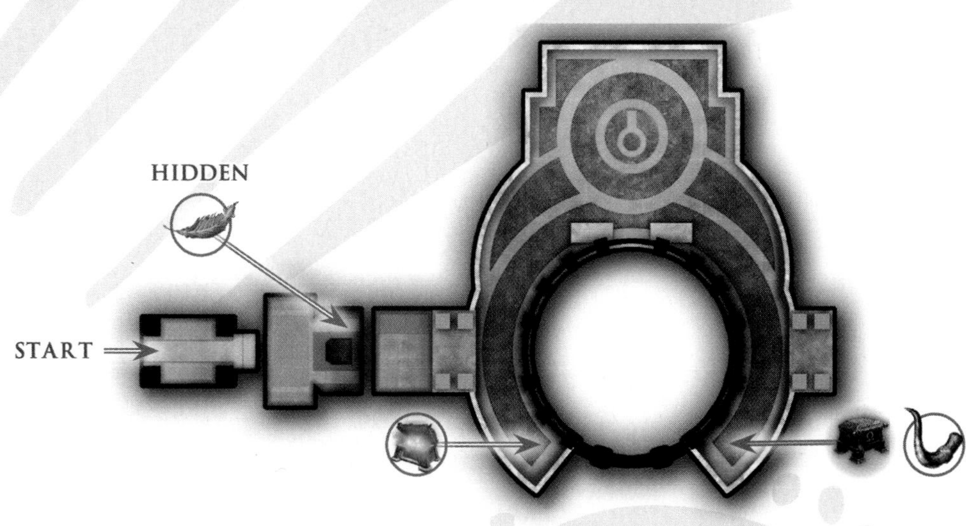
HIDDEN
START

SAVE ALTAR
START
PANDORA'S BOX
BENEATH ELEVATOR
X4
X2
SAVE ALTAR
HIDDEN

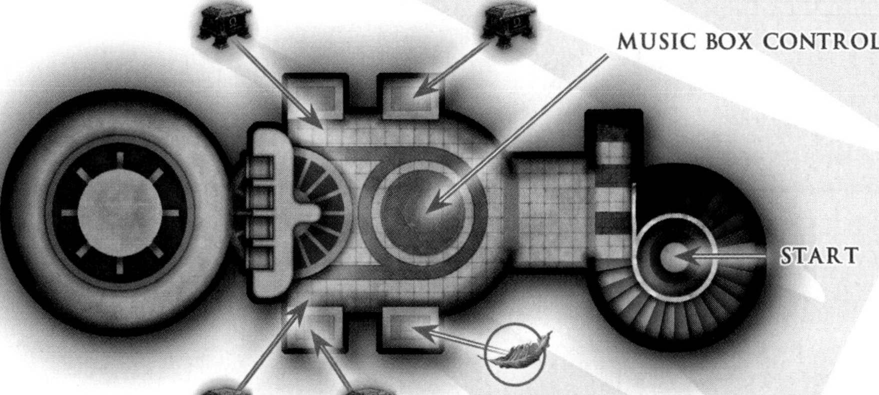
MUSIC BOX CONTROLS
START

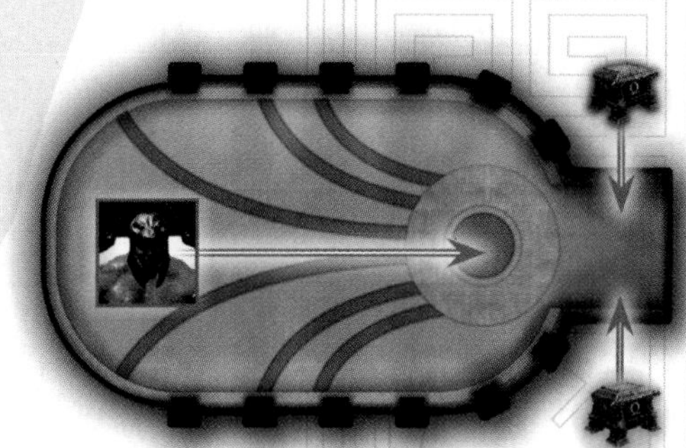

THE FLAME AND THE BOX

CATCH A GOD

A Child's Toy Box

Approach the blue flame's casing in the center of the chamber. Inside, Kratos finds the familiar sight of Pandora's Box. This doesn't seem quite real, but Kratos is assured by a familiar spirit that it is the box you used to defeat Ares. The flames that surround the container can only be removed by Pandora herself. She must be found if Kratos is to have access to its legendary powers.

The Ghost of Sparta cannot reach the cursed chest now, but there are other things you must do in this chamber. Six dust-covered alcoves are along the western wall. Use the Head of Helios to reveal the images behind the coverings. After all the frescos have been revealed, read the books at their bases. The words foreshadow the tasks that Kratos must brave in order to douse the flame.

Hermes appears partway through your reading. He taunts Kratos and waits by the chamber exit. As soon as the Spartan draws near, the God sprints farther away. Use the Save Altar and search the room thoroughly before giving chase.

There is a secret wall on the far side of the chamber in relation to where you entered. Shine the light of Helios on that wall to reveal a secret area. Inside are Red Orb chests and an Onyx wall that you can break some time in the future - after you find an item powerful enough to destroy this blue stone. After collecting these treasures, race after Hermes!

READING BETWEEN THE FRESCOS

It isn't necessary to read all the fresco descriptions. These give you insight, but they aren't required to proceed. Don't worry about Hermes; he's not going anywhere until Kratos approaches. Beyond that, Hermes won't stab Kratos in the back so fear not.

There are two chests here: a Magic Chest and a Health Chest. Kratos should have suitable reserves of these resources already. Save the chests for later; Kratos returns here in the future, and he's more likely to need the chests then.

So Close, Yet So Far

The chase is on! Kratos closes in on Hermes, but the mercurial god leaps ahead as Kratos crosses an open walkway. Continue down the path and sprint up the next set of stairs to find a viewing area. There are also two chests with Red Orbs. Use the pedestal to view the chaos created by the deaths of the last few Olympians.

Return to the middle of the walkway and leap through a break in the railing, floating down to the ledge where Hermes stands. The skittish god rushes away. Move to the climbable stone wall at the far end of the ledge. Slide down here with Kratos' blades. Fall to the stone lip, drop down, and continue to its base.

Approach the break in the molding on the right. Once there, lean toward the pulley where Hermes rests. Leap out and use the pulley's Grapple Point to sling onto the wooden plank walkway. A fire starts at the end of the walkway and rapidly spreads toward Kratos. Run forward but avoid sudden jumps or rolls. Flaming boulders damage the planks in front of Kratos, and you don't want to commit to any movement before you know what's going to fall apart.

The fire is too much for the simple structure, and it begins to splinter. The entire walkway suddenly collapses and Kratos holds onto the falling planks with all his might. Climb and leap up the broken wood speedily. A few Olympian citizens appear, dangling from the beams. Those immediately in Kratos' path should be uprooted swiftly so that you may continue.

Godly Race

Pull Kratos onto the stable platform at the top of the walkway. Dash past the frantic Olympians; Hermes is still on the move. The swift-footed god leaps to the small ledge above the platform. Follow suit and jump up to grab the molding. Have Kratos pull himself onto the thin strip of stone. Move to the right and jump again to grab another ledge.

WHEN IN DOUBT

Watch Hermes if you start to get confused about where you're heading. Hermes often takes a route similar to the one Kratos must use. The Spartan won't have any problems as long as he heads toward Hermes and stays on roughly the same path.

Continue toward the right until Kratos reaches for the ladder holding Hermes. Jump over and climb the ladder. The god continues bounding away, just out of reach. At the top of the ladder, jump to the upper molding and hustle to the right. Pull up when a statue blocks Kratos' path. Skirt the edge of the statue before dropping back down. Hermes sits on the other side of the statue, glaring at the Spartan.

As Kratos draws near, Hermes leaps down. Follow close behind, dropping (with **R1**) on the right side of the next section. Leap right to the broken column where the Messenger God stands. Hermes is too agile to be brought down here; he stays on the move. Jump to the right to continue the pursuit and keep moving across the stone molding. Jump down when you reach the wooden walkway.

The crane lurches across an open pit, spilling Hermes onto the nearby path. Chase him down using the Grapple Point on the swinging crane. As soon as Kratos lands on the path, the stone gives way.

THE CORRECT TIMING

Make sure that Kratos only leaps toward the Grapple Point when the **R1** command appears. Leap too soon (or too late) and you get a one-way ticket back to the Underworld. You won't escape Hades this time, so use some patience and take the jump when it's easiest.

Sprint along the wooden planks after Hermes. There are more Olympian citizens here, but there are enemies as well. Olympus Sentries block the path after a sharp turn. Dispose of them quickly before leaping onto a large, hanging crate. As soon as Kratos lands, the crate begins to give way. Use the Grapple Point on the crane overhead to avoid falling. The crane rises toward another wooden platform and comes to a jerking halt. Kratos lands on the platform while Hermes holds onto the crane, afraid to fall. Move left, toward the lever near the base of the pulley and pull it.

Headbanging

Jump to the next Grapple Point, on the wooden beam ahead. Swing to another Grapple Point, which launches Kratos back onto the crumbling stone path. Hermes continues his escape. You might get the feeling that this god is afraid to stand and challenge you. That's good—it means he's weak.

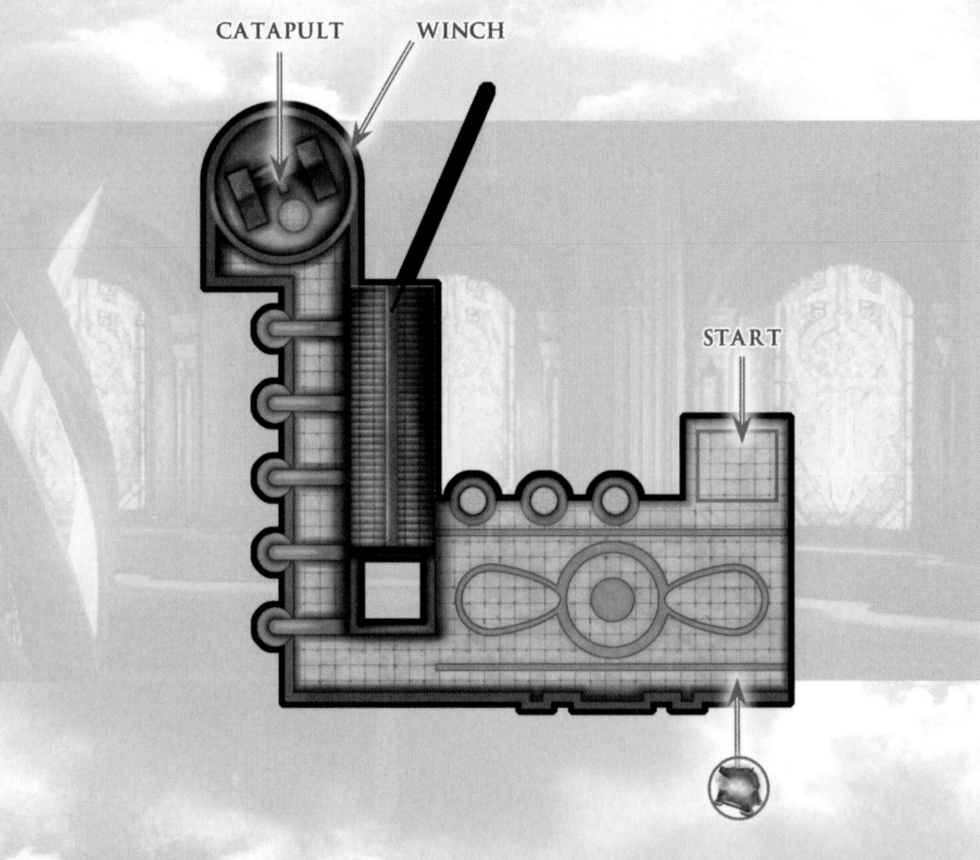

Follow close behind using the next Grapple Point. Kratos lands on an open platform, surrounded by Olympians, a few Harpies, and a group of Feral Hounds. Hermes quickly retreats behind a lowering portcullis, leaving Kratos to clear the area. Slaughter all the foes and decide what you want to do with the helpless Olympians.

Break all the vases in this area for extra experience, and remember that Olympians provide Green Orbs if you kill them by grappling them. Before moving on, look in the back, left corner of the platform to find an Alternating Chest. Use it before leaving.

Climb the ladder to the left of the portcullis. At the top, leap to the right and continue your ascent. Another jump is up to the left and it returns you to the path. Sprint after Hermes and watch as he runs along the taut wire overhead and lands on the statue of Athena.

Dash to the end of the path. Grab the pole at the base of the catapult and pull it toward Kratos. Line it up with the statue and get onto the platform. Use the catapult and perform the Context-Sensitive Action to grab onto the boulder you're launching. This hurtles Kratos through the air and into the nearby building.

FERAL HOUNDS

Feral Hounds are similar to War Hounds. They often appear in packs and lash out with their teeth and claws. They are fairly small and pose little threat compared with other similar foes.

That said, don't let them gather in a pack. When feeling brave, the pack attacks Kratos all at once, forcing him to shake them off with the left analog stick. Punt Feral Hounds by grabbing them. This hurts anything struck by the flying Hound.

FERAL HOUND 224

Kratos and Hermes fall with the broken statue, landing in the damaged room. By the time Kratos recovers, Hermes has disappeared. Search behind the head from the demolished Athena Statue if you'd like to pilfer **Hermes' Coin**. Start to leave the room and look at the floor. There's a blood trail! It seems that Hermes wasn't fast enough this time. Follow the blood around the corner, stopping briefly to open the nearby Health Chest.

HERMES' COIN

Look behind the head of Athena's broken statue. **Hermes' Coin** is there.

Running on Empty

Run around the bend to the break in the path. Leap over the breach and push toward a small incline. Pull Kratos up and stay on the blood trail. Kratos finds Hermes on the other side of a pile of rubble. Approach the panting God. He's not totally out of steam, but he can't flee now. It's time to end him.

Athena

Athena was the Goddess of Wisdom, and she oversaw duty, devotion, and obligation as well. She was also the patron of feminine craftwork, like weaving. She was a guiding spirit to a number of heroes and would help them on their quests.

The goddess was born directly from the head of Zeus, with no clear mother. One day, Zeus had a horrible headache, and nothing that he did would relieve it. In desperation, he split open his skull, and Athena, as a full adult woman, sprang out. Zeus was most impressed. When he asked her what she wanted, Athena replied that she wanted the arms and armor of a warrior. Pleased with her response and daring, Zeus had Hephaestus forge them for her right away, and Athena soon became known as a martial Goddess.

Athena was much concerned over the fate of the world, and had an immediate grasp of humanity's potential. There came a time when a city sent forth word that it was looking for a patron deity, someone to whom they could dedicate their worship. Both Poseidon and Athena set out to win over the city. Finally, it came down to a contest: who could produce the finest gift to the city? Poseidon struck out with his trident and produced a fine spring, which provided freshwater to the entire region. This was a fine gift, but Athena could do better. She reached forth and created the olive tree. Because olives could be used for so many purposes, it was decidedly the better offering. The city was named Athens in her honor.

Athena also features prominently in a number of stories where she aids those set on just courses. For instance, when Perseus tries to kill the Gorgon Medusa, Athena helps him by telling him where he has to go and how to obtain the weapons and armor needed to slay the monster. She also helps Odysseus by telling him of his family and helping to guide him on his journey home from the battle of Troy. Because of her generosity and intelligence, Athena was highly regarded, and her favor was widely sought.

HIDE AND SEEK

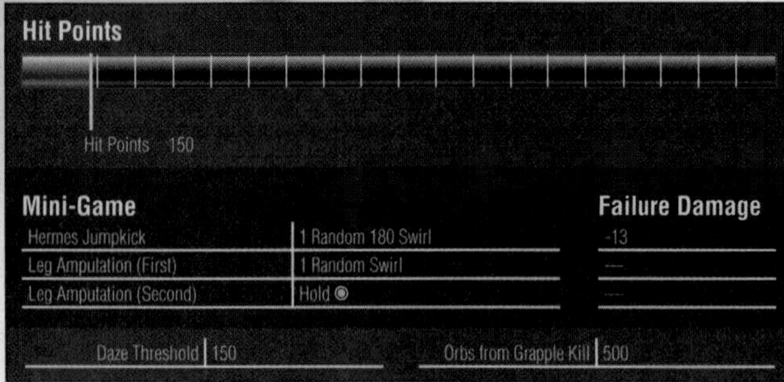

Hit Points

Hit Points 150

Mini-Game		Failure Damage
Hermes Jumpkick	1 Random 180 Swirl	-13
Leg Amputation (First)	1 Random Swirl	---
Leg Amputation (Second)	Hold ◉	---

Daze Threshold	150	Orbs from Grapple Kill	500

Even an injured Olympian is still a threat. The god has nowhere else to run, so he launches a full-out attack on Kratos.

Hermes sprints around the area, dodging a large number of Kratos' attacks. Arrows tend to find their mark, but inflict minor damage. In the end, it's best to stick to the Claws of Hades and wide-area magic. As Hermes is worn down, he becomes desperate and strikes out at Kratos. Be prepared for Context-Sensitive Actions when this happens. Roll your left analog stick quickly to damage Hermes and restore some of Kratos' health.

Repeat these attacks for a minute or two. The fight is not the most challenging, but it still takes time. After falling, Hermes offers Kratos a feeble speech, lecturing him on his so-called "honor." Allow the god his chance at an oratory and finish the battle.

BOOTS OF HERMES

A parting gift from Hermes, these shoes grant Kratos enhanced agility. Hold **L2** and press ⊗ to use the Boots to dash forward and run along walls. Sprint into the Hermes Brand Symbol to initiate these maneuvers. To perform the Hermes Air Evade, press the right analog stick while Kratos is airborne.

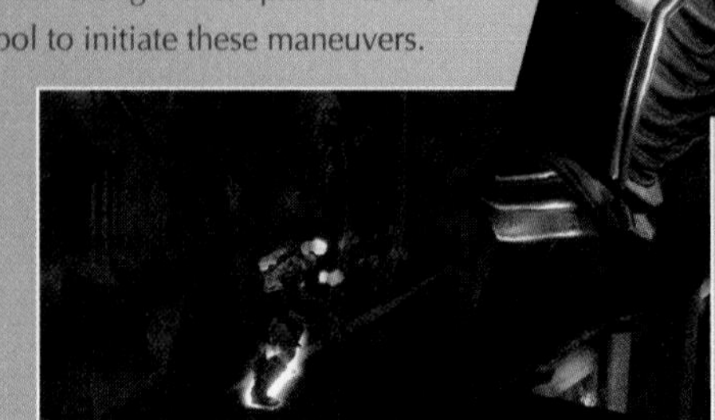

RETURN TO AN OLD FLAME

Sprinting Spartan

Something was awfully wrong within Hermes. His body erupts with a swarm of insects, and this plague spills into the city. Inside the room, a squad of Olympus Sentries appears; exterminate them while testing Hermes' Boots. When you're done, turn toward the scaffolding on the left. Run toward the Hermes Brand Symbol to dash up the planks to the upper level. Visit the nearby Save Altar and use the Hermes Brand Symbol along the wall to sprint across the fresco of the gods. Continue on the wall, past the bend, and dash up the short stone column.

There are chests on the upper platform: a Red Orb Chest and a Mixed Orb Chest. Kill the Sentries skulking about and practice your Hermes Air Evades.

PHOENIX FEATHER

The Item Chest at the left end of the balcony contains a Phoenix Feather.

Leave the area and take a look outside. There's an obstacle course laid out here and Kratos must navigate it to proceed. As you exit, open the nearby Red Orb and Health Chests and move onto a wooden walkway. Run along the walkway and make the turn at the bend. Yet another Red Orb Chest is along the way.

At the end of the walkway, dash up the Hermes Brand Symbol to the next level. Use the Boots again to run along the carved wall ahead. Hop down on the other side and continue to the right. Speed your way up another tier and slip out onto a balcony. Another Hermes Brand Symbol is there; use that to continue heading up.

Kratos is now as high as he can go. Walk to the right edge of the platform and leap down (toward the back right). That aligns you along a path against the back wall. Open an Alternating Chest and take the time to view the plague's effects on the Olympian citizens.

Leave the Olympians behind and enter an open area. Olympus Legionnaires are spawning. Remove them as quickly as possible. Save magic for the fights ahead and try to win this battle efficiently. After the majority of the Olympus Legionnaires have been killed, a Cyclops Enforcer arrives.

CYCLOPS ENFORCERS

These monstrous brutes are large and fierce. Their well-protected hide makes them particularly challenging opponents; few creatures endure as much damage as Cyclops Enforcers.

They aren't afraid to dish out damage. Their mace and chains cover a wide range and can knock Kratos around like a ragdoll.

Magical attacks and the Rage of Sparta are the quickest and most effective ways to dispose of these oversized foes. The Blade of Olympus is a good weapon against the Enforcers because of its massive damage potential.

CYCLOPS ENFORCER 220

If you don't have the Rage of Sparta ready, heavier combos from the Claws of Hades work well. Remember to allow as much room as possible for evasive rolls. Kratos can't always escape the reach of those long chains. You have to run and then dive if you plan on avoiding all that damage!

KRATOS' FINEST HOUR

There are three Cyclops Enforcers in this series of battles. Conventional wisdom is to kill the latter two with magic and the Rage of Sparta. Try doing it with only hit-and-run attacks.

After you've killed the Cyclops Enforcers, another wave of Olympus Legionnaires appears. They were smart; they brought *two* Cyclops Enforcers this time. Unleash the remainder of your magic and the Rage of Sparta here as available.

When those behemoths fall, a final group of Legionnaires spawns at Kratos' feet. Olympus Legionnaires can't be used as Battering Rams until their health is low, but this technique is still effective once it begins. Thin the ranks quickly as soon as you have a few targets with diminished health. The Spartan can trudge on once they're destroyed.

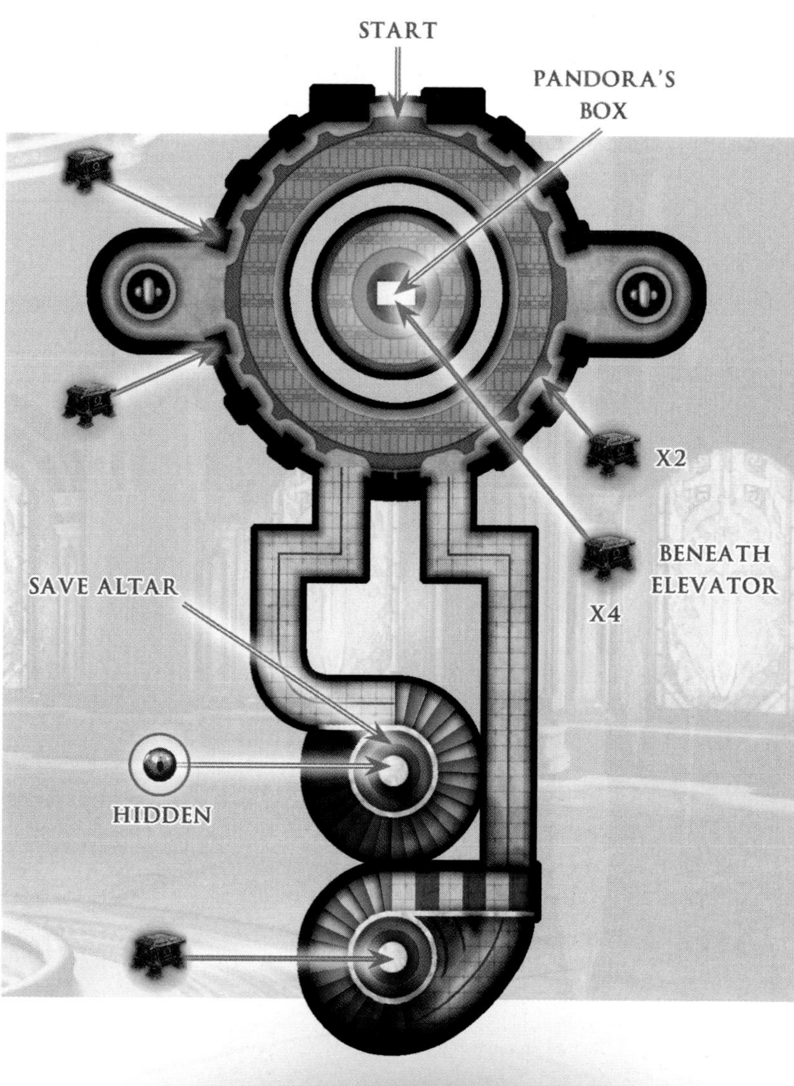

Search the left path for chests. Open the Red Orb Chest and Item Chest at the end of the walkway. A **Minotaur Horn** is inside the Item Chest. Return to the center of the area and use the door between two large statues. Kratos finds himself back in the Chamber of the Flame.

MINOTAUR HORN

The Item Chest at the end of the left path contains a Minotaur Horn.

Deadly Song

Use the Save Altar to the right of the chamber entrance. Continue around the circle and open the Magic and Health Chests you come across. Kratos eventually reaches an open archway, but leave that for a moment. Two Red Orb Chests are nearby; loot them before entering the archway. While searching through this area, keep on the lookout for four Archers. They pose little threat, and should be dealt with harshly.

The hallway winds through the building, leading Kratos toward two Siren Seductresses and a contingent of Olympus Legionnaires . Get ready for a cramped and somewhat challenging fight.

SIREN SEDUCTRESSES

These maidens are far from fair. They hide in the shadows and must be revealed with a Solar Flare from the Head of Helios. Only then can these alluring beasts be attacked normally.

The songs of the Siren Seductresses are enough to subdue even the Ghost of Sparta if he listens for too long. To break free of their spell, move the left analog stick back and forth rapidly.

This makes the Siren Seductresses a bit more like Gorgon Serpents in their style of fighting. You must constantly worry about being controlled and/or disabled by the enemies, so the best defense is an aggressive offense. Attack the Sirens aggressively to ensure that they don't have a chance to disable you.

SIREN SEDUCTRESS 229

Sirens

Sirens were women with the bodies of birds. They were sometimes depicted with full breasts and human arms in addition to their beautiful faces. There are different views on how the Sirens were formed.

Their father is said to be either Achelous (the River God) or Phorkys (the father of the Harpies, Graiai, and Gorgons). Sirens could sing with unearthly sweetness, but they are usually depicted as using this power to lure sailors to their deaths. Sirens were also associated with fevers and other delirious sicknesses.

In some legends, Sirens were the handmaidens of Persephone, Queen of the Underworld. In these tales they used their sweet voices to lure men into Persephone's presence.

Originally beautiful, Sirens were cursed with their monstrous bird-shape either by Demeter, to punish them for not saving Persephone from Hades, or by Aphrodite, to punish them for refusing to make love to any man or god.

The Sirens lived on an island named Anthemoessa, the location of which shifted from story to story. It's sometimes said to be around Sicily. Other stories say that the island is close to Scylla and Charybdis. The Sirens may have been exiled to Anthemoessa. Accounts of their numbers differ, but usually there were two to four Sirens on the island. The area itself was covered with the bleached bones and rotting flesh of their victims.

Two major legends involve these monstrous women. In the story of Jason and the Argonauts, the legendary musician Orpheus pits his music against the Sirens' song. Orpheus' music overpowers the Sirens. Because of this, only one of the Argonauts leaps overboard to swim to the Sirens' island. Some say that the Sirens killed themselves out of shame and disappointment.

The Sirens have another story in the Odyssey. Circe, a great sorceress, warns Odysseus that the Sirens are one of the dangers he must survive to make his way home. To resist them, Circe advised plugging all of his sailors' ears with wax so they couldn't hear the Sirens' song.

Odysseus wished to hear the song, so he had his men tie him to the mast of his ship so he couldn't throw himself overboard. The song promised foreknowledge of everything on Earth. This was irresistible to Odysseus and he screamed for his men to untie him. Luckily, he was bound too well to escape, and his men ignored his cries. Sometimes it is this disappointment that is said to drive the Sirens to their suicide.

Although diminished in later tales, the Sirens were once important deities. Their cult was probably overturned by the cult of Zeus and the Olympians at some point, thus there is a story where the Muses beat the Sirens is a competition of song.

Ancient vases depict both male and female Sirens, sometimes with sphinx-like lion's feet. They would play musical instruments like lyres and flutes as they sang, and sometimes such images appeared on ancient tombs. Sadly, the stories that inspired these images are lost.

Use Solar Flash by pressing **L2** and ◬. This reveals the Siren Seductresses. Focus on bringing the attack to them while relying on Army of Sparta and other wide-area attacks to dismantle the Olympus Legionnaires. It takes two rounds of Context-Sensitive Actions to kill each Siren, so be prepared and don't leave them at your back.

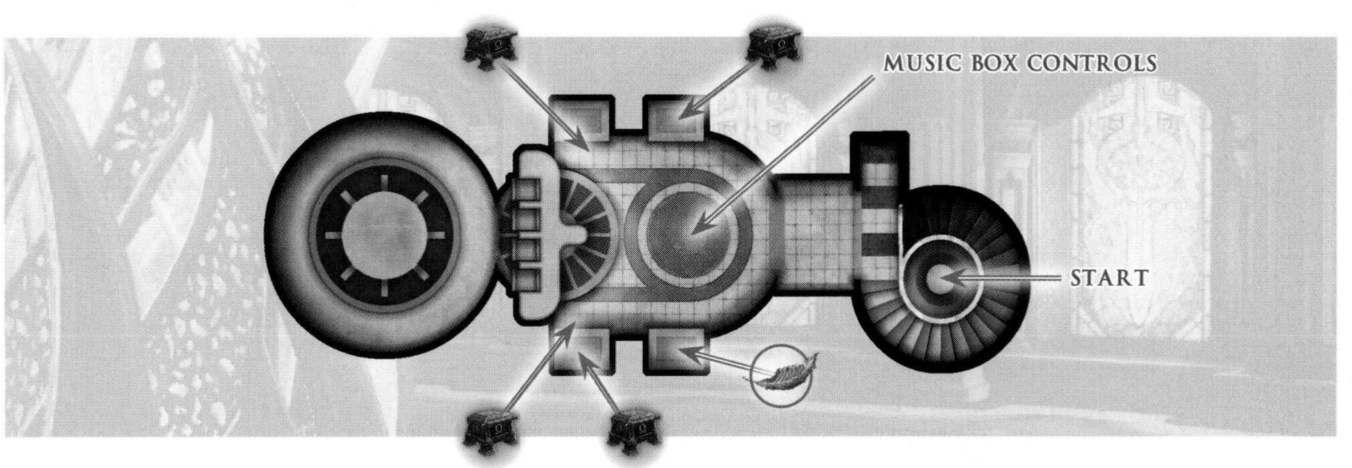

SOLVE THE RIDDLE OF THE MUSES

Open the Red Orb Chest at the end of the hallway and climb the stairs to the upper room of the chamber. Open the gate and enter. Inside, curtains draw back to reveal a set of Muse statues and a large crank. An oversized music box is beside the entrance. A viewing point gives Kratos a hint as to what he must do. Before attempting any puzzle solving, open the Red Orb Chest to the left and the Health Chest to the right. Now you're ready to go.

SMALL TIP

The sword is the key to this musical.

BIG TIP

When the sword is aligned, the notes follow and the Muses show the way.

The Musical

1 *Walk left and use the Wings of Icarus and the vent of air to reach the upper platforms.*

2 *Open the Red Orb Chest and the Item Chest on the platforms to either side of the vent. The Item Chest contains a Phoenix Feather.*

PHOENIX FEATHER

The chest to the left of the air vent contains a Phoenix Feather.

3 *Leap onto the metal ledge along the north wall. Grab the first bronze wheel (from the left) and turn it once. Leave the second wheel alone; it's already in perfect position.*

4 *Turn the third wheel three times.*

5 *Turn the fourth wheel three times as well. Now, an image of a sword is displayed below.*

6 *Jump onto the platform along the room's eastern wall. Hop over the vent to the next pillar and open a Red Orb Chest.*

7 *Drop to the ground and stand on the raised platform in the center of the room. There are now four buttons in front of Kratos.*

8 *Press **R1** to reveal the music bar under the image of the sword. Button commands begin to scroll across the bar. Press the correct buttons as they pass through the target zone.*

9 *The button presses are as follows:* ✕, ✕, ✕, ○, □, ○, □, ✕, △, □, ○, △, □ + ✕, □, △, □ + ✕, △, △ + ○, △ + ○, ✕, □, □ + ✕, ○, △, △ + ○

The Muses move the pillar above the Sacred Flame while Kratos plays. After the song, the statues pull the Flame and Pandora's Box to a higher floor, although it is still below Kratos' current position. This is soon rectified; the platform you're standing on transforms into an elevator. Take the lift to reach the Sacred Flame.

IV ATTEMPT TO FREE PANDORA'S BOX

A Stony Gaze

Pull the lever to start the elevator's descent. Partway down, the platform stops and a group of Olympus Sentinels appear before Kratos joined by a Gorgon Serpent. The Olympus Sentinels must be ignored. There is nothing that Kratos' weapons can do against the undead soldiers. Instead, focus on the Gorgon Serpent.

OLYMPUS SENTINELS

These defensive foes are similar to Olympus Legionnaires. With Kratos' current equipment it is nearly impossible to break their shields. However, a Gorgon Serpent's gaze has more than enough power to turn these enemies to stone.

OLYMPUS SENTINEL 227

Weaken the Gorgon Serpent quickly and use a Context-Sensitive Action to tear off her head. This action petrifies the Olympus Sentinels. Sentinel statues shatter with only a few heavy blows. Kratos should have no trouble clearing the first round of Olympus Sentinels in one go.

CHAOS UNLEASHED

The effects of the Gorgon Serpent's gaze are short-lived. Kratos has to attack the petrified victims immediately and rapidly. The Cyclone of Chaos (**L1** and ◉) is extremely effective. If Kratos takes too long to unleash heavy damage, the effect wears off, and the Olympus Sentinels are free to defend themselves once more.

Another Gorgon Serpent arrives with three more Olympus Sentinels in tow. Repeat the process to wipe the elevator clean. Finally, a third Gorgon Serpent appears. This time she is by herself (unless any of the skeletons survive the previous skirmishes). Destroy her without mercy and finish your ride on the elevator.

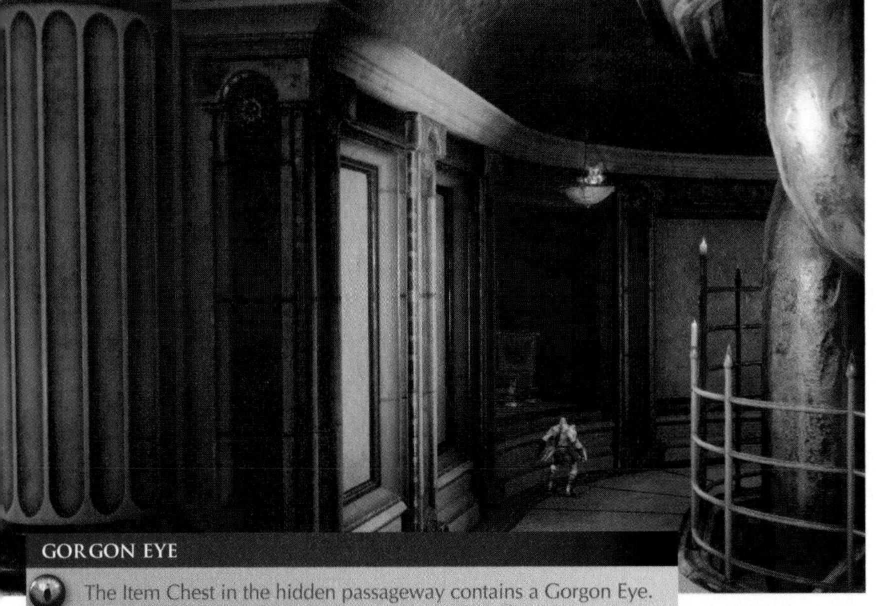

GORGON EYE

The Item Chest in the hidden passageway contains a Gorgon Eye.

The Flame: Round Two

On the bottom, take a second to find even more hidden treasure. Pull the lever to send the elevator back toward the top. Immediately race off the elevator and let it ride up without you. You've now revealed the bottom of the shaft; down there are four Red Orb chests! A wonderful discovery, is it not?

Enter the Chamber of the Flame; this takes you back to the original entrance. Don't immediately rush to the upper chamber if you're interested in finding powerful items. If you missed the treasure in here the first time, look at the oversized chain in the northwestern side of the room. There are several alcoves there; examine the third one. That faint shimmering means that a secret is close by. Use the Head of Helios to uncover the hidden passageway. Four chests are within: three Red Orb Chests and an Item Chest with a **Gorgon Eye**.

Use either of the unused chests from earlier. There are also a couple Olympus Archers here, if they weren't killed earlier, but they're a trivial nuisance.

When you're finished, climb the stairs to the upper level to see the Sacred Flame and Pandora's Box. Walk to the center of the room and grab hold of the crank. Push it around the Flame, away from Kratos. The crank lowers the protective barrier surrounding the Flame and causes the Chain of Balance to rise. Below you, the Three Judges pull the Chain back down, forcing the protection around the Flame back into place. It seems that Pandora's Box is still trapped.

Use the Save Altar here and take the northwestern exit afterward. Kill the Olympus Archers in the next passage and run down the hallway. Two Wraiths of Olympus attack! These enemies are a bit troublesome if Kratos doesn't know how to handle them. Their moon-shaped blades strike hard and fast and can be thrown at Kratos as well. Counterattack with the Golden Fleece or rip the foes from the ground with the Hyperion Ram or Soul Rip.

Another dependable method for fighting Wraiths is to hit them with Solar Flare before you initiate your attack routine. This seems to dramatically affect them, leaving Kratos with time to slice through his targets.

FIGHT THE LEGENDARY HERO

Sibling Rivalry

Take the stairs at the end of the hall and then move down into another corridor. Pause for a moment to use the nearby Save Altar and loot both the Health and Magic Chests. Both are needed, as a major boss fight is imminent.

HERA

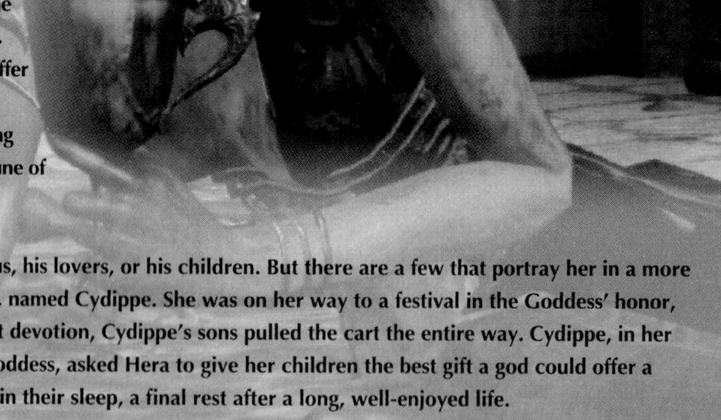

Hera was the Queen of the Gods, being both the sister and wife of Zeus. Her mother was the Titan Rhea and her father was the Titan Cronos. As such, she came from a long line of divinity.

Hera was happy with her status, but not especially satisfied with her husband. As the patron of marriage, she was interested in upholding fidelity. However, her husband Zeus was continually unfaithful, and she hated him for it. She gave him the authority he was due as King of the Gods, but she held little respect for him. She was known for her jealous and vengeful nature, particularly against Zeus' mistresses and the offspring he had with them.

Hercules, in particular, was a target for her rage, and she repeatedly tried to kill him or make him suffer. She also hated Dionysius, the God of Wine, another son of Zeus; she killed his mother Semele. Leto, the mother of Apollo and his twin sister Artemis, had to suffer through horrible childbirth pain because of her. And that's not all—many of Zeus' mistresses were forced to go through suffering and trials because of Hera. In fact, anyone who had the misfortune of gaining Zeus' affection was a "fair target" for her ire.

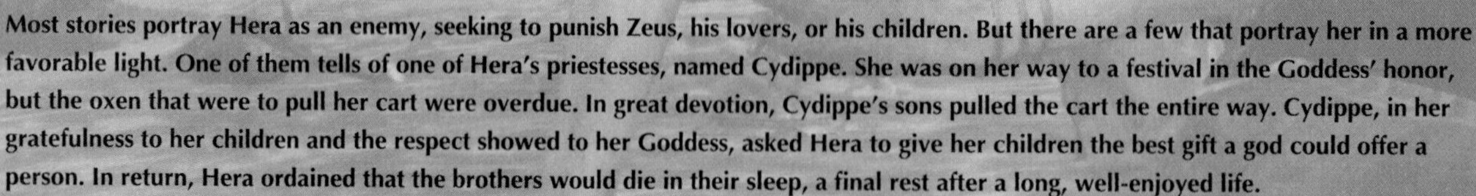

Most stories portray Hera as an enemy, seeking to punish Zeus, his lovers, or his children. But there are a few that portray her in a more favorable light. One of them tells of one of Hera's priestesses, named Cydippe. She was on her way to a festival in the Goddess' honor, but the oxen that were to pull her cart were overdue. In great devotion, Cydippe's sons pulled the cart the entire way. Cydippe, in her gratefulness to her children and the respect showed to her Goddess, asked Hera to give her children the best gift a god could offer a person. In return, Hera ordained that the brothers would die in their sleep, a final rest after a long, well-enjoyed life.

Hercules

The son of Zeus and a mortal woman, Queen Alcmene, Hercules was destined for greatness. He showed this very early on, when Hera, angry that her husband Zeus conceived a child with another woman, sent a giant snake into Hercules' crib. The intent was to have the serpent strangle the baby, but Hercules had other ideas. His mother found him playing with the snake's corpse like a rattle, having crushed it in his already mighty grip. This earned him two things: a reputation as a powerful warrior and Hera's enmity.

As a young man, Hercules trained with many other great heroes under Chiron. Chiron was a Centaur, but of all his people only he was wise and dedicated. Hercules soon stood out as a man of incredible strength—but not intelligence. Instead, Hercules was more a doer than a thinker; he was far more willing to solve problems with his fists than anything else.

It was with a great deal of happiness that Hercules wed a princess, Megara. He had several children with her. However, Hera was not about to let Hercules be happy. She sent a madness upon him, and Hercules killed his wife and children in a violent rage. After he saw what he had done, Hercules tried desperately to atone for his deed. He was told that he must complete twelve great labors, tasks that only a great hero could complete, to find peace.

The Twelve Labors of Hercules are the stuff of legends, and each of them is a story in itself. Needless to say, Hercules was successful in completing all of his tasks. Along the way, he helped many people, crushed some nasty monsters, and definitely accomplished more good than ill. There were a few unfortunate incidents, but Hercules was without a doubt a well-regarded hero. As you may imagine, this didn't make Hera happy at all.

In his travels, Hercules fell in love and married again, to a woman named Deianira. Hera put a great jealousy into Deianira, and the woman began worrying that Hercules would be unfaithful to her. Then Hera arranged matters so that Deianira was given a vial of poison. The woman wasn't told that it was poison, though; she thought it was a love potion.

Later, when Deianira thought there was another woman in Hercules' sight, she took the "love potion" and sprinkled it onto Hercules' shirt. The unsuspecting hero put it on and immediately was affected by the poison. It began to burn through his skin, causing him great agony. But Hercules was part immortal, and he couldn't die; he could only suffer. Finally, he made his friends build him an enormous pyre, and he climbed into it. The flames, however, only burned away the mortal part of Hercules. He was taken by Zeus to Mount Olympus to dwell with the gods. At this point, Hera gave up her quest for vengeance, and the two made some sort of amends. In fact, Hercules eventually wed Hera's handmaid, Hebe, the Goddess of Youth.

A Bitter Rivalry

Hera is lounging in the Forum when Kratos arrives. After he receives a cold welcome, Kratos turns the conversation toward Pandora. Hera is displeased by this, and she orders the Spartan's half-brother, Hercules, to put the Ghost of Sparta to rest.

GORGON EYE

A hidden Item Chest is at the bottom of the spiral staircase and it contains a Gorgon Eye.

TWO SONS OF ZEUS

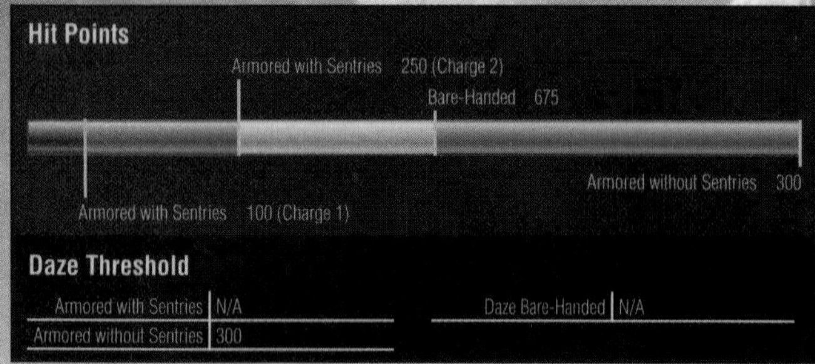

Hercules is a giant of a man. His strength is known throughout the land, and his experience in combat is equally impressive. While he's preparing to fight Kratos, a number of weaker foes leap into the ring to warm the place up.

Decimate the Lesser Combatants

These Olympus Sentries aren't a major threat, so hold back your magic and the Rage of Sparta; both are necessary in the fight to come.

Slaughter the weaker troops with Battering Ram assaults and wide-area attacks. Hercules orders the Olympus Archers on the upper tier to fire down at Kratos after a short time. Avoid these shots by fighting along the northern wall. Come out to return fire with the Bow of Apollo from time to time, but don't worry too much about this reprisal.

Hercules Takes the Field

Hercules enters the fight once the initial wave of enemies are killed. He's using the Nemean Cestus as a weapon, and he's wearing a protective helm and shoulder guard.

Though you've already defeated quite a few grunts, another squad of Olympus Sentries protectively surrounds Hercules. Use that to your advantage. Turn the troops into Battering Rams to break through each other and to annoy Hercules.

An alternative tactic is to light the weaker enemies on fire with the Bow of Apollo. Do this to distract the Sentries while you focus your stronger attacks on Hercules.

Between these runs, make use of wide-area attacks, striking both Hercules and the smaller pests. It doesn't take long for the demigod to become frustrated; he'll charge into Kratos. When this happens, push back by pressing ◎ repeatedly. Overcome Hercules' brute force and lift him up, ramming him into the nearest spike-covered vine (on the sides of the arena). Kratos then strips off his half-brother's shoulder guards, releasing a flow of Green Orbs.

Leveling the Field

Both siblings shake off their injuries and return to the center of the arena for the next round of battle.

OVERWHELMING ODDS

If left alone or ordered to swarm, the Olympus Sentries encircle Kratos, creating a solid wall of foes. Their overwhelming numbers are enough to shake even the Ghost of Sparta. If this happens, throw off the enemies by moving the left analog stick back and forth as quickly as possible.

Repeat the same tactics for the next round, this time ripping off Hercules' helm and releasing even more Green Orbs. You've now sundered most of Hercules' equipment. All that's left is the Nemean Cestus. But Hercules isn't daunted. In fact, he exclaims that "Armor is for weaklings." You'd better keep your guard up!

Disarm the Great Hero

This next round is a solo match between the step-brothers Kratos and Hercules. Expect plenty of action. Use the right analog stick to speed away from the demigod's powerful swings and jabs. Be even more cautious when Hercules tries to grab you.

Alternatively, Hercules uses heavy single attacks or a one-two swing that finishes with a slow ground-pounder. They are all easily dodged. After you recover, close and attack quickly to punish Hercules for his failure.

Don't use the Bow of Apollo in this part of the battle. Hercules is too tough to be affected by anything that trivial.

TWO CAN PLAY

Anything viscous enough to hurt Hercules is a threat to Kratos as well. The spiked vines on the sides of the area are best avoided. Don't turn your back, lest Hercules knock you back into them. If that does occur, press **L1** and **R1** repeatedly to set Kratos free.

The Claws of Hades are a fine weapon choice for Kratos in this stage. Hercules isn't a fast opponent, so make use of the Golden Fleece's Argo's Ram (**L1**, ◎). Continue to wear down Hercules until he begins showing signs of weariness and becomes sloppy. The demigod eventually launches a blinding white attack that stalls the battle and stuns Kratos. During this time, Kratos' brother brags to Hera while turning his back on the Spartan.

After Kratos recovers, rush up to Hercules and use a Context-Sensitive Action to strip off his Nemean Cestus. Though disarmed, Hercules now becomes quite invigorated. He was already having a good time, but now the fight is getting even more interesting. Hercules starts getting faster here, so take some time to get used to his new attacks.

Annihilate Him with His Own Weapons

Be on the lookout for back breakers and throws. Keep moving constantly, using the Nemean Cestus' light and heavy attacks to bash Hercules. Evade constantly to keep your edge.

If Hercules grabs a boulder be ready to dodge. You can't stand your ground against attacks that strong, so your best bet is to give ground and roll to the side. This avoids the boulder and lets you continue your assault.

Now that you're using the Cestus for yourself, get a feel for their might. These are the heaviest weapons you can wield. They throw most targets around (even heavier troops), and this gives them all the punch they need.

Attack Hercules again and again. It's a war of attrition, and he's the one losing. Make use of short combos, and then dodge away to let Hercules waste his attacks on thin air. There's a definite rhythm to it, and you shouldn't have problems as long as you don't get greedy and try to keep the attacks going indefinitely.

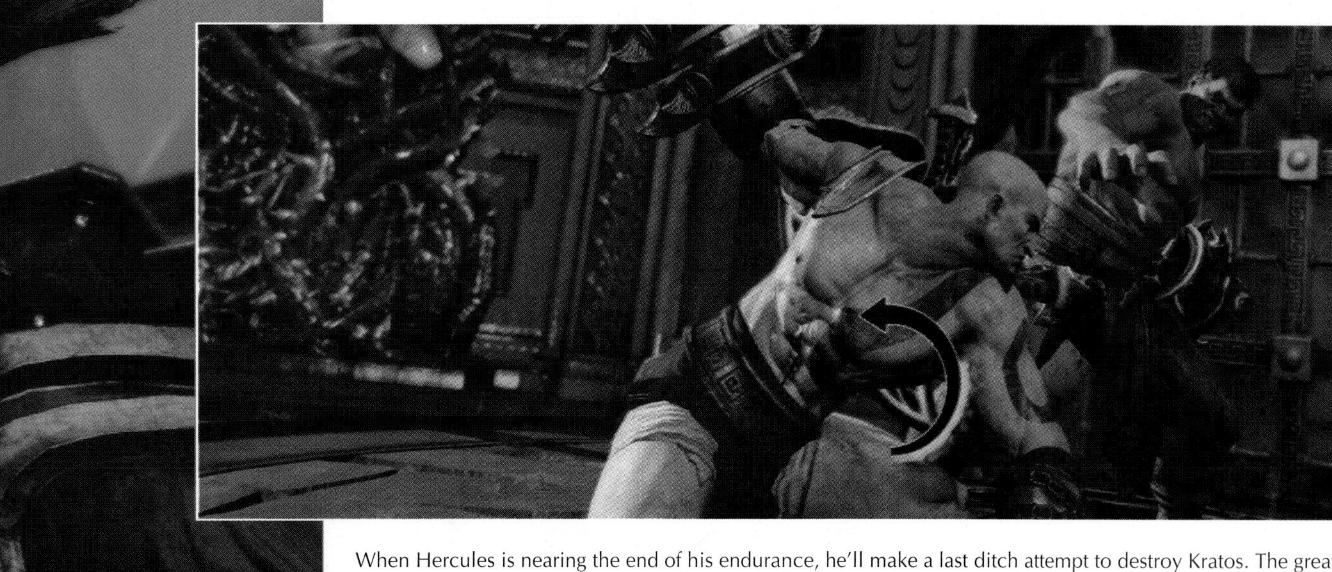

When Hercules is nearing the end of his endurance, he'll make a last ditch attempt to destroy Kratos. The great hero backs away and rips open the floor of the arena, lifting that (and Kratos) into the air like a child's toy.

Kratos tumbles toward the precipice, only saving himself if you make a quick press of the buttons. Hercules doesn't realize that Kratos saved himself, so the hero leaves himself exposed as Kratos climbs up the shattered floor.

And then, when Kratos reaches the top, he jumps. Show Hercules that he is nothing compared to Kratos. Destroy him where he stands.

Even in victory, Kratos tumbles through the floor, falling into a new area. Hercules doesn't fare nearly as well...

ACT VI

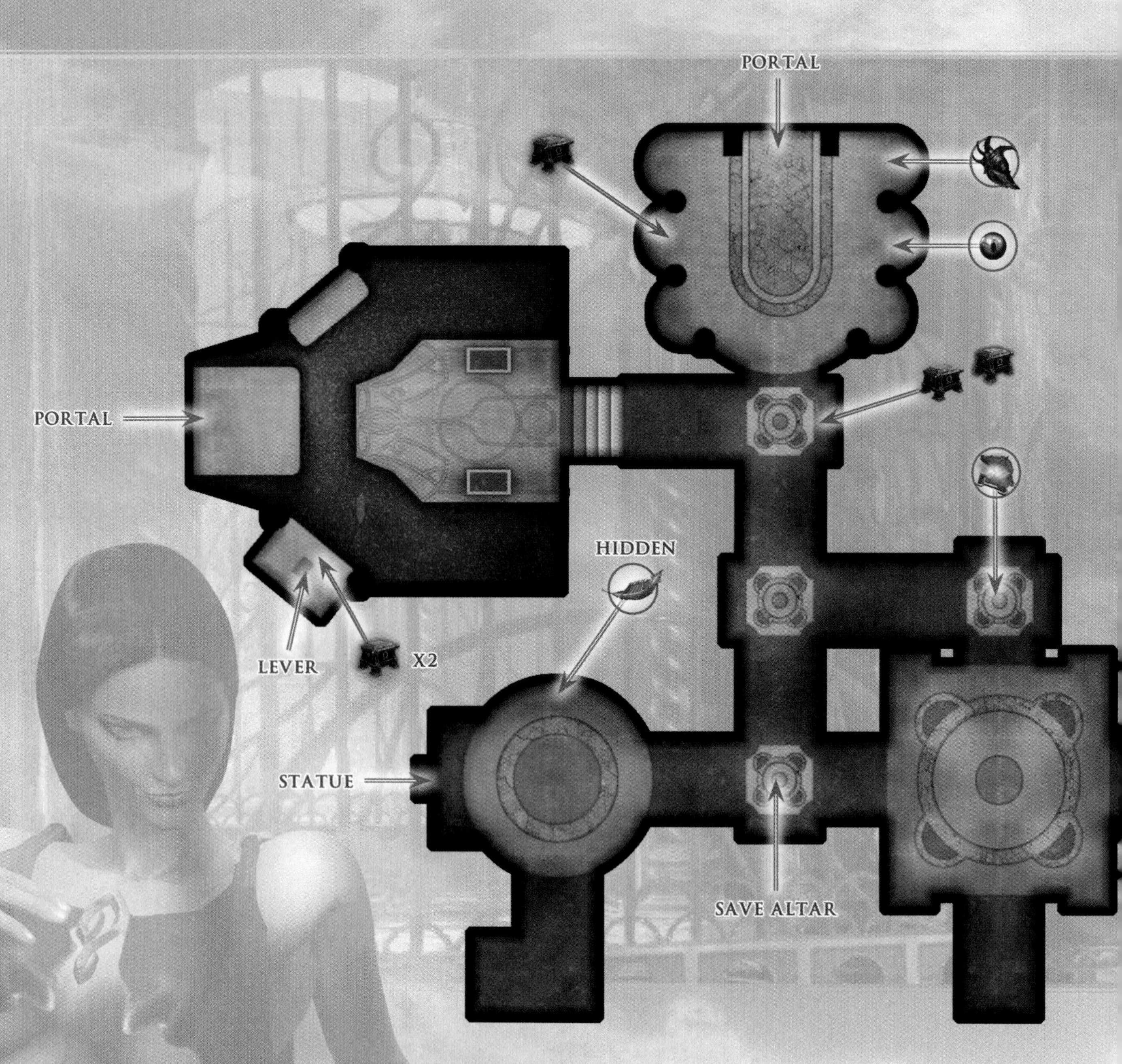

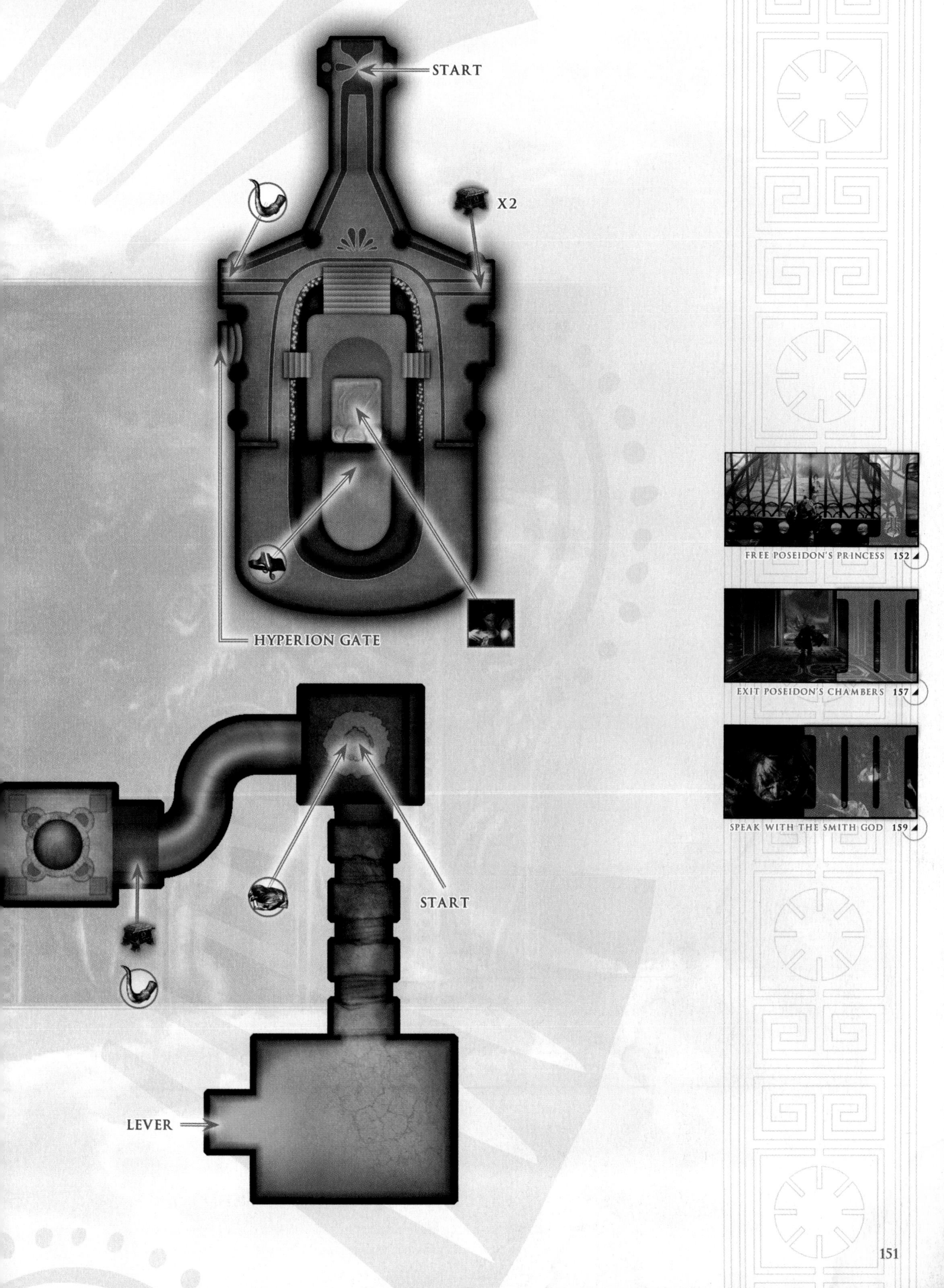
START
X2
HYPERION GATE
START
LEVER
FREE POSEIDON'S PRINCESS 152
EXIT POSEIDON'S CHAMBERS 157
SPEAK WITH THE SMITH GOD 159

POSEIDON'S CHAMBER

THE GODS' PERSONAL CHAMBERS

FREE POSEIDON'S PRINCESS

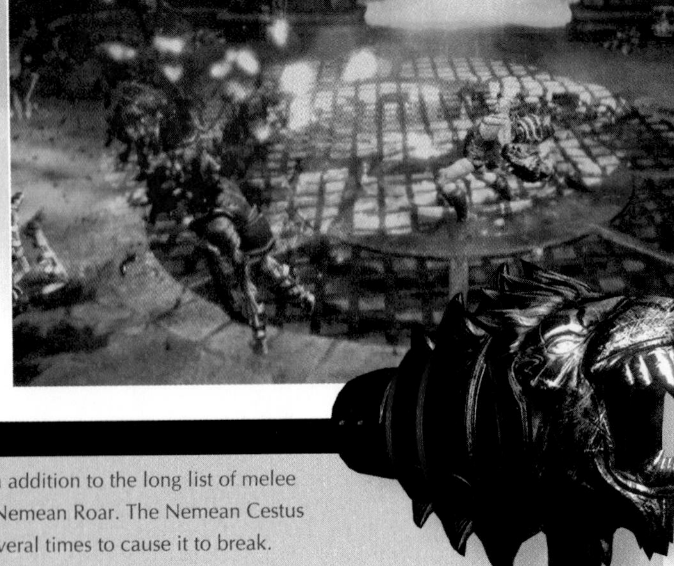

A Brief Swim

Kratos falls beside his brothers' body, landing in a deep pool of water. Search the bottom of the well to recover **Hercules' Shoulder Guard**. Surface and swim to the nearby ledge and climb up. Take the tunnel up an incline and into a small room.

HERCULES' SHOULDER GUARD

Hercules' Shoulder Guard is at the bottom of the pool, beneath Hercules' body.

NEMEAN CESTUS

The Nemean Cestus allows for close-quarters combat like never before. In addition to the long list of melee attacks, Kratos can create explosive waves by pressing **R2** to unleash the Nemean Roar. The Nemean Cestus can also break objects made of Onyx. To do this, attack the blue stone several times to cause it to break.

Let the Lions Roar

There are Olympus Sentries in the room up top. Kill these with the Nemean Roar, the magic attack from your newest weapon. Afterward, look in the back section of the room. A lever is covered in Onyx, so you can't use it yet. Break the Onyx with heavy attacks from the Cestus.

This opens a grate back in the well, but it also attracts the attention of Kratos' enemies. Olympus Sentinels rush toward Kratos to form a defensive wall by the exit. Heavy Cestus attacks finally allow Kratos to break their shields and make short work of the bunch.

Backtrack down the sewer, return to the pool of water, and descend. Journey through the newly opened tunnel and swim to its end. Ascend to an empty chamber. Before moving on, turn to the wall behind Kratos and open a Red Orb Chest and an Item Chest to be rewarded with a **Minotaur Horn**.

MINOTAUR HORN

The Item Chest behind the tunnel exit contains a Minotaur Horn.

NEMEAN LION

The Nemean Lion was the first of Hercules' twelve labors. The monstrous beast was sent to Nemea in order to terrorize the city. The lion's hide was rumored to be impenetrable, so the demigod, Hercules, needed to subdue the creature by other means. He eventually engaged the lion with his bare hands and strangled the beast, eventually being awarded the pelt as his own. In many depictions of Hercules during his twelve labors, he wears the pelt of the Nemean Lion over his shoulders as a sign of having completed the first labor.

The Mystery of the Hyperion Gates

Kratos enters Poseidon's Chamber and is immediately beset by Feral Hounds. Dispose of the beasts as well as the Olympus Sentinels that join the attack, and use the winch to the left of the gate to open the way. The gate closes quickly. Kratos can't get through the second part of the gate, but he'll be able to roll through the first, or dash under it with Hermes' Boots.

A Save Altar lies between the two gates. Turn down the right path when you're ready. Poseidon's Princess is calling out for help from beyond the gate at the end of the right path. Once she realizes who the Spartan is, however, she fervently changes her mind. Leave the woman and open the Magic and Health Chests nearby. There is also an Alternating Chest down a tiny side branch leading back toward the entrance.

Having looted those, take the hallway that leads left from the Princess' gate. The upcoming room has a small puzzle involving teleportation through the Hyperion Gates.

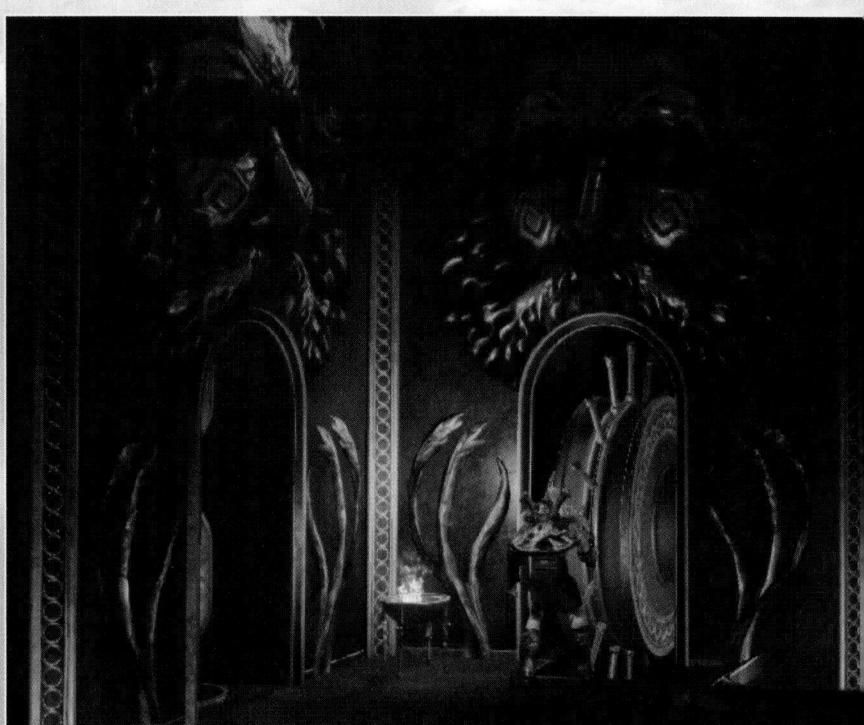

SMALL TIP

Feral Hounds are heavier than they look.

BIG TIP

Kratos doesn't have enough meat on him to bring down the upper platform. Luckily, he'll have help from the Feral Hounds.

1 *Three Hyperion Gates are located across a pool of water and spikes. Glide from Kratos' starting position to the gate on the right; this leads to the gate up high on the northern wall.*

2 *Kratos falls onto a platform underneath the gate. His weight lowers the platform just a few inches.*

3 *Leap to the lever on the western platform and give it a yank.*

4 *Several bridges extend toward the starting ledge. Jump back down as Feral Hounds appear.*

5 *Lure the Feral Hounds toward the eastern Hyperion Gate and press ◉ to kick them through one at a time. The dogs land on the upper platform, weighing it down even more.*

SPIN AND PUNT THE WHELPS

It's easy to kick Feral Hounds through the gate. You don't even need to lure them all the way to it. Grab each Feral Hound and spin Kratos toward the gate and quickly punt the hound; this sends the enemy flying in the desired direction.

6 *No more Hounds spawn after you've kicked four of them onto the platform. Quickly collect the Red Orbs from the two chests in the western wall and enter the eastern gate.*

7 *Kratos' weight is just enough to fully bring down the platform. Exit the area through the lower portal.*

DO NOT SLAUGHTER THAT WHICH SERVES YOU

Do not attack the Feral Hounds that are weighing down the platform. If they die, their corpses lose the weight causing the platform to rise. Kratos will have to complete the puzzle all over again.

BRONZE TALOS

These blue statues have stony exteriors that are difficult to penetrate, even compared with Stone Talos. Heat breaks down the Bronze Talos' defenses, causing them to glow white hot. This, in turn, indicates that they're ready to take damage. The Nemean Cestus' heavy attacks are wonderful for this. Pound the targets rapidly to warm them up, and watch them stagger as you break through to their interior.

The armor quickly cools when you land a damaging strike. It only takes a few of these staggering blows to daze a Bronze Talos, so don't despair when their shell needs to be heated again.

After a Bronze Talos is dazed, approach and grab the construct. A short mini-game ensues. Perform three-button presses in rapid succession to defeat the resilient construct.

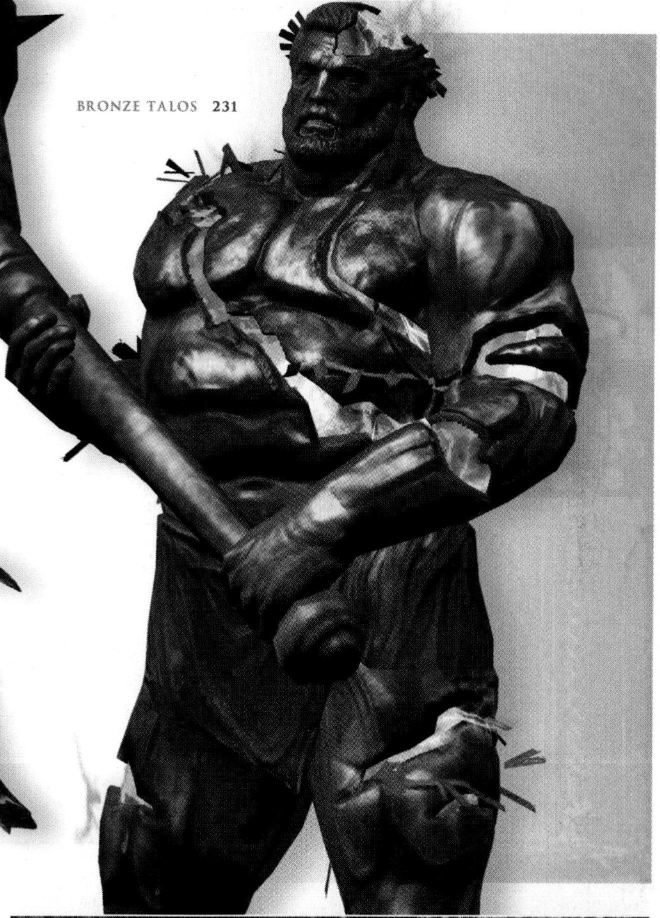

BRONZE TALOS 231

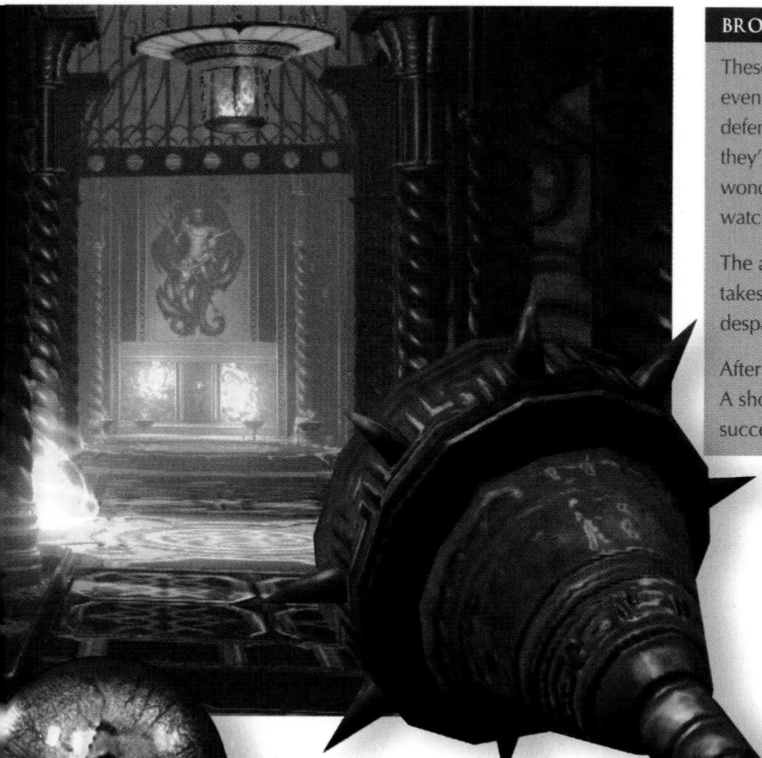

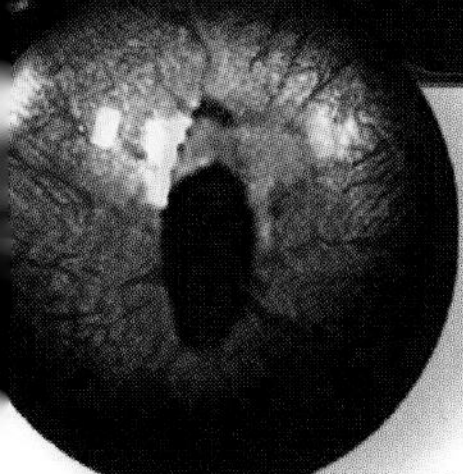

Guardian Spartan

Kratos enters the chamber of the frightened Princess and frees her. She leaves through the Hyperion Gate. Don't follow her yet! Search the chamber to find a letter from Poseidon to his mistress. His message is intriguing and he hints at a power hidden within the Labyrinth.

Loot everything else you find. There is a Red Orb Chest, an Item Chest with a **Gorgon Eye**, and **Poseidon's Conch Shell**. It's a fine treasure indeed.

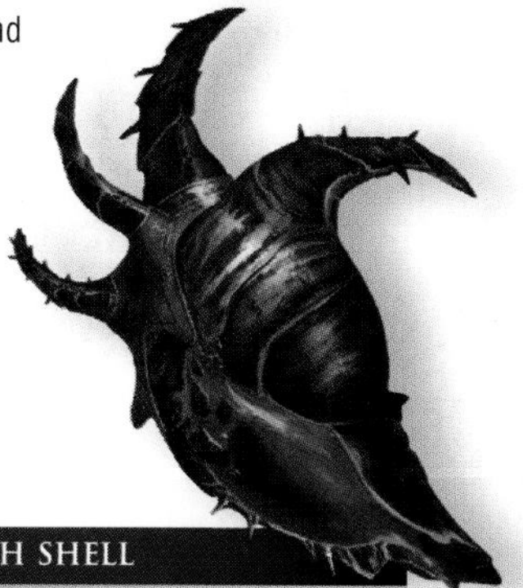

GORGON EYE AND POSEIDON'S CONCH SHELL

The Item Chest along the eastern wall holds a Gorgon Eye. Poseidon's Conch Shell is only a few feet away.

Return to the puzzle room to find the woman at the mercy of the Feral Hounds. Dispose of the dogs quickly; the Nemean Cestus is extremely effective. Another pack of dogs enters and knocks the woman onto the edge of the platform. The weight is too much, and the ledge descends rapidly. Kill the Hounds and immediately lend your assistance to the Princess.

Or, save her immediately and turn on the Hounds as soon as you can. If you wait too long the Princess will die and you are forced to repeat the elevator fight. Afterward, a few more Feral Hounds make an appearance, but Kratos is bound to slaughter them.

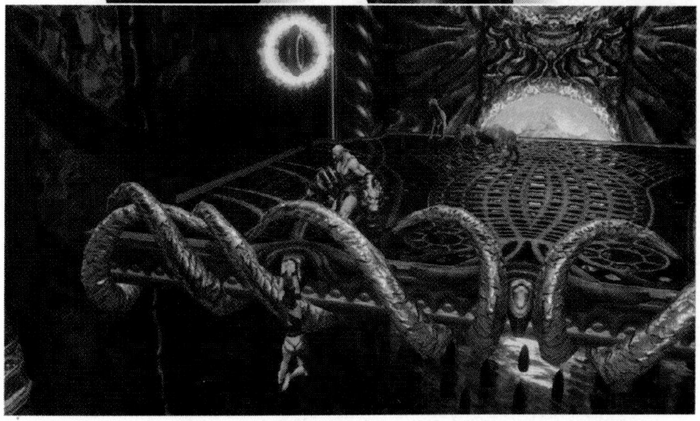

Art Imitating Life

Approach the woman again, this time initiating a Context-Sensitive Action. Shove her through the upper gate and follow close behind. The woman runs up the stairs to leave the room, but Kratos stays behind to fight the two Bronze Talos that spark to life.

BRONZE IS WEAK!

Use area-of-effect attacks to damage both Bronze Talos simultaneously. Why divide and conquer when you don't have to?

Attack these Talos individually. It takes several blows, delivered in quick succession, to break apart a Bronze Talos' protective shell. If Kratos attempts to engage both foes at once, he must spread out his attacks, giving the Bronze Talos time to cool down and harden.

Once one of the Talos is badly damaged; initiate a Context-Sensitive Action to finish the job. Repeat the process for the other construct.

Pass the Princess after climbing the stairs to face off against a squad of Olympus Sentinels. Use the Nemean Cestus to destroy their blockade and drive through. Open the chests here if you didn't loot them previously, and then start pushing the woman down the hallway. Use ◎ every time she stops to force her forward.

Open the gate where the Princess eventually stops. This takes you back into the entrance chamber. Two more Olympus Sentinels and another Bronze Talos launch another assault. Dispose of the foes and turn toward the cowering woman. Open the nearby gates again and use Poseidon's Princess to keep them open.

EXIT POSEIDON'S CHAMBERS

Failed Directions and Broken Bridges

Run beneath the gates and approach a figure of Pandora. The statue holds a familiar blue flame. Kratos calls out to Pandora and asks for her location. She is in the Labyrinth, but she doesn't have time to provide details. Her conversation is cut short and Kratos is left alone. Another letter from Poseidon is at his feet.

Before exiting to search for the Labyrinth, turn to the right and equip the Head of Helios to reveal an Item Chest. Get the **Phoenix Feather** from within and then leave via the left hallway. Exit to the Upper Gardens.

PHOENIX FEATHER

The hidden Item Chest contains a Phoenix Feather.

Plague-infected citizens lie at the Spartan's feet. Ignore them and continue onto the pillar ahead. Grab the pole extending from the pillar. This lets you rotate the attached section of bridge. Hop over to the next pillar and repeat the action. On the third pillar, pull the pole once, wait, and then use it a second time. This turns the bridge to its right side. Jump over and run toward the far doorway. Open this and enter Aphrodite's Chamber.

Taking a Break

Aphrodite's Chamber is a room of delights, not only for the senses, but also for Kratos' inventory. There are two Red Orb Chests to the left and an Item Chest (**Minotaur Horn**) to the right. Stay on the left side of the room and look behind Aphrodite's bed from there. You should see a glowing light. Double-jump and glide behind the bed to steal **Aphrodite's Garter**. Take everything you see and then approach the bed.

A MINOTAUR HORN AND APHRODITE'S GARTER

The Item Chest along the right wall contains a **Minotaur Horn**. Fly behind Aphrodite's bed for an even rarer treasure: one of **Aphrodite's Garters**.

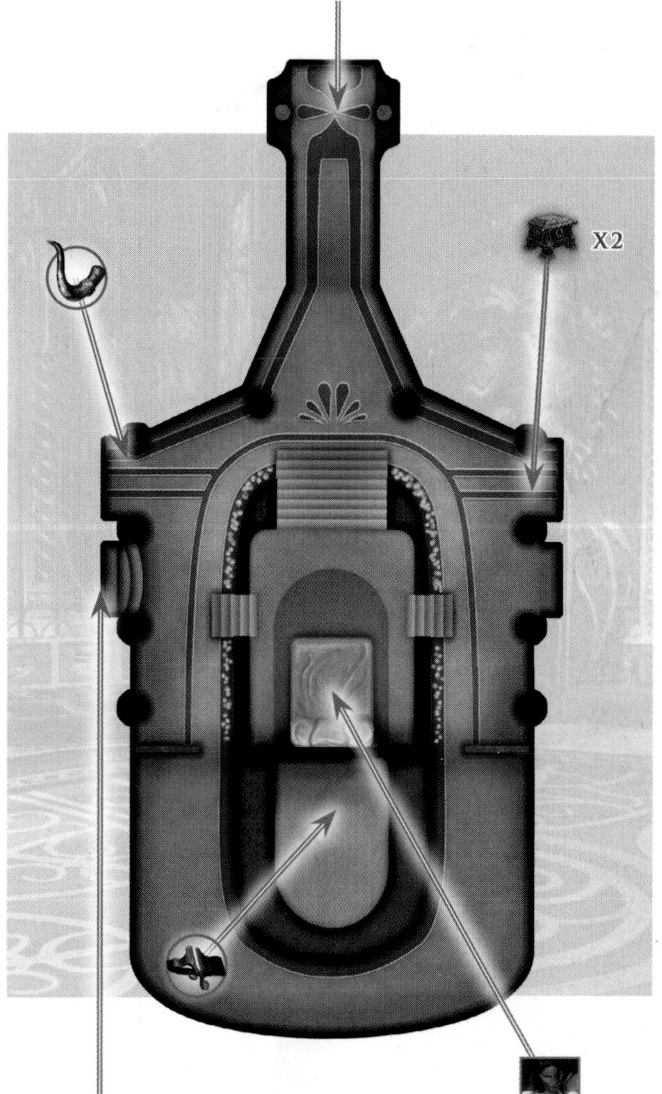

APHRODITE

Aphrodite is the Greek Goddess of love, beauty, and sensuality. She is surrounded by all the pleasures of the world, and she revels in the enjoyment and expression of them.

The goddess' birth was definitely an unusual one. When the Titan Cronos overthrew his father, Uranus, there was ruthlessly brutal fight. During the course of the battle, Cronos ripped off his father's genitals and threw them into the sea. Afterward, Aphrodite was born from the sea foam. She was carried on the waves until she landed on an island, either Cythera or Cyprus; both claimed her.

Because of her beauty and obvious divine nature, the Olympian Gods and Goddesses welcomed her as one of their own. However, it quickly became obvious that she would be a cause of tension. The other goddesses were jealous of her good looks, and the other gods continually vied with each other to impress her. Aphrodite herself was unconcerned about how the other goddesses viewed her, and she enjoyed flirting with all the gods—even the married ones. To keep the peace, Zeus had her married to Hephaestus, the Smith God.

Hephaestus considered himself a truly fortunate man, and he was devoted to Aphrodite. However, she was not happy to be the wife of such an ugly, misshapen creature, even if he was an incredible artisan. As such, Aphrodite was often unfaithful to Hephaestus, and she had affairs with a number of gods and mortals, some of which resulted in children.

Aphrodite had a long-time lover in Ares, the God of War. The two of them would often be seen in each other's company, and they would spend hours in bed together. Eventually it became a huge topic of Olympian gossip, and Hephaestus decided he had to assert himself, or risk having his masculine reputation forever tarnished. He devised a cunning plan to embarrass her.

He told Aphrodite that he would be in his smithy for some time, and then pretended to leave. She, predictably, sent for Ares. At that point, with the two - engaged - with each other, Hephaestus released a trap. A large net came down over the bed, trapping Ares and Aphrodite in a compromising position. Ares, with little hope of defending himself, was soundly thrashed. Aphrodite had to beg, plead, and promise until Hephaestus released her.

It wasn't long before Aphrodite resumed her seductive ways, but she at least tried to keep it a bit more discreet afterward.

The goddess dismisses her handmaids to address the Spartan. She spares a moment to complain about the broken bridges Kratos recently crossed. There are some that are still causing issues; coincidentally, the fallen God of War needs to cross them in order to reach the Labyrinth. Aphrodite holds no answers, but she suggests that Kratos speak with her husband, Hephaestus.

Before Kratos can leave, Aphrodite gives him an option: stay for a while to play with her or go and see Hephaestus. If Kratos chooses to stay and completes the following mini-game, he is rewarded with a flow of Red Orbs. When the deed is done, exit through the Hyperion Gate to the right.

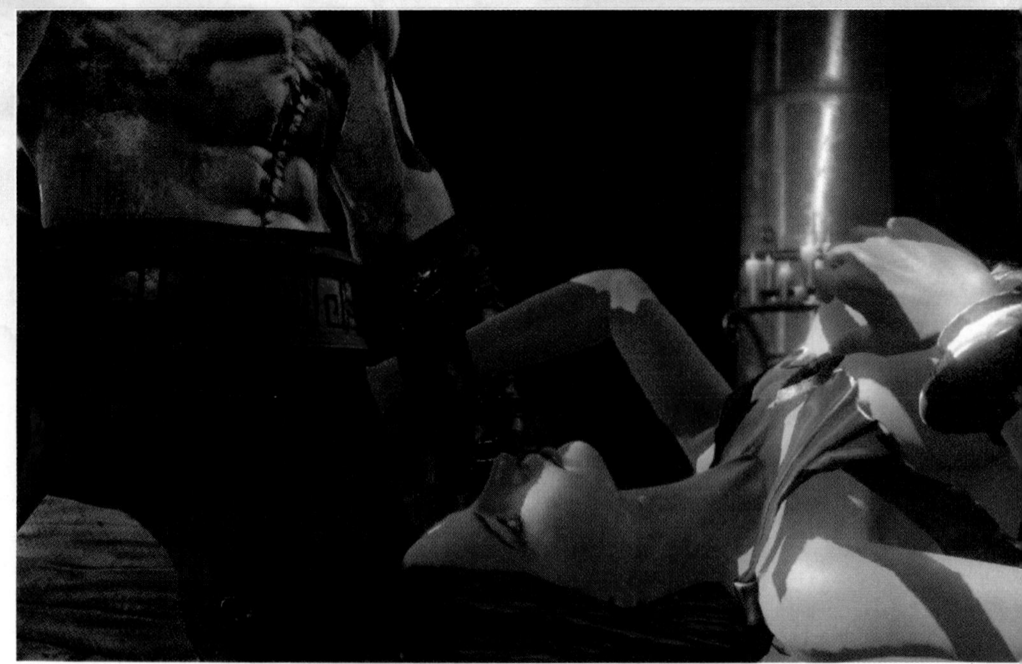

SAVE IT

You're allowed to play the mini-game with Aphrodite multiple times, but the experience reward for repeated successes is negligible.

SPEAK WITH THE SMITH GOD

The Origins of Pandora

Hephaestus is surprised, and a little miffed, to see Kratos exiting his wife's chamber. Kratos brings up the Labyrinth and the Smith God gets even hotter. He does not want Kratos anywhere near his beloved Pandora. Hephaestus tells the tale of Pandora and the box. Kratos shrugs him off.

Hephaestus changes his tune once Kratos states his plan. The Smith God is determined to help if it means killing Zeus. He is prepared to make the Spartan a weapon like no other. All he needs is the Omphalos Stone, which is located in the Pit of Tartarus. Move through the Forge and use the western gate to head out.

ACT VII

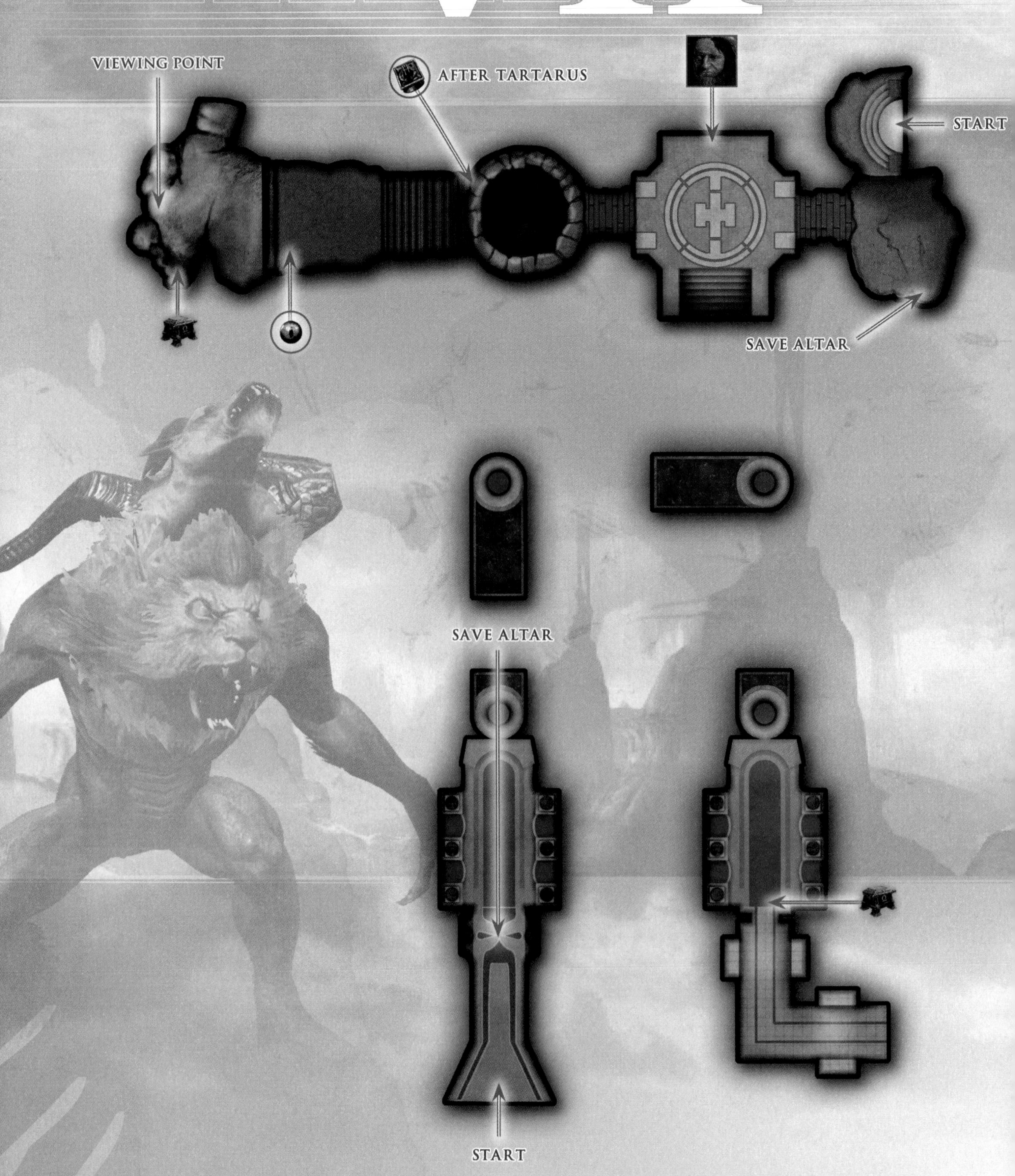

VIEWING POINT
AFTER TARTARUS
START
SAVE ALTAR
SAVE ALTAR
START

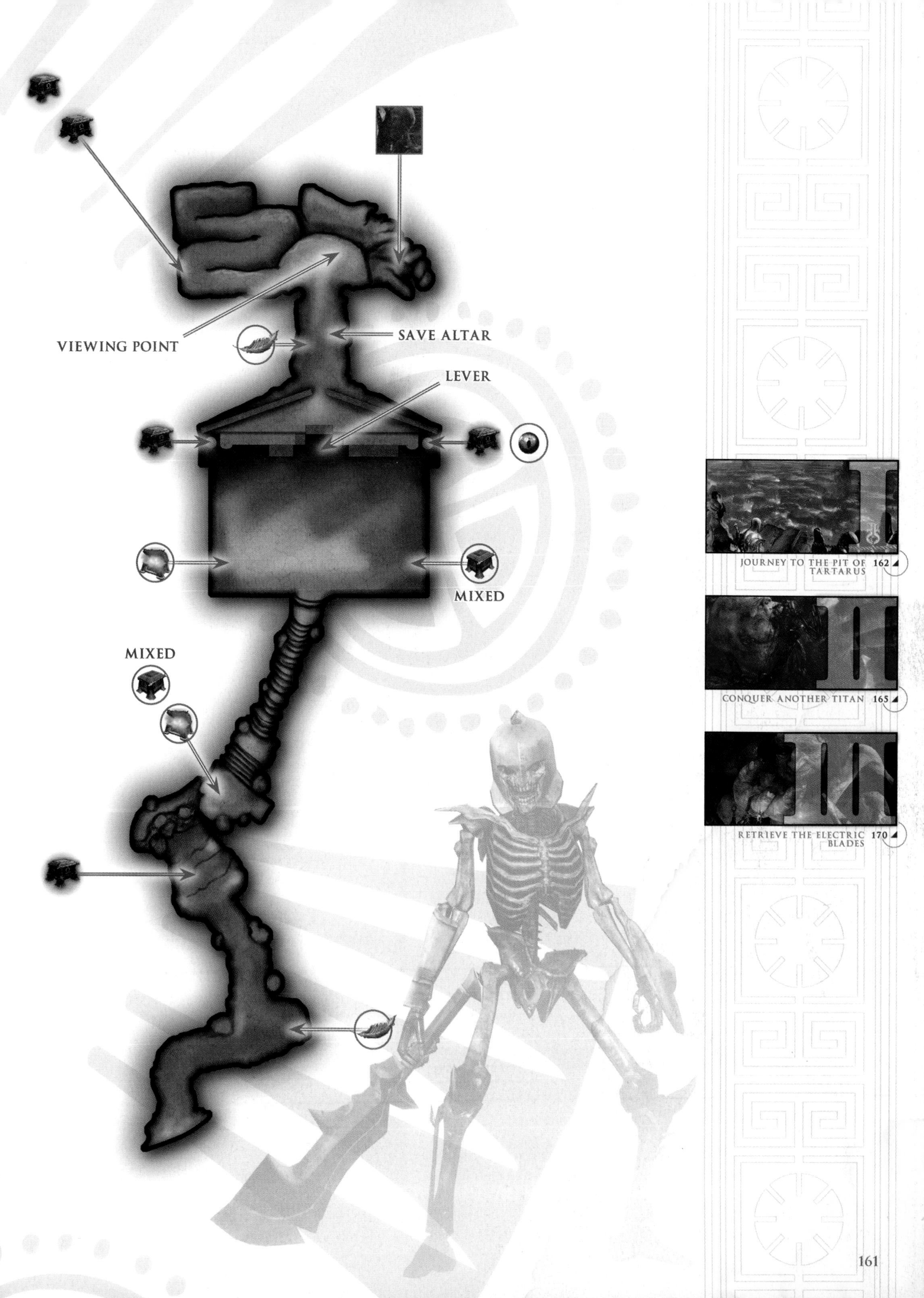
VIEWING POINT
SAVE ALTAR
LEVER
MIXED
MIXED

TARTARUS

COLOSSAL TASK

I JOURNEY TO THE PIT OF TARTARUS

The Ghostly Trail

Kratos leaves the Forge behind and enters the dismal realm of Tartarus, where the souls of the dead wander aimlessly now that Hades has been removed.

The entrance to Tartarus contains a few items of interest. Directly to the left is an Item Chest holding a **Gorgon Eye**. A little farther ahead, a Health Chest and a viewing spot can nab your attention. Open the chests and use the pedestal to observe the land. Down the trail to the right are a few harmless Lost Souls and another Item Chest. Keep an eye to the right side of the path and you won't miss anything. The second Item Chest contains a **Phoenix Feather**.

PHOENIX FEATHER

The Item Chest a bit farther down from the entrance contains a Phoenix Feather.

All that free loot might lull you into the sense that this is a safe place. Ignore that feeling; the trail leads into an ambush. The small area quickly fills with a Centaur General and a group of Olympus Sentries. The Sentries descend in droves in an attempt to overwhelm Kratos. Use wide-area attacks against the weaker enemies and then switch to the Nemean Cestus to pound the Centaur into submission.

Though the choice might seem too obvious, you still benefit heavily from using the Battering Ram tactics against the mighty swarm of Sentries. When the zone is cleared, open the Red Orb Chest to the left.

Leap onto the flat boulder on the right side of the area. Jump again to climb up top and open two more chests (one Alternating Chest and the other is a Mixed Orb Chest). Climb the stairs leading to the right. The steps take Kratos to the Gates of Tisiphone. Beyond is the Pit of Tartarus, but opening those bronze doors is no easy task. They are guarded by ferocious creatures that make their appearance shortly after Kratos enters the chamber.

Two Chimera attack the Ghost of Sparta. Oil pots are scattered throughout the room; make good use of them. Stay at range and fire to lure the first Chimera over to Kratos. Light it up the instant it is in range of a pot.

Use the Rage of Sparta during the earlier stage of the fight. Wait until after the second Chimera joins, then slam the initial Chimera with everything you have. Bring that beast down as soon as possible to simplify the rest of the battle. Once the first creature falls dead, the battle becomes a less lethal affair.

Use some of your magic to ensure that Kratos doesn't lose much health. There's a Mixed Orb Chest coming up, so there's no reason to maintain a full magic bar. When the fight is finished, loot the chests on either side of the area.

RESPOND WITH UNWAVERING FORCE

It's easy to forget about the Golden Fleece, but this is one fight where Kratos should make as much use of it as possible. The Chimera's charging melee attacks hit hard enough to knock the Spartan across the floor. However, these attacks can be deflected, and even countered, when using the Golden Fleece's Argo's Ram (**L1**, ◎).

Unlocking the Doors

It's not immediately obvious how to open the way forward. Kratos has to take stock of the situation and figure out how to proceed.

SMALL TIP

Take wing with the Harpy Queens.

BIG TIP

It's important to give and take. Give a gentle push to the blocks that need it, and take the wings right off the Harpy Queens' backs.

1 *Sprint to the chains on either side of the massive doors and pull them down; this moves sections of the bronze panels.*

2 *Two blocks are glowing at the base of the door. Push both of them into the structure and then climb up the left side.*

3 *Watch the blocks move in and out on the right panel. When the moving blocks retreat, grab the nearest Harpy Queen and ride it to the right.*

4 *Quickly jump onto the moving blocks and then leap onto the stable pillar in the center of the panels. Continue left and stop on the far left side. Kratos is now standing under a glowing handle.*

5 *Push the handle and turn to face the new blocks that appear on the right.*

HIDDEN TREASURES

At the top of the moving blocks there are two ledges: one on the top left and one on the top right. The ledge on the top right holds a red orb chest and the ledge on the right is home to another red orb chest as well as a **Gorgon Eye.**

6 *Ignore the Harpy Queen that approaches while you time your next flight. Wait until the block recedes, count to two, and then grab your Harpy Queen and fly across.*

7 *Kratos should land just as the block fully extends. Push the glowing handle to expose the top lock.*

8 *Leap to the lock and open the gate.*

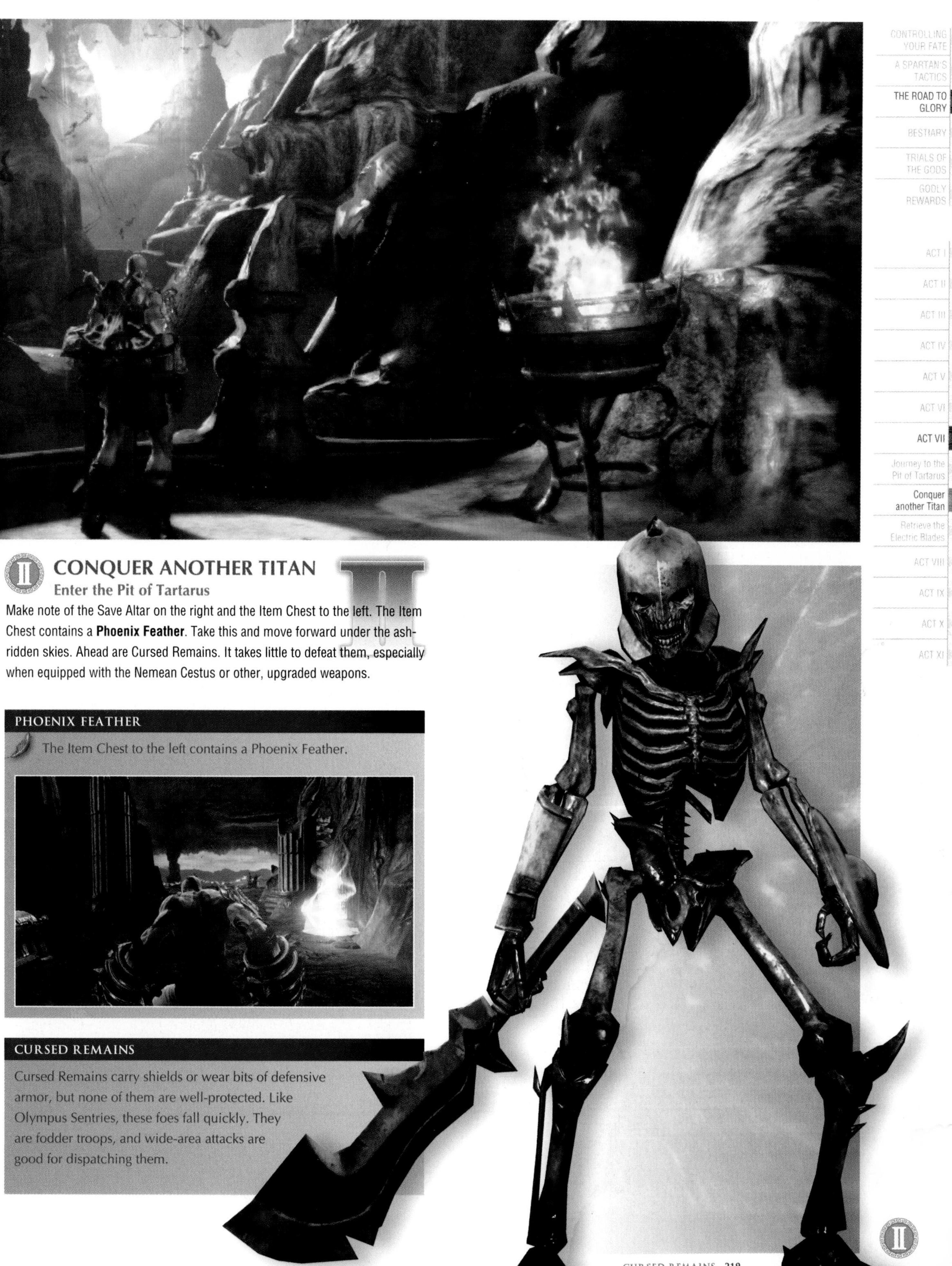

CONQUER ANOTHER TITAN

Enter the Pit of Tartarus

Make note of the Save Altar on the right and the Item Chest to the left. The Item Chest contains a **Phoenix Feather**. Take this and move forward under the ash-ridden skies. Ahead are Cursed Remains. It takes little to defeat them, especially when equipped with the Nemean Cestus or other, upgraded weapons.

PHOENIX FEATHER

The Item Chest to the left contains a Phoenix Feather.

CURSED REMAINS

Cursed Remains carry shields or wear bits of defensive armor, but none of them are well-protected. Like Olympus Sentries, these foes fall quickly. They are fodder troops, and wide-area attacks are good for dispatching them.

CURSED REMAINS 219

Look for a Stone, Find a Titan

After slaying the Cursed Remains, approach the viewing point and observe the legendary battleground of the Great War. When Kratos' view of the landscape is satisfied, continue down the path, destroying any Cursed Remains in your way.

Open the Magic Chest and Health Chest at the first bend. Continue along the winding path, crushing Cursed Remains as you proceed. Jump over a small gap partway down and keep moving when you land. The trail finally comes to an end as you reach the palm of a Titan's severed hand. Press **R1** after climbing onto the hand to continue.

Cronos is full of sorrow and plans to make Kratos pay for various sins. The Titan pins Kratos between his fingers, preparing to crush the life out of him. Fight back by pressing ◯ rapidly. Once free, hold down **L2** and charge a Solar Flare with △. This blinds the Titan and provides an opportunity for Kratos to escape his grasp.

The Spartan is flung into the air and lands on Cronos' hand. Cursed Remains appear nearby. Destroy the enemies and hold on when Cronos changes position. You're now suspended and must climb up the Titan's arm. The way in front of you opens as you approach. Beyond that is a boil that Kratos should rip apart with his blades. Unfortunately, this alerts Cronos to the Spartan's whereabouts.

Hit the Nail on the Head

The Titan raises his arm to address the problem as more Cursed Remains appear to hinder the Spartan. Fight the Cursed Remains; when they're about to fall, Cronos blows a gust of wind over Kratos and brings his hand smashing down close by. Move to the side to avoid the effects of Cronos' breath, then finish off any survivors.

Once Cronos' hand is in place, attack the nearest finger to chip the nail. Repeat this until Kratos rips the nail completely off using a Context-Sensitive Action.

Cronos and Rhea

Uranus was once the ruler of the Titans, but this violent and powerful lord was castrated and overthrown. In his stead, Cronos rose to lead the Titans and preside over the heavens and earth.

For a time, all was well. The Titans and the mortals beneath them lived in comfort, glad to be free of Uranus' rule. But this was not to last forever. Cronos knew of a prophecy. It was said that he would one day be struck down by his own child. Knowing the power of such prophecies, Cronos was afraid.

To protect himself, the Titan wouldn't let his wife Rhea raise any children. Each time she bore a son or daughter, Cronos would take the child and swallow them whole, keeping himself safe.

This was more than Rhea could bear. She begged Gaia to help her save her children from Cronos' cruelty. Gaia agreed. When Zeus was born, Gaia helped Rhea hide the child in a cave far away, in the mortal world. Cronos did not know of this deceit. Rhea wrapped a stone in blankets and fed it to Cronos to make him think the child was no longer a threat.

Zeus was raised by a pair of beautiful nymphs. He thrived on the milk of the legendary goat Amaltheia. As a reward for her service, Amaltheia was lifted into the heavens (she is seen in the night sky as the constellation Capricorn).

Zeus grew in strength. One day he formed a plan; he would make Cronos so ill that the Titan would vomit up all of Zeus' siblings. This succeeded. Cronos lost his hold on the Olympian children, allowing them into the world despite his best effort. Demeter, Hera, Hades, Poseidon, and Hestia emerged. He also vomited up the stone that had been eaten in Zeus' place. This rock was later known as the Omphalos Stone.

Zeus rose to become the leader of the Olympians. He fought against the Titans for years, enticing some of them to turn against their own kind. Eventually, the war ended and the Olympians were victorious. Many of the Titans were exiled to Tartarus.

FORCEFUL PUSH

If the struggle to remove the fingernail takes to long, Cronos becomes angry and attempts to knock Kratos off his arm. When this happens, be prepared to perform sudden actions using the left analog stick. If Kratos fails, he falls into eternal darkness...

After the nail is removed, Cronos smashes his hand over Kratos. The Spartan can avoid damage from this if you watch the shadows that appear and run toward an open area. This causes Cronos to miss.

Onyx Excavation

Look at the rocky patch on the side of Cronos' fingers. Climb onto that and clear any foes above. Soon enough, Cronos lifts the Spartan toward eye level. Watch Cronos' eyes and hold your ground until they start to glow. Then, use Solar Flare as soon as you can, even if there are still enemies nearby. If you succeed, Kratos is thrown off of Cronos but can sling himself onto the Titan's lower body. Take too long and you'll have to complete a Context-Sensitive Action. This sequence repeats until you blind Cronos again.

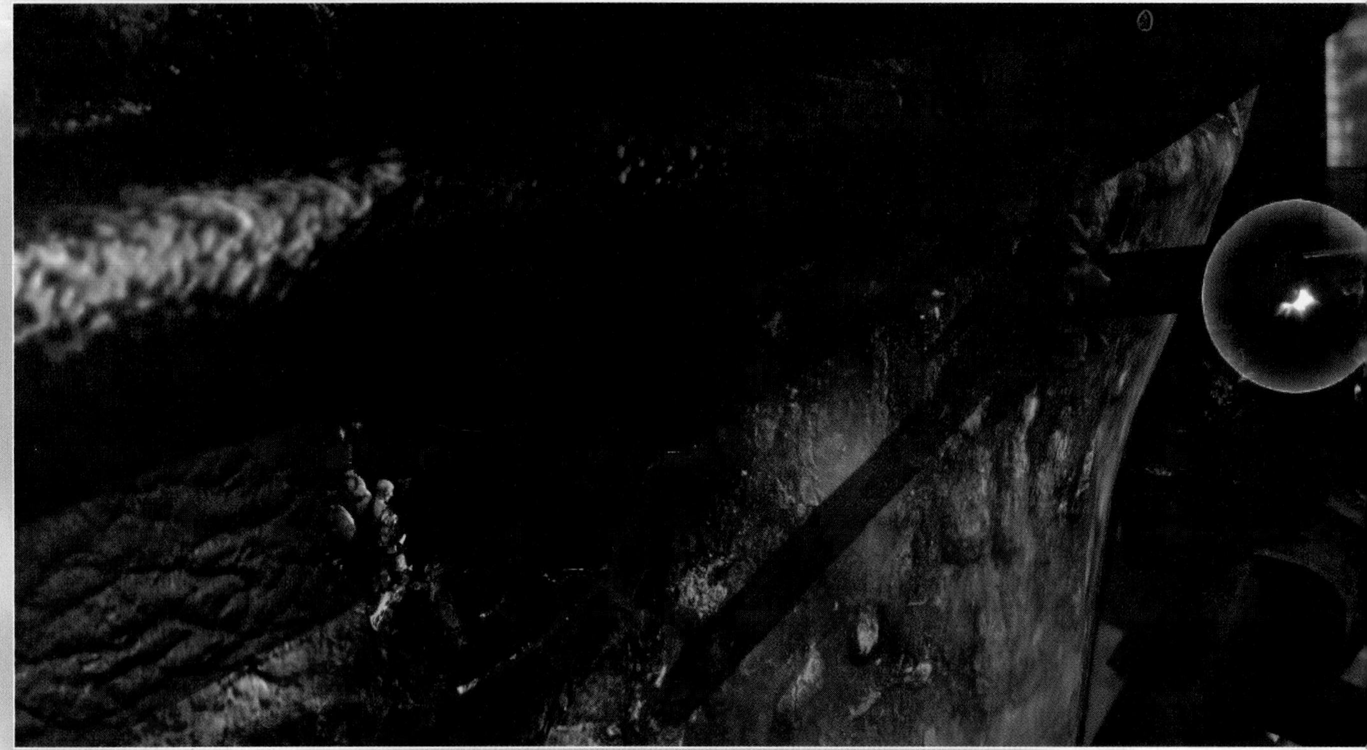

After grabbing Cronos' side, take a second to get your bearings back. Scale the skin path, either ignoring or killing the Cursed Remains in Kratos' way. When you can't climb higher, reach for the Grapple Point on Cronos' chains. These are on the right. Sling onto the iron platform connected to his chest. The jump is farther than it looks. Double-jump and glide onto the platform.

Two Stone Talos and a slew of Cursed Remains attempt to defend the Titan. Destroy them! Battering Ram attacks send Cursed Remains flying, and the Nemean Cestus is also quite effective.

After the fight, open the crest nearby and hack apart the fleshy exterior to expose the Onyx underneath. Another wave of Cursed Remains appears once the Onyx is revealed. Ignore the enemies while using area-of-effect attacks against the Onyx. This method holds off the enemies long enough to complete your assault.

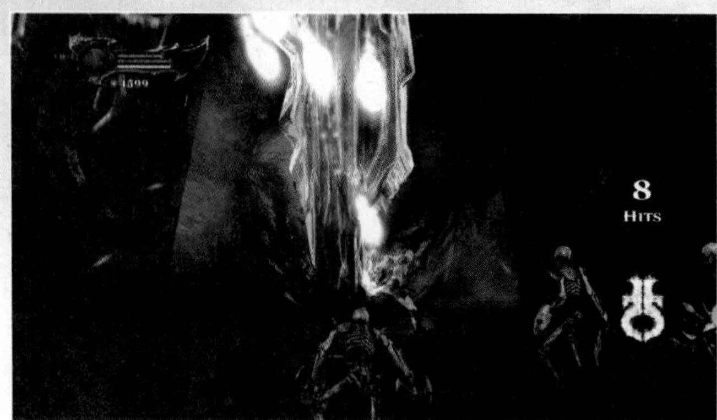

Cronos intervenes just before the Onyx breaks. The Titan grabs Kratos and cups the Ghost of Sparta in the palm of his hand.

FOCUSED ATTACKS

Kratos does not have to kill all the spawning Cursed Remains by the Onyx. If he simply focuses on the Onyx, it nears its breaking point quickly and causes Cronos to make his move with haste.

You won't get as many Red Orbs using this method, so completionists may prefer to kill everything first. That's fine too.

Chip on His Shoulder

More Cursed Remains spawn to continually tax Kratos and wear him down. You're hanging above these enemies at first. Use △ attacks to eradicate swaths of these monsters, and then press the attack after Cronos shifts his arm and gets Kratos upright again. Cronos' other hand soon comes crashing down. Avoid being crushed by completing a Context-Sensitive Action.

Cronos is temporarily disoriented and loses sight of Kratos. Use the confusion to scale his hand, moving toward the right. Once the Spartan nears the palm, he is flung into the air. Think fast and press **R1** to use the Grapple Point on the Titan's chains. Continue along to the next Grapple Point and make sure that you land all your jumps. None of these are hard if you take a moment to look around before you let go of your Blades of Exile.

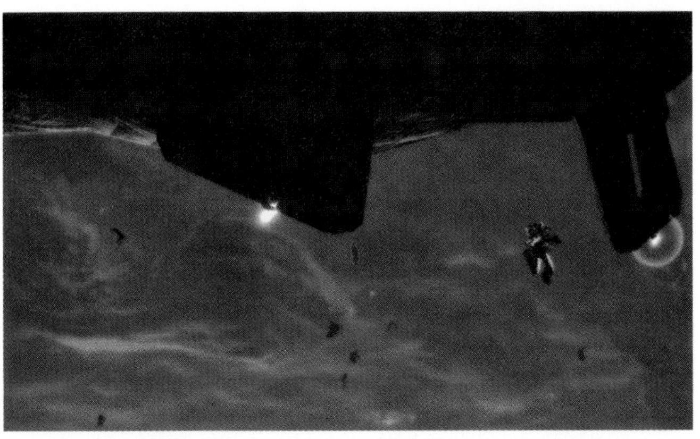

After several of these, Kratos lands on Cronos' shoulder. Immediately start running up the shoulder. The Titan spots Kratos and uses one of his cuffs to try and squash the Spartan against a series of obstacles. Don't let Cronos have his way; stay one step ahead of the cuff, leaping over the rocky barrier and then latch onto a Grapple Point. Kratos soon lands on an iron platform.

DEADLY GREED

Don't get greedy and attempt to slay the Cursed Remains along the edge of Cronos' shoulder. Fighting slows Kratos down, allowing the cuff to catch up to his position and crush him against a rocky barrier. Although Red Orbs are always tempting, ignore the Cursed Remains and prioritize moving to safety as the main objective.

Clear the smaller foes on the shoulder and prepare for the emergence of the Cyclops Remains. The festering mound of organs, muscle, and bone strikes at Kratos. Fight back, periodically using wide-area attacks to kill any skeletons. Once the Cyclops Remains is weak enough, grab it to gain control of this monstrosity.

Cyclops Remains are born from Cronos' wounds. Lacking skin, these disturbing creatures are merely the organs, muscle, and bone of a standard Cyclops Berserker. They react and attack much like normal Cyclops, and you may control them in the same fashion.

Once the Cyclops Remains are under Kratos' control, viciously attack the wound on the Titan's shoulder. Cronos reacts to the pain, listing somewhat and causing Kratos and the meaty Cyclops to slide toward the edge. Quickly perform a Context-Sensitive Action to prevent the Spartan's demise.

Ride the Cyclops Remains down as it grabs onto a section of the Titan's chain. Repeatedly strike the foe. Cronos soon makes his move, grabbing the Spartan and the Cyclops monstrosity and swallowing them whole.

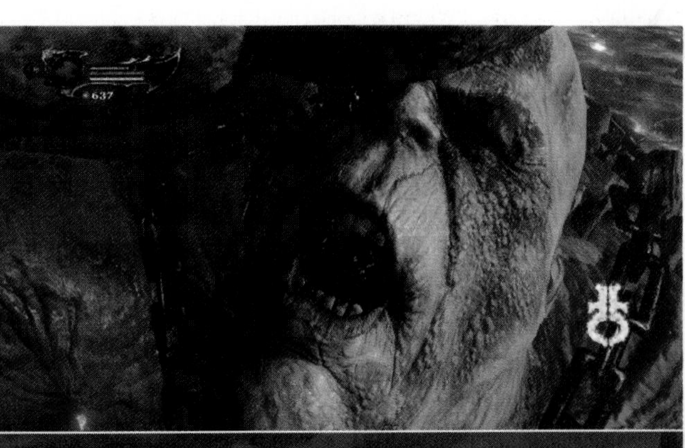

Indigestion

Slide down through the esophagus, avoiding the obstacles and finishing off the Cyclops Remains on the way down. The indigestion Kratos creates causes more than a simple stitch in the Titan's side. Follow the onscreen directions to pierce Cronos' stomach wall and rip a gaping hole in the Titan. Kratos emerges with the Omphalos Stone in hand.

BILE

A solid wall of bile follows Kratos down the Titan's throat. Slide along the esophagus walls quickly using **R1**. Each time you hit a stone barrier, dodge left or right with ◉. If Kratos takes too long... well, he better not take too long.

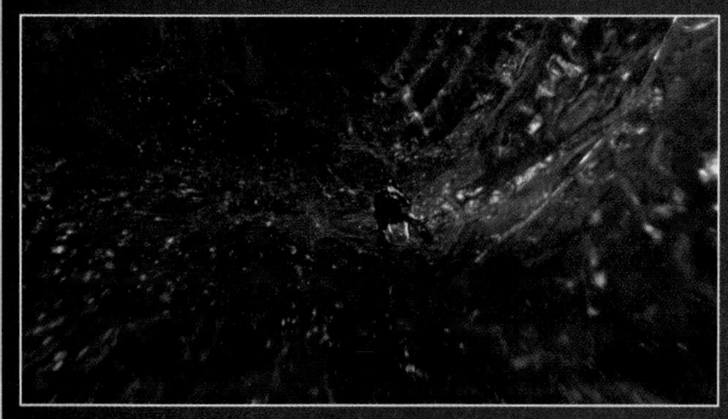

Cronos is now in quite a bit of pain. He asks the Spartan for mercy: an impossible request. Climb the Titan's fingers and drop to the iron platform on Cronos' chest once again.

Use the Nemean Cestus to break down the exposed Onyx. Be prepared when you start attacking; a sudden Context-Sensitive Action occurs soon. When completed successfully, the Onyx is bashed into the Titan's jaw. Destroy the exposed remains of the stone (this takes quite a few strikes) and then rush up to Cronos' forehead. The Titan speaks, but you're prompted to complete a short action and finish this engagement.

RETRIEVE THE ELECTRIC BLADES

Kratos lands at the edge of the Forge. Use the Nemean Cestus to remove the Onyx blocking his path. Continue forward to meet Hephaestus again. The Spartan is not happy about the quest that the Smith God sent him on, but Hephaestus promises that it was worthwhile. He creates the Nemesis Whip. But Hephaestus makes a mistake when he hands the Whip to Kratos: a dire and lasting mistake.

Favor Returned

Fight against the electric current running through the Spartan's body. Hephaestus does not give up. Deflect the iron tool that the misshapen god smashes down. Once free, the Spartan uses his new weapon to break Hephaestus' Ring and bind him in a wave of electric currents.

The pillar to the right is shining. Attack it with your Whip to activate the pillar and finish Hephaestus. The Smith God laments his death for unselfish reasons, then he collapses.

Test out the Nemesis Whip on the Olympus Sentries that appear in the Forge. Once all foes are cleared, jump left and look near the cooling pool that Hephaestus used to use. **Hephaestus' Ring** is there. Take it as a trophy, and then use the Save Altar to the right. Run up the wall with Hermes' Boots and return to Aphrodite's chamber.

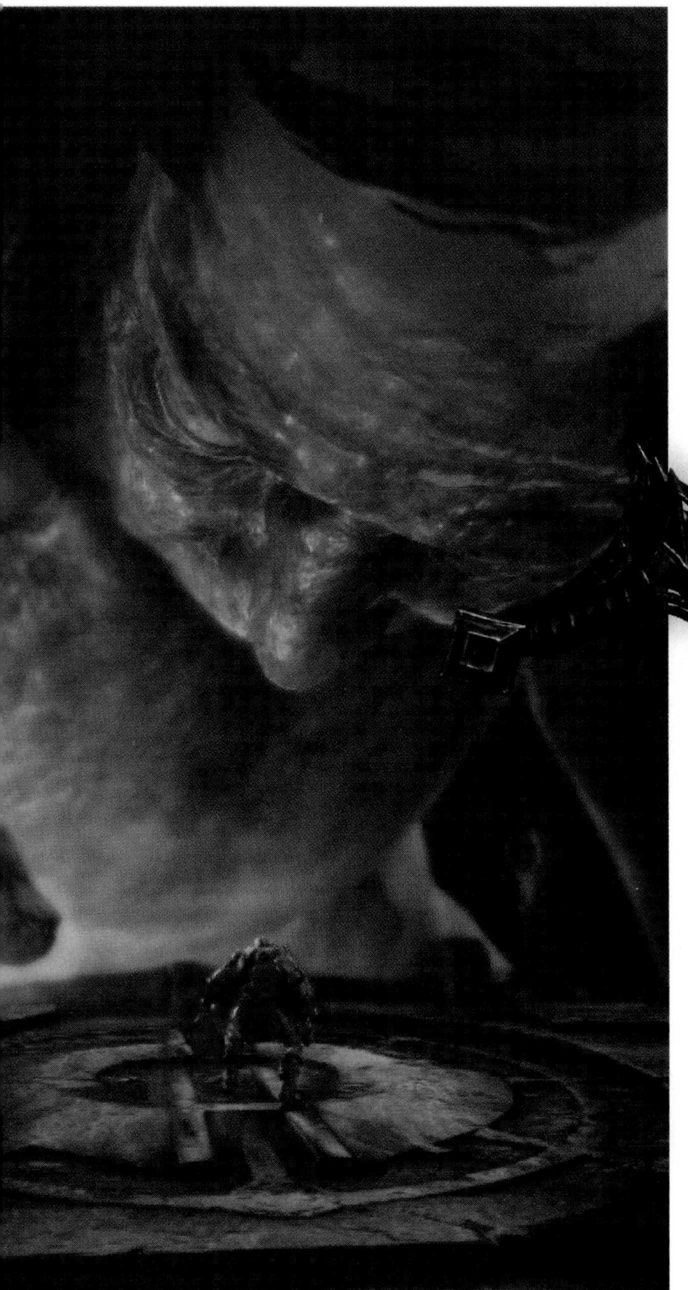

Crossing Bridges

Exit the chamber to return to the Upper Garden. With the Nemesis Whip in hand, Kratos has the power to finish navigating the broken bridges. A squad of Olympus Sentries assaults the Ghost of Sparta. Release Nemesis Rage with **R2** to kill them.

Jump back to the main portion of the bridge. Turn the crank to reorient the bridge and get to the far side. Leave the Nemesis Whip equipped and strike the pillar on that bridge segment to activate it. Get onto the edge of the platform and jump toward the right to approach a new door. Open the Health Chest nearby, and then enter Daedalus' Workshop.

SAVE ALTAR

START

NEMESIS WHIP

The Nemesis Whip was forged by Hephaestus using the power of the Omphalos Stone. This electrically charged weapon shocks foes with powerful currents. Hold either □ or △ at the end of a combo to keep the blades spinning. Press **R2** to release Nemesis Rage and send an electric shock into surrounding enemies.

Return to Aphrodite and don't mention what you just finished cleaning up. Whatever her feelings, it wouldn't be in good taste. Besides, it's never wise to invite the wrath of a goddess.

ACT VIII

SECOND STORY LOFT

X4

START

LEVER

LEVER

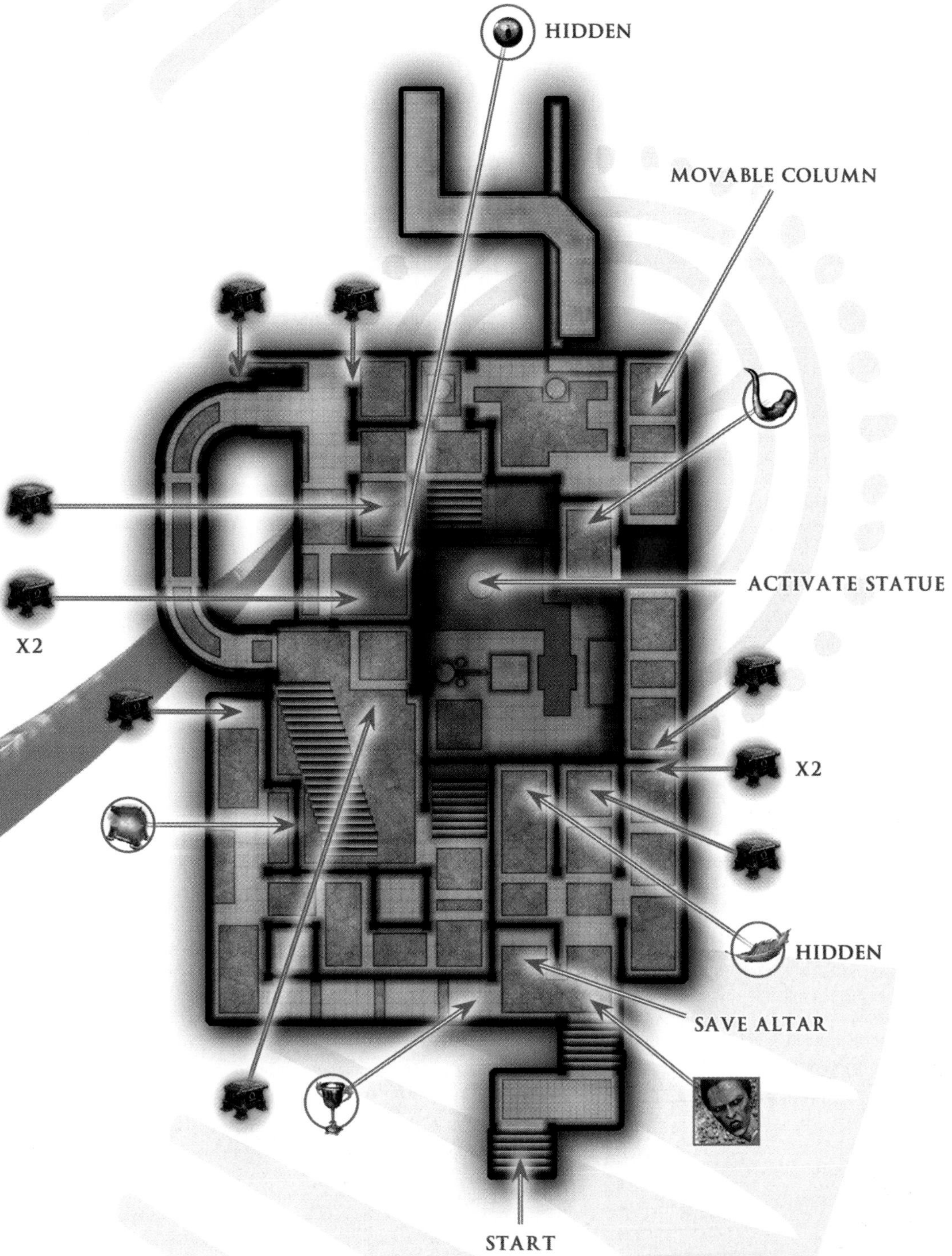

HIDDEN

MOVABLE COLUMN

X2

ACTIVATE STATUE

X2

HIDDEN

SAVE ALTAR

START

SOLVE THE MYSTERIES 174

ESCAPE HERA'S GARDEN 176

DAEDALUS' WORKSHOP

THE WORKSHOP AND THE GARDEN

SOLVE THE MYSTERIES

Bolt Action

With the help of Kratos' newest weapon, he is able to continue toward the Labyrinth. His path brings him to Daedalus' Workshop.

Daedalus kept records of his time spent on the creation of the Labyrinth. Review the documents and drawings around the room. They are excellent clues as to what Kratos may face in the near future. In addition to the notes scattered around the room, there are six portals, a locked gate to the north, and a ballista in the center.

SMALL TIP

The ballista can fire more than one bolt.

BIG TIP

Aim low before bringing the ballista up for a high shot. Remember, good things come in threes...

1 *Rotate the ballista to face west and fire. The cable stretches through three blue portals and latches to the alcove in western wall.*

2 *Climb the cable to the blue portal on the eastern wall.*

3 *Drop onto the caged balcony to open the Red Orb Chest and rush to the opening in the bars. Double Jump and deploy the Wings of Icarus to return to the cable.*

4 *Navigate to the alcove in the western wall and open the Red Orb Chest and Item Chest to receive a Minotaur Horn.*

MINOTAUR HORN

The chest by the western wall contains a Minotaur Horn.

5 *Drop to the ground floor. Pull the lever on the eastern wall and move onto the raised platform.*

6 *Fire the ballista.*

7 *Climb the cable to its end to reach the upper alcove on the eastern wall.*

8 *Open the Item Chest and remove the Gorgon Eye from within.*

GORGON EYE

The Item Chest in this alcove contains a **Gorgon Eye**.

9 *Return to the ballista and turn it to face north. Fire it once to lower the gate, exposing the portal behind it.*

10 *Turn around to face east and dash up the Hermes Brand Symbol to pass through an orange portal. Exit into the caged area on the northern wall.*

11 *Pull the lever there to lower two Item Chests from the ceiling. Rush back to the ballista and fire through the blue portal to the north. The cable strikes the crane holding the chests, causing them to fall.*

12 *Open the Item Chests to get Daedalus' Schematics and a Phoenix Feather.*

13 *Fire the ballista again through the north portal.*

14 *Reach the eastern alcove using the portals. Double jump and attach to the rope.*

15 *Once attached, head south to find four Red Orb chests.*

DAEDALUS' SCHEMATICS AND A FEATHER TOO

These Item Chests have some of Daedalus' plans. There's also a Phoenix Feather. An appropriate find in the lair of the inventor, no?

Exit through the lowered gate to the north. Drop through the open hole and slide down the pole. The hallways below are free of enemies, but that doesn't mean you should speed through them. Walk toward the camera and search for a Red Orb Chest and an Item Chest containing a **Minotaur Horn**.

MINOTAUR HORN

The Item Chest in the back of the hallway holds a **Minotaur Horn**.

II ESCAPE HERA'S GARDEN

Through the Maze

Exit the hall to enter Hera's Garden. Move down the steps and approach the goddess. Hera gives Kratos a piece of her mind, blaming him for the fall of her family and the destruction of man. She may have a point there, but that is irrelevant. She plans to trap the Spartan in her garden, stopping him from completing his revenge.

Use the Save Altar just ahead and turn to the right. A squad of Olympus Legionnaires strike. Fight back with Kratos' weapon of choice and then walk down the path to the far right. Open the two Red Orb Chests there. Next, move to the adjacent corridor to the left and open another Red Orb Chest. The last corridor in that area contains a hidden Item Chest. Equip the Head of Helios to reveal it. A **Phoenix Feather** is inside. Once you have snagged it, return to the Save Altar and record your progress.

PHOENIX FEATHER

The hidden Item Chest contains a Phoenix Feather.

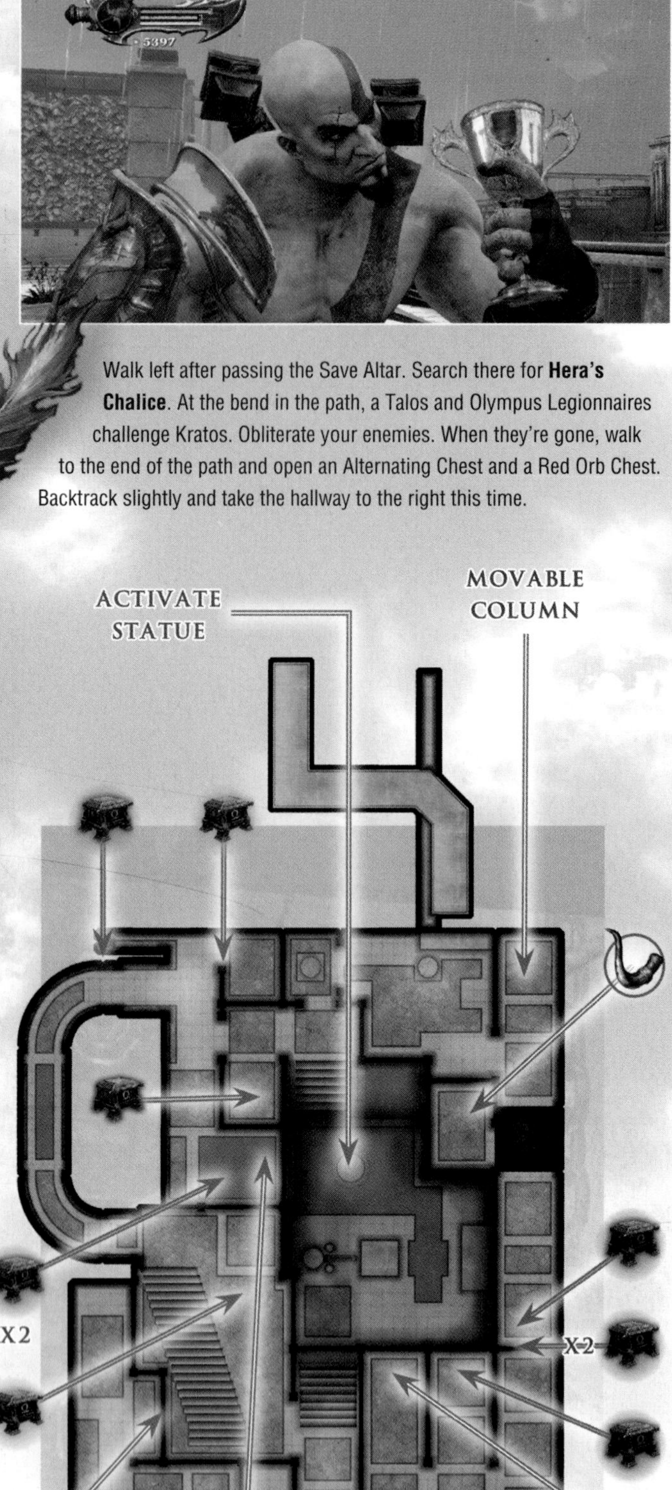

Walk left after passing the Save Altar. Search there for **Hera's Chalice**. At the bend in the path, a Talos and Olympus Legionnaires challenge Kratos. Obliterate your enemies. When they're gone, walk to the end of the path and open an Alternating Chest and a Red Orb Chest. Backtrack slightly and take the hallway to the right this time.

Icarus and Daedalus

Daedalus was an astounding inventor, and a man highly regarded for his intelligence, creativity, and skill. He was especially known for his work on the Labyrinth, which he constructed for King Minos.

Icarus and his father, Daedalus, worked together in the service of King Minos. This relationship soured after the Minotaur was slain. King Minos realized that Daedalus had made it possible for Pasiphae to give birth to the Minotaur; he was more than a little put out by this. Minos blamed the inventor, locking both him and his son inside the Labyrinth. However, the entire Labyrinth was not closed in; some areas were open to the air. This gave the inventors an idea of how to obtain their freedom. They hoped it would be possible to fly over the guards and escape the island.

Daedalus and Icarus spent long weeks gathering feathers from passing birds. They built two wooden frames and used wax to fix the bird feathers onto them. After a few simple tests, the inventors decided that the wings were good enough for flight. Before attempting to escape, Daedalus warned his son that Icarus mustn't fly too high to the sun, or the heat would melt the wax on the wings. He also couldn't fly too low, otherwise the ocean spray would wet the wings and disturb the feathers. To be safe, Icarus must keep to a middle course and follow his father.

Things went well initially, but Icarus had too much fun flying. He forgot his father's words and let himself soar higher and higher into the clouds. The wax on his wings began to melt, but the young inventor had even more problems. The sun was so hot against the wings that Icarus burst into flames. He plummeted from the sky while Daedalus watched, helpless.

Daedalus was already being chased by King Minos' ships, and he had to flee instead of gathering his son's body. Daedalus arrived safely in Sicily, where he was welcomed by King Cocalus. The inventor built a temple to Apollo and hung up his wings as an offering to the god. Icarus' body was later found by Hercules, who was moved by the man's sad fate. Hercules gave Icarus a proper burial and due honors. Daedalus later heard of this and built a statue in tribute to Hercules. The state was so amazing and lifelike that Hercules thought it was a threat when the statue was presented to him. He knocked the statue's head off before he could be convinced otherwise.

Minos, meanwhile, stilled hunted for Daedalus. He went from city to city, asking for something that could be accomplished by only an amazing inventor. It was a challenging riddle: he presented a spiral seashell and asked for a string to be run through it. When he reached Sicily, King Cocalus, knowing Daedalus would be able to solve the riddle, fetched the old man to him. Daedalus tied the string to an ant, which, lured by a drop of honey at one end, walked through the seashell. The string was then passed through the shell. That was all Minos needed; he knew Daedalus was there and demanded his return.

Cocalus was unwilling to part with such a creative genius, though, and stalled for time. He managed to convince Minos to take a bath first, where Cocalus' daughters killed the tyrant. However, some people say that it was Daedalus himself who poured boiling water over Minos.

HERA'S CHALICE

Found along the left path, Hera's Chalice is a prized possession of the Goddess.

More Legionnaires block the way. Lay waste to them with your usual tactics. Continue following the path and veer to the left. A pair of Stone Talos and a handful of Olympus Legionnaires lie in wait for Kratos. Slay them where they stand and then open the nearby Health Chest.

YOU DON'T NEED TO BE FAIR

If you're playing on higher difficulty levels and want to be mean here, read the following tip. The enemies can't make it to your side of the short staircase. Kratos can launch attacks from his position and take out the enemies without risking much in return. Only the Stone Talos have a chance to counter. Avoid their attacks and repeat your own until victory is assured.

The path leads to a narrow enclosure guarded by two Satyrs. Combine launches and heavy attacks to remove the threat. Start heavy combos from maximum range (or even beyond it). This allows Kratos to avoid counterattacks during the weak startup time of these combos and brings the Satyrs into range just in time to punish them. Once the Satyrs are busy incurring heavy damage it's easier to press them and keep the combos going. Continue down the cleared corridor and lift the gate at its end.

SATYRS

These half-goat creatures wield large spears and are well-skilled in melee. It takes more than a few strikes from Kratos' weapon to defeat these foes. Powerful hits and combos throw them off balance. Launching attacks, such as the Blades of Exile's Olympic Ascension, are effective as well.

PURE SKILL AND PERFECT TIMING

Beat your first Satyr using only counterattacks from the Golden Fleece. It's not the easiest way to kill these foes, but nobody can argue that it is an impressive feat.

Chasing Waterfalls

Remove the Olympian in front of the Health Chest and recover any Green Orbs lost during the recent fights. Take a short trip to the left and turn the corner to find an unguarded Red Orb Chest. Open it and return to the area's entrance. This time take the path on the right.

Satyrs

Satyrs were the male counterparts of the Nymphs. These creatures were companions of Dionysus, the mysterious God of Wine. Rites to Dionysus involved wine, dancing, sex, and sometimes violence. Little is known about the worship of Dionysus—compared to many of the other Greek gods. The cult of Dionysus began elsewhere, outside of Greece.

Satyrs were closely associated with the goat-like god Pan; they may even have been derived from him. Satyrs were usually described as human-like, but small in stature, with horse or goat-like qualities. They have a horse's tail, cloven hooves, horse ears, and goat-like horns.

While Nymphs represented idealized females, so the Satyrs embody the masculine sex drive. They maintain a constant state of sexual excitement and were known to fall upon attractive women - and boys - in gangs. When they weren't out hunting for sexual conquest, Satyrs over-indulged in wine, played wild songs, danced, and coupled with Nymphs.

Satyrs were sometimes quite vicious. Occasionally they would harass travelers, or intentionally try to lead them into the wilderness. There, the unlucky victim would be lost and eventually die from hunger or exposure.

Open the Magic Chest and turn right again to enter a side area of the garden. Follow the path around a bend to find two more Red Orb Chests and an Item Chest. The Item Chest won't be visible at first, but that's why you still have the Head of Helios. Open all of the chests to steal another **Gorgon Eye**.

GORGON EYE

The hidden chest in the side area has provides a wonderful treasure: a Gorgon Eye.

Return to the recently opened Magic Chest. Pass through here to reach the end of the garden. The gate slams shut as soon as Kratos enters. Descend some small steps and stand on a large pressure plate. The plate is linked to the statue towering over the garden. The stone in the statues' eye and the stone from Hera's Chalice glow, altering the view of the land. Steps that were too distant from each other now seem connected. Paths form where there were none before.

SMALL TIP

Everything is in the eye of the beholder.

BIG TIP

Chase the waterfalls and let the steps carry them to their destinations.

1. Move away from the pressure plate and head south toward the raised gate. Lower it with **R1** and climb the stairs leading to the second floor walkway.
2. As Kratos reaches the top of the steps, the statue closes its eyes and ends the area effect.

SLOW POKE

Don't take too long to climb the steps. Once Kratos leaves the plate it's only a matter of time before the statue closes its eyes and ends the effect. Make sure the Spartan reaches the top of the steps before this happens.

3. Walk to the gate at the end of the platform. Lift this gate to get into the next area. Slip down the ladder and open the Red Orb Chest to the south.
4. Double jump off the ledge and glide west through the opening in the gate. Beyond is a chest with a **Minotaur Horn**.

MINOTAUR HORN

Fly west from the ledge to get another Item Chest.

5. Leap back to where you were and make another double-jump to head north.

6. Grab the pillar of steps and drag it to the east, by a small waterfall. Rotate the pillar once, to the left, and slide it under the water.
7. Water flows down the steps and pools into a nearby basin, lowering another platform as well as a gate to the south.

8. Move past the gate to find Hera.
9. Hera is dealt with, and the garden loses much of its beauty. The grass and flowers dry up, leaving the only brambles, crisp and ready to burn.
10. Use the Bow of Apollo to destroy the brambles.
11. Grab Hera and throw her on the pressure plate.
12. Return to the pillar of stairs and move it under the newest waterfall, near the cleared brambles. The stairs guide the water into the adjacent basin, causing another waterfall to appear. The basin near the pressure plate moves.

13. Grab the pillar of stairs again and move it to the south, past the pressure plate. Rotate the stairs twice and push them into the nearby slot.
14. Collect Hera again and climb the steps to the basin. Place her inside to lower the final platform.
15. Grab the pillar one last time and place it on top of the plate. Now Kratos can climb up the winding stairs and platforms to reach the garden's exit.

A Wing and a Prayer

Kratos crushes the stone from Hera's Chalice, breaking the statue's effect once and for all. Move along the platform to reach a broken section of the bridge. A Harpy Queen rests on the column to the right, just begging to be of use. Get her attention with an arrow and then grab hold of her. Ride the Harpy Queen over the gap.

A flock soon gathers, and Kratos can hop from Harpy Queen to Harpy Queen until he finally lands on solid ground. A winch, a Magic Chest, and a Health Chest are before him. Open the chests and then turn the winch. The path above opens, exposing a dark cavern. Climb the stairs toward the entrance and make a slight detour to open the Red Orb Chest to the right. Use the Save Altar nearby.

Next, equip the Head of Helios and move left to uncover a hidden Item Chest. Take its **Gorgon Eye** before entering the cavern.

GORGON EYE

The hidden chest contains a Gorgon Eye.

ACT IX

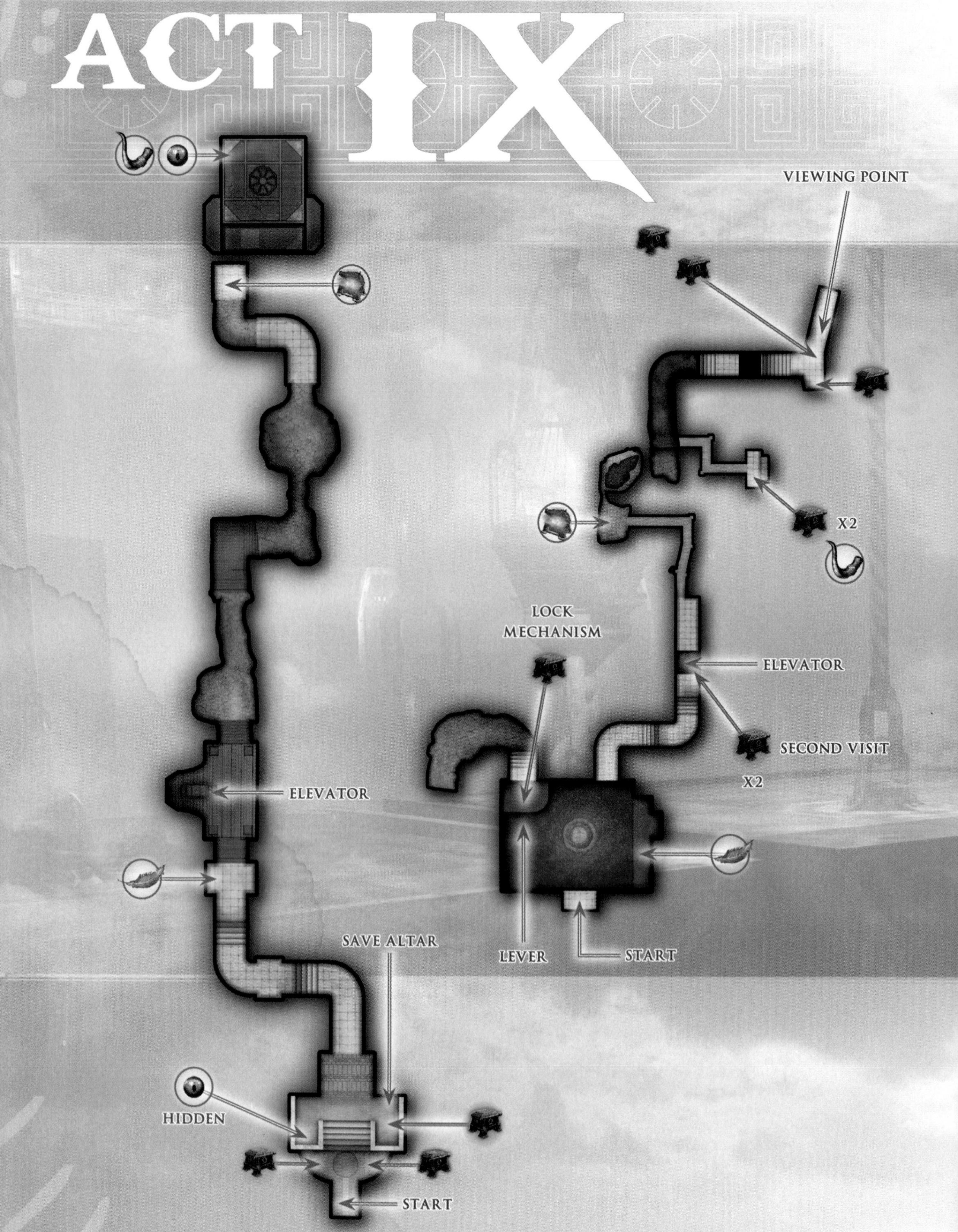

VIEWING POINT
X2
LOCK MECHANISM
ELEVATOR
SECOND VISIT
X2
ELEVATOR
LEVER
START
SAVE ALTAR
HIDDEN
START

BOREAS
ICESTORM
HIDDEN
LOCK MECHANISM
PLATFORM ABOVE
SAVE ALTAR

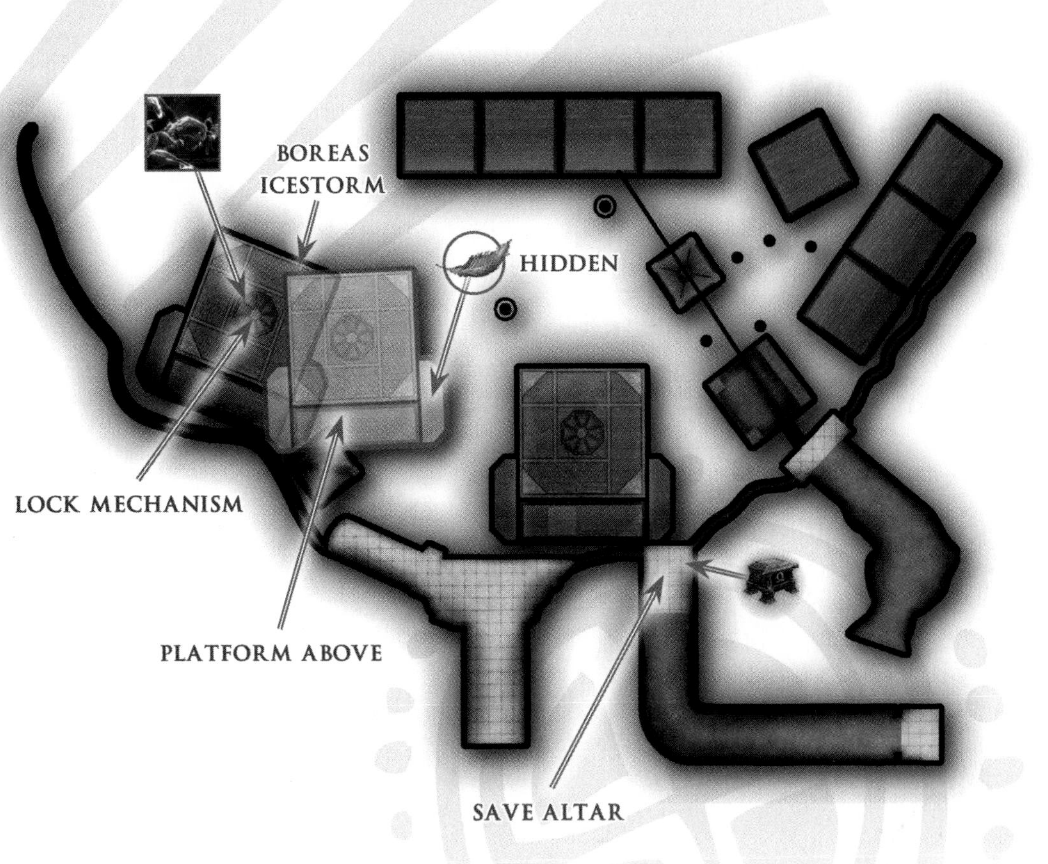

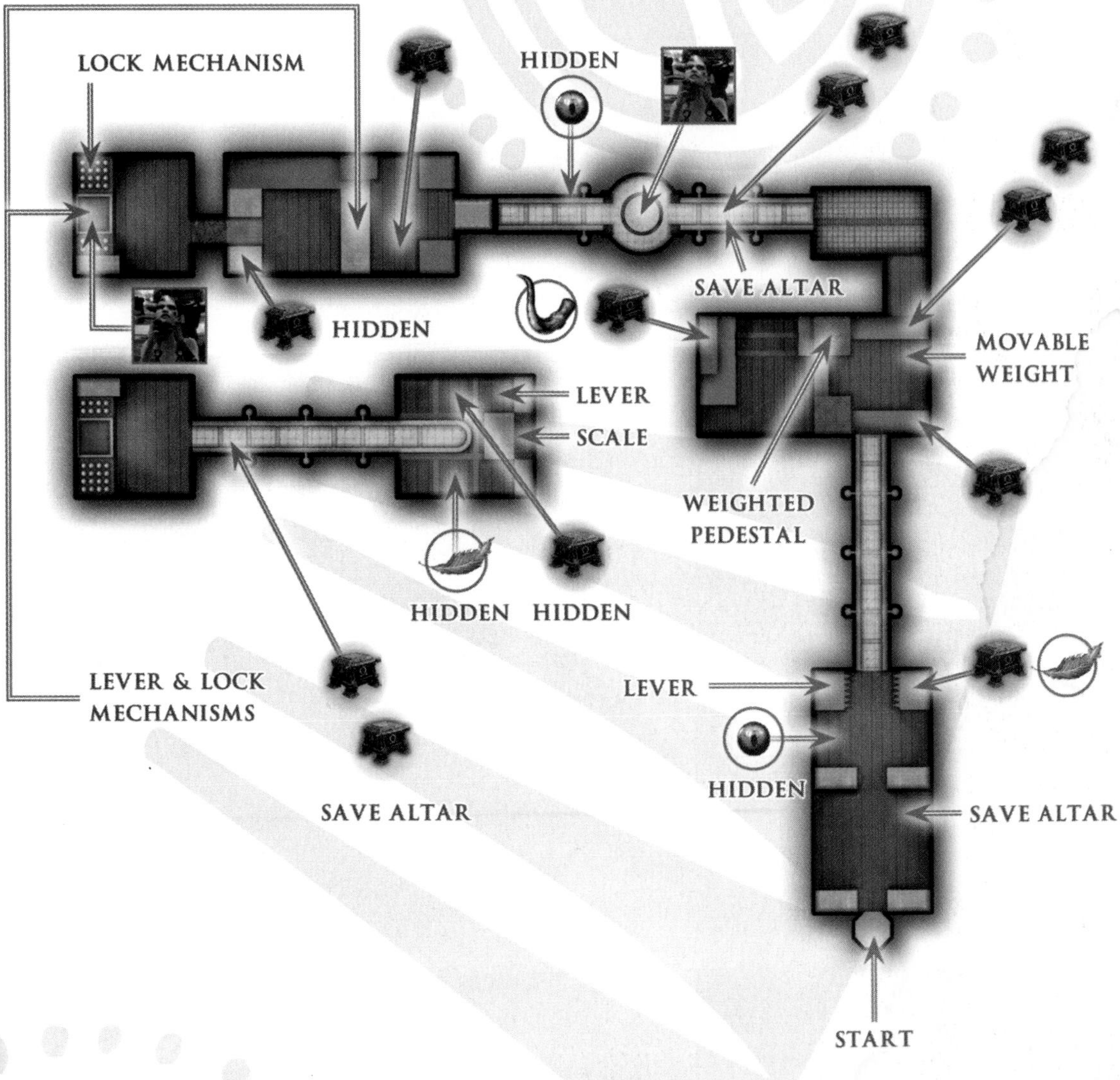

LOCK MECHANISM
HIDDEN
SAVE ALTAR
HIDDEN
MOVABLE
WEIGHT
LEVER
SCALE
WEIGHTED
PEDESTAL
HIDDEN
HIDDEN
LEVER & LOCK
MECHANISMS
LEVER
HIDDEN
SAVE ALTAR
SAVE ALTAR
START

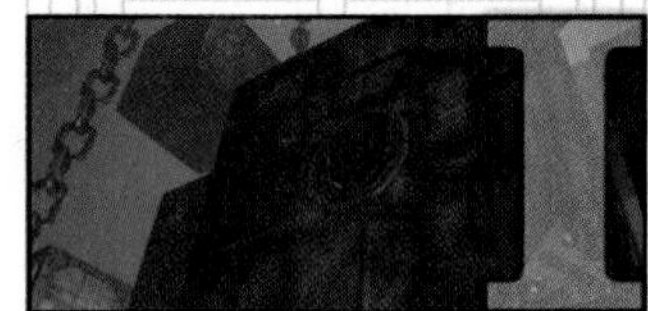

ENTER THE LABYRINTH 184

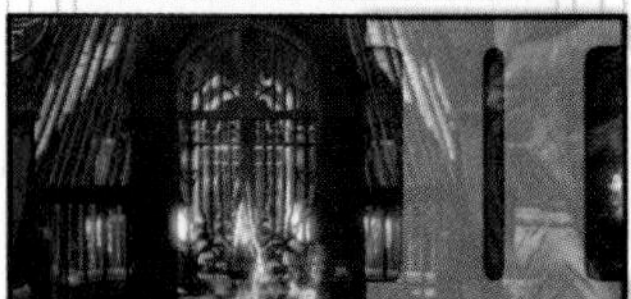

FIND PANDORA 192

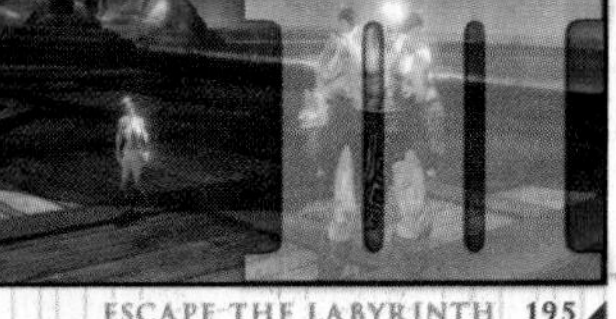

ESCAPE THE LABYRINTH 195

THE HIDDEN PASSAGEWAY

THE LIGHT IN THE DARK

ENTER THE LABYRINTH

Pest Control

Walk down the pathway to discover what protects the Labyrinth. These Skorpius Spawn look terrifying, but they are really more of a gift than a curse. Kratos can quickly kill these creatures by grabbing them or hitting them with his blade.

Skorpius Spawn release Green Orbs when they die, healing Kratos. Continue battling the Skorpius Spawn and proceed to the end of the hallway. The number of creatures grows exponentially, but Kratos can handle them easily with heavy Cestus attacks or sweeping Blade combos.

SKORPIUS SPAWN 230

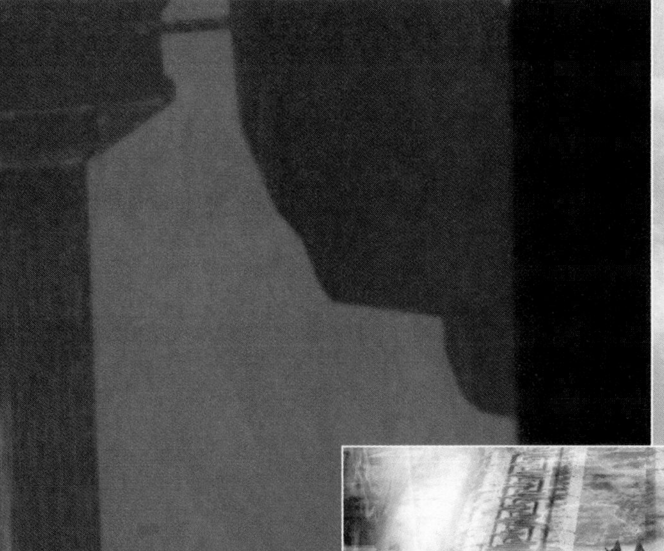

A Familiar Stage

Kratos must fight several waves of enemies while riding on top of the platform. After Kratos' arrival, two Cyclops Enforcers rise from the floor to challenge the Spartan. Equip the Blades of Exile and begin working on one of the monstrous beasts immediately. The best strategy is to jump above the creature and use the Cyclone of Chaos all the way down. The Cyclops Elites' weapons usually stay low to the ground, so Kratos is relatively safe while airborne.

Once the Cyclops Elite is dazed, grab him and bring him down. After the first Cyclops Elite falls, a Cyclops Berserker and another Cyclops Elite spawn as reinforcements. Focus all Kratos' attacks on the Cyclops Berserker. Use Cyclone of Chaos in the air and keep attacking until you daze the enemy. Once the creature's weakened, grab the Cyclops Berserker and ride him!

DON'T STOOP TO THEIR LEVEL

Cyclops Berserkers are foul creatures. Don't use one of them as a mount! Beat all the cyclopean beasts on your own for a genuine sense of accomplishment.

Turn left at the end of the corridor and search for an Item Chest. Loot the **Phoenix Feather** from within.

PHOENIX FEATHER

At the end of the corridor is an Item Chest.

Walk across the wooden planks and press **R1** at the giant cog to use the elevator. This takes Kratos down to the lower level. Exit the elevator and take the path leading north. It's shrouded in darkness, so use the Head of Helios to see where you're going. Kill any Skorpius Spawn that approach and keep moving until Kratos comes upon an infestation of the cursed monsters.

Quickly move into the center of the small chamber. When the Skorpius Spawn are close, unleash Army of Sparta (or a similar magic attack) to slaughter most of them in one simple move. Eliminate the stragglers and move through the caverns, back into the light. Open the Health Chest on the right and read the note to left. When ready, use the Wings of Icarus to glide to the top of the platform up ahead.

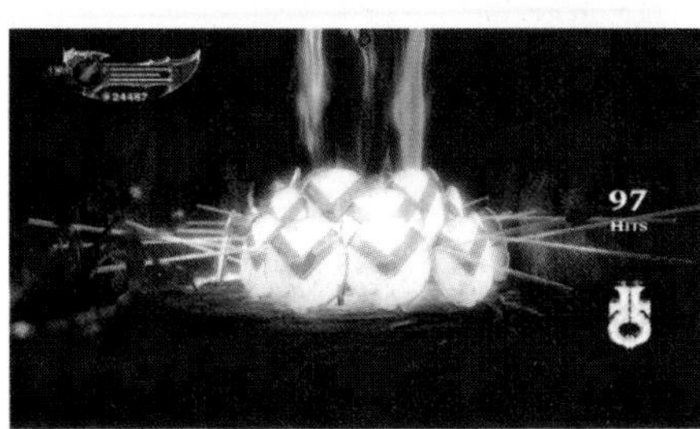

More Cyclops Elites arrive. Make every attack count and inflict as much damage as possible while riding the Cyclops Berserker. Time is of the essence, because the blows from your enemies quickly bring down your mount.

Pull out the stops once you're on the ground again. Hit the Rage of Sparta and slice away, then rely on magic to finish the battle. When the battle ends, search the right side of the container for its Item Chests. Take the **Minotaur Horn** and **Gorgon Eye** from within.

MINOTAUR HORN AND GORGON EYE

Collect these two items as spoils of war after the Cyclops fight.

Proceed to the cave beneath the bust of Icarus. Use the Wings of Icarus to reach the cave and then read the note on the ground. Open the Health Chest on the wall and utilize the Save Altar in this room. Shine the Head of Helios on the giant rock face in front of Kratos; a new path is revealed.

The Path to the Labyrinth

Head down the path until Kratos enters a chamber designed by Daedalus. There are Red Orb Chests on both sides of Kratos, and you find a note here as well. Read that, then explore the upper platform. When you're done, drop to the lower level.

Look along the far east wall. Locate an alcove with an Item Chest inside. This contains a **Phoenix Feather**.

PHOENIX FEATHER

Search the eastern alcove for another treasure.

Walk to the left and use the lever on the northern wall. This raises the water inside the room. Float up and jump onto the platform on the western side to grab a Red Orb Chest. Examine the lock on the floor; an intense heat radiates from its core.

Swim to the eastern side of the room and climb up the lattice on the northern wall. Move all the way down the hallway to reach an elevator with a lever. Pull the lever to ride the platform up. Kill the small pack of Skorpius Spawn once the platform stops and then proceed into the darkness.

Hazardous Path

Use the Head of Helios to guide Kratos. Walk out to the wooden plank and follow its path to a new stone platform. Read the note on the ground, open the Alternating Chest, and jump to the netting on the north wall. Climb up.

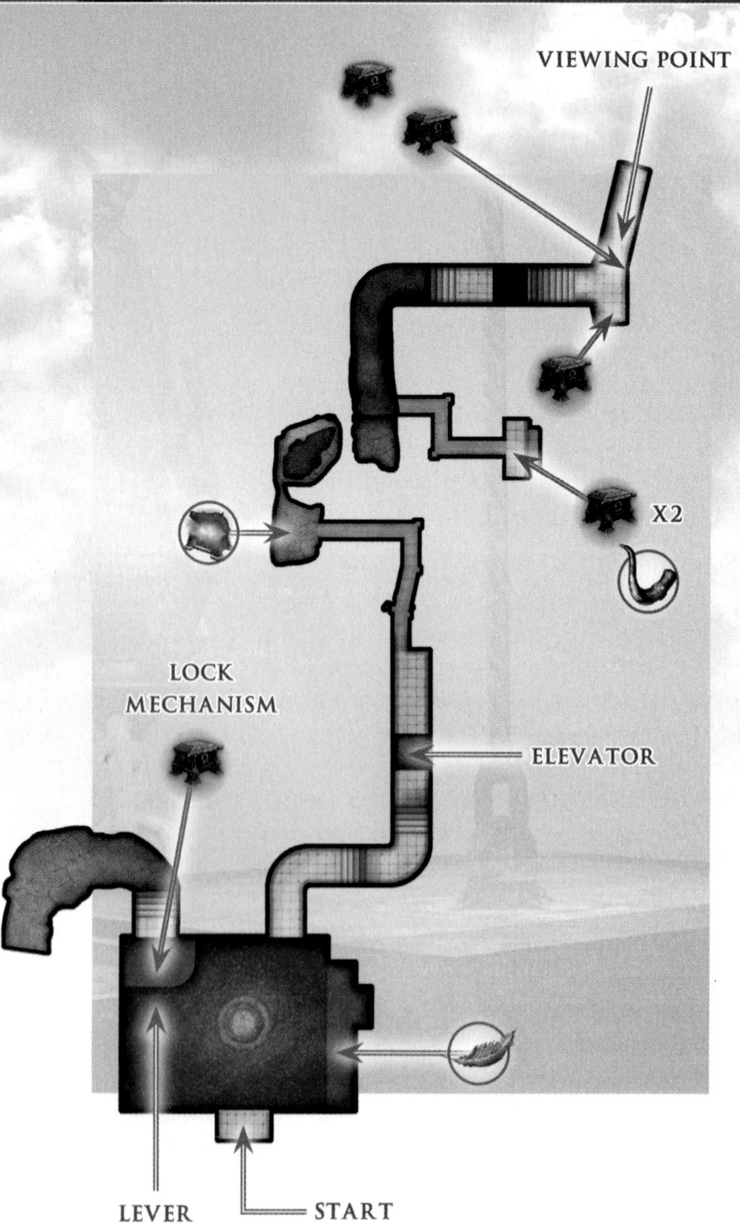

GORGONS

Gorgons fight much like their larger sisters. These serpentine creatures slither across the ground and attack Kratos with their slowing gaze. This effect slows Kratos, making him more susceptible to being petrified.

When facing off against Gorgons, keep your combos quick. This allows you to roll aside at a moment's notice, avoiding the Gorgon's gaze.

Use combat grapples and magic to end the fight quickly. Gorgons have a similar death as the Gorgon Serpents if you grapple them. Use this to petrify nearby enemies.

After scaling the rock face, Kratos finds himself in a dark pool of water. Two Gorgons, joined by a couple Harpies, emerge from the murky puddle. Use quick combos and dash in circles around the sinuous beasts. Rely on combat grapples to knock back the Gorgons and lay into them until everything falls silent.

After the battle, take out the Head of Helios and locate the path to the right. Jump over the gap and onto a wooden platform. Move toward the camera and then take the path right. Investigate them all prior to using the Hermes' Brand Symbol. There are three chests on a ledge if you continue searching. Two of them are Red Orb Chests. The other has a **Minotaur Horn**.

MINOTAUR HORN

Go toward the camera and then east after passing the Hermes' Brand Symbol. Collect all the treasure there.

Return to the symbol and use the Boots of Hermes to scale the wall to the north. Open a heavy door and proceed down the path, killing Skorpius Spawn on the way. Jump over a fiery gap and then open the door at the end of the hallway.

Back for More

Open the Health and Magic Chests in the next room. Also open the Red Orb Chest to the right. Head down the path to the left and then jump down to the container below.

TIME FOR AN UPGRADE

Now would be the time to upgrade the Nemean Cestus as much as possible. Kratos is about to face a fiend covered in Onyx, and the Nemean Cestus is going to play a major role in its destruction.

SKORPIUS

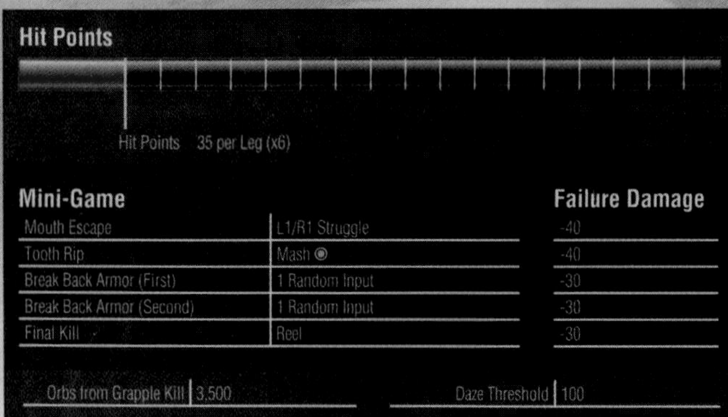

Hit Points

Hit Points: 35 per Leg (x6)

Mini-Game		Failure Damage
Mouth Escape	L1/R1 Struggle	-40
Tooth Rip	Mash ◉	-40
Break Back Armor (First)	1 Random Input	-30
Break Back Armor (Second)	1 Random Input	-30
Final Kill	Reel	-30

Orbs from Grapple Kill: 3,500

Daze Threshold: 100

Kratos is swarmed by a pack of Skorpius Spawn as soon as he lands on the box. Equip the Blades of Exile and use the Cyclone of Chaos to massacre these vile pests. Things seem to be going well, but that soon changes.

In moments, Skorpius joins Kratos on the container. This is a huge Scorpion; far larger and more powerful than the spawn you've been facing. This monstrous beast is no immortal, but it sure fights like one. Skorpius grabs onto Kratos and throws him into its mouth. Quickly perform the Context-Sensitive Action to escape the Skorpius' jaws.

The mouth is Skorpius' weak spot, but you must avoid its claws to make a proper assault. Ignore the small Skorpius Spawn on the field and flank their master. Equip the Nemean Cestus and start hammering into the creature's legs.

Watch out for a few attacks during this phase. The first is a simple claw attack. Skorpius quickly stabs at anything in front of it.

The second attack is a grapple (like the one Skorpius used to start the battle). If you're close to the creature's mouth while hitting the legs, roll away to try and avoid this retaliatory attack.

Finally, Skorpius has a devastating ground pound. Keep an eye on the beast's tail to see this coming. Jump high and fly away from the tail when you see it rise.

BEST DEFENSE IS A STRONG OFFENSE

Sometimes Kratos isn't able to get out of range during a tail attack. When this happens, use a magic attack to make yourself temporarily invulnerable.

Overall, the ground pound is the easiest to dodge, so Kratos should work on the hind and middle legs instead of the front ones. Move to the back of Skorpius and start chipping away.

Use the Vicious Maul attack if you've leveled the Nemean Cestus. This allows you to simultaneously damage two legs.

When two legs have been exposed on one side, move to the other side and repeat the process. Skorpius may jump into the air and relocate. When this happens, follow its lead and move back to its side and continue attacking. Once you've destroyed three of the monster's legs, Skorpius buckles under its weight and collapses.

Go for the Mouth

While stunned, Skorpius' mouth is exposed. Hurry to the front of the monster and use the Rage of Sparta. Start chopping into the mouth of the beast and take out as many tiny Skorpius Spawn as possible while damaging the giant version.

By killing Skorpius Spawn with Kratos sweeping attacks, he regains health while damaging his primary target. Once Skorpius is dazed, hit ◎ to move in and rip out one of its fangs.

Skorpius charges Kratos and keeps going out the top of the container. Dash to either side to avoid the monster and then kill Skorpius Spawn that swarm the area. This helps replenish Kratos' health.

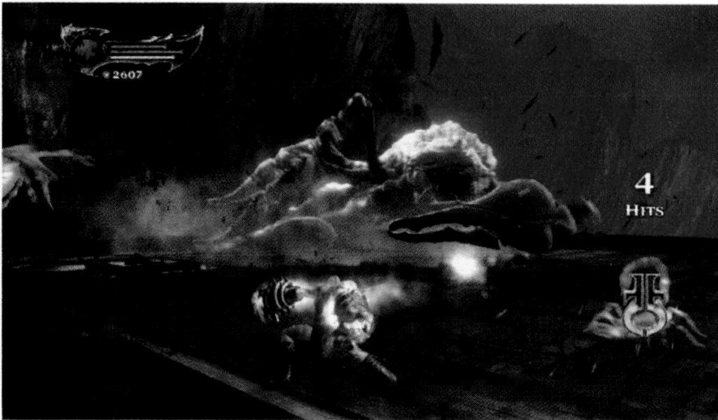

Soon, Skorpius reappears and performs a gale attack. Avoid its ghastly breath by dodging to either side. Afterward, resume your attack on the boss' legs.

The Beast Returns

Skorpius has gained new attacks. The creature's tail can now stab at Kratos from above, and Skorpius will often leave the container (appearing later from a different angle). These attacks add a dangerous layer of variety.

When Skorpius disappears, slaughter his tiny minions to regain health. Once the creature returns, break all of its legs and then start tenderizing its face. Once it has been dazed again, grapple Skorpius and push it off the container.

Kratos plummets over the edge but soon regains his composure. He flies back toward Skorpius with the Wings of Icarus. Dodge the flying icicles and then reinitiate a Context-Sensitive Action when Kratos is close to the enemy.

Once Skorpius is frozen, finish it off in style with a strong attack. Find the creature's severed tail and then break it open. The Boreas Icestorm is your reward.

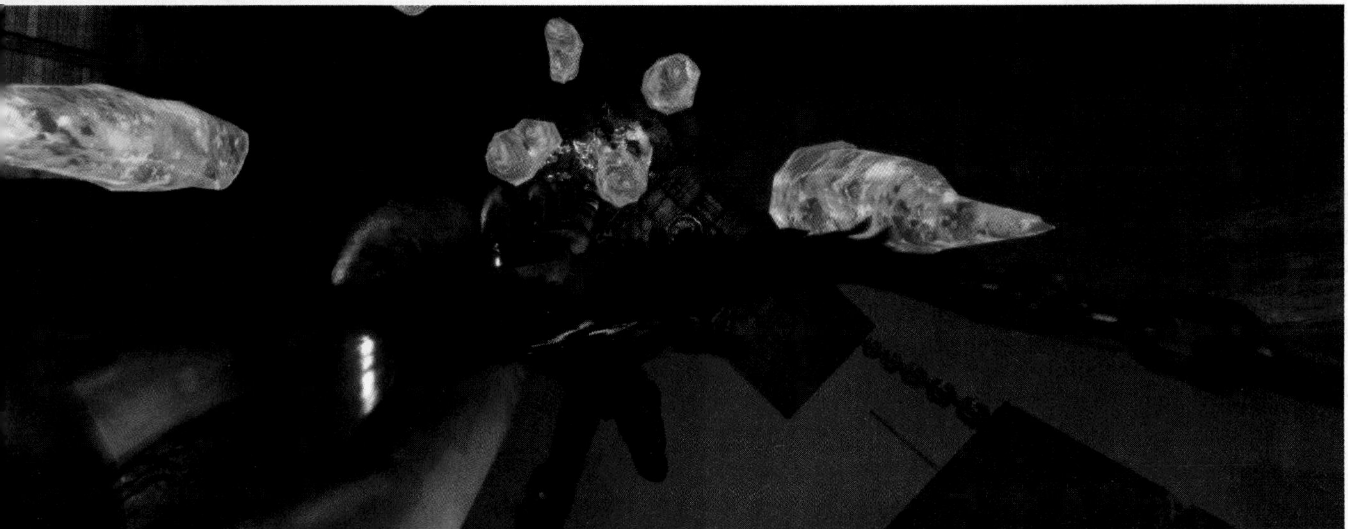

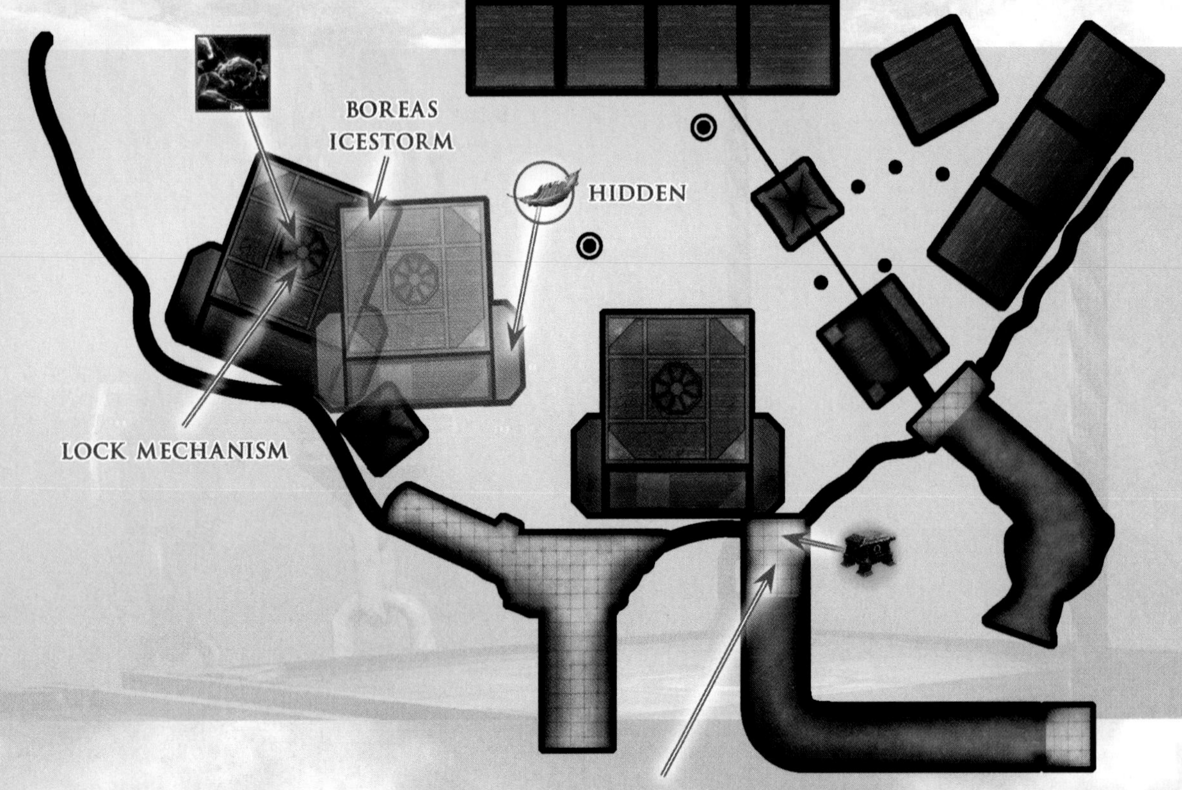

The Key to the Labyrinth

With the Boreas Icestorm, Kratos is able to cool down the heated lock mechanisms in the outer Labyrinth. Walk to the center of the platform and use the Boreas Icestorm to open the first lock. Once unlocked, an Icarus Vent opens in the northeast corner. Use the vent to glide up to a large metal clamp.

Cross the metal clamp and jump onto its elevated side, past the heated lock. Turn left and use the Head of Helios to uncover an Item Chest with a **Phoenix Feather** in it.

PHOENIX FEATHER

A hidden chest is sitting to the side of the large metal clamp.

Move to the center of the clamp and cool down the lock with the Boreas Icestorm. This unhinges the clamp and sets the boxes in motion. Run back to where Kratos first landed and then use the Grapple Points to swing to a container on the other side of the caverns. Cool the lock on the wall and wait for the box to move.

As it moves, a Gorgon, Minotaur Elites, and some Olympus Sentinels arrive en masse. Concentrate all your energies on killing the Gorgon first. Destroying the Gorgon allows Kratos to use her head and turn all other enemies to stone.

The Nemean Cestus works splendidly in this fight; it's good at knocking people into the air. Fight near the edge of the container to throw enemies off, killing them instantly with your heavy attacks.

WAITING FOR THE PERFECT OPPORTUNITY

After beating the first Gorgon into a weakened state, keep her alive until the second pack of Olympus Sentinels and another Minotaur arrive. Once the second wave has arrived, use the Gorgon to petrify them.

If Kratos has to fight the enemies one-on-one, the best strategy is to skirt around the perimeter and attack from the outside. Keep fighting until every enemy has been killed. Kratos reaches his destination soon after.

Use Grapple Points to swing onto an old clamp and then climb to the top. Jump across and reenter the cave beneath the statue of Icarus. Follow the path back into the water chamber. Swim across to the platform on the northwest side of the chamber and cool the lock on the ground.

Take the path on the right to reach two Red Orb chests. These are beneath the lift that you used earlier.

You now have access the column in front of Kratos. Use the Boots of Hermes to run up the side of the wall and reach a new hallway. Run through the hallway and grab a note written by Daedalus. Exit back to the caverns. Health and Magic Chests are at the end of the hallway.

When you're ready, move into the light to talk to Daedalus. When the conversation ends, look to the right for an Item Chest. There are also two Red Orb Chests over there. Grab your **Gorgon Eye** and move out.

GORGON EYE

On the right side of Daedalus' room are several chests.

Dadealus' Advice

Jump to the rope near Kratos and use it to climb past Daedalus to a hanging platform. From there, use Grapple Points to reach the box above Daedalus. These Grapple Points aren't stable. You must jump quickly. Pay attention and stay calm. Cool the lock on the northeastern side and get ready for another ride. Climb down some wire netting and jump to the door that opened on the side of the container.

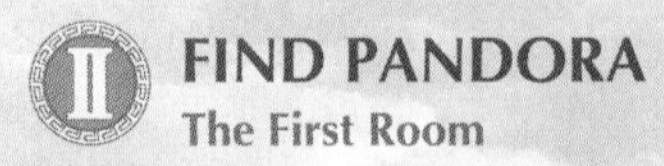

FIND PANDORA

The First Room

Use the Save Altar as you come in. Afterward, cool the lock in the northwest corner of the room. The room shifts, and Kratos is dropped onto a wall that has now become the ground floor.

Use the Head of Helios in the left corner (closest to the camera). This reveals a Red Orb Chest if you've already finished upgrading your health and magic.

Two Bronze Talos stand before Kratos as soon as he lands and offer a challenge. Equip the Nemean Cestus and use heavy attacks to break through the Talos' armor. Focus on one at time and turn these monsters into rubble. A Cerberus Mongel arrives as soon as you kill your first Bronze Talos. Keep the surviving Talos between Kratos and the Cerberus while you finish the next kill.

Finally, beat the Cerberus Mongrel into a weakened state and then mount the beast. Two more Bronze Talos and some Feral Hounds appear, but this time you have the Cerberus under your control. Continuously pour flame over your enemies, killing them quickly. Once the Cerberus drops, finish any remaining enemies without the assistance of fiery breath. When all enemies are slain, giant spikes descend from the ceiling. The doorway opens.

The Next Challenge

Open the Health and Magic Chests in the small passageway beyond. Jump into the adjacent room and use the Head of Helios along the left wall. This reveals an Item Chest. Again, if you've finished collecting your upgrades this chest will contain Red Orbs instead of a Gorgon Eye.

Cool the lock on the floor. This causes the room to rotate. There are currently no enemies in the room, but Kratos now faces quite an obstacle course. Wait for the fire to extinguish on the left side of the room and then quickly climb up the steel lattice on the wall. Use ⊗ to climb as fast as possible to prevent Kratos from getting cooked. Scale the lattice as far as you are able.

Once Kratos is on the moving platform, climb to the right side and wait. The platform starts smashing into the eastern platform repeatedly. Just after the platforms crash together, jump the gap.

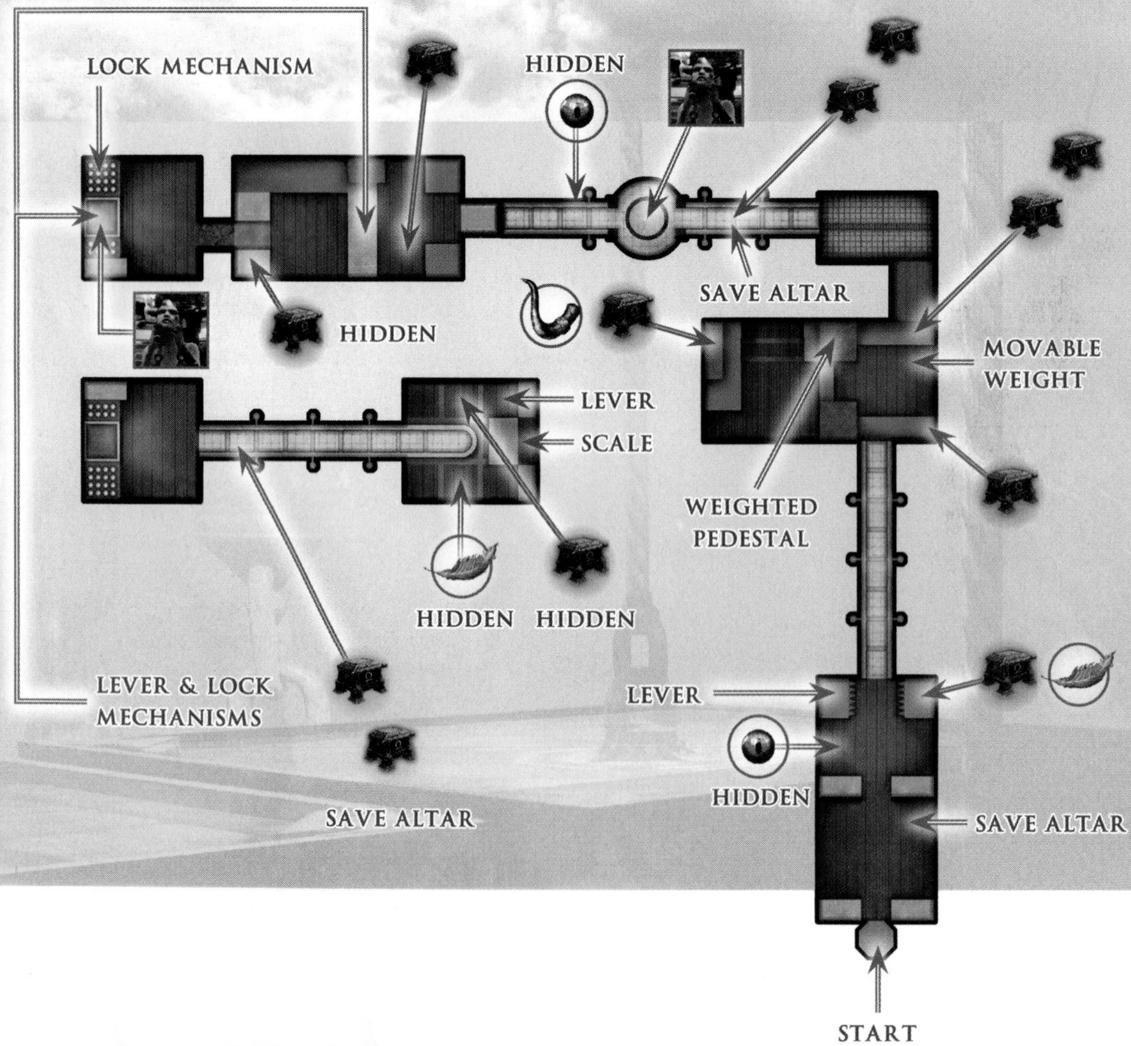

LOCK MECHANISM
HIDDEN
HIDDEN
SAVE ALTAR
MOVABLE WEIGHT
LEVER
SCALE
WEIGHTED PEDESTAL
HIDDEN HIDDEN
LEVER & LOCK MECHANISMS
LEVER
HIDDEN
SAVE ALTAR
SAVE ALTAR
START

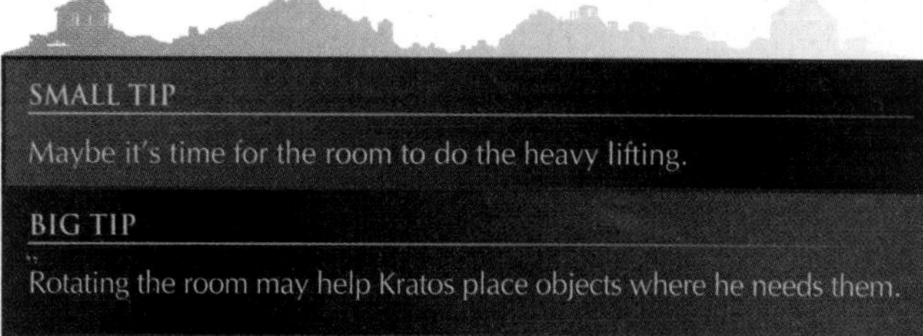

SMALL TIP

Maybe it's time for the room to do the heavy lifting.

BIG TIP

Rotating the room may help Kratos place objects where he needs them.

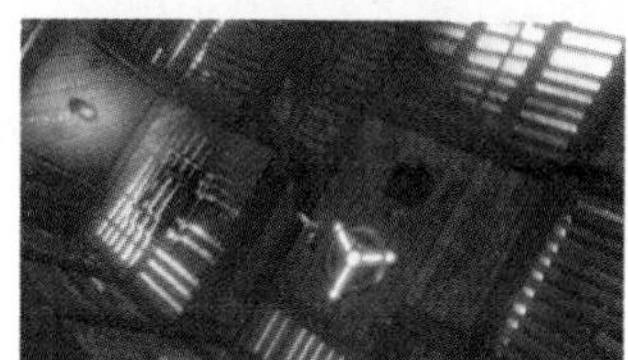

Notice the opposite platform that comes rushing above Kratos. Be wary of it. That platform can spike you against the wall. Wait for the platform above Kratos to draw back. Climb onto your current platform and scurry up the lattice on the far wall.

When the highest platform moves beneath Kratos, drop onto the platform and pull the lever there. The fire below is quenched, and the platforms stop moving. Open the Item Chest and Red Orb Chest on the ground level now that the fire isn't protecting them. This gets you a **Phoenix Feather** (if you still need any). Drop to ground level and enter the doorway. Walk along the catwalk until you reach the next room.

PHOENIX FEATHER

Once the fire is quenched you can open an Item Chest on the room's lower floor.

A New Perspective

The following chamber is complex. Give it some time if you want to uncover everything on your own or read on to find out what has to be done.

1 *Grab the weight in the center of the room and push it next to the lock to the west.*

2 *Cool the lock to rotate the room. After rotating the room the first time, move the weight to the eastern wall, just south of the lock. Jump on the weight and jump again to get onto a ledge.*

3 *Leap across the gap to the north and then use the Wings of Icarus to glide down to the northwestern platform. There are chests there: a Red Orb Chest and an Item Chest with a **Minotaur Horn**.*

MINOTAUR HORN

The northwestern platform contains this Item Chest.

4 *Grab the weight again and push it to the northern wall. Leave the weight against the wall, underneath a lantern.*

5 *Cool the lock in the center of the floor to rotate the room back to its original position.*

6 *To open the door, push the weight onto the scale.*

7 *Open the chests along the eastern wall: health, magic, and Red Orbs are inside them. Use the Boots of Hermes to climb the northeastern wall and exit the room.*

LET HELIOS CLEAR THE WAY

If you have the Orbs to spare, upgrade the Head of Helios. Using the Head as a weapon in the next room is extremely helpful.

A Thorny Situation

Cool the lock on the far wall and get ready for one hell of a fight. Minotaur Elites and Olympus Legionnaires flood the room, but this is the least of Kratos' problems. Spikes rise from the floor and can instantly kill Kratos—or his enemies. Keep an eye on the floor and watch for signs of the spikes. If Kratos sees the spikes starting to pop out of one quadrant, immediately rush to a safe area.

Use the Head of Helios to repel enemies. This occasionally pushes the hapless monsters onto the spikes. The Cestus works well too because you can push enemies around. Be warned though. It's important to switch back to the Blades of Exile when you're getting ready to launch a combat grapple. Practice switching weapons on the fly!

Use Olympus Legionnaires that are dazed as Battering Rams. This is another good way to throw your victims around, automatically killing some of them.

Eventually, the entire floor shows signs of the deadly traps, and it seems like Kratos' doom is imminent. Look for a single Harpy Queen above. Use a combat grapple to start riding it. Stay on the Harpy Queen as the room rotates, providing Kratos with a safe place to land.

Once you're back on solid ground, Olympus Legionnaires, Minotaur Elites, and now Siren Seductresses launch an attack. The spikes no longer show up in one quadrant. They now rise in two quadrants at the same time! Fight with similar tactics while waiting for the floor to fill up with spikes again. Use another Harpy Queen for a safe flight.

THE SONG THAT DECEIVES

Use the Head of Helios to knock Siren Seductresses out of their insubstantial state. This has the added benefit of stunning nearby foes. Spikes won't kill Siren Seductresses because they float above the floor, so these enemies are the best ones to target if you're using resources like magic or the Rage of Sparta.

The room rotates again, and this time Kratos lands on a floor without spikes. If any Siren Seductresses have managed to survive the attacks, they'll come after Kratos now. Finish them and then climb up to the doorway that opened. Run down the catwalk. Use the Save Altar and open the Health and Magic Chests in that spot. Next, approach Pandora's cage. Use the Nemean Cestus to break the lock on the cage. Go inside!

ESCAPE THE LABYRINTH

Pandora's Path

Watch the next scene. Kratos leaves the cage afterward, and that's a good time to use the Head of Helios. To the right is an Item Chest with a **Gorgon Eye**. Get that as you head out.

GORGON EYE

The hidden chest near Pandora's Cage is revealed with the Head of Helios.

Open the door in front of Kratos and follow Pandora down the path. Pandora isn't able to scale the wall ahead. Press ◎ to lift her onto Kratos' shoulders and then press **R1** to lift her up. Jump up to the ledge and then continue through the doorway into the next room.

Inside, a Gorgon Serpent and some Olympus Sentries spawn. Grab the Olympus Sentries and use them as Battering Rams to attack the Gorgon Serpent. Keep attacking the sinuous monster and use her head to turn all other enemies to stone. Break apart the petrified foes and finish any survivors.

Two more Gorgon Serpents, along with more and more Olympus Sentries, appear after the first one has been slain. Attack the Gorgon Serpents first and only focus on the Olympus Sentries if Kratos is going to use them as a Battering Ram.

Once all the enemies in the room lie dead, shine the Head of Helios along the left wall exposing a chest. Follow Pandora to the lever on the wall. Pull back the lever to allow Pandora through the small doorway in the cage. Pandora steps on the cage, making the far wall descend. Cool the lock beside Kratos to cause the room to rotate.

You now have a new path to traverse, but Pandora is trapped in her cage. Giant, bladed pendulums are quickly descending toward her.

Quickly scale the wall and jump to the platform with the pendulums. Move left and drop to the platform that houses Pandora. Return to the ground level and use the lever to release Pandora from her cage. Now that everyone is relatively safe, grab onto Pandora and push her through the fence on the northern wall.

Use the Head of Helios to reveal a hidden chest on the left wall.

Damsel in Distress

Pandora scales the ladder and Kratos soon hears that she has gotten herself into trouble. As soon as the fence descends, climb the ladder in front of Kratos.

Pandora is trapped in a cube that is about to fill with water. If Kratos doesn't hurry, she will surely perish. Use the Head of Helios while scanning the wall to the right. Dead center on the wall is a hidden area with an item chest. In there is a **Minotaur Horn**. Grab the handle on the northwestern wall and pull the pillar out as far as it can go.

MINOTAUR HORN

Use the Head of Helios to find an Item Chest on the right side of the room.

The next section is timed, so be ready to use the Boots of Hermes. Sprint around the pillar and run up its side with the Boots of Hermes. Once on top, jump onto Pandora's cube and then jump onto the metal fencing to the right. The metal fencing slides down, and a column juts out above Kratos. Climb up the fencing and climb along the underside of the exposed column. Hurry to the top and cool the lock there to rotate the room.

This, by itself, doesn't solve any of Kratos' problems. However, it opens new paths. Quickly climb back onto the column before the spinning blades chew Kratos to pieces. Run to the far wall and use it to climb under Pandora's position. Watch the moving spiked box to the right; immediately after it descends, perform a gap jump to the right and begin climbing the wall.

Climb onto Pandora's cube. Rotate the winch as fast as possible to drop the cube. A heated lock appears before Kratos. Quickly cool it to save Pandora's life. Jump to ground level and break the glass with any of Kratos' weapons. Grab Pandora; she's survived the ordeal. Leave with her and open the Health and Magic Chests during your escape. Use the Save Altar as well, then continue to follow Pandora. The two have a short conversation as they leave.

Room From Hell

Enter the next doorway and approach Daedalus. Three Siren Seductresses arrive as Kratos advances, and more enemies surge forward without much delay.

SHE CAN FEND FOR HERSELF

There is no need to worry about Pandora during these battles. She's quick on her feet and is able to avoid all attacks that come her way.

After Kratos kills the first Siren Seductress, Olympus Guardians enter the room. Equip the Nemean Cestus and launch heavy attacks throughout the room. Focus on the Olympus Guardians but treat the Siren Seductresses as targets of opportunity. If they get too close to Kratos, punish them.

Wraiths of Olympus are the next fiends to arrive. The Blades of Exile are a good choice for this next stage of the battle. Use combat grapples and strong attacks to launch your victims into the air. If Kratos is overwhelmed, escape by dodging instead of using magic. Kratos needs to save his magic and the Rage of Sparta for a later stage.

When more Olympus Guardians reinforce their fallen comrades, reequip the Nemean Cestus and meet them head on. Don't kill these warriors yet. Wait for Minotaur Elites to further reinforce the enemy forces. With their appearance, pick up the Olympus Guardians and treat them like Battering Rams.

Cleaning Up the Mess

Search the room for loot once your enemies are gone. The Head of Helios reveals an Item Chest with a **Phoenix Feather** on the right side. Similarly, there is a Red Orb Chest on the left.

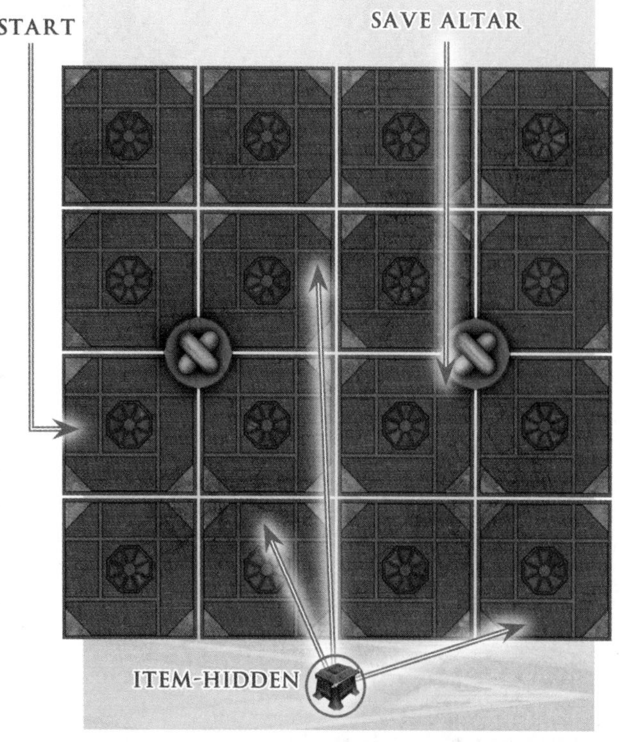

PHOENIX FEATHER

Use the Head of Helios to find an Item Chest on the right side of the room.

Wraiths of Olympus and Siren Seductresses follow the Minotaur Elites. Switch to faster weapons, such as the Blades of Exile or Nemesis Whip, and go back to using combat grapples and air attacks. If any of the Siren Seductresses disappear, use the Head of Helios to bring them back to the light.

A small legion of Olympus Guardians arrives, but Kratos knows how to deal with them. The Soldiers shouldn't be a problem, but things get dicey if you don't thin their numbers quickly. More Minotaur Elites are on their way. If Kratos is starting to hurt, start using magic or even unleash the Rage of Sparta. Kratos is nearing the end, but there are still enemies barring your way.

Use Olympus Sentries as Battering Rams and then focus Kratos' attacks on the Minotaur Elites. Wraiths of Olympus and Siren Seductresses should also reinforce the force shortly after the Minotaur Elites. Let loose with magic and the Rage of Sparta to clear the room of all the enemies.

Pull a lever on the left side of the room. This allows Pandora to slip through a small cage. She steps on a scale and brings out a pressure plate for Kratos to stand on.

Before jumping on the plate, there is a note from Daedalus on the floor. Read that if you wish. Leap on the pressure plate. The platform Kratos is on begins to rise. Once back on top of the container, Pandora runs toward the Chain of Balance.

Record your progress at the next Save Altar. Following Pandora triggers a scene and sends you into the next area.

WHATEVER YOU DESIRE

Before joining Pandora, explore and look on the other boxes. Hidden on these are chests with each of the major collectible items: a **Gorgon Eye**, a **Phoenix Feather**, and a **Minotaur Horn**.

Join Pandora when you are done with this area. She tells Kratos about the Chain of Olympus and why he must destroy it. Kratos is once again bound for Hades.

ACT X

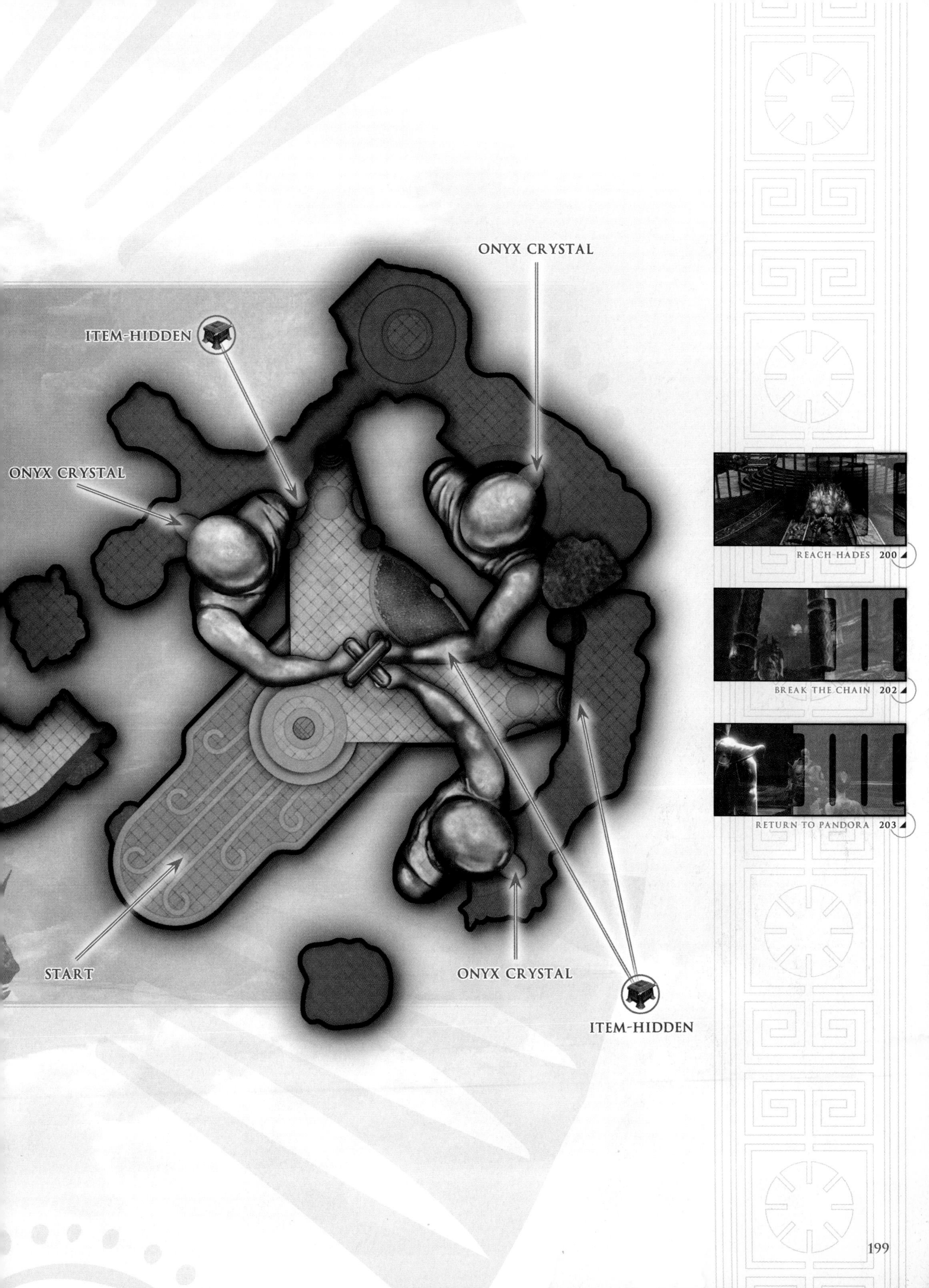

REACH HADES 200
BREAK THE CHAIN 202
RETURN TO PANDORA 203

CHAIN OF BALANCE

BREAKING THE CHAIN

REACH HADES

The Descent

After talking to Pandora, Kratos realizes what he must do. The Ghost of Sparta takes the plunge and dives back into the Underworld. Falling is a lot like flying, so you should be fairly comfortable with the controls. Dodge the obstacles ahead to the best of your ability. The openings are tinier and the obstacles more frequent, but with proper foresight, it's entirely possible to pass through the area unscathed.

Eventually, falling boulders litter the tight space, and Kratos must carefully navigate between them. Find the opening and squeeze through. The end of the column is filled with a series of spokes. Move slowly up and down, and strike to one side of the spokes. Get ready for action, because once Kratos lands…

One More Trail

After landing, Kratos is greeted by a Hades Cerberus Breeder. This monstrosity is tougher than earlier ones and has the ability to spew Feral Hounds from its mouth. While the enormous Cerberus is busy birthing pups, launch your attack! Get ready to block if you see the Cerberus' front legs brace for an attack. Immediately counterattack after blocking its assault to inflict some damage.

Note the difference between this attack and the heavier claw stomp that the Breeder tries periodically. This attack is not blockable! Make sure to get out of the way of the stomp using evasive rolls. Try flinging the Feral Hounds back into the Cerberus Breeder during this fight. It's a move that Kratos pulls off with genuine style, and it helps to kill two...dogs...with one stone.

Continue this until the Cerberus Breeder is dazed. Grapple with it to proceed in the fight. Once Kratos has removed the first of the three heads, things get more difficult.

Two More Heads

A Satyr arrives and immediately rushes at Kratos. Switch to your favorite weapon for killing Satyrs (the Blades of Exile or the Nemean Cestus are fantastic options) and turn your attention to this new foe.

If you're a juggler, use the Head of Helios to stun the Satyr and then try to juggle it into the air. Hit the fiend with aerial combos to damage it and keep it from landing. Or, if you're more interested in ground tactics, back away as much as possible to give yourself space and then use heavy combos (△, △, △ with the Blades of Exile) to kill the Satyr.

Once the Satyr is dead, resume your attack on the Cerberus Breeder. It'll soon be dazed. Close for another grapple and decapitation.

Only One Remains

With the second head removed, two more Satyrs challenge Kratos. This is the final stage of the battle and it's time to give everything you have. Use all of Kratos' magic and then unleash the Rage of Sparta. If Kratos is ever pinned, jump into the air and use the air dodge to escape. Don't forget to use the Head of Helios to give yourself space from time to time.

AN EASIER FIGHT?

There's an alternative strategy if you're gutsy. Instead of killing the Satyrs first, go after the Hades Cerberus Breeder during each wave. This causes only one Satyr to spawn in the final phase, meaning that you only have to kill two Satyrs instead of all three. The downside is that you have the Satyrs on your back for two full phases of the fight.

Focus on taking out the Satyrs first and then return to the Cerberus Breeder. Once the final head has been chopped off, the gates to the north open. You're ready to face the Three Judges.

HADES CERBERUS BREEDER

Hit Points

Hit Points 900

Mini-Game

Right Head Decapitation	1 Random Button
Left Head Decapitation	1 Random Button

Daze Threshold	225 (Head 1)
	375 (Head 2)
	300 (Head 3)
Orbs from Grapple Kill	200 (Head 1)
	200 (Head 2)
	400 (Head 3)

Defense Tactics	Counter
Burn Time	1.5

II BREAK THE CHAIN

Removing the Judges

Enter the Judges' area *but don't trigger anything yet.* Search to the right, near the doorway to the Hyperion Gate. There is a hidden chest there. It's probably a Red Orb Chest now that you've gathered so many items, but originally it was an Item Chest.

MORE ITEM CHESTS AHEAD

There are Item Chests (with Red Orbs if you're full) all over this area. Search with the Head of Helios at the following spots.

- To the right edge of the pool, near the Chain of Balance.

- To the right just after you pass through the first Hyperion Gate.

- After the Olympus Sentinel, go through a tunnel and search to your left.

- The only other chest isn't hidden, but you have to pass through another Hyperion Gate to get it. Look near the lever for this final chest.

Step on the pressure plate near the Judges to get them to release their grip on the chain. Get off the plate and notice two things: the Judges grab the chain again, but a gate opens, revealing a new path to the right.

Walk to the left side and record your progress at the Save Altar. Look the Alternating Chest to the right and the Mixed Orb Chest to the left. Finally, enter the new gate and walk up to the Hyperion Gate.

After exiting the Hyperion Gate, follow the path to the left and smash the Onyx crystal on the back of the Judge's head with the Nemean Cestus. With the crystal destroyed, the Judge is deactivated and no longer holds onto the chain.

Walk back toward the Hyperion Gate. Some Feral Hounds and two Siren Seductresses ambush Kratos. Silence the Hounds and then start working on the Siren Seductresses. Once everything lies dead, move down the path to the right. Faster weapons with sweeping attacks work well here because all of the enemies are quite mobile.

Grab the hidden chest nearby with the Head of the Helios (as mentioned in the previous note). Afterward, double-jump across the gap in the path. Continue to the right. Kill the Olympus Sentinels that attack Kratos and then destroy the second Judge's Onyx crystal. This leaves only one more Judge to deactivate.

When Kratos gets close to the third Judge, Satyrs and Olympus Sentinels attack. This battle should be straightforward. Use the Nemean Cestus to blast the Sentinels while damaging anything else that closes in. Annihilate everything, then walk to the right and climb down the vines on the rock face.

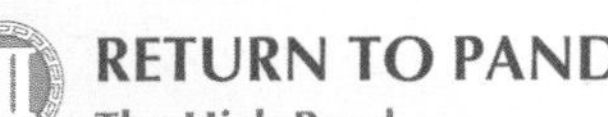

RETURN TO PANDORA

The High Road

It's time for one final trip up the Chain of Balance. There are two stages in this flight. Initially, watch for falling boulders and choose the correct side of the tunnel to hide. Avoid the wooden beams as you go.

Once Kratos has made it through the beams, things open up. It gets easier at this point, as you only have to dodge the boulders. Continue all the way up. Record your progress at the Save Altar and then use a Grapple Point to latch onto the Chain of Balance. Use the Chain of Balance to climb back into the Chamber of the Flame. You are now back on top of the Labyrinth.

Jump off the vines to reach the lower platform. Move to the back of the Judge and break the final Onyx crystal on its neck. After destroying the crystal, climb back up the vines. Look for the next Hyperion Gate; this leads to the gated area back by the entrance. Grab the Item Chest there and use the lever to open the gate. You now have access to both sides of the Judges' platform. This is also the fastest way to get back to the Judges.

Save again and walk toward the Chain of Balance. Break the Onyx rings that hold the chain in place. Kratos flies back toward Pandora when this is complete.

ANOTHER ATTEMPT TO LOOT

If you missed the spare Item Chests your first time through the Labyrinth, make time to get them now. Search with the Head of Helios to find these before you use the Grapple Point. All three chests are on top of the containers.

ACT XI

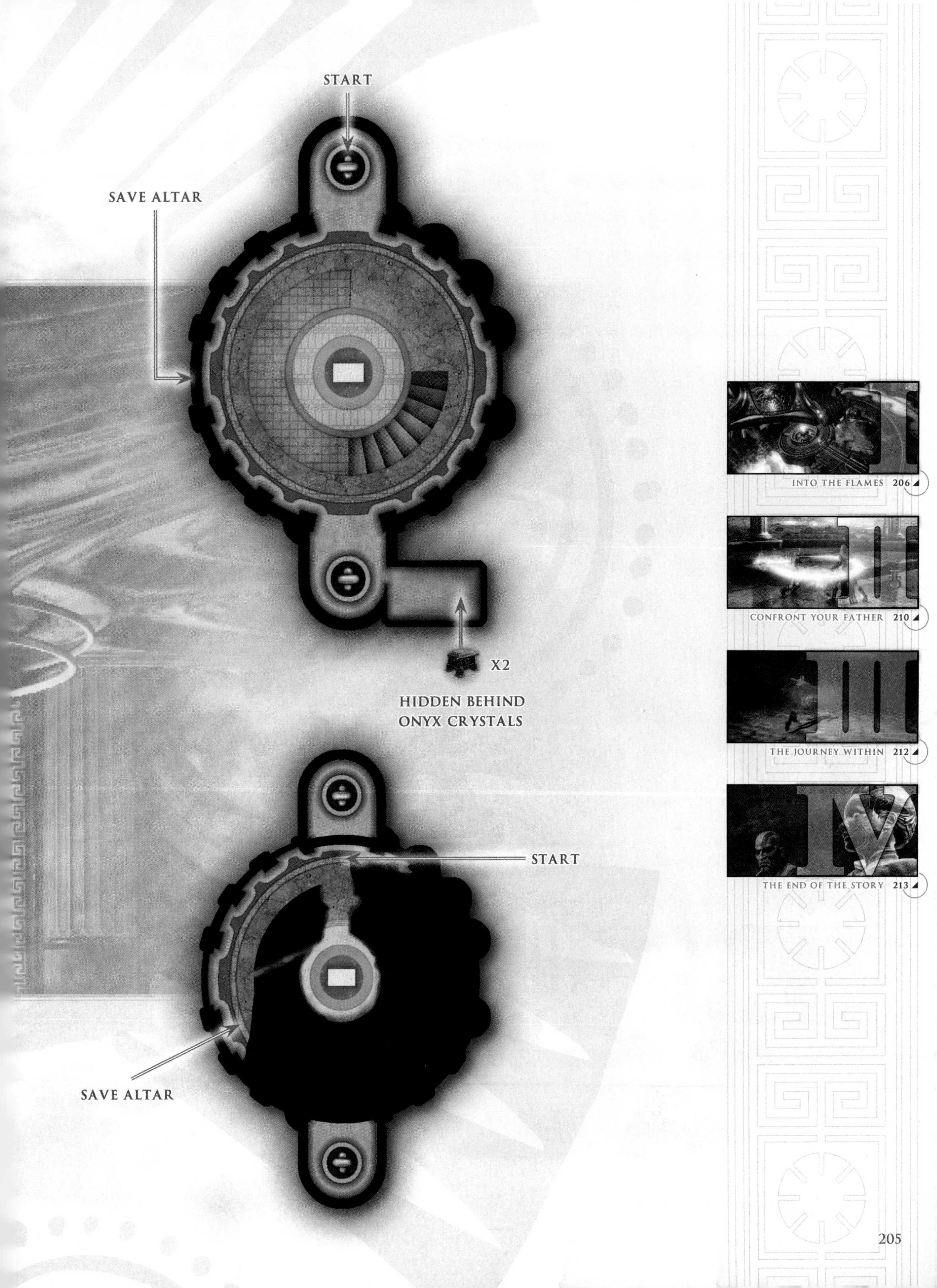
START
SAVE ALTAR
X2
HIDDEN BEHIND
ONYX CRYSTALS
START
SAVE ALTAR

DESTROYED CHAMBERS

MY VENGEANCE ENDS NOW

INTO THE FLAMES

The Return

There is a large staircase before you. Before taking it, walk to the back of the room and slip into an elevated alcove. Open the Red Orb Chests and the Item Chest (if you didn't find them earlier) and then use the Nemean Cestus to break the Onyx barrier. You find two more Red Orb Chest behind the Onyx barrier.

REDEEMING RED

Before proceeding onward, make sure that the Spartan's weapons are as powerful as possible. Use the remainder of your Red Orbs to upgrade as many weapons and items as possible.

If you haven't maxed out your favored weapon at level 5, do so now. The Blades of Exile and the Nemean Cestus are the most common choices for the final battle, but you're absolutely free to use whatever you enjoy and fits your play style.

Climb to the second level of the chamber. Grab hold of the previously unresponsive crack in the center of the room. With the Judges disabled, Kratos' efforts expose the Flame and bring the Labyrinth crashing through Mount Olympus. Most of the chamber is destroyed as a result.

Though shaken by her journey, Pandora now stands ready. An important scene follows, as Kratos decides what he must do. This is interrupted by Zeus, the God of Thunder, Lord of Olympus.

ZEUS

Known to the Greeks as the King of the Gods, Zeus was the master of weather and ruler of the heavens. The symbol of his power was his thunderbolt. He is also charged with upholding laws and justice. Anyone who defies the laws of the world has to face Zeus disapproval (or even worse, the Furies).

Zeus was the youngest son of the brutal Cronos. As Cronos defeated Uranus, so Zeus defeated Cronos. Cronos' wife Rhea was forced to watch as he devoured her children one by one. Zeus was the youngest, and Rhea hid him from his father by sending him to be raised by the Nymphs Adrasteia and Ida, fed by milk from the divine goat Amaltheia.

Zeus defeated his forebears and took control of the heavens. His brother Poseidon was given control of the world below, and Hades took to the Underworld. Between the three of them all things are kept under control.

Gaia had helped Zeus when he was young, but the god's war against the Titans angered her. He'd slain and exiled quite a few of her children, so Gaia went to the giants. She asked them to attack the Olympians. In that battle, the hero Hercules came to lead the Olympians to victory.

Gaia sent Typhon against Zeus as well, but Typhon was defeated. After this victory, Gaia seemed to accept Zeus' mastery of gods and mortals.

Zeus took Hera as his wife. She bore four children for him: Ares, Eilethyia (Goddess of Childbirth), Hebe (Goddess of Youth), and Hephaestus (God of Blacksmiths). Ares was the God of War. In Kratos' mythology, Ares is now dead, slain with the Blade of Olympus.

Zeus' dalliances with other Goddesses and mortals are legendary, and these encounters produced Athena, the Fates, the Muses, Apollo, Artemis, Hermes, Persephone, and Dionysus. His encounters with Greek women often resulted in the birth of Greek heroes and heroines. Perseus and Helen of Troy are good examples.

The Greeks venerated Zeus from ancient times, and so the body of myths and legends about him has grown to be enormous. The Romans incorporated him completely into their pantheon, where he often went by the name of Jupiter or Jove. Ancient art usually depicts him as a powerfully built man with a long beard, bearing a thunderbolt. Sometimes he is accompanied by an eagle. He is also associated with bulls and swans, sometimes taking their form when he visits the world.

An enormous ivory and gold statue of Zeus, fashioned by the great sculptor Pheidias, stood at his enormous temple at Olympia. Although that statue is lost to history, it was at the time regarded as one of the Seven Wonders of the World.

ZEUS PHASE I

Hit Points

?

Even the Oracle at Delphi cannot fathom the true powers of the Lord of Olympus. His abilities are both supreme and unknowable.

The Ghost of Sparta and the King of the Gods enter battle without much delay. The two knock each other back, landing on a small walkway.

This is a narrow spot offering little room for maneuvering. You can only move backward or forward during this stage of the fight. This limited maneuverability means that Kratos is going to have to be in top form with his positioning and evasion.

The Blades of Exile are Kratos' weapons of choice in this battle. Their long reach and the quickness of Olympic Fury, matched with the power of the Spirit of Hercules, are a good combo.

PROVE YOUR WORTH

When Kratos uses his best weapons, magic, and the Rage of Sparta, Zeus has the odds stacked against him. Practice for a short time and he'll even have trouble getting many hits on Kratos.

Spice things up. See how many of Zeus' phases you can beat without using ANY magic or the Rage of Sparta.

Other options include the Nemesis Whip, which is unrivaled in quickness; its Righteous Ascension strikes at exactly the height of Zeus' flight-based attacks.

The Nemean Cestus boasts unrivaled stopping power. Its heavy blows knock Zeus off his feet and into a vulnerable position. Erymanthion Rage and the Nemean Roar are both deadly.

Regardless of your weapon choice, this is a poor time for magic or the Rage of Sparta. Use both sparingly, or not at all, because Zeus is going to come at you several times. Save your strength and pace yourself.

It Begins

Initially, Zeus has four powerful attacks at his disposal: a double punch and thunder clap combo, a furious charging grapple, an aerial lightning assault, and an air-to-ground, lightning-powered melee attack.

There are two strategies to countering Zeus' double punch and thunderclap. The best option is to block and counter the attack. To deal even more damage, wait for Zeus to begin his pounce and then evade toward him just before the hit lands. With perfect timing, Kratos rolls past the god and is free to attack with heavy combos while Zeus swings wildly forward.

Another deadly technique is to grab Zeus while he's in the air. This isn't easy, but practice makes the tactic quite effective. Use Hermes Dash while airborne by pressing the right analog stick toward Zeus. This lets Kratos slip behind Zeus. Grab him before you land and take full advantage of the situation.

THREE STRIKES

Zeus only unleashes his powerful thunderclap if both early hits connect with Kratos. Kratos cannot block this third attack, and there is no time to jump out of the way. Only a well-timed evade can save Kratos.

There are two good counters to Zeus' aerial attacks. The bolts from his lightning assault can all be sent hurling back using Argo's Return. This defensive maneuver is also used to repel Zeus if he dives toward Kratos. Alternatively, use combat grapples to pull Zeus out of the sky.

Don't forget about Zeus' grappling attack. If Kratos has time, jump out of the way when Zeus charges to initiate this attack. If Kratos is grabbed, Zeus drags him across the floor and slams him into the wall. A desperate Context-Sensitive Action is all that prevents Kratos from being brutally crushed against the marble. Move the right analog stick back and forth as quickly as possible to limit the damage to Kratos and toss the Lightning God back against the other wall.

Kratos Stands Defiant

Once Zeus has been sufficiently beaten back, initiate a Context-Sensitive Action. Zeus and Kratos struggle and exchange blows. The skirmish ends with Kratos launching Zeus into the southern wall. Zeus releases a few precious Blue and Green Orbs before returning to the fight. He's now even stronger.

Zeus only adds one new attack to his arsenal, but it is a powerful move indeed. Zeus occasionally uses an electrical attack that affects a wide area. Don't try to counter this. Put all your attention into avoiding damage. Roll or block this electrical assault to give yourself the best chance of survival.

While Zeus prepares the attack, jump and use Hermes Dash to avoid the lightning. Use the Rage of Sparta and follow with your best magical attacks. Kratos is restored if he survives this phase, so there's no need to hold anything back.

After a grueling battle, Zeus' defenses are broken. Grab the God and follow the onscreen directions to destroy the chamber around him.

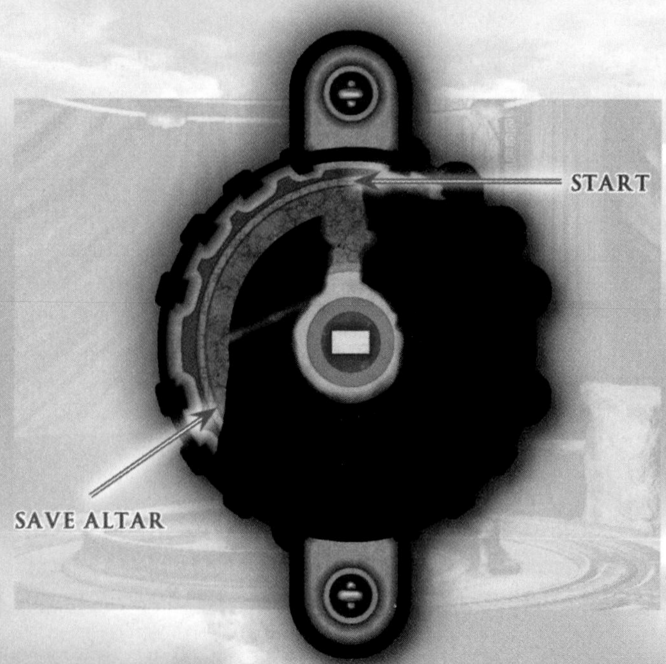

During the fight, Pandora made her way back to the main landing. She's now near the Flame. Another important scene unfolds. When it ends, use the Save Altar by the southern exit. Zeus is waiting outside. Go after him!

CONFRONT YOUR FATHER

Revenge Nears

Nothing stands between Kratos and his revenge. All that's left is to reach out and grasp it. Double-jump and glide over the next gave. Approach the pavilion where Zeus is waiting and destroy what little he has left in this world.

ZEUS PHASE II

Equip Kratos' weapon of choice and ready the Golden Fleece. The god strikes with powerful lightning blows. The attacks are slow enough to counter. Zeus' hands spark with energy before an attack. This is an obvious tell, and it gives you a chance to block and counter the attacks.

There are three types of attacks in this phase: a three-hit melee and lightning combination, a charged punch, and a ground lightning strike.

The three-hit combo is the most troublesome. It can be stopped during the first punch if Kratos blocks it with the Golden Fleece. However, if allowed to hit, the second punch launches the Spartan and you won't be able to avoid the lightning bolt that follows unless you activate a Hermes Dash as quickly as the Messenger God himself.

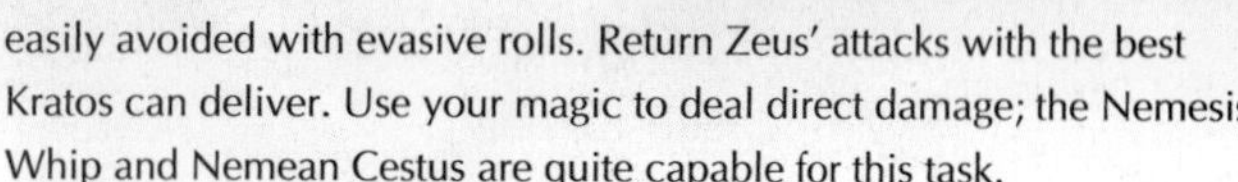

The charged punch and ground lightning strike are easily avoided with evasive rolls. Return Zeus' attacks with the best Kratos can deliver. Use your magic to deal direct damage; the Nemesis Whip and Nemean Cestus are quite capable for this task.

SHORT VERSUS LONG

Don't bother with long combos when attacking Zeus. Chained attacks like the Nemesis Whip's Furious Contempt, Claws of Hades' Hades Agony, or the Blades of Exile's Olympic Fury are all ineffective against the god. Use short combos to maintain an active defense.

A Titan's Rage

While the battle rages, Gaia rises in the background. Once the camera pans back and you see Gaia moving in, stop all offense and focus entirely on survival. The scene ahead is already determined, and getting a few more hits in won't make a difference.

Gaia grips the pavilion. The Titan crushes the structure like it's made of twigs. Zeus and Kratos escape, both falling into Gaia's shoulder, through the wound she received during her ascent.

Kratos lands in a familiar place. Slip through the narrow crack to the left and climb along the vine-covered walls. Return to Gaia's heart. Use the Nemean Cestus to break the Onyx protecting Gaia's heart. Charge a flaming arrow afterward and launch that into the brambles that were just exposed.

Attack the heart directly when the fire dies down. Green Orbs flow from Gaia and into Kratos. Before your task is done, Zeus descends, ready to continue the epic battle.

Zeus Relentless

The Thunder God has added a few maneuvers to his previous list of attacks. The most obvious addition is the ability to create multiple copies of himself. None of these copies are powerful or have the same stamina as the original, but they are a nuisance.

Zeus' copies often begin with an air-to-ground strike, causing the area around them to ripple with waves of lightning. Avoid this by hanging in the air. Use Cyclone of Chaos with the Blades of Exile to increase your hang time.

If too many copies appear, use Army of Sparta to kill many of them simultaneously.

HEALING HEART

During the battle, Gaia's heart plays an important role. When glowing brightly it can be attacked to release Green Orbs. This keeps Kratos healthy during the brutal fight against his father. Make haste when the heart glows; Zeus is just as capable of stealing Gaia's life force!

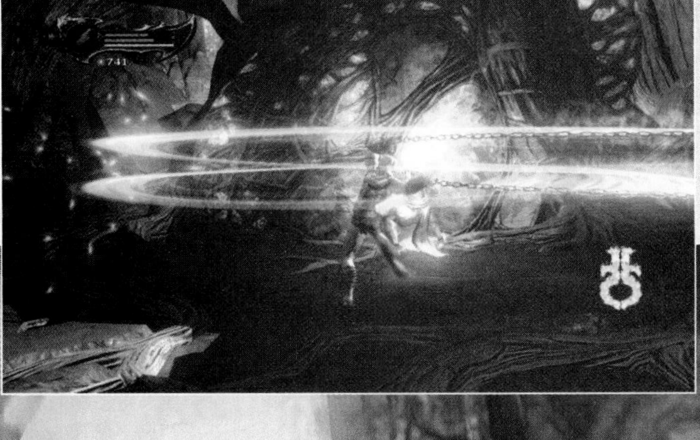

Zeus also unleashes a light volley in the final battle. This attack consists of three small lightning blasts. These attacks are easily deflected or reflected if Kratos uses the Golden Fleece with perfect timing.

Heavy attacks from the Nemean Cestus juggle Zeus with amazing results. This stage of the fight is easy if Zeus doesn't have time to deploy copies. Take the upper hand and juggle Zeus as often as possible. If Zeus gets a moment to himself, he'll protect himself with a lightning blot before racing up to Gaia's heart. To interrupt this, slam the Olympian with heavy attacks before he finishes charging. Failing that, run after Zeus and batter him to knock the deity away from Gaia's heart before he can heal substantially.

Once the god is weary and dazed, go for the kill. The series of button commands in the final sequence is challenging. This requires extreme concentration and a swift hand. If Kratos falters more than a couple times he'll be killed immediately. Luckily, you just passed a checkpoint and won't have to redo the entire area.

When you succeed, Zeus and Gaia are both mortally wounded. Gaia falls, taking Kratos and Zeus with her.

THE JOURNEY WITHIN

Realization

After a time, Kratos recovers. He's now on a cliff side, facing the destruction he's wrought. Nearby is the body of Zeus. Step forward and grip the Blade of Olympus with **R1**. While the Ghost of Sparta walks away, the spirit of Zeus rises. The spirit strikes at Kratos, disarming him and stealing his strength.

Left defenseless, Kratos can do nothing but protest weakly. The scene changes again. There is nothing but darkness around Kratos. Run through the shadows and follow the path that appears at the Spartan's feet. Ahead, he hears a cry and sees a lantern. Pass the object and continue into the gloom.

Kratos stumbles upon a thick trail of blood. Follow it and listen. A fire illuminates a small patch in the distance. Continue forward toward it. As you advance, Pandora speaks, acting as the Spartan's guide. Follow her voice as she creates a path in the darkness. Kratos returns to the lantern, but this time Pandora is there. Press **R1** to hold her.

The trail of blood returns. Walk along the path and meet other specters. Stay on the path. Ahead, another light burns and Pandora creates another path. Move toward the flame. As Kratos draws near, the light is replaced with another memory. Pass this. As you begin to move away, a spirit stirs behind you. Return to the ghost and interact with it. Now you may continue.

Finding Hope

Pandora's voice calls out again, urging Kratos forward. Rush toward the distant flame at the end of the path. The Ghost of Sparta finds himself at the edge of nothingness. He lets his lantern fall and follows soon after it. He hits a red pool of water, and voices from his past cry out from all sides.

Swim to the floating light, reclaim the lamp, and continue. Soon, Pandora's gentle words chase away the other voices. Follow her light toward the water's edge. You have to swim for some time for all of this to occur. Kratos leaves the water afterward.

Climb the steps beyond to find Pandora's Box. Open it with **R1**. Inside, a blue light glows and is reflected in the Spartan's eyes.

THE END OF THE STORY

Fate

We now return to the real world. Kratos pushes back against his father with a strange new power and picks up his Blades of Exile. Swing the blades to banish the spirit.

When it's done, the Spartan throws his weapons aside and charges at his father. Perform the Context-Sensitive Action until Kratos' vision is completely covered in blood. Let go of the controller at that point and rest. You've done it.

FOREVER AND A DAY

Kratos is so filled with vengeance that he gets carried away. The attack sequence continues as long as you keep pressing the button that appears onscreen. To continue, you must let go.

Hope for Mankind

With Zeus dead, Kratos stops to look over the land. Another scene occurs. A brief action concludes this sequence. Follow the directions to complete your quest.

DESTINY'S HAND

One final scene is shown after the credits.

WHO DARES DEFY THE GOD OF WAR!

One of the best ways to improve your performance in *God of War* games is to master decimating each enemy type. Learn their attacks, their weaknesses, and how to turn these against these creatures. This chapter lists all the non-boss enemies in *God of War III* and provides a wealth of information for defeating them.

1 Name of Monster

This is, obviously, the name of the subject. However, they're grouped together by enemy type.

2 Hit Points

There's a wide variance of hit points from the minor grunts you face in the beginning of the game, to the monstrous Cerberus or Cyclopes you battle later. There's a numerical representation of the creature's hit points, but there's also a graphical representation of how tough they are compared to the other non-boss enemies. Obviously, if you see a fully green Omega symbol for the creature, it's no pushover.

Daze: During Context-Sensitive (CS) Actions, there are often stages to the fight that provide an indication of how far you've progressed in the battle. A rotating [CR] appears over the enemy's head indicating that they're dazed. The marks on some of the Omega symbols show how much damage a creature must incur to initiate a "dazed" status. These are often labeled with more descriptive indicators, as is the case with a Hades Cerberus.

3 Mini-Game

These are the types of Context-Sensitive Actions that one may face against the monsters. Some require random button commands, while others may require you to mash [CR]. Take a peek at these to be prepared for what comes.

4 Orb Data

This chart is a graphical representation of how many Orbs are released when the monster falls. The majority of the Orbs released are Red Orbs, or experience. However, a few situational kills provide Green (Health), Blue (Magic), or Yellow (Rage) Orbs. For instance, if you kill a Gorgon Serpent with a CS Kill, both Blue and Red Orbs are released. Keep an eye out for these variances.

Kill: A Kill is an old-fashioned beat down. Inflicting enough damage on most enemies, most, is enough to kill them. This generally provides Red Orbs.

Context-Sensitive (CS) Kill: CS Kills require some type of command to be entered after the enemy is dazed. These often provide different types of Orbs. It's a fantastic strategy to learn and remember what types of Orbs certain creatures release when killed with a CS Kill. It could be enough to turn the tide of battle or provide that little bit of health that allows Kratos to survive for another day.

Stone Shatter: A Stone Shatter is a unique kill that requires a little help from a nearby Gorgon or Gorgon Serpent. Upon their deaths, Kratos rips the heads from the monsters and flash-petrifies any nearby creature susceptible to stoning. Enemies typically are weak at this stage and can be killed easily. Killing monsters in this fashion may provide an Orb variance.

BOSS DATA

The boss data are listed throughout the walkthrough and is not repeated here. The strategies involved in defeating each boss are also provided during the explanation of that boss encounter.

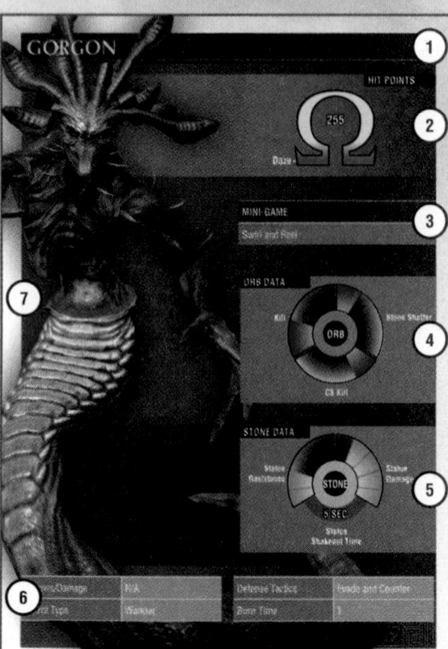

5 Stone Data

This relates to an enemy's susceptibility or resistance to being petrified, how much damage it takes to kill them in this manner, and how long it takes for them to shake out of the stoning.

Stone Resistance: Some enemies are resistant, or even invulnerable, to being petrified. This is a five-stage scale indicating whether they're strong against this or if they're weak. A full five-bar rating indicates a creature that is invulnerable to being stoned. A one-bar rating indicates that it's likely that the enemy will become a statue with little trouble.

Statue Damage: Statue Damage is another five-bar scale indicating how much damage is required to destroy an enemy while they're in their statue form as a result of stoning. A single bar indicates that the enemy will shatter with ease, while a five-bar rating indicates that it'll require much more damage to shatter the statue.

Statue Shakeout Time: This is a simple time limit indicating how long it takes an enemy to shake out from their stone form. A value of N/A probably means that they're invulnerable to petrification.

6 Additional Data

Throws/Damage: Some enemies are instantly killed when thrown, while others may have a CS Action available. This section provides what options are possible.

Patrol Type: Monsters may stroll in a certain pattern while others just roam. This is a general example of what they do.

Defense Tactics: Certain creatures have specific tactics to use against Kratos when challenged. They may block an attack and immediately counter, or dodge around evading Kratos' attacks.

Burn Time: While a few enemies more susceptible to burning, like from the Bow of Apollo's charged shot, while others douse themselves quickly. This is a quick reference showing how long they burn for. A longer burn time indicates that they'll take more damage over time.

7 Enemy Image

This image of the creature may vary between individual creatures, but provides a chance to identify the different creatures at a quick glance.

ENEMY CATEGORY

These are the generic types of enemies. However, just because multiple enemies fall under the same category, Cyclopes or Centaurs, it doesn't necessarily mean that the strategies to defeat them are the same or that they're the same strength. Standing off against a Cerberus Mongrel is definitely a cake walk when compared with a Hades Cerberus Breeder.

CENTAUR GENERAL

HIT POINTS

375

First Daze
Second Daze

MINI-GAME

4 Random Buttons

ORB DATA

Kill | Stone Shatter | ORB | CS Kill

STONE DATA

Statue Resistance | STONE | Statue Damage | 5 SEC | Statue Shakeout Time

Throws/Damage	N/A	Defense Tactics	Block and Counter
Patrol Type	Wander	Burn Time	1.5

CENTAUR COMMANDER

HIT POINTS

375

First Daze
Second Daze

MINI-GAME

3 Random Buttons

ORB DATA

Kill | Stone Shatter | ORB | CS Kill

STONE DATA

Statue Resistance | STONE | Statue Damage | 5 SEC | Statue Shakeout Time

Throws/Damage	N/A	Defense Tactics	Block and Counter
Patrol Type	Wander	Burn Time	1.5

CENTAURS

Centaurs are large creatures that are half-horse, half-man. They wield large, heavy spears and their physique is quite daunting. Kratos is best served by avoiding a toe-to-toe encounter with Centaurs. Instead, he inflicts his best damage by charging at their flanks, or by striking them at maximum range. This avoids the direct spear attacks that Centaurs utilize and it also limits their ability to use their hind legs to kick the Ghost of Sparta.

It's wise to play a hit-and-run game with Centaurs. Roll to their sides, hit them with several attacks, and then roll again even before the Centaur turns to retaliate. This exploits one of the biggest weaknesses of the beast: their inability to turn and retarget quickly.

Charging into Centaurs with the Battering Ram technique is extremely effective. This allows you to frontload your damage, hit hard and fast, and then retreat without worrying about reciprocative attacks. Use any Olympus Sentries in the area to assist in annihilating the Centaur!

Both Centaur Commanders and Generals lack ranged weapons. That's a big advantage for Kratos because he can pick at them at range with the Bow of Apollo. This provides relatively safe damage and a good way to lure Centaurs toward Kratos. Do some damage, then roll away when the Centaur charges.

If you're caught by a Centaur, prepare for a mini-game. Quickly give the left analog stick a half turn in the direction indicated on-screen. This is one of the tougher events and the timing is unforgiving. Kratos incurs damage if you fail, but it's not life threatening unless you're already in awfully bad shape.

CERBERUS

It was once thought that there was only a single Cerberus: a great canine guardian of the underworld. In the realm of *God of War*, that has proven to be most inaccurate. These three-headed dogs are rare, but they are by no means unique. The gods use these creatures to guard their most sacred locations and items. To kill them, Kratos must either remove all three of their heads, or find a way to rip their bodies to shreds.

Because fights involving Cerberus are often long, it's best to learn and identify their attacks quickly so you don't get worn down. Fireballs have plenty of range, while the Fire Breath has more spread to the sides. Both of these attacks are easy to dodge. Roll past the Cerberus each time they stop moving. If you evade early, it's easy to avoid damage.

A Cerberus is a moderate threat while engaging Kratos in melee combat. Avoid getting right on top of the Cerberus because you limit your defensive options. Instead, keep the hound at full blade length and peck away at it.

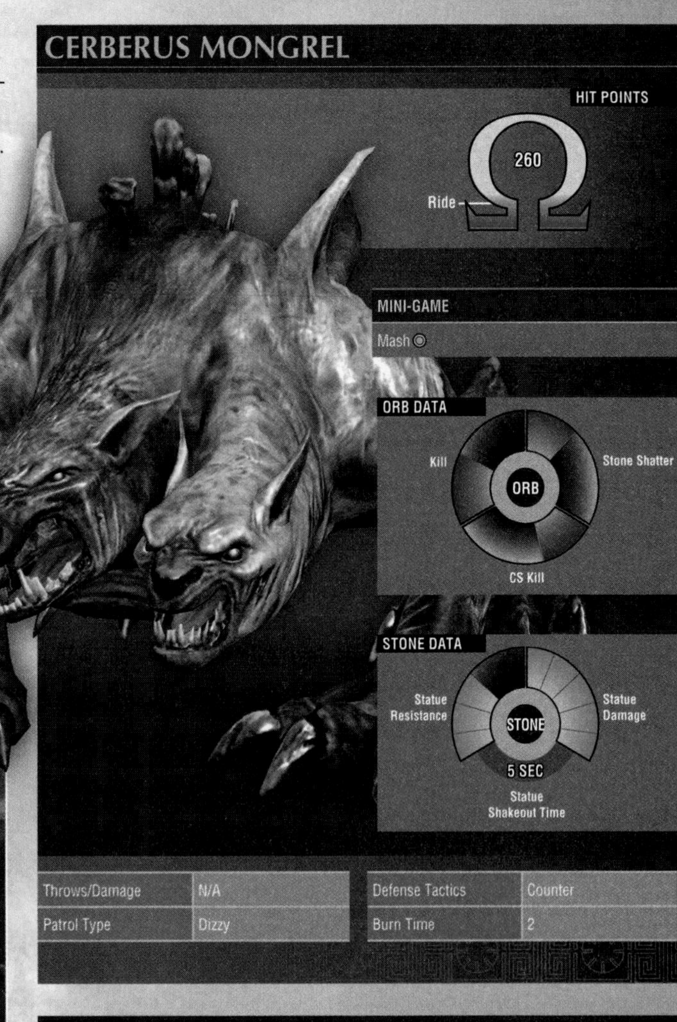

During a standard fight, each Cerberus head becomes vulnerable after roughly a third of the creature's total health is depleted. Approach and grapple the beast to initiate a mini-game that ends with the decapitation of one of the beasts. This doesn't immediately diminish a Cerberus' powers, but it's a necessary step.

The more damage a Cerberus incurs, the more likely it is to unleash its fire attacks. Be aware of this and keep rolling! Keep enemies between yourself and any Cerberus in a battle. This prevents the canines from leaping on Kratos and pinning him down. It also ensures that their attacks hit other targets; that's a bonus for Kratos.

Cerberus Mongrels are the weakest of this breed. The white warrior won't have to rip all their heads off to kill them. Even more interesting, it's possible to ride these creatures after they've been beaten down to a certain point. Once the Cerberus is dazed, there's a Context-Sensitive Action that lets Kratos ride the creature. At this point, you can direct fire attacks against anything else in the fight. It's an enjoyable way to turn the tables against your foes. When the Cerberus takes too much damage, Kratos is forced to destroy it rather than let it run free.

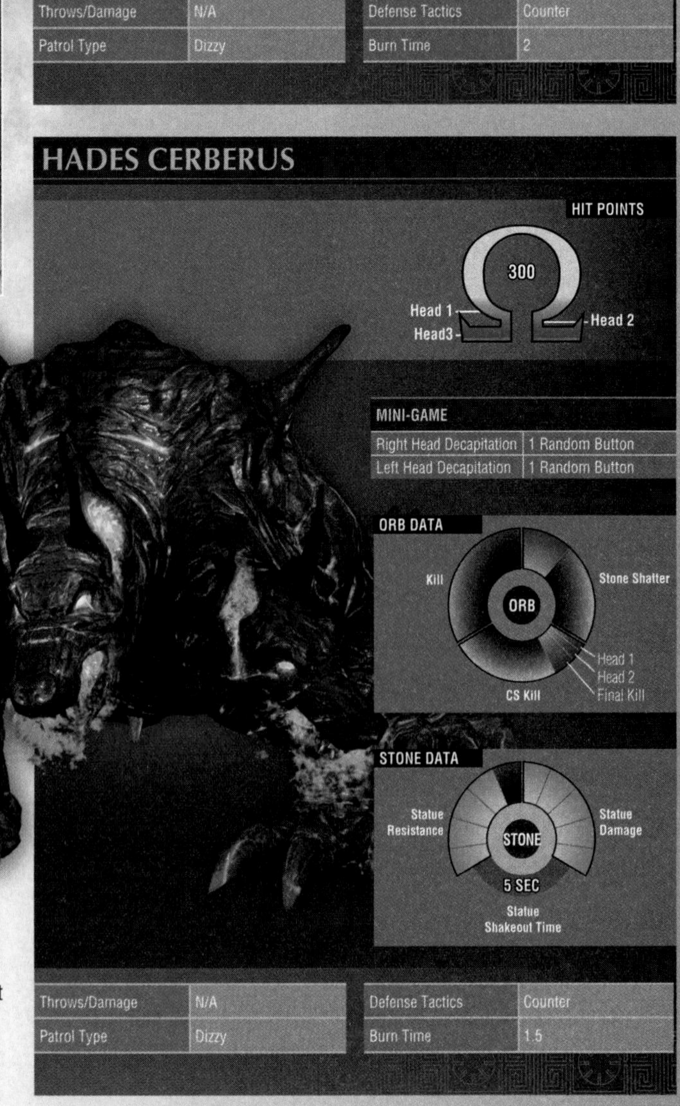

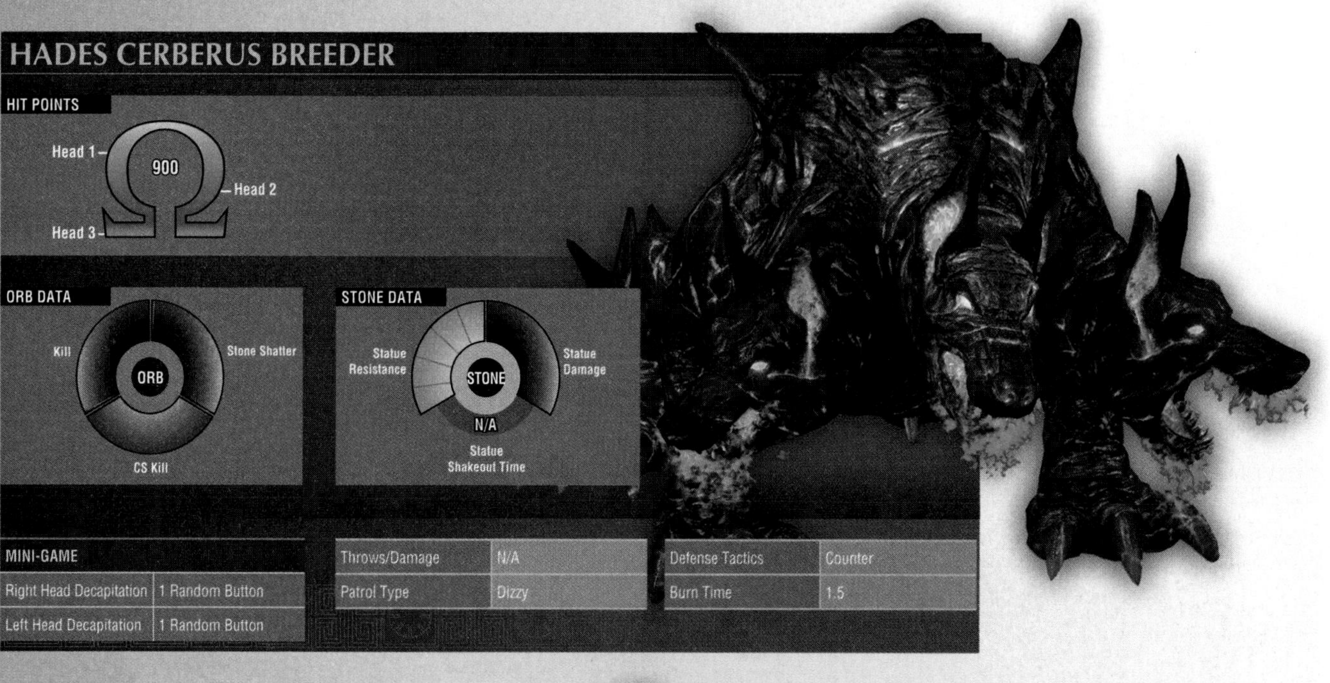

HADES CERBERUS BREEDER

HIT POINTS

Head 1 – 900 – Head 2
Head 3

ORB DATA: Kill, Stone Shatter, CS Kill

STONE DATA: Statue Resistance, Statue Damage, Statue Shakeout Time: N/A

MINI-GAME	
Right Head Decapitation	1 Random Button
Left Head Decapitation	1 Random Button

Throws/Damage	N/A	Defense Tactics	Counter
Patrol Type	Dizzy	Burn Time	1.5

CHIMERA

HIT POINTS

390
Snake – Lion
Goat

MINI-GAME	
Snake	1 Random Button
Lion	Mash ◎
Goat	1 Random Button
Final Kill	Mash ◎

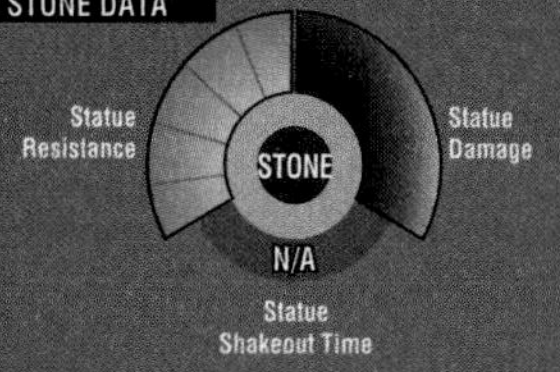

ORB DATA: Kill, Stone Shatter, CS Kill

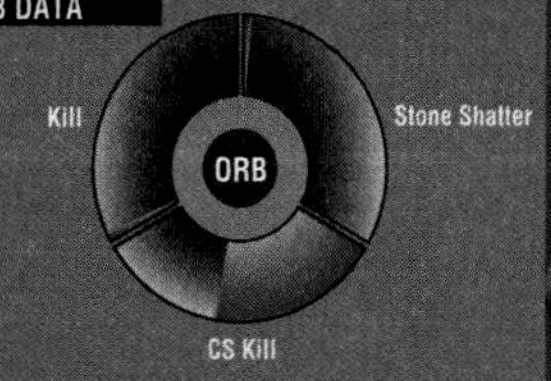

STONE DATA: Statue Resistance, Statue Damage, Statue Shakeout Time: N/A

Throws/Damage	N/A	Defense Tactics: Goat	Evade and Counter
Patrol Type	Dizzy	Burn Time	1
Defense Tactics: Snake	Block		

CHIMERA

Chimera are dealt with in three stages. At first, you must fight their serpent head/tail. During this phase, Kratos must dodge venomous spit and block, or evade, the creature's raking claw attacks. This is the easiest stage of the fight, so it's wise to save magic or the Rage of Sparta for later.

When the Chimera is dazed, run up to it and tear the creature apart. This won't kill the Chimera, but it stops the beast from spitting at you; that's a victory unto itself.

During the next phase, the Chimera rears up and relies on its fire attacks. Expect to evade often while attempting to keep Kratos at full health. Side-to-side rolls are especially good for remaining within combat range while avoiding the flames.

Attack in short bursts and wait for another opportunity to daze and grapple the Chimera. This second attack during the beast's dazed status tears another piece from the beast. The Chimera drops to all fours, ready to fight to its last breath.

Use magic and the Rage of Sparta in the final phase. This damages the Chimera quickly and ends the fight before Kratos can lose a battle of attrition.

CIVILIANS

There are creatures throughout the game that are primarily non-combatants. They can be attacked and killed by Kratos, but they pose almost no threat to him. In Hades, these targets come in the form of Lost Souls. Above ground, they are either healthy Citizens of Olympia or Plagued Citizens.

Killing these enemies yields no experience. However, Kratos receives a small amount of health if he kills the Olympian Citizens or Lost Souls with a grab/throw action.

LOST SOUL

HIT POINTS: 4

MINI-GAME: N/A

ORB DATA: Kill / Stone Shatter / CS Kill

STONE DATA: Statue Resistance / Statue Damage / Statue Shakeout Time: 10 SEC

Throws/Damage	Instant Kill Throw
Patrol Type	N/A

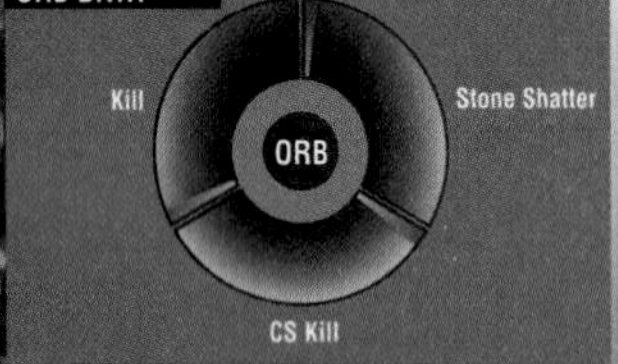

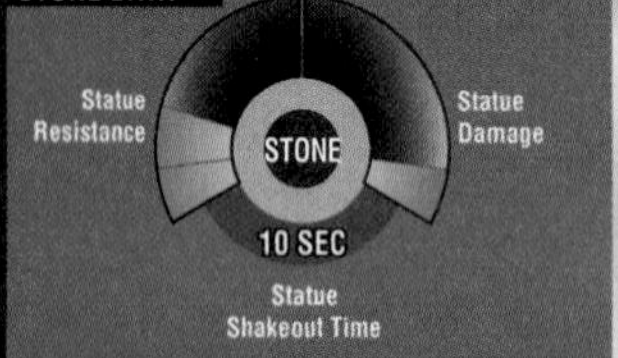

Defense Tactics	N/A
Burn Time	5

OLYMPIA CITIZEN

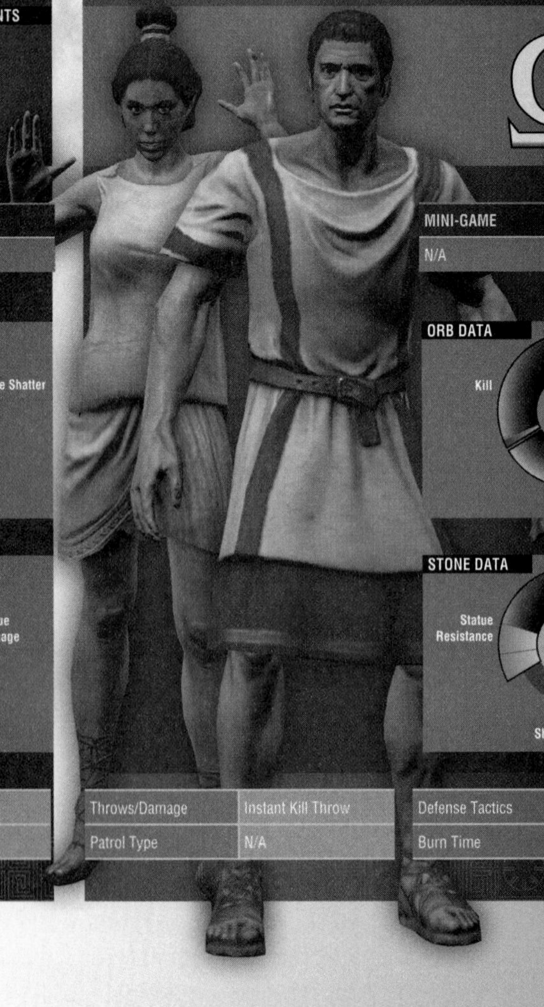

HIT POINTS: 4

MINI-GAME: N/A

ORB DATA: Kill / Stone Shatter / CS Kill

STONE DATA: Statue Resistance / Statue Damage / Statue Shakeout Time: 5 SEC

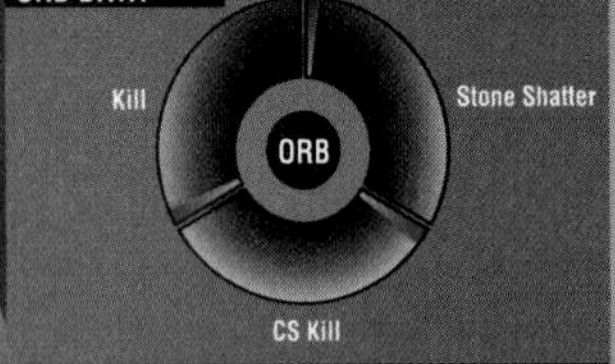

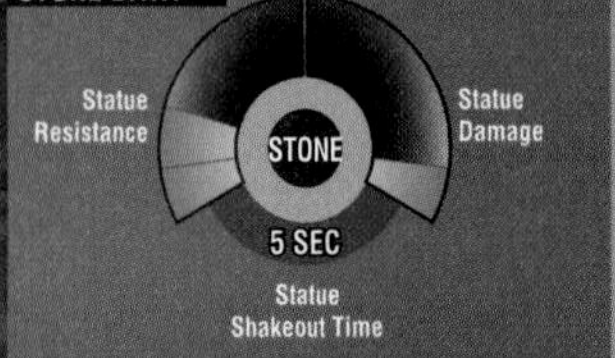

Throws/Damage	Instant Kill Throw
Patrol Type	N/A

Defense Tactics	N/A
Burn Time	5

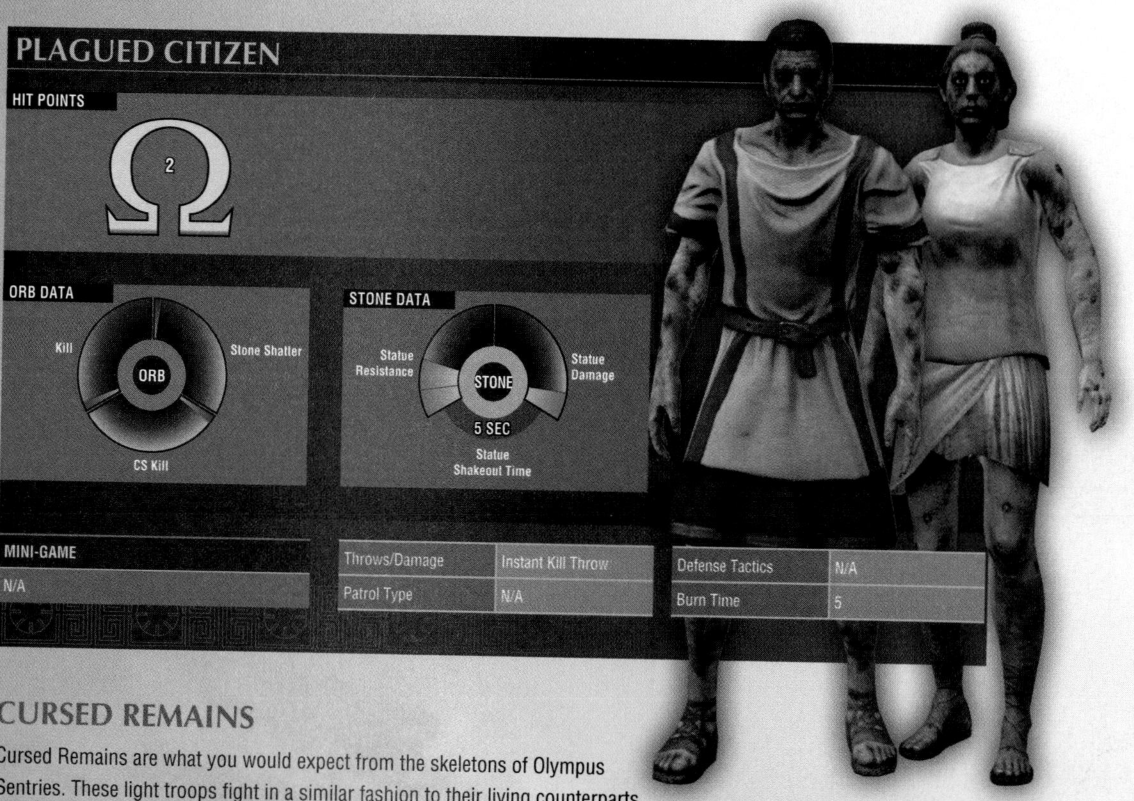

PLAGUED CITIZEN

HIT POINTS

2

ORB DATA

Kill
Stone Shatter
ORB
CS Kill

STONE DATA

Statue Resistance
Statue Damage
STONE
5 SEC
Statue Shakeout Time

MINI-GAME
N/A

Throws/Damage	Instant Kill Throw
Patrol Type	N/A

Defense Tactics	N/A
Burn Time	5

CURSED REMAINS

Cursed Remains are what you would expect from the skeletons of Olympus Sentries. These light troops fight in a similar fashion to their living counterparts, and they're just as easy to push around. Their attacks are blockable, they're extremely susceptible to grapples that kill them, and the Battering Ram technique is incredibly effective when used against groups of Remains.

The only major change when facing Cursed Remains is in their statistics; these enemies inflict slightly more damage and have higher health. If you use upgraded weapons against them you aren't even likely to notice that difference.

CURSED REMAINS

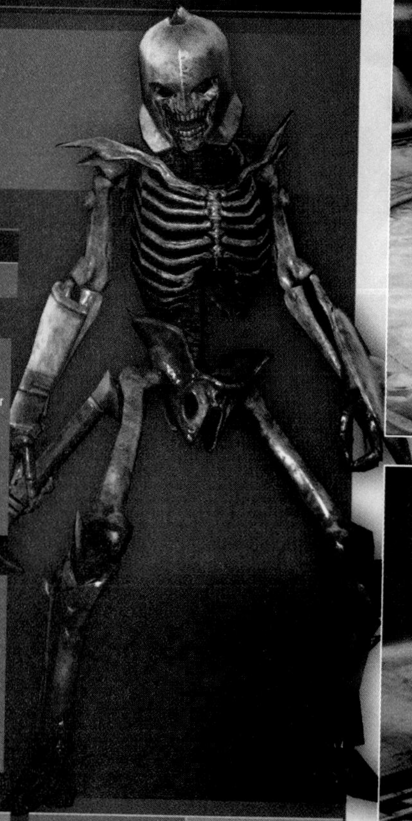

HIT POINTS

60

MINI-GAME
Option Select

ORB DATA

Kill
Stone Shatter
ORB
CS Kill

STONE DATA

Statue Resistance
Statue Damage
STONE
5 SEC
Statue Shakeout Time

Throws/Damage	Instant Kill Grab or Throw for damage
Patrol Type	N/A

Defense Tactics	N/A
Burn Time	3

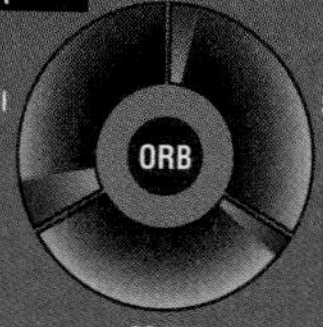

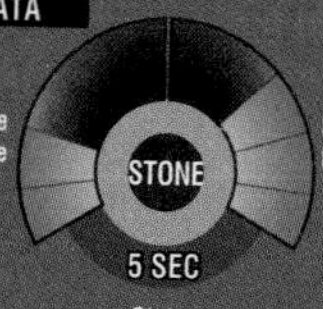

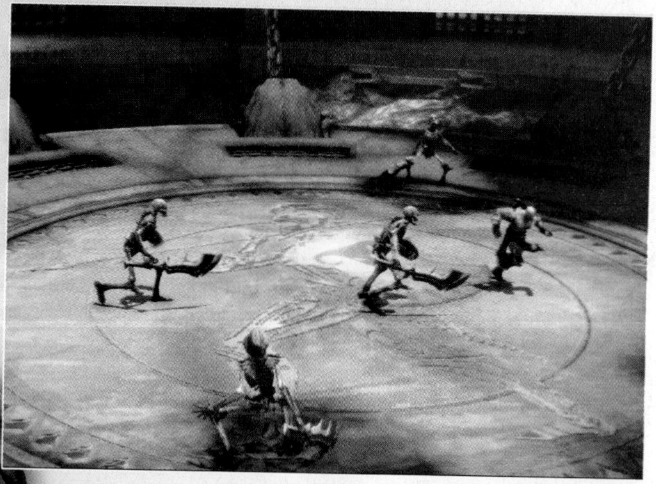

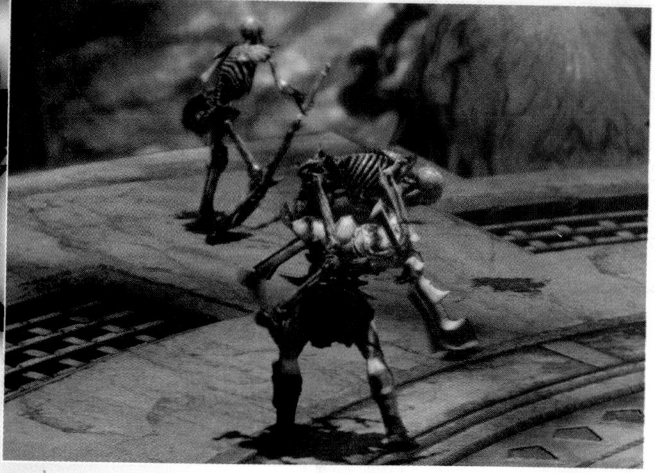

CYCLOPES

Cyclopes are some of the most damaging enemies in the world of *God of War*. Their swinging strikes are devastatingly powerful. Any connecting hit from a Cyclops is likely to knock Kratos back, dealing massive damage in the process. Don't block any of their attacks.

Instead, use short combos and evasive techniques, or take to the air and unleash aerial combos. Cyclopes spend most of their time swinging their monstrous bludgeons near the ground; this is especially true of Cyclops Berserkers. Kratos doesn't need to dodge to avoid their ground attacks if he's already in the air. Attacks like Cyclone of Chaos are useable while airborne and tend to flay Cyclopes without mercy. You must still avoid overhand swings, but that's less of a challenge once you obtain the Boots of Hermes. The Messenger God's boots let you tap the right analog stick to evade even while you're in the air.

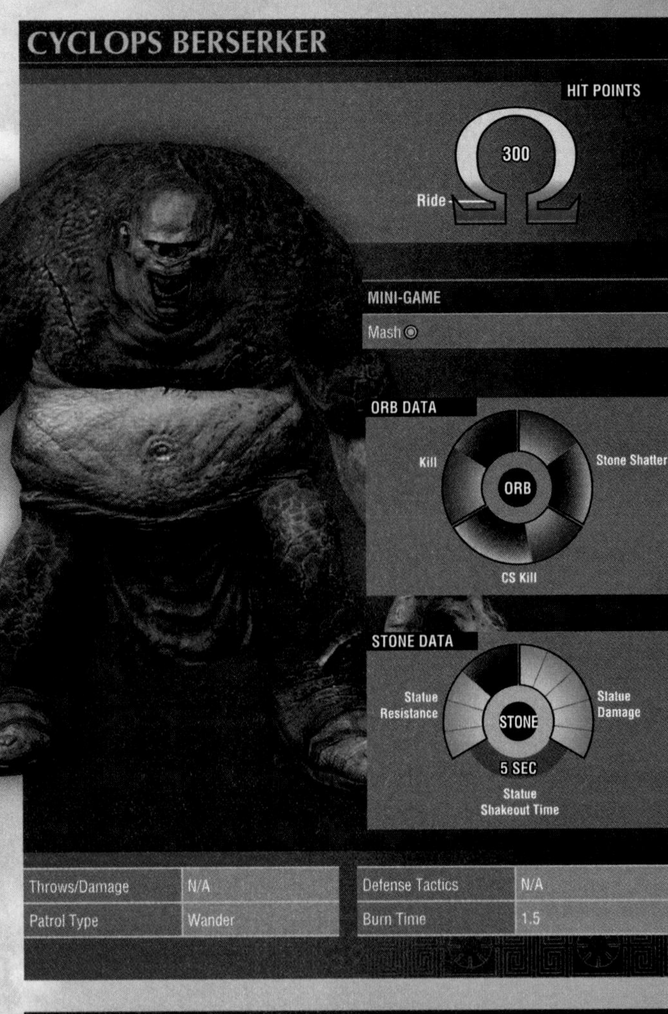

Throws/Damage	N/A	Defense Tactics	N/A
Patrol Type	Wander	Burn Time	1.5

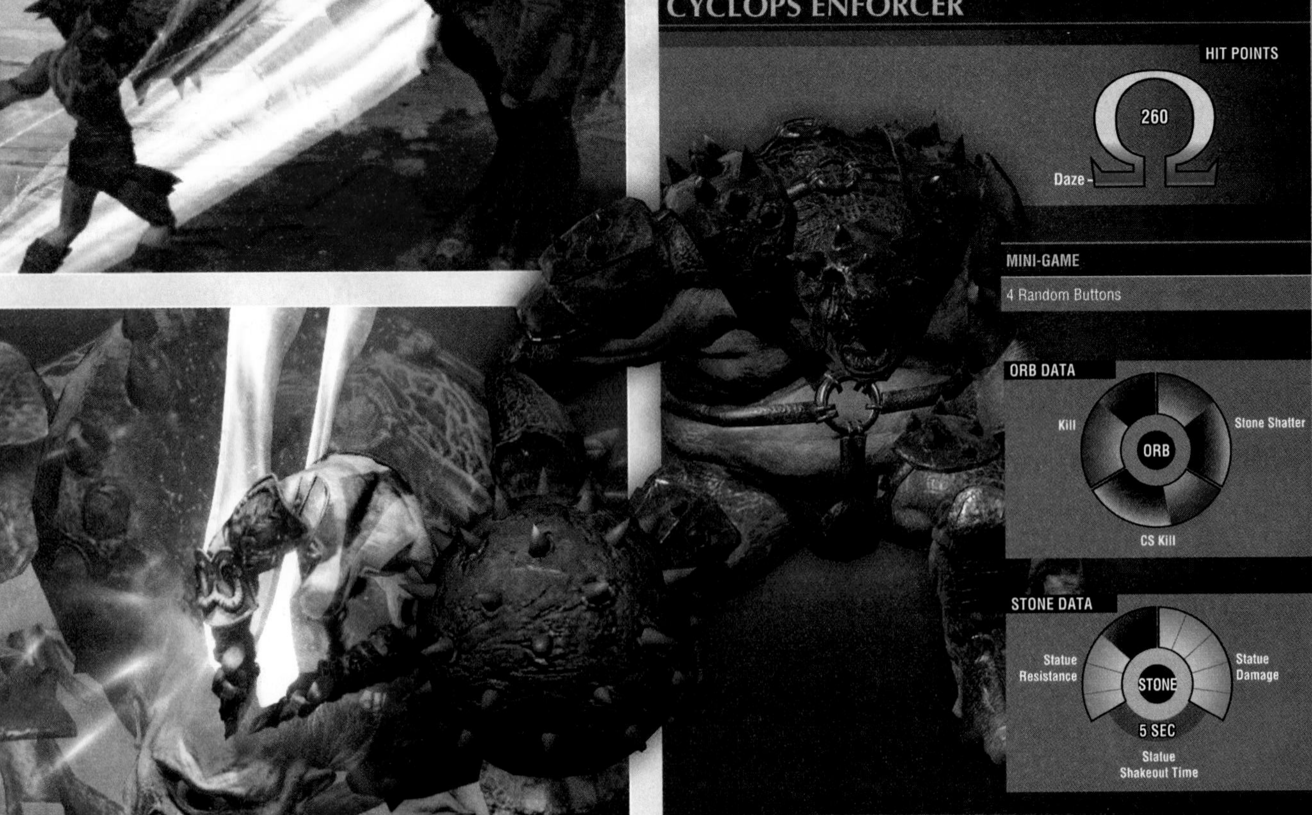

Throws/Damage	N/A	Defense Tactics	Counter
Patrol Type	Wander	Burn Time	1.5

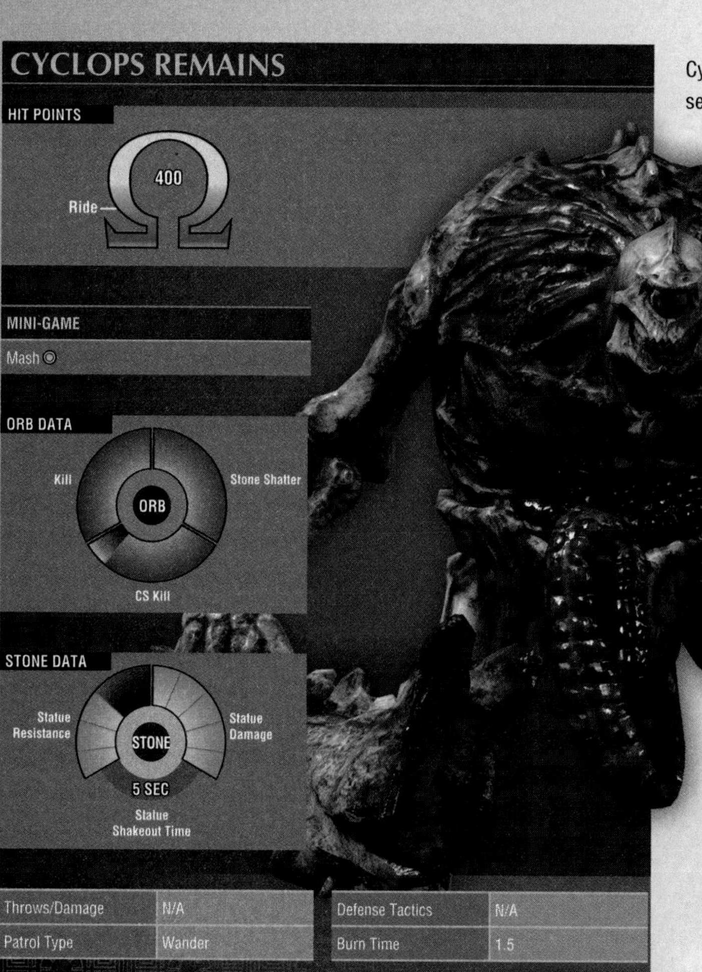

Throws/Damage	N/A	Defense Tactics	N/A
Patrol Type	Wander	Burn Time	1.5

Cyclops Berserkers become unwilling allies in your battles. Wounded Berserkers can be grabbed, mounted, and controlled. Kratos gets to ride them around and force them into combat with their former allies. Use light attacks to push things out of your way and employ heavy attacks to splatter everything with impunity.

Cyclops Enforcers are much more dangerous than their ill-equipped Berserker brethren. They have a mace and chain that covers most of the screen when they swing. They'll attack aerial targets more aggressively, so Kratos is better off utilizing more hit-and-run attacks. Enforcers can't be mounted and ridden, so the fights against them are longer. Fight even more cautiously, back off and roll as they prepare their swings, and use magic to give yourself an edge.

Cyclops Remains rise from the wounds of the Titan Cronos. Lacking skin to cover their bodies, they are animated mounds of muscle, organs, and bone. They appear to have once been Cyclops Berserkers. Like their still-skinned brothers, they react and attack much like the Berserkers and Kratos may mount and control them in the same way.

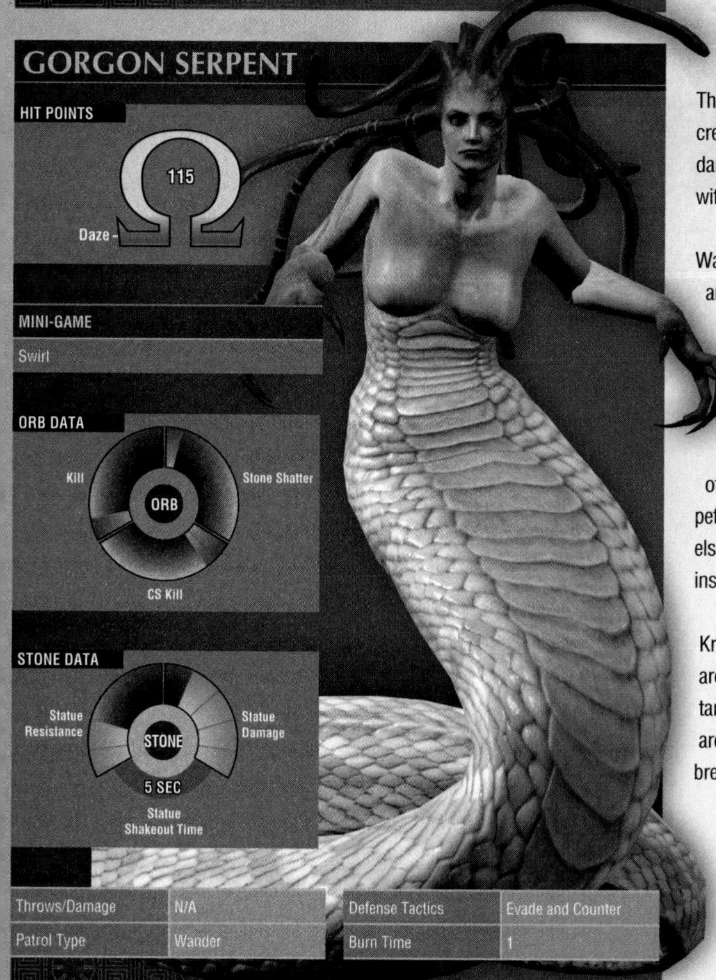

Throws/Damage	N/A	Defense Tactics	Evade and Counter
Patrol Type	Wander	Burn Time	1

GORGONS

These female warriors are serpentine in appearance and have the power to turn living creatures to stone. Though they are quick in melee combat, and inflict moderate damage, their attacks can be blocked without much danger. Block and then counter with Kratos' melee combos when battling Gorgons Serpents by themselves.

Watch carefully for a Gorgon Serpent's tail sweep. This attack covers a huge amount of territory. You can block it, but Kratos has to be on the ball because the sweeps don't take long to lash out.

Both types of Gorgons use their stone gaze differently in *God of War III* compared with earlier titles. Instead of a single beam, Gorgon Serpents send two pulses of energy toward Kratos. Roll to either side, or put plenty of distance between him and the scaly creature, to avoid being stoned. If you're petrified, wiggle left and right with your analog stick to break free before anything else hits you. A solid attack from any other source against a statue of Kratos is instantaneous death and the end of the Spartan's quest.

Kratos encounters Gorgon Serpents before he must face the real thing. Gorgons are more dangerous than their sisters. Instead of unleashing two pulses to turn targets to stone, Gorgons shine their gazes over an area. This slows anything in the area-of-effect and eventually turns any targets to stone. Roll away from this cone to break its debilitating effect.

Both types of Gorgons are substantially more troublesome when joined by creatures to support them. It's harder to stand and block when you must worry about enemies attacking from multiple fronts. Once you start dodging, it's difficult to judge when to stop and block. For this reason, a more mobile defense without blocking is better against Gorgons that have supporting troops. Evade frequently and counter when an opening presents itself.

All weakened Gorgons can be grappled and killed without much trouble. In previous *God of War* games this came at a slight cost to your experience. That is no longer the case. Gorgons and Gorgon Serpents are worth full experience when grappled and killed; in addition, they provide Blue Orbs to restore some of your magic.

Also new to *God of War III* is a secondary benefit for killing Gorgons by grabbing them. Kratos finishes his mini-game by ripping the Gorgons' heads off. This discharges a burst of their Gorgon Gaze, nailing everything nearby—except for Kratos. If there are many weaker enemies surrounding the Gorgon, this becomes an effective way to suppress them. Shatter their statues afterward for bonus experience and easy kills.

GORGON

HIT POINTS: 255 (Daze -)

MINI-GAME: Swirl and Reel

ORB DATA: Kill / Stone Shatter / CS Kill

STONE DATA: Statue Resistance / Statue Damage / 5 SEC Statue Shakeout Time

Throws/Damage	N/A	Defense Tactics	Evade and Counter
Patrol Type	Wander	Burn Time	1

HADES ARM

Anyone who spends time in Hades gets to know these spirits. Hades Arms rise from the ground and try to grapple their victims or swipe at them. These things aren't especially dangerous, but they're worth a tiny amount of experience and take little time to kill. Stay at medium range to kill Hades' Arms safely.

The only time you're at risk from Hades Arms is when they grab and hold Kratos in place during a big fight. This gives heavier enemies a chance to get free hits against Kratos. Wiggle your left analog stick left and right to break free before that happens.

During the Hades boss fight, these Arms are worth Green Orbs (for health). This allows Kratos to restore himself from damage during the long encounter.

HADES ARM

HIT POINTS: 4

ORB DATA: Kill / Stone Shatter / CS Kill

STONE DATA: Statue Resistance / Statue Damage / 5 SEC Statue Shakeout Time

MINI-GAME: N/A

Throws/Damage	Instant Kill Throw	Defense Tactics	N/A
Patrol Type	N/A	Burn Time	N/A

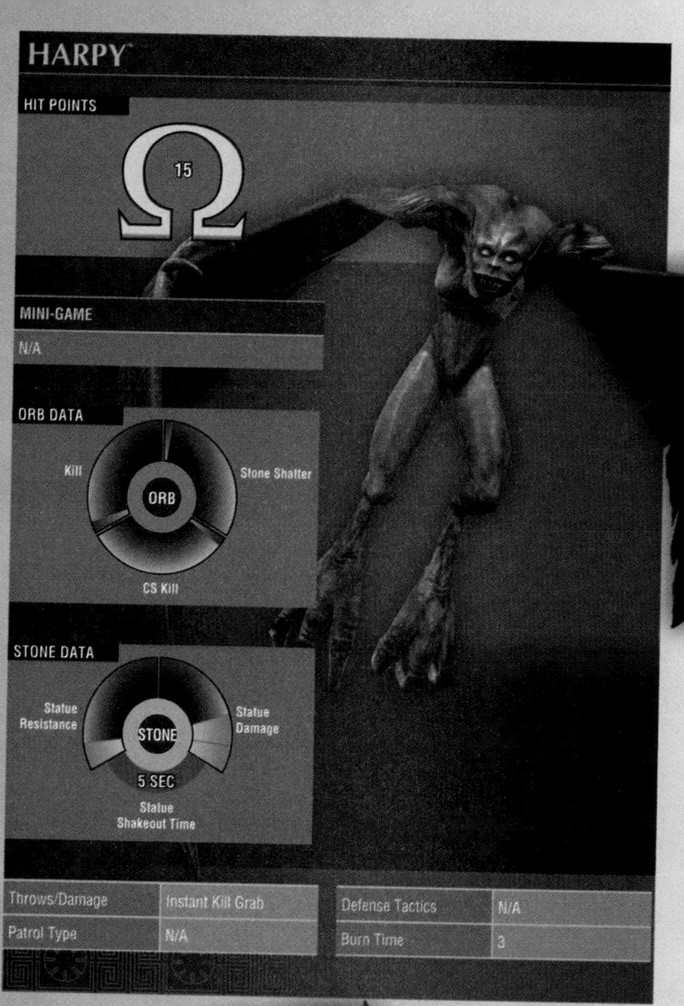

HARPY

HIT POINTS: 15

MINI-GAME: N/A

ORB DATA: Kill / Stone Shatter / CS Kill

STONE DATA: Statue Resistance / Statue Damage / 5 SEC Statue Shakeout Time

Throws/Damage	Instant Kill Grab	Defense Tactics	N/A
Patrol Type	N/A	Burn Time	3

HARPIES

Harpies don't usually impose much of a threat, but they excel at distracting Kratos. These flying beasts remain in the air where it's harder to hit them. Leap to get some altitude and use either light weapon combos or grapple attacks. When dealing with Harpies that are spread out, it's easier to grab one at a time and kill them instantly. You won't miss if you get close and use ◎. If the Harpies group together, weapon combos are more effective because they kill a few simultaneously. Aerial attacks, such as Cyclone of Chaos, are quite effective in these fights.

Watch the ground while you're fighting Harpies. A red icon appears when Harpies ready their dive attacks. Either roll away if you're inside the red circle or jump into the air to avoid the diving assault. This attack is especially ruthless if Kratos has become stoned by a Gorgon's Gaze.

Harpies also use a sweeping attack as they strafe along the ground. This isn't as hard to avoid as the dive, and Kratos won't take heavy damage even if struck by the attack. This is a blockable move, so counters work well against it.

Once the Harpies miss with their attack they remain near the ground for a short time. This makes them especially vulnerable; kill them before they take to the sky again unless you're threatened by other targets.

When Harpies are airborne you can still grab them, but this won't instantly kill the creatures. Instead, Kratos throws them down. Land and finish off the Harpies before they take to the air once again.

HARPY QUEEN

HIT POINTS: 80

MINI-GAME: N/A

ORB DATA: Kill / Stone Shatter / CS Kill

STONE DATA: Statue Resistance / Statue Damage / 5 SEC Statue Shakeout Time

Throws/Damage	Instant Kill Grab (While Riding)	Defense Tactics	N/A
Patrol Type	N/A	Burn Time	2

Harpy Queens are more of a blessing than a bane. Use these tougher flying monsters cross large gaps. Lure them toward Kratos by firing at them with the Bow of Apollo. Incensed, the Harpy Queens fly over and expose themselves to attack.

Leap toward the creatures and grapple with them. This gives Kratos control of the bird—temporarily. Use the left analog stick to fly toward the far side of any nearby gaps. Harpy Queens drop Kratos if he doesn't stab them frequently while flying, so you can only go so far on a single Queen. If the path is too long for the Harpy Queen to survive, kill the first and leap to a second before Kratos falls.

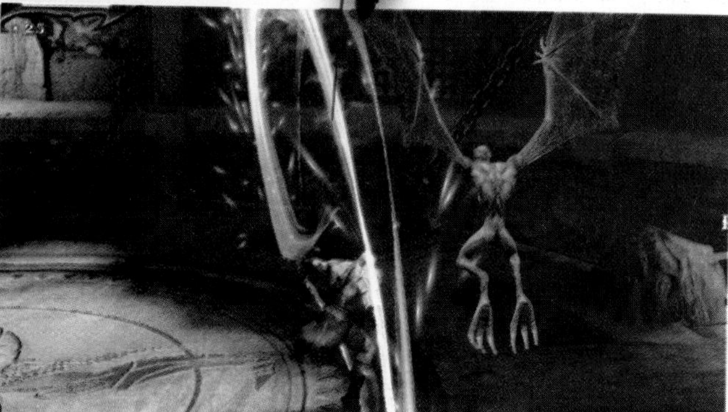

HOUNDS

All Hounds are fairly easy targets, whether you're fighting them in Hades or elsewhere. They attack in large packs and that's the only way that they pose a serious threat. Don't let the group circle around you; this makes it easier for them to dogpile on the Spartan. All the creatures leap onto Kratos and nip at him until he's able to throw them off.

Use heavier attacks that cover a wide area to slaughter multiple Hounds at once. If you're in a more desperate situation with other enemies as well, use Army of Sparta to kill the Hounds while damaging heavier troops.

When Kratos has room to retreat, backpedal and fire the Bow of Apollo to kill pack members without taking any risks. The Hounds won't catch up to Kratos, and he'll eventually thin the ranks enough to make his fight less of a concern.

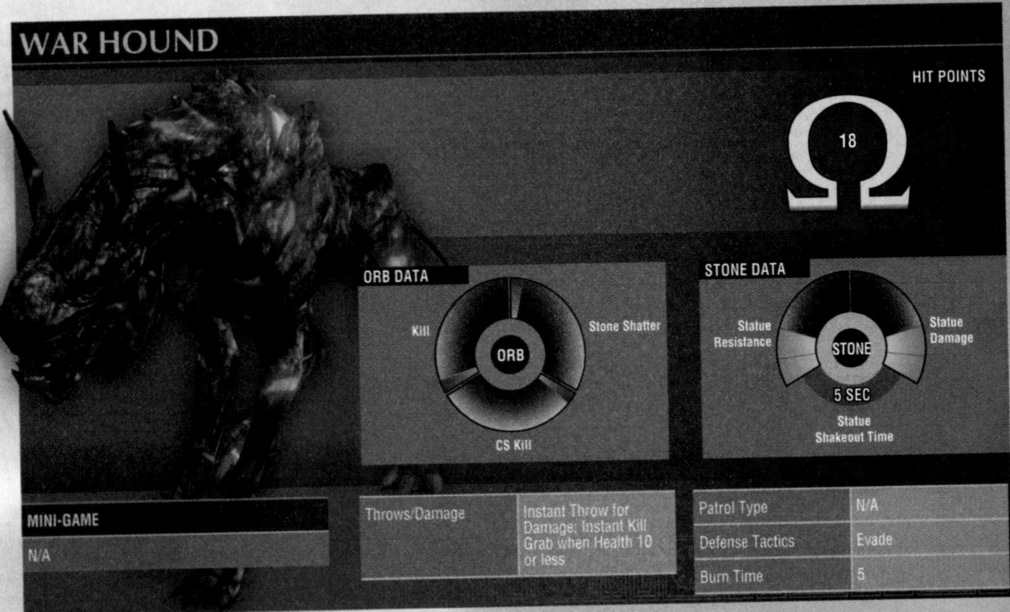

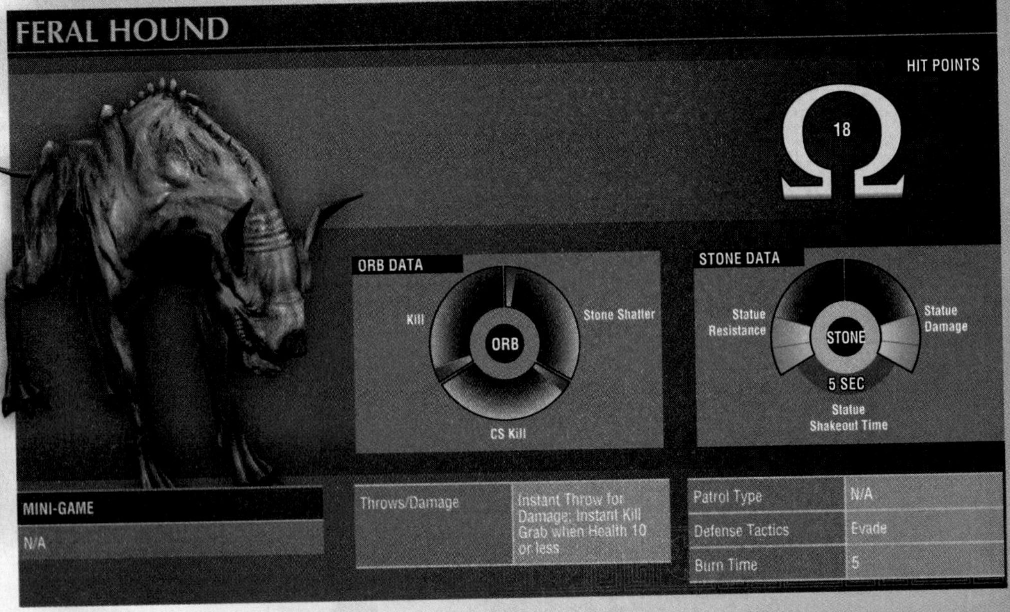

MINOTAURS

All Minotaurs are exciting to fight, but they're not easy targets to take down. They often arrive with support, either from other Minotaurs or from lesser troops in the area. Your first goal is to eliminate the easiest targets first. If there are Olympus Sentries around, grab them and use them as Battering Rams against the Minotaurs and each other.

When Minotaurs are alone, you must deal with two fundamental problems: their heavy attacks and their charges. Roll to avoid both of these, and be aware that Minotaurs can change direction when charging, especially if they run into a wall or obstacle.

MINOTAUR ELITE

HIT POINTS

225

Daze

MINI-GAME

Swirl

ORB DATA

STONE DATA

Throws/Damage	N/A	Defense Tactics	Block and Counter
Patrol Type	Wander	Burn Time	1

LABRYS MINOTAUR

HIT POINTS

375

Daze

MINI-GAME

Swirl

ORB DATA

STONE DATA

Throws/Damage	N/A	Defense Tactics	Block and Counter
Patrol Type	Wander	Burn Time	1

Kratos' heaviest attacks are suitable against Minotaurs because they break through their defenses. Otherwise, you waste a fair amount of your damage against them. Weapons like the Nemean Cestus are quite good, as are heavy attacks from the Blades of Exile.

Minotaur Brutes and Minotaur Elites are similar except in sheer power. Minotaur Elites have more health, a reflection of the heavy armor they wear. For faster kills against these foes, master block-and-counter techniques instead of relying purely on defensive rolls. Properly countered attacks open the way for heavy damage without wasting much time.

Labrys Minotaurs are the heaviest brutes of the bunch. They have hand axes that launch throw at Kratos, augmenting the Minotaurs' offensive options. They won't do this often, so keep it in mind unless you want to be caught off guard. Kratos is able to grab fallen Labrys from the ground and return the favor against his enemies!

OLYMPUS ARCHER

Olympus Archers are quite similar to Olympus Sentries in that they're easy for your enemies to deploy, but take little work to bring down. Archers stand their ground wherever they spawn and use their bows to harass Kratos from range. Staying in motion allows Kratos to avoid most of their attacks.

Remember that you lose some of your opportunities while Olympus Archers are active. For instance, you can't start a long combo without fear of being shot. Taking a hit does damage; it also breaks your combo and leaves Kratos open to damage from nearby enemies.

To avoid that entire scenario, it's usually best to kill Olympus Archers first. They're easily dispatched at close range with a grab attack (◎) or any simple combo. Another option is to kill the Archers from long range. Kratos eventually receives the Bow of Apollo! It's incredible for turning enemy Archers into pincushions. Fire a few shots into each and watch them disappear.

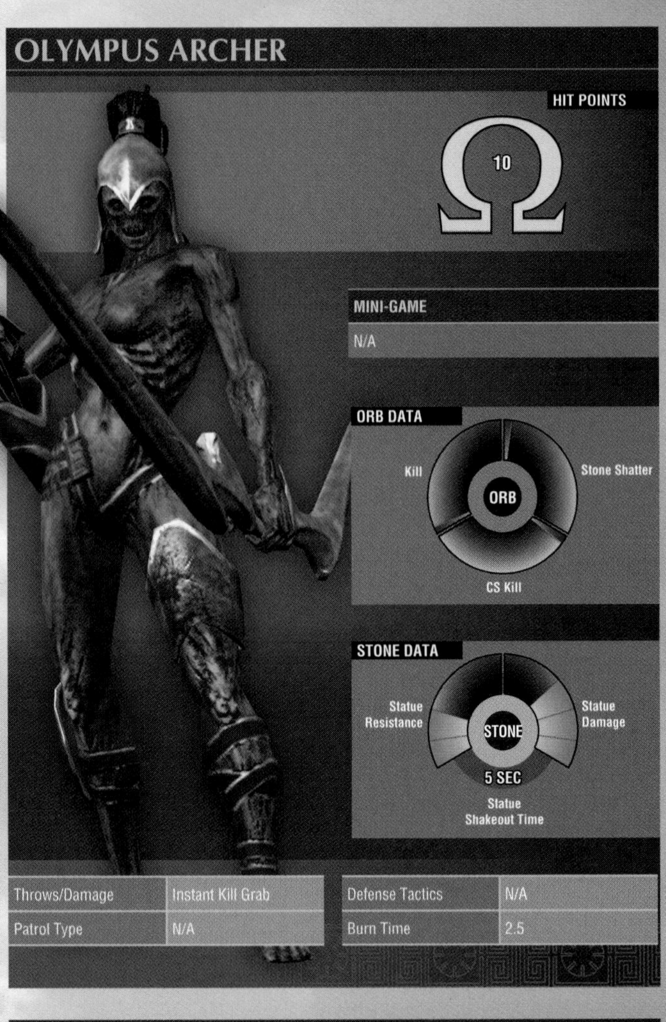

OLYMPUS FIEND

Olympus Fiends are only found in a few places. They utilize a mixture of melee attacks and thrown grenades to do their damage. Kratos has a hard time dealing with them up close because their blasts damage things over an area-of-effect. To avoid this, backpedal while facing Fiends and kill them with ranged attacks. This is an economical way to survive fights against Olympus Fiends.

Don't approach the bodies of these enemies. There is a chance that the foe is still partially alive, ready to make a final attack against Kratos. These troops occasionally use grenades when they're on the ground. Steer clear of their crawling torsos to play it safe.

OLYMPUS GUARDIANS AND SENTINELS

OLYMPUS GUARDIAN

HIT POINTS

30

MINI-GAME

Option Select after shield is broken

ORB DATA

STONE DATA

Throws/Damage	Instant Kill Grab or Throw for Damage after Shield is Broken
Patrol Type	N/A

Defense Tactics	Block
Burn Time	2.5 - 3

Olympus Guardians and Sentinels have very different stats, but their purpose is identical. These troops carry massive shields that prevent almost all damage from getting through. Both types of enemies group together and protect each other's flanks—quite effectively.

To defeat these enemies early in the game, Kratos must use allies. He'll ride Cyclops Berserkers into their midst and blast the shielded troops aside. Or, he'll fight against Gorgon Serpents and let the Gorgon's stony gaze petrify the Olympian troops.

OLYMPUS SENTINEL

HIT POINTS

90

Daze -

MINI-GAME

Option Select after Shield is Broken and Circle Appears

ORB DATA

STONE DATA

Throws/Damage	Instant Kill Grab or Throw for Damage after Shield is Broken and Circle Appears

Patrol Type	N/A
Defense Tactics	Block
Burn Time	2.5 - 3

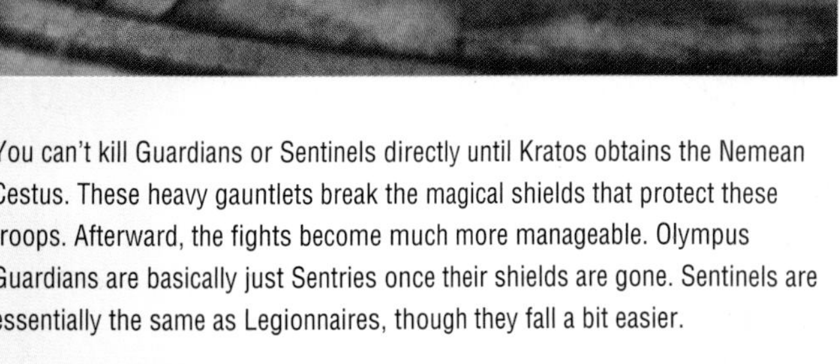

You can't kill Guardians or Sentinels directly until Kratos obtains the Nemean Cestus. These heavy gauntlets break the magical shields that protect these troops. Afterward, the fights become much more manageable. Olympus Guardians are basically just Sentries once their shields are gone. Sentinels are essentially the same as Legionnaires, though they fall a bit easier.

OLYMPUS LEGIONNAIRE

Olympus Legionnaires are armed with heavy axes that pose a genuine threat to Kratos. These enemies wear heavy armor, take longer to kill than Sentries, and cannot be grappled until their health is low.

Olympus Legionnaires' faster attacks are blockable. Block and counterattack to inflict substantial damage against these enemies if you're experienced with the Golden Fleece. If that isn't your style, damage a single Legionnaire, grab them when they're badly wounded, and use them as a Battering Ram to damage their entire legion.

If you have magic that you're willing to spend, Army of Sparta works quite well. Olympus Legionnaires often come in large squads, and this spell damages them all equally, especially if your Blades of Exile have been upgraded.

The worst thing about Olympus Legionnaires is their charged attack. This swing takes a moment to prepare, giving Kratos time to roll away. Do so with haste! Blocking won't work, and the strikes produce a modest shockwave. Rolling to either side works better than rolling backward, but either method succeeds as long as you start early.

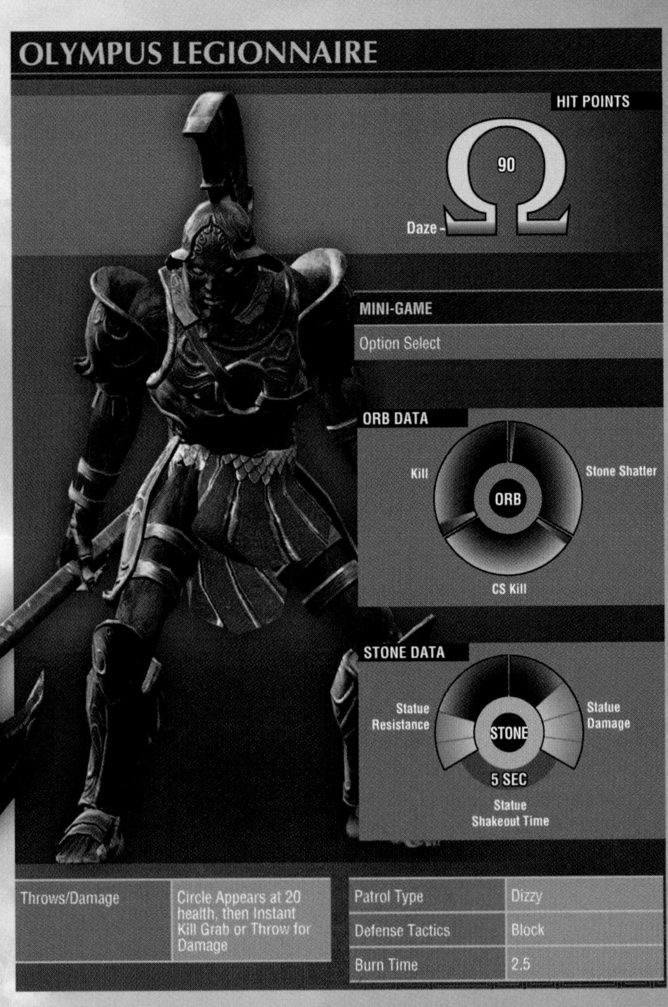

Throws/Damage	Circle Appears at 20 health, then Instant Kill Grab or Throw for Damage	Patrol Type	Dizzy
		Defense Tactics	Block
		Burn Time	2.5

OLYMPUS SENTRY

These are the basic ground troops of Olympus at this stage of the war. Zeus has countless numbers of these troops at his disposal, and he'll throw them against you with fair consistency and outright impunity. They aren't powerful. They use basic attacks at fairly short range, and everything in their repertoire is blockable and easy to dodge. Only in large numbers do these foes pose any threat, and even then there are quite a few ways to get out of danger.

First, combos that cover a wide area are especially good for disrupting and killing groups of Sentries. The time-tested Plume of Prometheus (□, □, △) works wonderfully. Many types of magic are effective as well, though it's sometimes a waste of your resources to use magic in these "lighter" engagements.

A new trick in *God of War III* that clears rank-and-file enemies is the Battering Ram. Grab the nearest Sentry (○) and press □ to begin a Battering Ram charge. Kratos picks up his victim and mows through nearby enemies. This inflicts damage to the "ram" and everyone that can't avoid it.

Use this to clear large groups of Olympus Sentries quickly. Also, consider its use against mini-bosses. A good example is the first Centaur Commander that Kratos faces early in the game. The Centaur appears with Olympus Sentries as his support. Turn this against him by repeatedly ramming the creature with his own troops. This allows Kratos to remain mobile, deal damage, and pick off some of the Sentries while retaining his focus on the Centaur!

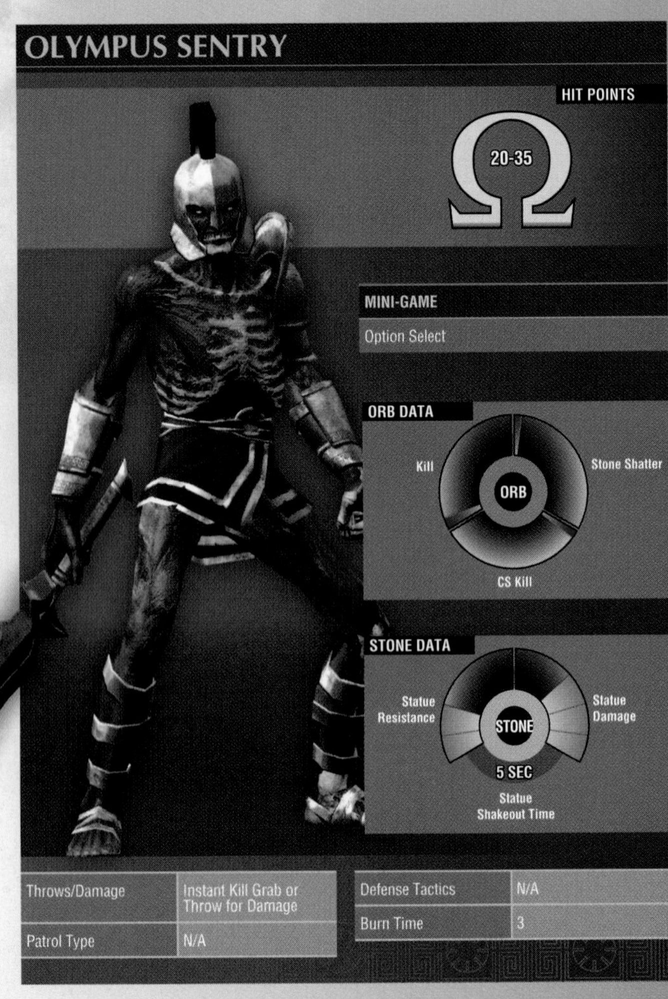

Throws/Damage	Instant Kill Grab or Throw for Damage	Defense Tactics	N/A
		Burn Time	3
Patrol Type	N/A		

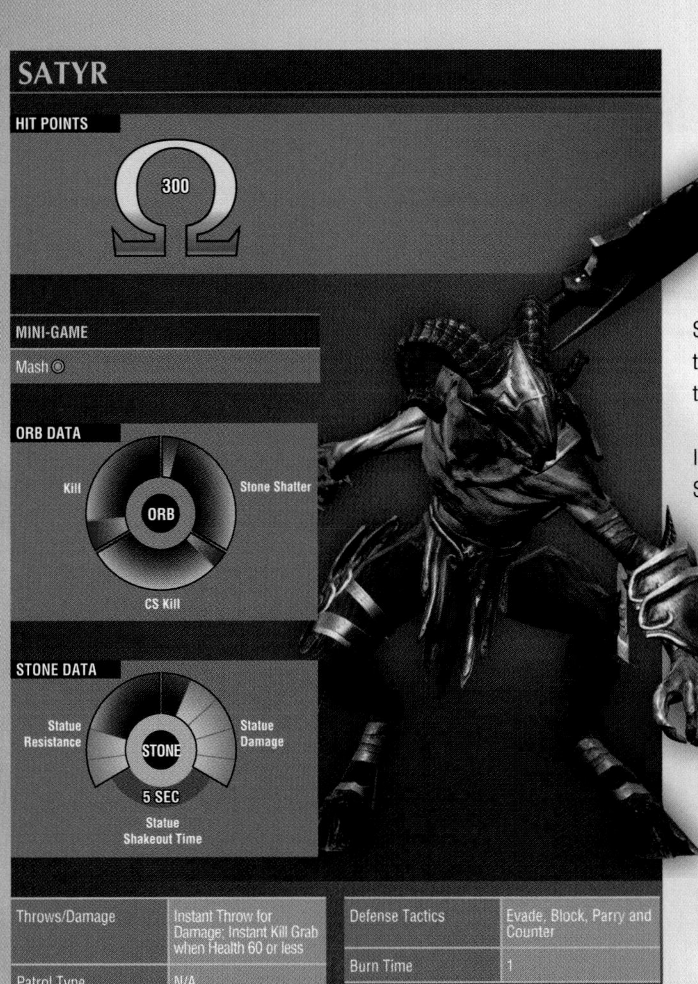

Throws/Damage	Instant Throw for Damage; Instant Kill Grab when Health 60 or less
Patrol Type	N/A

Defense Tactics	Evade, Block, Parry and Counter
Burn Time	1

SATYR

Satyrs have always been deadly adversaries, and *God of War III* provides no exceptions. They don't inflict too much damage with individual attacks, but they're darn hard to avoid and they launch long combos. Defensively, these are tough enemies as well because they're so good at blocking.

Kratos should avoid fast, light attacks; they're practically worthless against Satyrs. The heaviest combos are much better. Don't flank Satyrs or attack from the air; they have counters against all these tactics. They can hook Kratos out of the air with their halberds, and they pivot quickly if you get behind them.

Instead, rely on range to give Kratos the upper hand. Start heavy combos before Satyrs get into attack range. It doesn't matter if you miss the first attack in a series. The latter attacks are often the deadliest, and those are the ones you want to connect. Let the Satyrs walk right into it. When you finish, roll away from the Satyr and repeat the process.

Launch Satyrs and punish them while they're airborne for additional damage. If you're a fan of really close-range melee, this is slightly preferable to the previous tactic.

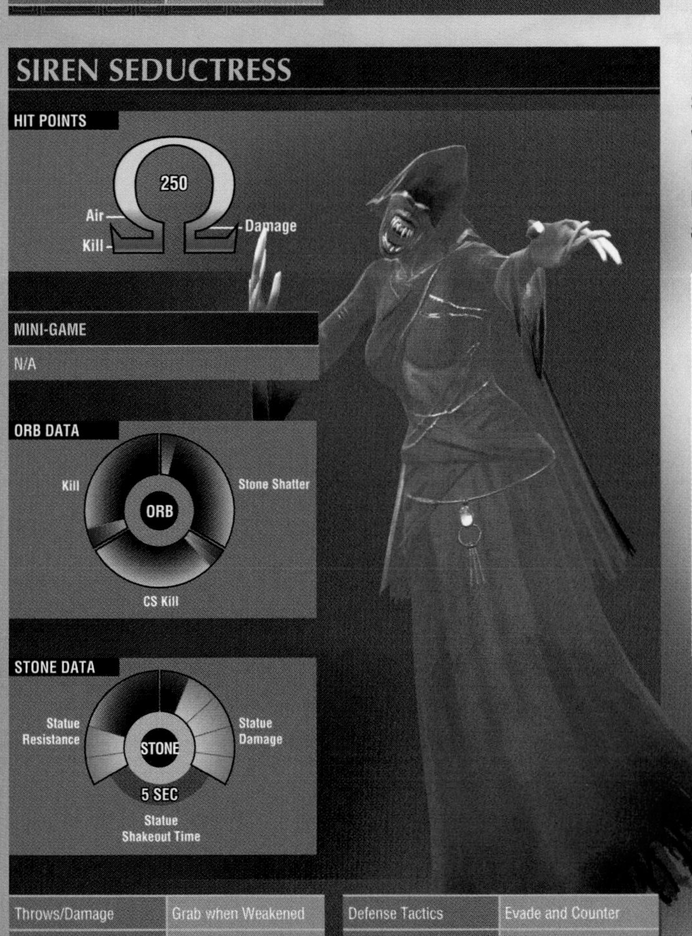

Throws/Damage	Grab when Weakened
Patrol Type	Dizzy

Defense Tactics	Evade and Counter
Burn Time	1.5

SIREN SEDUCTRESS

Sirens Seductresses are tougher than rank-and-file enemies, but they don't kill with heavy, unblockable attacks. Instead, they use speed and subtlety to bring Kratos down. The first defense of a Seductress is to become intangible. You know when they're doing this because they turn black. Destroy the shadows around them with the Head of Helios; hold **L2** and press ◬ to light the area.

Sirens Seductresses also fly. They'll rise above Kratos and attempt to daze him with their songs. If you're affected, wiggle the left analog stick back and forth to break the spell. Or, if you realize what they're doing ahead of time, jump into the air and Combat Grapple the Seductresses to stop their flight.

As long as you counter these attacks, Sirens Seductresses won't give you much trouble. They don't block your attacks, their health is relatively low (for a higher tier enemy), and Kratos can dispatch them without too many strikes.

SKORPIUS SPAWN

These pests aren't a match for the God of War. Their health is relatively low and they don't move particularly fast. Use ranged attacks to kill them quickly. If they swarm around Kratos, slam the area with something heavy to kill the Spawn en masse. Skorpius Spawn are a minor pain if enough of them gather around Kratos; their tail strikes interrupt the Spartan and allow the others to connect with their attacks.

Any health you lose against Skorpius Spawn can be replenished. Kill the Spawn to gather a tiny amount of health from each. This especially helps during a certain boss fight. You'll know it when you see it!

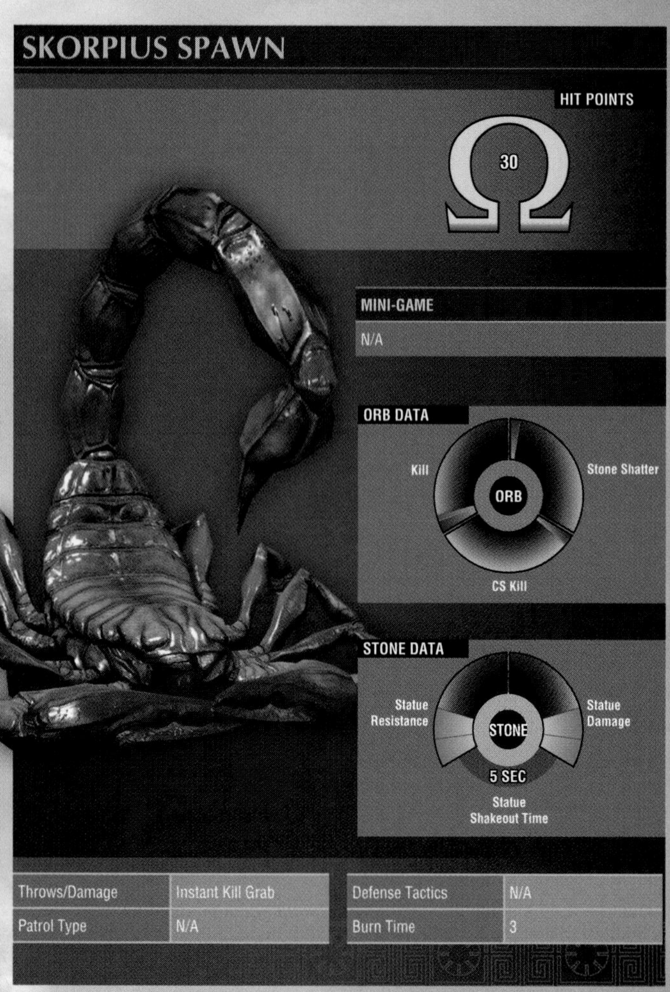

Throws/Damage	Instant Kill Grab	Defense Tactics	N/A
Patrol Type	N/A	Burn Time	3

TALOS

Talos are heavy hitters. They fight at close range with two-handed hammers. Don't try to stand still and block their attacks. It's easier and more effective to roll around the enemies and strike at their flanks. The Nemean Cestus is good for this, but all weapons are suitable. It's hard to stagger or interrupt both types of Talos. Use your most powerful attacks (heavy combos and attacks with the Nemean Cestus) to knock them around.

Kratos falls into a pattern while fighting Stone Talos. Dodge when they launch their double attacks and make sure they aren't going to nail you with the ground pound. Slip back in to punish them, and repeat the process as they recover and start a new combo of their own.

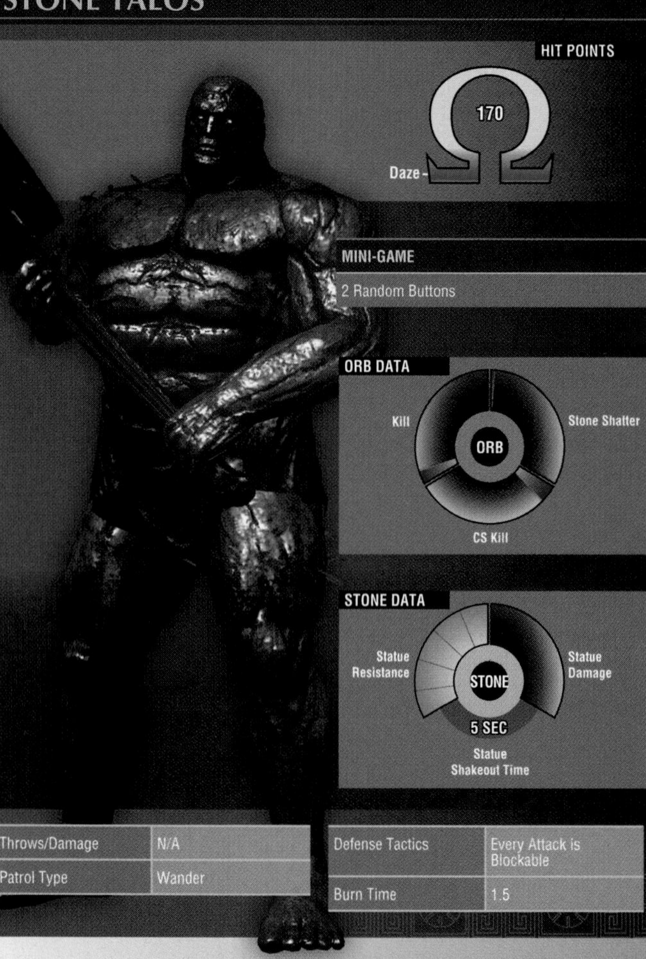

Throws/Damage	N/A	Defense Tactics	Every Attack is Blockable
Patrol Type	Wander	Burn Time	1.5

BRONZE TALOS

HIT POINTS

510

Daze

MINI-GAME

3 Random Buttons

ORB DATA

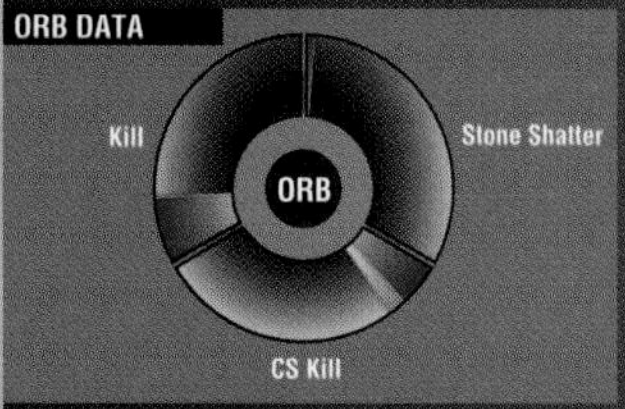

Kill / Stone Shatter / CS Kill

STONE DATA

Statue Resistance / Statue Damage / Statue Shakeout Time: N/A

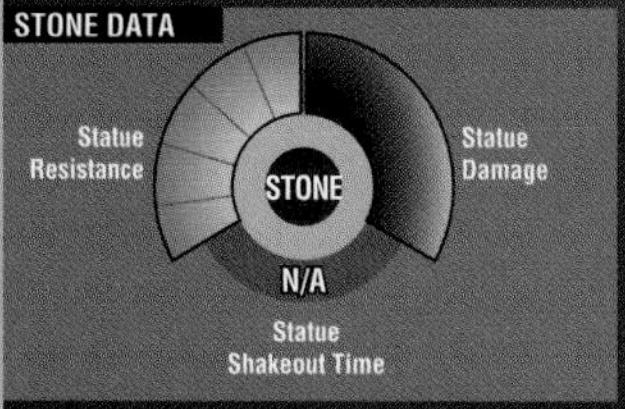

Throws/Damage	N/A	Defense Tactics	Every Attack is Blockable
Patrol Type	Wander	Burn Time	1.5

Bronze Talos have an added mechanic. Though their offensive abilities are similar, you must damage them in stages. Attack quickly and watch a single Bronze Talos change color. Their armor heats up, glowing red and then eventually blazing in white. Continue hitting a white Bronze Talos to stagger them and inflict lasting damage.

This process resets once a Bronze Talos takes damage. Repeat it several times to daze the creature, then grapple with them to secure the kill. Because of this process, it's wise to kill lesser enemies first. It's also sensible to destroy Talos individually, focusing on one target until it's fully destroyed.

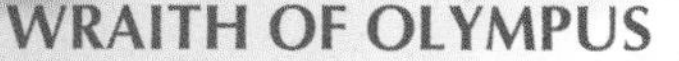

WRAITH OF OLYMPUS

HIT POINTS

240

MINI-GAME

N/A

ORB DATA

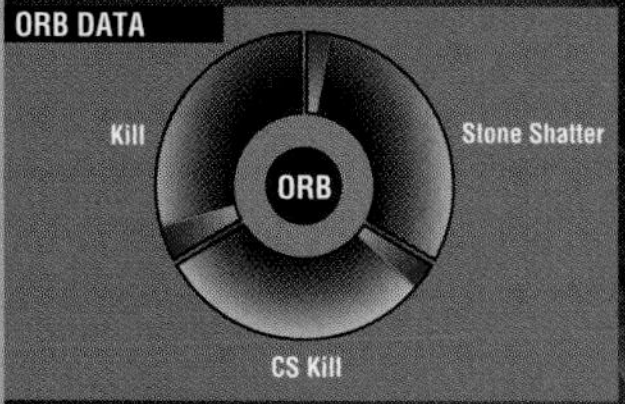

Kill / Stone Shatter / CS Kill

STONE DATA

Statue Resistance / Statue Damage / Statue Shakeout Time: 5 SEC

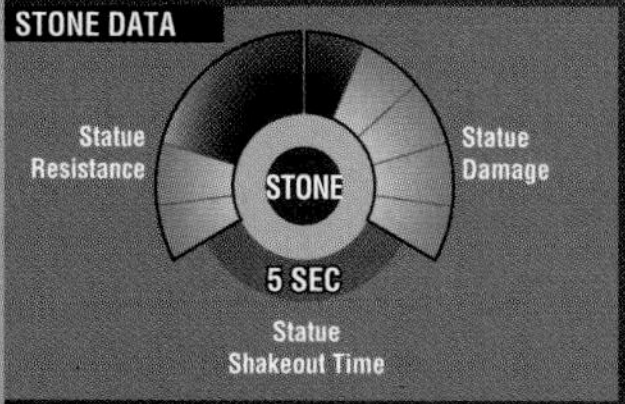

Throws/Damage	Instant Throw Launch when Health at 41 or more; Instant Kill Throw when Health at 40 or less	Defense Tactics	Burrow, Evade, Block and Counter
		Burn Time	1.5
Patrol Type	N/A		

WRAITH OF OLYMPUS

Wraiths of Olympus are melee fighters. They dash in close to Kratos quickly and hound him with constant attacks. Though all their moves are blockable, you can end up in a situation where it's hard to stop blocking, not seeing an opening for reprisal in return.

Combat Grapples are the best tools against Wraiths. These attacks stop the Wraiths' momentum and expose them for a short time. Have Kratos knock them into the air and juggle the Wraiths to death, either from the ground or with aerial attacks. Heavy Nemean Cestus attacks or jumping attacks from the Blades of Exile are equally wonderful.

Combat Grappling also rips Wraiths out of the ground when they hide. If you see a Wraith burrow into the earth, approach and use your Combat Grapple to snatch them before they ambush Kratos. Once revealed, return to the method of juggling them to prevent them from launching a counterattack of their own.

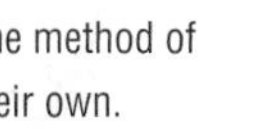

TRIALS OF THE GODS

Several items unlock after you beat *God of War III* for the first time. Kratos gets at least one of his special costumes (with more to come) and you gain access to the Challenges of Olympus. After beating these special scenarios, you also get access to an arena. This chapter lets you know what to expect from all of these and how specifically to beat the Challenges.

THE CHALLENGES OF OLYMPUS

POPULATION CONTROL

CHALLENGE RULES

Don't allow there to be more than 50 enemies at the same time. Kill them before too many spawn.

This challenge is quite basic. Kratos must keep the population of enemies beneath 50 for 90 seconds. There are two strategies that turn Kratos into the ultimate executioner. Using the Nemean Cestus, it is entirely possible for Kratos to beat this Challenge by simply mixing strong and weak attacks into the densest pockets of Olympus Sentries. A couple attacks can quickly kill an Olympus Sentry, but if Kratos isn't hitting more than three at a time, he isn't going to make it.

An alternative strategy is to repeatedly use the Battering Ram attack. Grab onto an Olympus Sentry and use him as a ram while running in a long U-type path. Never let Kratos' dash end at a wall; this slows Kratos as he bashes his victim to death without worrying about the other soldiers. After Kratos chucks his Sentry over the edge, grab another and repeat the tactic. The Ghost of Sparta wants to end his trajectory near the end of the dial so that he may push off as many Sentries as possible.

Either of these strategies allows Kratos to complete the challenge with as little frustration as possible.

By the time the Cyclops Enforcer arrives, at least one of the Talos needs to be destroyed. Eliminate any remaining Talos and spend the last 20 seconds unleashing everything to damage the Cyclops Enforcer with constant Battering Ram attacks. Keep up the pressure to win the challenge.

BARE HANDS

CHALLENGE RULES

Before time runs out, kill all the enemies without using any weapons.

Plenty of skill and a bit of luck are required for Kratos to accomplish the Bare Hands challenge. It's all about the Battering Ram; simple as that. There is no room for mistakes here and if Kratos can't kill both of the Stone Talos within the first 40 seconds, then this challenge is over. Grab an Olympus Sentry and use it as a Battering Ram as Kratos pinballs between the two Talos. If Kratos gets lucky, it is possible to knock a Talos with full health off the edge with a single charge.

GET STONED

CHALLENGE RULES

Allow the Gorgons to turn you to stone 15 times without dying.

Get Stoned is most definitely a challenge worthy of the God of War. This challenge is a test in patience. The goal is to get petrified by the Gorgons and survive the process 15 times.

Begin the challenge by dazing the Gorgon without killing her. Kratos must do this before getting petrified twice, or else Harpies arrive and throw a wrench into the works. After the Gorgon is weakened, concentrate on getting Kratos turned to stone. Do nothing but this until the Satyrs spawn. Satyrs usually arrive once Kratos has achieved becoming a statue five times.

By the time the Satyrs arrive, a second Gorgon enters the fray. Use the Golden Fleece to reflect gaze attacks and hope that this petrifies the Satyr. Kratos should kill the Satyr, but realize that more are on the way once one is killed. In the short respite between Satyrs assailants, attempt to get turned into a statue once more.

After being stoned about seven times, Cyclops Enforcers appear. Initiate the Context-Sensitive Action against the weakened Gorgon from earlier in the challenge and then destroy the now-stoned Cyclops Enforcers. Attempt to be petrified during the brief respite and then prepare for absolute chaos.

Kratos must deal with Satyrs, Cyclopes, Harpies, and Lost Souls. Grab and kill Lost Souls to regain small bits of health and then find open areas in which to safely become petrified. Use the Golden Fleece to reflect gaze attacks back at nearby enemies.

Kill the most dangerous enemies any time they become statues and stay on the defensive the rest of the time. Expect to repeat this challenge several times; it's certainly one of the most difficult.

KNOCKOUT

CHALLENGE RULES

Score 1,000 Points by knocking enemies out of the arena. Sentries = 15 Points, Minotaurs = 30 Points, Wraiths = 60 Points.

This challenge requires a ruthless and persistent offense. Run up to the Cyclop Berserkers and use Cyclone of Chaos in the air to bring him down in a flash. Once the Cyclops is weakened, jump on him and start riding.

Circle around the perimeter of the arena and use nothing but quick attacks. Funnel the enemies into tight pockets and then knock them out in one giant attack. If Kratos can, aim for the Wraiths of Olympus to get an even higher score.

HADES' KIDS

CHALLENGE RULES

They don't die, they multiply. Get 5 Cyclops Enforcers to spawn.

Hopefully, Kratos is well-acquainted with Tartarus Rage and Cyclone of Chaos, because these keep him alive during this challenge. Initially, there is only a single Cyclops Enforcer. Once Kratos kills that beast, two more Enforcers reinforce their fallen brother. Eventually, Kratos may simultaneously be dealing with up to four Enforcers.

Eliminate the Cyclops Enforcers as quickly as possible. Kratos must use Tartarus Rage repeatedly. The ending blow from Tartarus Rage knocks back the Enforcers and prevents them from attacking. Practice this against the first Cyclops Enforcer to see its effectiveness.

When the next two Cyclops Enforcers appear, dash to their flanks. Attack from the side to ensure that your strikes nail both targets. It's possible to destroy both Enforcers without letting them attack a single time.

After killing the next two Cyclops Enforcers, four of the goliaths enter the arena. Tartarus Rage is not going to work against four Enforcers at the same time. Instead, jump into the air and pick one of the Cyclopes to attack. Use Cyclone of Chaos, pausing only to dodge or position. Repeat this to overcome the challenge.

SIMPLY SMASHING

CHALLENGE RULES

Destroy all the urns before time runs out.

Kratos has 30 seconds to destroy all the urns in the room. This seems simple, but the challenge requires precision. There aren't many seconds to spare, so you require a path to be mentally mapped out ahead of time.

Use the Blade's fast attacks and reach out in a clockwise manner. Think of Kratos' reach as the minute hand on a clock and methodically break the urns in a full circle. Plan Kratos' attacks and don't get frustrated if he fails his first attempt. After getting to know the layout of the arena, Kratos should be able to hit urns that the camera isn't even focused on. Keep it simple and stay calm. There is enough time to get everything done.

CHALLENGE OF EXILE

Do you still have a thirst for being tested to your limits? The Challenges listed here are downloadable content and only unlocked after beating the game.

OLD BIRDS

CHALLENGE RULES

Kill 15 Crows before time runs out. Hitting the ground will reset the counter.

SWITCH BLADE

CHALLENGE RULES

Kill all the enemies before time runs out. Your weapon will be switched every 30 seconds.

PANDORA ON FIRE

CHALLENGE RULES

Don't let Pandora's Cage hit the floor. Kill enemies to make the cage rise.

HANDS OFF

CHALLENGE RULES

Kill all the Hades Arms before time runs out.

USE PROTECTION

CHALLENGE RULES

Break all of the shields without killing any enemies.

HADES' KIDS 2

CHALLENGE RULES

They still don't die, they still multiply. Get 5 Chimeras to spawn.

FEAR ITSELF

CHALLENGE RULES

Kill Fear Kratos.

THE ARENA: PRACTICE MAKES PERFECT

The Combat Arena is a place for Kratos to sharpen his blades and hone his skills. In the Combat Arena, you can create custom battles swarming with the monsters of your choice. Use this to practice new moves, improve strategies, and test Kratos' battle skills.

Besides selecting the monsters you wish Kratos to fight, you can also customize Kratos' health, magic, item meter, and the difficulty of the encounter. If you would like to customize the Combat Arena further, set the arena to night and try fighting in the dark!

MANY FACES OF KRATOS

Know that upon donning a different guise, Kratos looses all opportunities to achieve Trophies through gameplay. However, the costumes definitely have their advantages…

FEAR KRATOS

HOW TO UNLOCK

Fear Kratos is received upon beating the game.

Bonus: Fear Kratos Inflicts 400% Attack Damage
Penalty: Enemies Inflict 400% Attack Damage

APOLLO

HOW TO UNLOCK

Downloadable Content

Bonus: Enemies Inflict 50% Attack Damage
Penalty: Apollo Inflicts 50% Attack Damage

MORPHEUS ARMOUR

HOW TO UNLOCK

Downloadable Content

Bonus: All Orbs worth 200% Normal Value

PHANTOM OF CHAOS

HOW TO UNLOCK

Downloadable Content

Bonus: Red Orbs worth 500% Normal Value

FORGOTTEN WARRIOR

HOW TO UNLOCK

Downloadable Content

Bonus: Enemies Inflict 25% Attack Damage

DOMINUS

HOW TO UNLOCK

Downloadable Content

Bonus: Dominus Inflicts 200% Attack Damage; Enemies Inflict 50% Attack Damage, All Orbs worth 200% Normal Value

GODLY REWARDS

BRONZE TROPHIES

TROPHY	HIDDEN UNTIL EARNED	HOW TO UNLOCK
Releasing the Floodgates	Yes	Kill Poseidon
Burnt to a Crisp	Yes	Acquire the Bow of Apollo
Mr. Hand	No	Find the secret Hades' Arm Room
The walkthrough for Act II details the location of this hidden area. Make sure you explore it before you leave.		
Shine Lord	Yes	Kill Helios
Shoe Delivery	Yes	Kill Hermes and Acquire His Boots
I Didn't Do It...But I Wish I Did	Yes	Kill the Poseidon Princess
Ladies Man	Yes	Successfully Entertain Aphrodite
This is a choice; Kratos doesn't have to complete this mini-game with Aphrodite to proceed, but you earn experience for it and a free Trophy. Keep your cool, hit the right buttons, and enjoy the scene.		
Handy Man	Yes	Sever Gaia's Hand
Open Sesame	Yes	Open the Gates of Tisiphone
Rescue Me	Yes	Save Pandora
Three Wise Men	Yes	Solve the Puzzle of the Three Judges
Hit Man	No	Perform a 1000-Hit Combo
Kratos needs to find a small group of enemies, Cursed Remains in the Pit of Tartarus work well, and then equip the Claws of Hades. Have all the enemies positioned in front of Kratos and use the Soul Rip move to start the combo. The Soul Rip grab inflicts very little damage and keeps enemies at bay, allowing Kratos to perform it endlessly. Attract about six enemies in front of Kratos so that he has some insurance in case one of them does meet their demise. You may not get this combo on the first try, but practice makes perfect.		
Rip One!	No	Rip Apart One Olympus Sentry With a Throw
Nice Tan	No	Blind 100 Enemies With the Head of Helios
Use Solar Flash/Flare repeatedly toward the end of the game if you haven't unlocked the Trophy yet. It's easy to get, but some people don't naturally use the attacks often and miss their chance for the Trophy if they don't stop to ensure they're using it enough.		
Obedience School	No	Deliver 50 Kicks to Hounds
There are a fair number of Hounds in the game, but you only get to kick each one a couple times unless you're playing on the highest difficulty. Thus, Trophy hunters should always grapple Hounds to punt them around.		
It's Getting Hot In Here	No	Burn 100 Enemies with the Bow of Apollo
This Trophy isn't hard to get if you want it. The Bow of Apollo doesn't use magic so you're free to charge its attacks to burn enemies at any time. Slower targets are the best to practice on because you don't have to worry about them closing the distance while you're charging.		
Souled Out	No	Summon Every Soul With the Claws of Hades (Level Five)
Bloody Hell	No	Cover Kratos in 500 Buckets of Blood
This is a Trophy that you eventually get regardless of play style.		
No Guts, No Glory	No	Gut 3 Centaur Generals
Hitting Your Stride	No	Upgrade Any Weapon

SILVER TROPHIES

TROPHY	HIDDEN UNTIL EARNED	HOW TO UNLOCK
Sibling Rivalry	Yes	Kill Hercules
Titan Slayer	Yes	Kill Cronos
Retribution	Yes	Kill Zeus
Hooker	Yes	Kill Hades
Freezer Burn	Yes	Acquire the Boreas Icestorm
Seeing Things From a Different Perspective	Yes	Solve Hera's Gardens
Eye Candy	No	Collect All Gorgon Eyes
Feather Plucker	No	Collect All Phoenix Feathers
Are You Horny to Win?	No	Collect All of the Minotaur Horns
The walkthrough has information for collecting all Gorgon Eyes, Phoenix Feathers, and Minotaur horns well before the end of the game. Even if you miss several chests, the system lets you "make this up" by finding spares until you've hit the full count. It's easy to get everything you need.		
Maxed Out!	No	Completely Upgrade All Weapons
Play the game on the lowest difficulty if you want to receive this Trophy. Though far less of a challenge, you have the benefit of getting much more experience during your playthrough. This makes it astoundingly easy to get weapon upgrades. In addition, make full use of combos to receive bonus experience. Kill enemies with grappling attacks for more Red Orbs and search all levels thoroughly. Not only does this yield more Red Orb chests; it also lets you get collectible items earlier. That translates to accumulating far more experience later on when you open item chests and receive bonus experience instead of collectibles.		

GOLD TROPHIES

TROPHY	HIDDEN UNTIL EARNED	HOW TO UNLOCK
Vengeance Complete	No	Beat the Game
Up to the Challenge	No	Beat the Challenge of Olympus
Look in the starting menu to find these extra events. We've documented all of these with tactics to help you win, or you can go it alone and defeat them without any help. Either way this Trophy is fun to get.		
Unhuman	No	Beat the Game in Titan Mode
Priceless	No	Collect All of the Godly Possessions
aMAZEd	Yes	Beat the Labyrinth Without Dying or Failing
Save before you enter the Labyrinth! This way you can always reload after any deaths and retry the area. That is much more efficient than hoping for a success and having to replay the whole darn event in a future playthrough. This is a good Trophy to hunt while you're trying to achieve the Maxed Out! trophy. Play for both of them while on the lowest tier of difficulty to increase your chances of getting both.		

THE PLATINUM TROPHY

TROPHY	HIDDEN UNTIL EARNED	HOW TO UNLOCK
King of the Hill	Yes	Unlock all other Trophies

GOD OF WAR III

OFFICIAL STRATEGY GUIDE

Written by Michael Lummis and Peter McCullagh, Stacy Dale, James Manion, & Samuel Chartier of Off Base Productions

DK/BradyGames, a division of Penguin Group (USA) Inc.
800 East 96th Street, 3rd Floor
Indianapolis, IN 46240

ISBN 13: 978-0-7440-1192-0
ISBN 10: 0-7440-1192-2
UPC Code: 7-52073-01192-5

Printing Code: The rightmost double-digit number is the year of the book's printing; the rightmost single-digit number is the number of the book's printing. For example, 10-1 shows that the first printing of the book occurred in 2010.

13 12 11 10 4 3 2 1

Printed in the USA.

BRADYGAMES STAFF

Publisher
David Waybright

Editor-In-Chief
H. Leigh Davis

Licensing Director
Mike Degler

International Translations
Brian Saliba

Team Coordinator
Stacey Beheler

CREDITS

Sr. Development Editor
Christian Sumner

Screenshot Editor
Michael Owen

Book Designers
Dan Caparo
Tim Amrhein

Production Designer
Tracy Wehmeyer

Map Illustrations
Argosy Publishing

Ultimate Edition Title Manager

MICHAEL LUMMIS' ACKNOWLEDGEMENTS

I'd like to thank Edwin Kern and Kathleen Pleet for their support. I'd also like to thank Aristophanes for being such a skilled writer, and Homer (whether a man or a group) for creating some of the best poetry ever made.

BRADYGAMES ACKNOWLEDGEMENTS

A fantastic relationship that began with *God of War II* three years ago has come full circle and I find myself, once again, editing an incredible guide for an awe-inspiring game. Plenty of people pitched in to bring this guide together and, while I can't name them all, their efforts culminated with what you're currently holding in your hands.

I have to say, the folks in Santa Monica always amaze me. They're just great to work with and show a passion for what they do. This easily comes through to those of us lucky enough to play their games, giddy with excitement, sitting on the edges of our seat waiting to see what comes behind the next corner. In particular, I have to mention that William Weissbaum stepped up in a colossal way. While everyone on the Santa Monica development team that chipped in gets a robust "Thanks a million!" from me, I will be buying Mr. Weissbaum dinner when next we meet.

I must offer a sincere thank you to everyone at Sony Computer Entertainment America that helped on this guide. Ken Chan was the behind-the-scenes master at making miracles happen and getting everything done. It's been a few years since I was introduced to Ken. He was a bachelor at the time, working himself to the bone on his end to help us make our guide top-notch. The only thing that's changed is that he's now married.